UK countries

England

Capital: London
Population: 53 million
Area: 130,400 km²

Scotland

Capital: Edinburgh
Population: 5.3 million
Area: 78,800 km²

Wales

Capital: Cardiff
Population: 3.1 million
Area: 20,800 km²

Northern Ireland

Capital: Belfast
Population: 1.8 million
Area: 14,100 km²

Not part of the UK

Republic of Ireland

Capital: Dublin
Population: 4.6 million
Area: 70,300 km²

Atlantic Ocean

Galway

REPUBL
OF IRI

Cork

THE BRITISH ISLES

ORKNEY ISLANDS

0   100   200   300 km
0   100   200 miles

■ Inverness
Loch Ness
▲ *Ben Nevis*

Highlands

■ Aberdeen

SCOTLAND

UTER
BRIDES

Firth of Forth

■ Glasgow

■ Edinburgh

Edinburgh Castle

Hadrian's Wall   ■ Newcastle
     Tyne

Giant's Causeway

■ Belfast

THERN
IRELAND

ISLE OF MAN

Lake District

Pennines

■ York

■ Hull

Irish Sea

Liverpool

■ Manchester

Humber

■ Dublin

▲ *Snowdon*

■ Nottingham

The Wash

Trent

ENGLAND

St. George's Channel

WALES

Cambrian Mountains

■ Birmingham

■ Cambridge

THE NETHERLANDS

North Sea

Severn

■ Swansea
■ Cardiff

Oxford ■

■ London

Big Ben

Heathrow

Thames

Stonehenge

■ Dover

BELGIUM

Devon

■ Brighton

Cornwall

ISLE OF WIGHT

■ Plymouth

■ Penzance

ISLES OF SCILLY

English Channel

FRANCE

CHANNEL ISLANDS

Blue Line 3 Lehrerausgabe

für Klasse 7

Das Lehrbuch versteht sich als Gesamtangebot. Welche Texte und Aufgaben verpflichtend sind, wird durch die schulinternen Curricula festgelegt.

Zusätzliche Informationen in der Lehrerausgabe:
- Lernwortschatz für alle: history
- Differenzierungswortschatz: pet shop
- Kein Lernwortschatz (fakultativ): traveller
- Grammatische Strukturen: Language detectives
- Lösungen für geschlossene Übungen: 2. That's York.
- Aussprachehinweise: [ˌlɒx ˈneɪ]
- Hilfreicher Wortschatz zur Bildbeschreibung: **Helpful words:** statue, knight's armour, battleaxe
- Verweise auf Kopiervorlagen im Lehrerband: → KV 13
- Für weitere Informationen zu Blue Line: Code 6nn4xt auf www.klett.de

---

1. Auflage   1 5 4 3 2 | 20 19 18 17

Alle Drucke dieser Auflage sind unverändert und können im Unterricht nebeneinander verwendet werden.
Die letzte Zahl bezeichnet das Jahr des Druckes.

Herausgeber: Dr. Frank Haß, Kirchberg
Autorinnen und Autoren: David Brimage, Brighton; Geraldine Greenhalgh, Hamilton; Wolfgang Hamm, Marktredwitz; Melanie Ku, Hanau; Howard Rayner, London; Clare Treleaven, Castellón sowie Chris Caridia, Bangkok; Andrew Cowle, Glasgow; Jo Cummins, London; Michael Meisenzahl, Karlstadt; Karen Seekings, London; Konstanze Zander, Großenehrich
Beratung: Brunhilde Biek, Leonberg; Karin Braun, Dortmund; Wilma Brings, Bedburg; Amanda Chisnell, Lollar; Ulf Degen, Braunschweig; Tanja Frank, Ulm; Sandra Haberland, Recklinghausen; Wolfgang Hamm, Marktredwitz; Ulrike Heringhaus, Altheim; Michael Herrmann, Ludwigsfelde; Christa Kathmann-Fuhrmann, Bonn; Dr. Margitta Kuty, Greifswald-Eldna; Grit Machut, Berlin; Michael Meisenzahl, Karlstadt; Beatrix Pierce, Eppingen; Annegret Preker-Franke, Bielefeld; Dr. Hubert Schwandt, Parchen; Christian Straukamp, Nordhorn; Ines van Hove, Oldenburg; Dieter Vilimek, Helmstadt-Bargen

Redaktion Schülerbuch Lehrerausgabe: Dr. Rudolf Erben; Perdita Geier, Senden
Redaktion Schülerbuch: Claudia Schwarz-Brownbill, William Sears, Joanne Popp
Herstellung: Ulrike Wursthorn

Umschlaggestaltung und Gestaltungskonzept: know idea, Freiburg; Koma Amok, Stuttgart
Umschlagfoto: plainpicture GmbH & Co. KG (Ableimages/Jutta Klee), Hamburg; plainpicture GmbH & Co. KG (Bias), Hamburg
Fotografen: Thomas Weccard, Ludwigsburg
Illustrationen: Marek Blaha, Offenbach; Kirill Chudinskiy, Köln; Marcus Wilder, Hamburg; sowie Friederike Ablang, Berlin; Lars Benecke, Hannover; Thomas Binder, Magdeburg; Gilles Bonotaux, Paris; Vera Brüggemann, Bielefeld; Christian Dekelver, Weinstadt; Thorsten Droessler, Leipzig; Andreas Florian, Lübeck; Anke Fröhlich, Leipzig; Josef Hammen, Trierweiler; Christian Hansen, Berlin; Susann Hesselbarth, Leipzig; Carmen Hochmann, Bielefeld; Martin Hoffmann, Stuttgart; Hendrik Kranenberg, Drolshagen, Cleo-Petra Kurze, Berlin; Sven Leberer, Altenberge; Dorothee Mahnkopf, Berlin; Karin Mall, Berlin; Helga Merkle, Albershausen; Pawel Miedzinki, Kozieglowy; David Norman, Meerbusch; Katrin Oertel, Münster; Liliane Oser, Hamburg; Sven Palmowski, Barcelona; Katja Rau, Berglen; Bettina Reich, Zwenkau; Sandra Schmidt, Berlin; Carolin Ina Schröter, Berlin; Jaroslaw Schwarzstein, Hannover; Manfred Tophoven, Straelen; Jacqueline Urban, Eisenach; Ulrike Vetter, Leipzig; Aurel Voigt, Waiblingen; Martina Vollhardt, Kamenz; Sylvia Wolf, Wiesbaden; Steffen Wolff, Brohl-Lützing; Dorothee Wolters, Köln

Satz: Satzkiste GmbH, Stuttgart
Reproduktion: Schwabenrepro GmbH, Stuttgart
Druck: Passavia Druckservice GmbH & Co. KG, Passau

Printed in Germany
ISBN 978-3-12-547953-1

Blue Line 3

Lehrerausgabe

Herausgeber: Dr. Frank Haß

Ernst Klett Verlag
Stuttgart • Leipzig

Inhalt

L = Listening   S = Speaking   R = Reading   W = Writing   V = Viewing   I = Intercultural

L = Listening S = Speaking R = Reading W = Writing V = Viewing I = Intercultural

Inhalt

L = Listening   S = Speaking   R = Reading   W = Writing   V = Viewing   I = Intercultural

So lernst du mit Blue Line

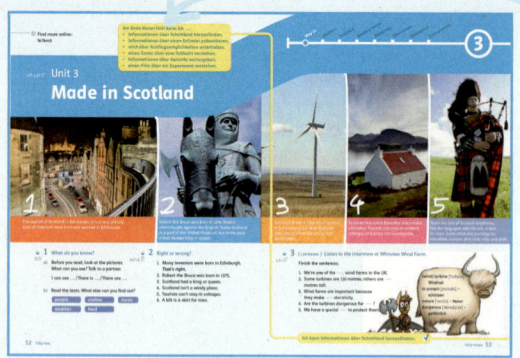

Hier zeige ich dir, wie du dich in deinem Buch gut zurechtfindest. Das Buch hat fünf Units (Kapitel). Jede Unit ist gleich aufgebaut.

Way in

Hier steigst du in das neue Thema ein. Dazu gibt es auch einen kurzen Film.

Im gelben Kasten siehst du, was du in der *Unit* lernst.

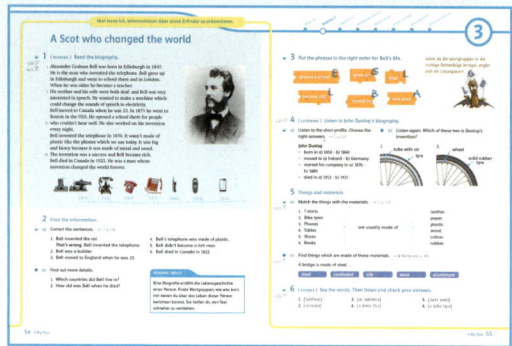

Stations

In jeder *Unit* gibt es zwei *Stations*, in denen du viele neue Dinge lernst. Diese Symbole zeigen dir, wie schwer die Übung ist und ob es im Anhang eine leichtere Variante gibt:

 → ○ p. 137 ●

In der *Your turn*-Aufgabe kannst du zeigen, dass du alles verstanden hast, und deine eigenen Ideen einbringen.

Reading corner

In der *Reading corner* gibt es verschiedene Geschichten, Dialoge und andere Texte.

Mediation/Film corner

Auf der linken Seite geht es darum, englische Informationen auf Deutsch weiterzugeben oder umgekehrt.

In der *Film corner* geht es um einen englischen Film.

Checkpoint

Auf dieser Seite kannst du überprüfen, ob du in der *Unit* alles verstanden hast. In der *Checklist* sind alle Lernziele noch einmal aufgelistet.

Die Abschluss-Aufgabe (*task*) sollt ihr zu zweit oder in der Gruppe lösen.

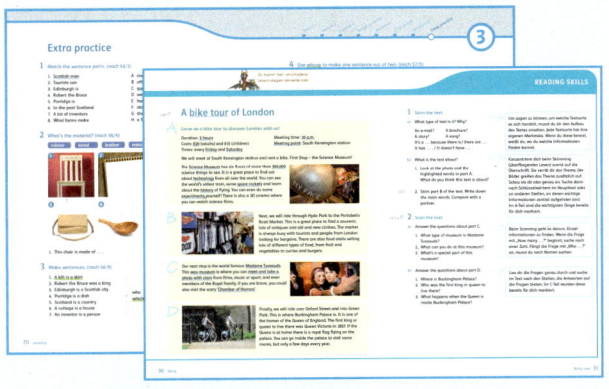

Extra practice

Hier findest du zwei Seiten mit Zusatz-Aufgaben,
z. B. zur Vorbereitung auf die Klassenarbeit.

Skills

Auf einige *Units* folgt eine Doppelseite, auf der ihr eine
bestimmte Fertigkeit (*skill*) besonders trainieren könnt,
also z. B. das Lesen, Schreiben, Sprechen oder die
Wörterbucharbeit.

More about

Hier findest du interessante weiterführende
Informationen zur Region der Unit.

Im Anschluss an die fünf *Units* gibt es noch weitere nützliche
Seiten:

Extra: Hier erwarten dich weitere Lesetexte: eine Geschichte, ein Theaterstück und vieles mehr.

Grammar: Hier findest du alle Regeln und Erklärungen
zur Grammatik sowie weitere Übungen.

Methods: Manche Übungen könnt ihr auf eine bestimmte
Art und Weise bearbeiten.
Das erkennt ihr an diesem Symbol: → M
Wie es genau funktioniert, kannst du hier nachlesen.

Vocabulary: Im *Vocabulary* findest du alle neuen Wörter in der
Reihenfolge, in der sie in der *Unit* auftauchen,
und die wichtigsten Arbeitsanweisungen.
Im *Dictionary* sind die Wörter noch einmal
alphabetisch aufgelistet: zuerst Englisch–Deutsch
und dann Deutsch–Englisch.

Am Schluss des Buches findest du noch
- Sätze, die du im Unterricht sagen kannst, z. B. bei der
Gruppenarbeit
- Lösungen zu den Übungen der *Extra practice*-Seiten
- eine Liste mit den unregelmäßigen Verben

Symbol	Erklärung
○ ◑ ●	leicht/mittel/schwer (Niveaudifferenzierung)
✳	individualisierende Aufgabe (natürliche Differenzierung)
→ ○ p. 131	Verweis auf leichtere Parallelübung auf der *Diff corner*-Seite
OR	Aufgabe zur Auswahl (Wahldifferenzierung)
⌐○	Entwicklung von Schlüsselkompetenzen
P	Hier entsteht ein Produkt für das Portfolio.
4/1 🗐	Verweis auf eine Übung im *Workbook*
→ G13, p. 172	Verweis auf den Grammatikanhang (*Grammar*)
→ M	Verweis auf die Methodenseite (*Methods*)
→ V	Verweis zum Wortfeld im Vokabular (*Vocabulary*)
☺☺	Partnerarbeit
☺☺	Gruppenarbeit
☺	Verweis auf die Lehrer-CD (Audio)
🎞	Verweis auf die Lehrer-DVD (Film)
⊕ Find more online:	Code auf www.klett.de eingeben und Zusatzinformationen erhalten

Zoom in – <u>The British Isles</u>

[ˈðə ˌbrɪtɪʃ ˈaɪlz]

The British Isles

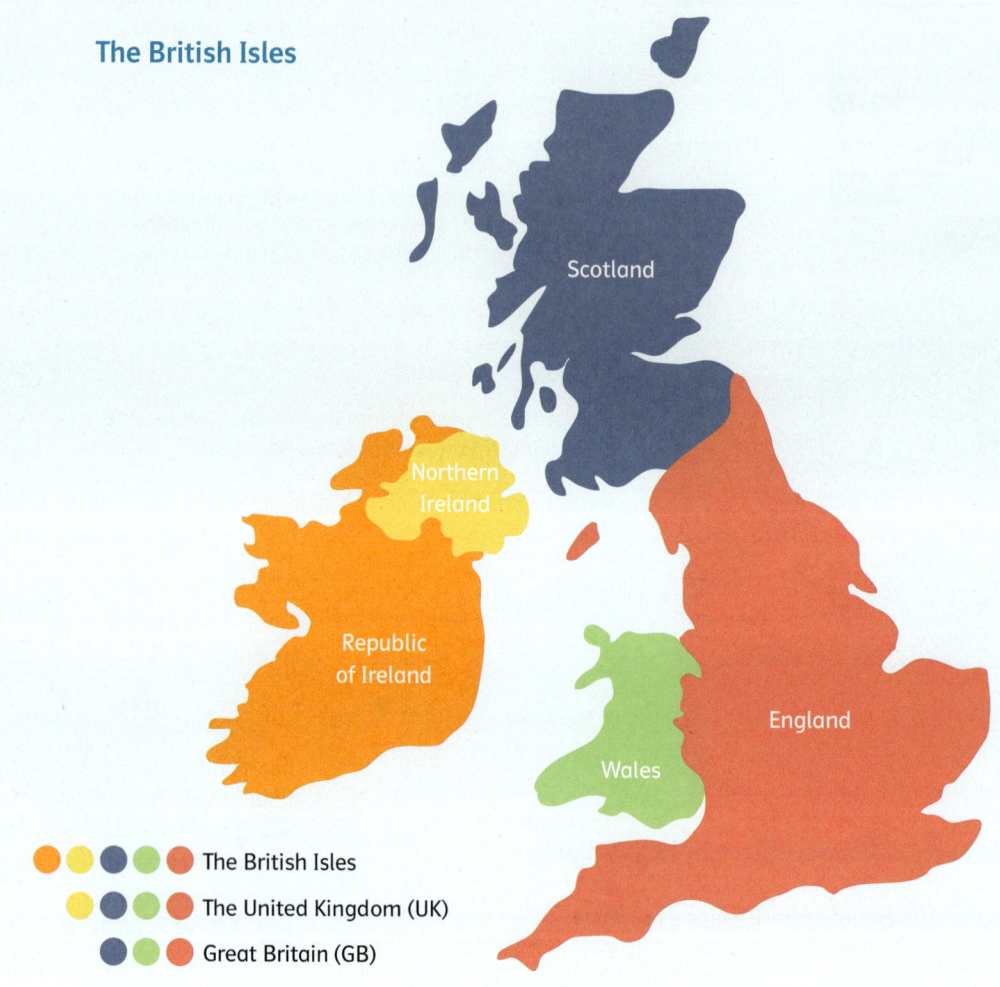

Scotland

Northern Ireland

Republic of Ireland

Wales

England

● ● ● ● ● The British Isles
● ● ● ● The United Kingdom (UK)
● ● ● Great Britain (GB)

☺☺ **1** **Do the British Isles quiz with a partner.**

1. What are the names of the five countries of the British Isles? England, Wales, Scotland, Northern Ireland, Republic of Ireland
2. Which is the biggest country in <u>the United Kingdom</u> (UK)? England
3. Which is bigger, <u>Northern Ireland</u> or <u>the Republic of Ireland</u>? The Republic of Ireland
4. Which is bigger, Scotland or <u>Wales</u>? Scotland
5. Which country is in the UK but not in <u>Great Britain</u> (GB)? Northern Ireland
6. Which country has more people, Wales or Scotland? Scotland
7. Which is the biggest city in the UK? London
8. Which country is not in the UK? The Republic of Ireland
9. The Channel Tunnel goes from France to which country? England

Sieh dir die Karte auf der Vorderseite an. Du kannst deine Antworten auf Seite 270 überprüfen.

Helpful words:
deckchair
pebble beach
pier

England

Wales

Helpful words:
Highland cattle

Scotland

Northern Ireland

Ireland

1,1 🎧 **2** (LISTENING) **Listen to five teenagers from the British Isles.**

Make a table. Then listen and take notes.

Name		From?	Age?	Hobbies?	Plans?
Emily					
Dylan					
Lewis					
Sophie					
Patrick					

Emily: England (Brighton); 14; horse riding, swimming; work with animals (not sure)
Dylan: Wales; 15; rock climbing; police officer
Lewis: Scotland; 13; take his dog for a walk, ski; cook in a hotel restaurant
Sophie: Northern Ireland; 14; take photos; singer or dancer
Patrick: Republic of Ireland; 15; hang around or play football with friends; shop assistant in a sports shop

Die fünf Teenager kommen aus den verschiedenen Ländern der Britischen Inseln. Sie haben unterschiedliche Akzente. Welche Akzente findest du am einfachsten zu verstehen? Welche am schwierigsten?

🌐 Find more online:
fe76m3

Am Ende dieser Unit kann ich ...
- Informationen über historische Orte in England herausfinden.
- Wegbeschreibungen geben und verstehen.
- meinen Wohnort ausführlich vorstellen.
- eine Geschichte aus der Vergangenheit verstehen.
- Informationen über die Geschichte eines Sports weitergeben.
- einen Film über Greenwich früher und heute verstehen.

1 🎞 1,2 🎬 Unit 1

England now and __then__

1

Stonehenge is an old stone circle in the south of England. It's more than **4,000 years old**. No one knows why it is there.

2

In **122** the Romans started to build **Hadrian's Wall** in the north of England. It took six years to build it.

◔ **1** What's the oldest building or sight that you know?

◔ **2** Name the place.

2/1-2 🏃

1. There was lots of industry here during the Industrial Revolution. That's **Manchester**.
2. Some Vikings came to this town from Denmark in 866. That's York.
3. No one knows why this stone circle is there. That's Stonehenge.
4. The Romans built this place in 122. That's Hadrian's Wall.
5. The Normans won a battle against the English there in 1066. That's Hastings.

3 In **866** the Vikings invaded the English city of **York**. They came from Denmark, Norway and other countries. Some stayed in England and York became their home.

4 In **1066** the Normans came from France and invaded England. They won a battle against the English near **Hastings**. A Norman became king of England.

5 There was lots of industry in **Manchester** during and after the Industrial Revolution (**1780 – 1840**). Now there are also shops, cafés and parks in the city.

🔈 **3** (LISTENING) **Stonehenge: Choose the right answers.**

1,3 ⚙
2/3 ▱

1. The biggest stones weigh
   45 tonnes • ~~100 tonnes~~.
2. The biggest mystery is
   ~~how old Stonehenge is~~ • what Stonehenge was for.
3. Some people think the circle was
   a big clock • ~~a big building~~.
4. Maybe people came there when they wanted to
   ~~meet their friends~~ • feel better.
5. Near Stonehenge there are
   graves • ~~houses~~.

Diese Wörter helfen dir,
den Hörtext zu verstehen.

tonne [tʌn] – Tonne
sun [sʌn] – Sonne
sick [sɪk] – krank
grave [greɪv] – Grab
million [ˈmɪljən] – Million

Ich kann Informationen über historische Orte in England herausfinden. ✔

Around York

1 Look at the pictures of York.
What can you find in the city?

'The Shambles' is an old street in York with overhanging timber-framed buildings.

2 (READING) Read the dialogue.

1,4
3/1

1 **Sam:** Excuse me. I'm here on holiday. Do you know the <u>way</u> to the tourist information?
Mrs Jenkins: I do, but maybe I can help you. What <u>are</u> you <u>interested in</u>?
5 **Sam:** I would like to <u>learn</u> more <u>about</u> the <u>history</u> of the city.
Mrs Jenkins: Well, we are near the Viking Centre. It shows <u>what</u> the city <u>was like</u> about a thousand years ago. Just <u>cross</u> the road. After
10 that you can go to the tourist information. Walk <u>past</u> the post office and turn <u>right</u> at the end of the road. Then take the first road on the <u>left</u>.
Sam: OK. And do you know a good clothes shop?

15 **Mrs Jenkins:** Yes, I do. The best shops are on the Shambles. I often go there too. Why don't you go to the <u>souvenir shop</u>? It sometimes has cheap Viking helmets.
Sam: Brilliant! <u>How do I get there?</u>
20 **Mrs Jenkins:** That's easy. Turn right and walk <u>down</u> the road … it's on the left.
Sam: Is it <u>far</u> away?
Mrs Jenkins: No, it doesn't take long. It's just <u>a five-minute walk</u>.
25 **Sam:** Oh good. Thank you.
Mrs Jenkins: You're welcome.

3 Match the sentence parts.

1. The boy would like to know more about
2. The woman and the boy are very near
3. It shows what the city was like
4. The best shops are
5. The souvenir shop sometimes has
6. The souvenir shop is just

a five-minute walk away.   6
on the Shambles.   4
cheap Viking helmets.   5
the Viking Centre.   2
the history of the city.   1
about a thousand years ago.   3

4 (WRITING) Where can you buy these things?

3/2a)

a) Match the things with the right shops. Write them down. → ○ p. 112

A   B   C   bread   D   a birthday card   E

a football

shoes

shoe shop E   clothes shop ✓   card shop D   baker's B   sports shop C

1. You can buy jeans at the clothes shop. 2. You can buy …

3/2b)

b) Where can you buy these things? Copy the shopping list and complete it. → V Shops, p. 174

newsagent's   greengrocer's

butcher's   pet shop

jeweller's

Things to buy	Shop
sausages, ham	butcher's
magazines, comics	newsagent's
fruit, vegetables, salad	greengrocer's
pet food	pet shop
jewellery	jeweller's

5 (LISTENING) Find the way to the card shop.

1,5
3/3

a) Listen to the dialogue. Find the way on the map. Tell it to a partner.

turn left   turn right

go straight on   walk past …

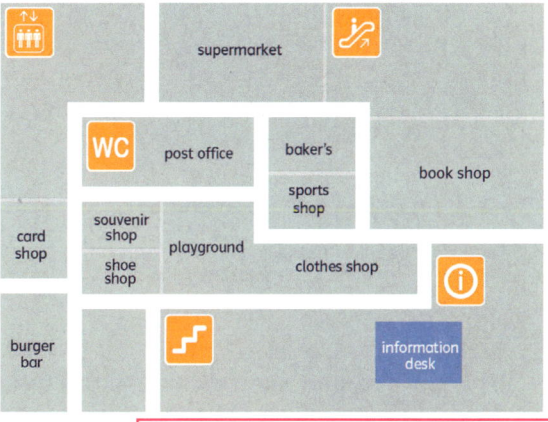

b) What's the fastest way to the card shop? Tell a partner.
Turn left here in front of the clothes shop. Walk past the playground. Turn right at the shoe shop. The card shop is on the left.

6 (SOUNDS) How quickly can you say this tongue twister?

1,6

Sharon <u>sells</u> shoes in the shoe shop. The shoes in the shoe shop aren't Sharon's size.

5 a) Go straight on. Turn left at the book shop and then right at the sports shop. Walk past the baker's. Then turn left. Walk on until you get to the supermarket. Turn left there. Look for the post office. Turn right there. Walk until the end. Then turn left again. The card shop is just opposite the souvenir shop.

Language → **G1**, p. 150

Do you remember?

I often <u>go</u> there.
It <u>doesn't take</u> long.
<u>Is</u> it far away?
<u>Do</u> you <u>know</u> a good clothes shop? - Yes, I do.

Schau dir die Sätze an. Welche Zeitform ist das? Wie wird sie gebildet?

7 **Complete the sentences with one of the verbs.**

4/4

He, she, it – das -s muss mit!

> go ✔   be (2x)   not arrive   have   prefer
>
> wait   not like   meet

1. I sometimes <u>go</u> shopping with my friends at the weekend.
2. We always —— at 11 a.m.   meet
3. My best friend usually —— before 11:30, but we always —— for him.   doesn't arrive – wait
4. In the afternoon we often —— something to drink at a café.   have
5. My favourite shop —— The Busy Bookworm.   is
6. My friends —— it. They —— the sports shop.   don't like – prefer
7. Our favourite shops —— on the Shambles.   are

8 (SPEAKING) **Interview your partner.** → **M** Double circle, p. 167

4/5

a) Ask a partner. He or she answers. → ◯ p. 112

A:			B:
	you	go to the cinema?	Yes, I do.
	your friends sometimes	do your homework?	No, I don't.
Do + they + often +	play football?	Yes, he does.
Does	your dad usually	watch TV?	No, he doesn't.
	he	go shopping?	Yes, they do.
			No, they don't.

b) Make more short dialogues. Use these words.

> buy clothes online   look for bargains
>
> spend money on . . .   get comics at a newsagent's   . . .

A: Do you sometimes buy clothes online?
B: No, I don't. They don't usually fit.

9 (WRITING) Make questions.

a) Complete the dialogue. → ○ p. 112

5/6

1. (know) Do you <u>know</u> where the football stadium is? – Yes, I do.
2. (take) —— it —— long to get there? – Yes, it does. But there's a bus. Does – take
3. Where (be) —— the <u>nearest</u> bus stop? – It's just five minutes down that road. is
4. When (leave) —— the buses ——? – I think it's every five minutes. do – leave
5. (be) —— bus <u>tickets</u> expensive? – No, they aren't. Just 90p. Are
6. Where (can) —— I buy a ticket? – On the bus. can

b) Make three more questions and answers. Use the words for help.

toilets   food stalls   …

Where are …? / Where can I find …?

�֍10 (YOUR TURN) Directions → V Directions, p. 178

5/7

a) You are at X on the map. Work with your partner. Ask for directions to:

post office   swimming pool   café   …

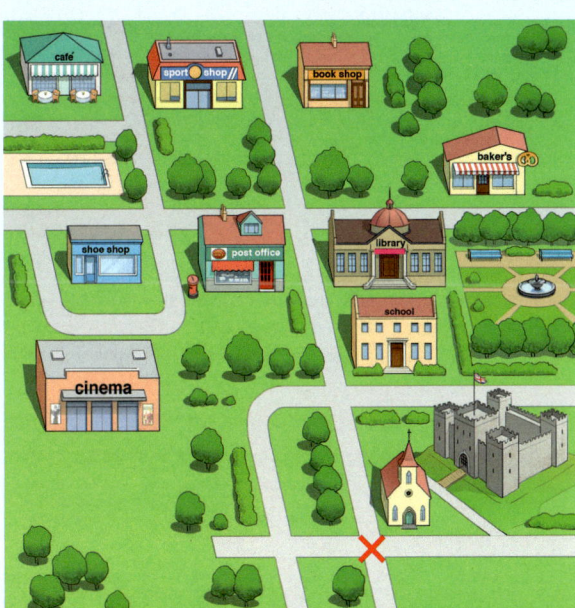

A: Excuse me, please. Is there a <u>shoe shop</u>
  near here?
B: Yes, there is. Go past the church.
  Then <u>walk down the second street</u>
  <u>on the left</u>. After that <u>turn left</u>.
  The shoe shop is <u>opposite</u> the <u>cinema</u>.
A: OK. Thanks for your help.
B: You're welcome.

turn right   go straight on

cross the road   …

left   next to the …   …

b) Present one of your dialogues in class.

Ich kann Wegbeschreibungen geben und verstehen. ✔

Manchester and Bramford

1 (READING) **Read about where Hannah and Tom live.**

1,7
6/1

1 Hi! I'm Hannah and I'm from Manchester, in the northwest of England. It's a large city with more than half a million inhabitants. There's lots of traffic. It's noisy too – I don't like that!
5 But there are many buses.

In the past Manchester had lots of industry. There were dirty factories. There were coal mines near Manchester too.

I live in a flat with my mum and my little
10 sister. It's in the centre of the city and it's very small! Mum works in a supermarket. She often has to work in the evening.

The best thing about Manchester? Football! Manchester City is great!

My name is Tom and I live on a farm in Bramford. That's a small village in the north of England, near Hadrian's Wall. We used to live in Newcastle, but my parents didn't like the city. They wanted to live in the country. 5 Did they ask me? No, they didn't.

It's hard work on the farm. There are two goats, Bert and Daisy, and a lot of cows.

It's quiet in the village. Only about 400 people live here. The country is boring, but 10 I like the animals on the farm!

The worst thing about our village? There are only two buses a day. It's difficult to see friends at the weekend! It's so unfair!

2 **Take notes about where they live.**

a) Make a table and put in the information.

	name of place	town, city or village?	where in England	good/bad things
Hannah	Manchester	city	northwest	good: many buses; footb· bad: lots of traffic; noisy
Tom	Bramford	village	north	good: animals bad: the country is boring only two buses a day

b) What more can you remember? Close your book and write one more sentence about Hannah and one about Tom.

Hannah's mum works in a supermarket.
Tom's parents didn't like the city.

3 Sort the words into groups. → M Peer correction, p. 169

6/2 a) Copy the table. Put the words and phrases into the right groups. → ○ p. 113

places 1	where 2	words for the size of places 3
village		

in the centre of 2   village ✓ 1   miles away from 2   big 3

small 3   near 2   in the north/south/east/west of 2   town 1

large 3   city 1   in the mountains 2

6/3 b) Add these words to your list. → V Talking about places, p. 175

tiny 3   close to 2   a two-hour drive from 2   huge 3   on the coast 2

4 (SPEAKING) Where would you like to live? → M Think-pair-share, p. 171

6/4 a) Collect adjectives for the city and the country.

city:	country:
exciting	boring
noisy, interesting	quiet, beautiful

b) Talk with a partner.

A: I'd like to live in a city. Cities are exciting.
B: Yes, but they are noisy too!
   I'd like to live in the country.
A: Really? That's interesting.

town

quiet   small

near   in the mountains

That sounds boring/nice.

5 (SONG) The City

1,8 Listen to the song. What does the singer think about his home?

1 This city never sleeps
I hear the people walk by when it's late
Sirens bleed through my windowsill
I can't close my eyes
5 Don't control what I'm into
This tower is alive
The lights that blind keep me awake
With my hood up and lace untied
Sleep fills my mind
10 Don't control what I'm into

London calls me a stranger
A traveller
This is now my home, my home
I'm burning on the back street
15 Stuck here sitting in the backseat
I'm blazing on the street
What I do isn't up to you
And if the city never sleeps
Then that makes two

7/5-6 **6 Make Tom's story.**

a) Complete the sentences. → ○ p. 113

1. Last Saturday morning things <u>went</u> a little crazy on our farm. (go)
2. I —— a noise in the garden (hear) and I —— . (get up) *heard – got up.*
3. I —— my dad in the garden. (see) *saw*

4. He —— to put Bert and Daisy, our goats, in his tractor. (want) *wanted*
5. Suddenly he —— in the mud, <u>head first</u>. (fall) *fell*
6. It —— so funny. (be) I just —— to laugh. (have) *was had*
7. Dad —— very happy. (not be) *wasn't*

b) What happened next? Write an ending.

shout at **be angry** **help** **...**

7/7 **7 (WRITING) What did Hannah and Kilkenny do on Saturday?**

a) Look at the pictures. Correct the sentences. → ○ p. 113

2. Hannah wasn't ... She was in the garden. 3. Hannah didn't do ... She played a computer game. 4. They didn't make ... They cooked a meal. 5. Later she didn't write ... She listened to music. 6. They weren't ... They were at the shoe shop.

1. Hannah walked to the baker's in the morning.

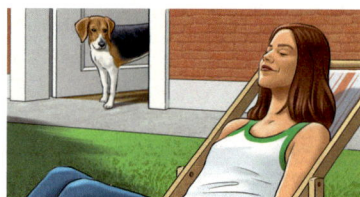

2. Hannah was in the living room at two o'clock.

3. Hannah did her homework in the afternoon.

4. She and her sister made jewellery at five o'clock.

5. Later she wrote a text message.

6. Hannah and her sister were at the cinema.

1. Hannah <u>didn't walk</u> to the baker's in the morning. She <u>watched</u> TV.

b) Look at the pictures again. What did Hannah's dog, Kilkenny, do?

Kilkenny <u>didn't watch</u> TV. He <u>played</u> with a ball.

b) 2. Kilkenny wasn't in the garden. He was in the house. 3. He didn't play a computer game. He ate a sausage. 4. He didn't cook a meal. He slept in the kitchen. 5. He didn't listen to music. He looked out of the window. 6. He wasn't at the shoe shop. He waited in the street.

8/8-9

8 (SPEAKING) **Talk to a partner about the weekend.** → M Milling around, p. 168

a) Make questions.

1. have • you • a nice weekend? • Did
   Did you have a nice weekend?
2. at home all weekend? • Did • stay • you   Did you stay at home all weekend?
3. you • anything nice with your family? • Did • do   Did you do anything nice with your family?
4. What • you • do together? • did   What did you do together?
5. the weather like on Sunday? • What • was   What was the weather like on Sunday?
6. did • What time • get home? • you   What time did you get home?
7. Were • tired on Sunday evening? • your parents   Were your parents tired on Sunday evening?

b) Talk to a partner. Use the questions from a).

Did you have a nice weekend?

Yes, I did, thanks! I visited my aunt and uncle.

do your homework   go shopping

watch TV   be at home   . . .

9 (YOUR TURN) **A short talk** → V Where I live, p. 179

9/1-2

Give a short talk about where you live.

I live in … . It's a … . It's in … Germany. It has about … inhabitants. In the past … . My favourite place is … . I like it because I can … .

name of place: Hamburg/…
size: small village/large town/city …
where: the north/the east/the south/ the west of …
number of inhabitants: 5,000/50,000/ a million/…
history: there was …/there were …/ we didn't have …/people worked in …/…
favourite place: cinema/…
what I can do there: play football/hang around/…

CULTURE

Auf englischen Straßenschildern stehen die Angaben für Entfernungen in Meilen (miles) statt in Kilometern. Eine Meile sind 1,6 Kilometer. Wie viele Meilen sind es von deinem Zuhause bis zur Schule?

Ich kann meinen Wohnort ausführlich vorstellen. ✔

A <u>deadly</u> <u>silence</u>

1 **What do you know about Manchester – now and in the past?** → M Think–pair–share, p.171

2 (READING) **Read the story.**

1,9

The Rushy Park Coal Mine, near Manchester. September 1850

1.

1   My name is Jonas Fox. I'm twelve years old and I work in the
     mines. I sit near a door in the <u>tunnel</u> every day. I open the door
     when the coal arrives. Then I close the door again. I sit in <u>the dark</u>
     every day, but I'm never scared because my friend Billy is there
5   with me. Billy sings all day long. He's yellow with black eyes. Billy
     is a <u>canary</u>. I would love to sing too, but I can't even talk.
     [kəˈneəri]

2.

     Sometimes there is <u>gas</u> in the mine, and gas can <u>explode</u>. Last year
     a gas <u>explosion</u> <u>killed</u> 30 <u>miners</u> and ten boys. A canary <u>smells</u> gas
     sooner than a man. So when the canaries sing, the tunnels are
10 OK. But if they don't sing, there's gas in the mine. Everyone must
     leave the tunnels very fast.

READING SKILLS

Dies ist eine längere Geschichte, aber sie ist in mehrere kurze Teile aufgeteilt. Lies dir jeden Teil kurz durch und versuche zu verstehen, worum es in diesem Teil der Geschichte geht.
Schau dir dann die Teile noch einmal genauer an und stelle
W-Fragen. **Wer** kommt in diesem Teil der Geschichte vor?
Wo sind die Figuren, **was** passiert und **wann** passiert es?

3.

My brother, Bart, worked in the mine too.
One day Bart started to cough. Bart coughed   [kɒf]
all the time after that. Soon he died. And I
stopped talking. I don't know why, really. I

15 opened my mouth, but I couldn't speak. The
men in the mine called me 'Silent' Jonas'
after that.

4.

Billy was singing like he always did. I heard
the people in the tunnels and the noise of

20 the coal trucks. I opened the door. There was
a cold wind in the tunnel. I closed the door.
Billy stopped singing. There was gas in the
mine!

5.

I had to tell everyone in the mine.

25 I opened my mouth and tried to say, "Gas."
Nothing came out. I closed my eyes and
opened my mouth again. Nothing. I had to
speak! I tried again. This time I made
a noise. I opened the door and suddenly

30 I could shout, "Gas. Gas. GAS!" A moment
later I heard the miners in the tunnels.
I took Billy's cage and ran too.

6.

I ran through the tunnel. My head hurt. I couldn't
breathe in the gas. Suddenly I heard a voice. "Come
35 on, boy!" it said. One of the miners picked me up.
He took me out of the mine. I had Billy's cage with
me, but I was sure he was dead. At last we got out
and I could breathe again.

7.

BOOM! The noise of the explosion was awful. My ears hurt.
40 I closed my eyes. Then I opened them again. I saw that the
men and boys were all OK. A miner asked, "Who shouted?"
"Me!" I said. They were so surprised! Then everyone said
thank you. "Silent Jonas found his voice!" a miner shouted.
But how could I feel happy? My friend Billy was dead. I
45 looked in his cage to say goodbye to him. Suddenly I heard a
small 'Tweet'. Billy was alive! I opened the cage …

There were canaries in mines until 1987. Today miners use
machines to find out if there is gas in the mine.

3 Did you like the story? Say why or why not.

> I liked/didn't like the story.   I think the story was exciting/boring/interesting.

> l like stories about the past.   …

4 Match each heading with a section of the story.

A Everything is OK if the canary sings.   2
B Gas in the mine!   4
C Jonas must find his voice.   5
D The explosion – and after   7
E Meet Jonas Fox – and Billy!   1
F Silent Jonas   3
G Can they get out?   6

5 Choose the right answer.

1. Jonas works in a ~~factory~~ • **mine**.
2. He is never scared because **his canary Billy** • ~~his brother Bart~~ is with him.
3. If the canary doesn't sing, **there's gas** • ~~there are people~~ in the mine.
4. When his brother died, Jonas ~~started talking~~ • **stopped** talking.
5. One day there was gas **in the mine** • ~~at home~~ and Billy stopped singing.
6. Jonas wanted to **tell everyone** • ~~run away~~ but he couldn't speak.
7. **Suddenly** • ~~A day later~~ Jonas shouted and the miners left the mine.
8. One of the miners took Jonas and Billy **out of the mine** • ~~into the tunnels~~.

READING SKILLS

Du hast die Geschichte schon einmal gelesen, deshalb musst
du dieses Mal nicht jedes Wort lesen.
Schau dir jeden Teil kurz an. Lies genauer, wenn du die
Informationen findest, nach denen du gesucht hast.

6 Look at the story again. Make a mind map about Jonas.

How old?
12 years old

Jonas

good things friend and canary Billy

job
works in
the mines

bad things sits in the dark every
day, can become ill,
explosions

family brother Bart died

7 Choose one of these tasks.

10/1
11/2-4

a) Work in groups. Make freeze frames for
each part of the story. Let other groups
guess.

OR

b) Work in groups. Practise the text.
Read it in class.
→ **M** Dramatic reading, p. 167

Ich kann eine Geschichte aus der Vergangenheit verstehen. ✔

The history of football

INTERNET

Football now and then

['tsuju]

1 Some people think the English invented football, but they
didn't. More than 2,500 years ago the Chinese played a game
with many similarities to football. Its name was cuju. The
English did do one thing though: they wrote down the first
5 rules for the game.

Football was a popular sport in 19th-century England. When
players from different schools played, there was one big
problem: they all had different rules! For example, the players
from Rugby School carried the ball; others used only their
10 feet. Players often disagreed about who won the game.

['fʊtbɔːl,
ə,səʊsɪˈeɪʃn]

To make the game fair for everyone, they wrote down the
rules. They were called the Cambridge Rules. The Football
Association (FA) used these to make their own rules in 1863.
This is when Association Football (called football in England
15 and soccer in the USA) and rugby became two different
sports.

Nowadays it isn't just boys who play football in England.
Many of the big English football clubs such as Arsenal,
Liverpool and Chelsea have their own female teams and the
20 Women's National Team is one of the best in the world.

1 Beantworte die Fragen.

12/1-2

1. In welchem Land spielte man eine frühe Form von Fußball?
2. Warum wurde es nötig, die Fußballregeln niederzuschreiben?
3. Was erfährt man über Frauenfußball in England?

2 What do you know about the history of football in Germany?

1. China
2. Jede Schule hatte unterschiedliche Regeln: Einige Spieler haben den Ball getragen, andere haben nur ihre Füße benutzt.
3. Viele der großen Fußballklubs wie Arsenal, Liverpool und Chelsea haben auch Frauenmannschaften. Die Frauennationalmannschaft ist eine der besten weltweit.

Ich kann Informationen über die Geschichte eines Sports weitergeben.

Girl from the past

1 **How did children live in Germany or England about 150 years ago?**

→ **M** Think-pair-share, p. 171

Think about these things.

work

school — children

home

> **CULTURE**
>
> Königin Viktoria war von 1837 bis 1901 britische Königin. Man nennt diese Zeit das „Viktorianische Zeitalter", und viele Gebäude in London stammen aus dieser Zeit. (Eine der wichtigsten Bahnhöfe in London ist z. B. Victoria Station.) Welche Königinnen kennst du?

Now watch the film. Was there anything new to you?

2 (VIEWING) **Watch the film.**

2 🎬

a) Which summary is correct?

1. Laura reads about the <u>Victorian era</u> in a book. Then she and Marley travel back in time.
✔ 2. Marley <u>falls asleep</u> in the library. He <u>dreams</u> that he meets a girl from the past.
3. Violet meets Laura in the library. Laura tells her about life in the 21st <u>century</u>.

b) Who says it?

1. <u>I'd rather</u> work than go to school. Marley
2. I <u>wish</u> I could go to school! Violet
3. Look, we've just travelled through time. Marley
4. You've <u>been asleep</u> <u>almost</u> an hour. Laura

Laura   Marley   Violet

['vaɪələt]

3 (SPEAKING) **Talk about the film.**

👥

a) Watch the film again from 1:30 to 3:25.

How does Marley feel?
First he is confused.
Later he is surprised. Then he is happy.
At the end he is surprised.

surprised	confused
happy	...

> **VIEWING SKILLS**
>
> Worte sind wichtig in einem Film, aber du solltest auch auf die Gesichter und die Körpersprache der Personen achten. Sie können dir viel darüber sagen, was passiert oder wie die Personen sich fühlen.

b) Would you like to travel back in time? Where would you like to go? Who would you like to meet?

Ich kann einen Film über Greenwich früher und heute verstehen. ✔

Checklist

Ich kann Informationen über historische Orte in England verstehen. ✔

13 🗐

Ich kann Wegbeschrei-bungen geben und verstehen. ✔

Excuse me. • Is there a shoe shop near here? • Go past the church. • Then walk down the second street on the left. • It's opposite the cinema. • Thanks for your help. • You're welcome.

13 🗐

Ich kann meinen Wohnort ausführlich vorstellen. ✔

I live in .... • It is a town/city/ village. • It is in the north/ south/… of Germany. • It has about … inhabitants. • In the past there was ....

14 🗐

Ich kann eine Geschichte aus der Vergangenheit verstehen. ✔

14 🗐

Ich kann Informationen über die Geschichte eines Sports weitergeben. ✔

15 🗐

Ich kann einen Film über Greenwich früher und heute verstehen. ✔

✿ (TASK) A film project
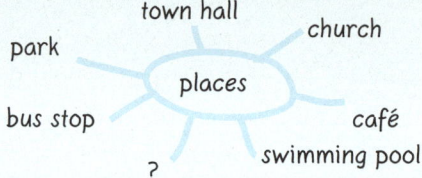

Work in groups of four to six students. Each group makes a short film about a sight in your home town or village.

Step 1

Collect ideas. → M Placemat, p. 169

First collect ideas and make a mind map of the sights you can film.

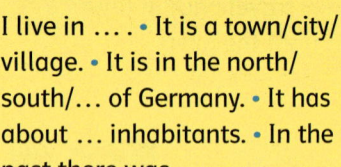

town hall church
park church
places
bus stop café
? swimming pool

Talk about the ideas. Choose a sight.
You can choose an old or a new sight or building.

Step 2

Find people for the different film jobs.

Who can:
- write 2–3 sentences about the sight?
- say the sentences (the presenter)?
- film the presenter and the sight?
- be a director?

STUDY SKILLS

Gib jeder Person die Möglichkeit zu sagen, welche Aufgabe sie gerne übernehmen oder nicht übernehmen möchte. Versucht euch in der Gruppe über eure Ideen für Drehbuch, Titel, Musik etc. zu einigen.

Step 3

Write the script and get ready.

a) Write two or three sentences about your sight.

b) Check the sentences and correct them if you need to.

c) The presenter must read the sentences in a clear voice. Practise this.
   → M Read and look up, p. 170

Step 4

Make your film.

Use a phone or a camera. Go to the sight and film the presenter there.
Wait until everyone is ready before you start, then say "Action!"
Make two or three versions ('takes') of the film. Keep cool if the presenter makes a mistake.

Step 5

Present your film.

Watch all the films together. Then make new groups.
The new group has one student from each film group.

Ask for feedback. Make a checklist like this.

Go back to the film group and look at the checklists. What would you do differently in your next film?
→ M Tip top, p. 171

Feedback checklist
The film is

O exciting   O easy to understand
O informative   O interesting
O fun   O not very interesting.

I like
O the presenter
O the …

Extra practice

1 Write the name of the places. (nach 11/3)

1. H *adrian's*   Wall

2. Y *ork*

3. M *anches*   ter

4. St *one*   he *nge*

5. H *astings*

2 Where do you go to . . . (nach 13/4)

1. buy bread?
2. buy some tennis balls?
3. look for a new coat?
4. buy a birthday card?

Which shop don't you need?   *a shoe shop*

sports shop	2	card shop	4
clothes shop	3	shoe shop	
baker's	1		

3 Write Ben's sentences. (nach 14/7)

| walk | fly | have | get up | eat | go |

1. I never —— before 8 p.m. *get up*
2. I usually —— to different places. *fly*
3. But sometimes I also —— . *walk*
4. I always —— little animals for breakfast. *eat/have*
5. Cheese? No, I never —— that. *have/eat*
6. I usually —— to bed in the morning. *go*

4 Do or Does? (nach 15/9)

1. ~~Do~~ / Does your friend sometimes buy T-shirts at the new clothes shop?
2. Do / ~~Does~~ you sometimes go shopping in the York Sweet Shop?
3. Do / ~~Does~~ they often play football after school?
4. ~~Do~~ / Does she usually buy bread at the baker's on the weekend?
5. ~~Do~~ / Does the new shoe shop always open at 10 p.m.?
6. ~~Do~~ / Does your family usually walk to the card shop?

5 Find the way. (nach 15/10)

a) Start at the X on the map. Where do you go?

1. Walk down the second road on the left. It's on the right, opposite the shoe shop. swimming pool
2. Walk down the first road on the right and walk past the school. It's on the left. park
3. Go straight on and walk down the second road on the left. Turn right and then left. It's on the right. café

b) Complete the sentences about the map.

1. The library is —— the baker's. opposite
2. The church is —— the castle. next to
3. The school is on the —— of the first road on the right. corner
4. Go past the post office and —— the road. The shoe shop is on the —— . cross – left

6 Write sentences about Hannah. (nach 18/7)

go +	meet +	get up –	go +	call –	go –

1. Hannah —— at 9 a.m. So she was late. didn't get up
2. She —— her friend on the bus. met
3. They —— shopping and had lots of ice cream. went
4. Hannah —— her mum at 4 p.m. didn't call
5. They —— back home at 5 p.m. Hannah's mum was angry. went
6. So they —— to the cinema in the evening. didn't go

7 Write the questions. (nach 19/8)

1. Did you forget your mobile?
2. Did you buy a new T-shirt?
3. Did you go to the library?
4. Did you have a good time together?
5. Did you buy cheese and tomatoes?

1. you – forget – your mobile – Did
2. a new T-shirt – Did – buy – you
3. to the library – you – Did – go
4. have – you – Did – a good time – together
5. you – buy – cheese and tomatoes – Did

No, I forgot to call you. I'm sorry, mum.
No, I didn't like them.
No, we met friends from school.
Yes, we had some ice cream. Yummy.
Yes, here you are.

1,10 ⌕

A bike tour of London

A

Come on a bike tour to discover London with us!

Duration: 3 hours
Costs: £20 (adults) and £15 (children)
Times: every Friday and Saturday

Meeting time: 10 a.m.
Meeting point: South Kensington station

We will meet at South Kensington station and rent a bike. First Stop – the Science Museum!

The Science Museum has six floors of more than 300,000 science things to see. It is a great place to find out about technology from all over the world. You can see the world's oldest train, some space rockets and learn about the history of flying. You can even do some experiments yourself! There is also a 3D cinema where you can watch science films.

B

Next, we will ride through Hyde Park to the Portobello Road Market. This is a great place to find a souvenir, lots of antiques and old and new clothes. The market is always busy with tourists and people from London ['bɑːgɪnz] looking for bargains. There are also food stalls selling lots of different types of food, from fruit and vegetables to curries and burgers.

C

Our next stop is the world famous Madame Tussauds. This wax museum is where you can meet and take a photo with stars from films, music or sport, and even members of the Royal Family. If you are brave, you could also visit the scary 'Chamber of Horrors'.

D

Finally, we will ride over Oxford Street and into Green Park. This is where Buckingham Palace is. It is one of the homes of the Queen of England. The first king or queen to live there was Queen Victoria in 1837. If the Queen is at home there is a royal flag flying on the palace. You can go inside the palace to visit some rooms, but only a few days every year.

1 Skim the text.

a) What <u>type</u> of text is it? Why?

An e-mail?	A <u>brochure</u>?
A story?	A song?

brochure It's a … because ~~there is~~ / there are big pictures.
It has … . / It doesn't have … .
a list with different activities

> Um sagen zu können, um welche Textsorte es sich handelt, musst du dir den Aufbau des Textes ansehen. Jede Textsorte hat ihre eigenen Merkmale. Wenn du diese kennst, weißt du, wo du welche Informationen finden kannst.

b) What <u>is</u> the text <u>about</u>?

1. Look at the photo and the highlighted words in part A. What do you think this text is about?

2. Skim part B of the text. Write down the main words. Compare with a partner.

> Konzentriere dich beim Skimming (überfliegendes Lesen) zuerst auf die Überschrift. Sie verrät dir das Thema. Die Bilder greifen das Thema zusätzlich auf. Schau sie dir also genau an. Suche dann nach Schlüsselwörtern im Haupttext oder an anderen Stellen, an denen wichtige Informationen zentral aufgelistet sind. Im A-Teil sind die wichtigsten Dinge bereits für dich markiert.

19/1-4

2 Scan the text.

a) Answer the questions about part C.

1. What type of museum is Madame Tussauds?
2. What can you do at this museum?
3. What's a special part of this museum?

> Beim Scanning geht es darum, Einzelinformationen zu finden. Wenn die Frage mit „How many …?" beginnt, suche nach einer Zahl. Fängt die Frage mit „Who …?" an, musst du nach Namen suchen.

b) Answer the questions about part D.

1. Where is Buckingham Palace?
2. Who was the first king or <u>queen</u> to live there?
3. What happens when the Queen is <u>inside</u> Buckingham Palace?

> Lies dir die Fragen genau durch und suche im Text nach den Stellen, die Antworten auf die Fragen bieten. Im C-Teil wurden diese bereits für dich markiert.

1 b) 1. It's about a bike tour in London. There are different times. One stop is the Science Museum. 2. market, souvenirs, antiques, busy, bargains, different types of food

2 a) 1. a wax museum 2. meet and take a photo with stars 3. the Chamber of Horrors

2 b) 1. in Green Park 2. Queen Victoria 3. a royal flag flies on the palace

→ KV 1

🌐 Find more online:
fe76m3

3 📖 1,11 ☞

Unit 2

Adventures in Wales

1 Learn a language. Get ready and learn some Welsh! We will read menus and road signs, and you will learn how to get to know people.

Bore da! – Good morning!

2 Ride down a mountain. Mount Snowdon is the highes mountain in Wales (1,085 metres). The longest zip line in Europe is near here. It's a mile long and you travel very fast! You can do skiing here too.

🔘 **1** Look at the pictures.

20/1 ⤴

a) Which activities would you / wouldn't you like to do?

☺ I'd like to ... because ... .
☹ I wouldn't like to ... because I think ... .

b) Which activities do you do in your free time?

☺ I often/sometimes ... because ... .

🔘 **2** (READING) Find the right words.

1. Canoeing and rafting are —— activities. popula
2. Cardiff is the —— of Wales. capital
3. We will read road signs.
4. Lifeboats help people in trouble at sea.
5. The highest mountain is Mount Snowdon.

Visit Cardiff Castle. The capital city of Wales is Cardiff. Visit Cardiff Castle in the city centre. It's almost two thousand years old! People often make films here too.

Try a water sport. Wales has a very long coast and many rivers, so you can try many different water sports. Canoeing and rafting are popular activities.

Be a volunteer. Lifeboats are very important in Wales. They help people in trouble at sea. The people on lifeboats are usually volunteers.

3 (LISTENING) Right or wrong?

1,12
20/2

1. Teenagers learn Welsh until they are 15.
2. About 20 % of the Welsh people are fluent in Welsh.
3. A lot more people speak Welsh in the north and in the south.
4. There are no Welsh computer games.
5. The Welsh word 'plant' means children.

1. wrong: They learn Welsh until they are 16.
2. right
3. wrong: A lot more people speak Welsh in the north and west.
4. wrong: There are Welsh computer games.
5. right

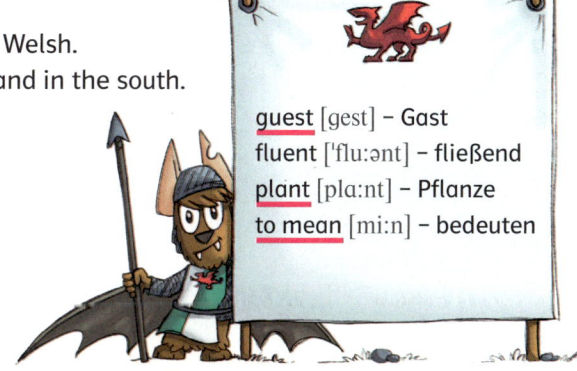

guest [gest] – Gast
fluent ['fluːənt] – fließend
plant [plɑːnt] – Pflanze
to mean [miːn] – bedeuten

Ich kann Informationen über Freizeitaktivitäten in Wales herausfinden. ✔

Hier lerne ich, Informationen über eine Sportart zu präsentieren.

Outdoor activities

1 (READING) **Read the information.**

1,13

INTERNET

BLACK MOUNTAIN ACTIVITY CENTRE, POWYS, WALES
['pəʊɪs]

SUMMER ACTIVITIES

Take a canoeing trip on the river. We go slowly and the trip is six hours. We will have picnic lunch too.

If you like fast and tough sports, try rugby! It's a popular sport. We play in teams of girls and boys. You can learn the rules quickly.

The Welsh country is great for horse riding. Our team is friendly, and the horses are too!

We do outdoor rock climbing and we have an indoor wall – very good in wet Wales! You can borrow the equipment.

2 **Name the activities.**

21/1

a) Which activity is it?

1  horse riding

2  rock climbing

3  rugby

4 canoeing

b) Which activity …

1. … can you do on a wall? **2** 2. … is with animals? **1** 3. … is a water sport? **4** 4. … is with a ball? **3**

3 (READING) **Read the dialogue.**

1,14
21/2

1 Beth: I tried rugby myself for the first time last week. Why don't you come with me next time?
Mark: Rugby? That's cool. But isn't it a tough sport? Are you big and strong enough for it?
5 Beth: Don't be cheeky! I'm small but I'm fit. I can run fast and I'm strong. I had lots of fun.
Mark: *Rock climbing* is fun. I can climb quite well already. It isn't dangerous if you are careful, and you wear a helmet!
Beth: No, thanks. I'm scared of heights. I'd like to try horse
10 riding.
Mark: Horse riding? I did that last year and I hurt myself! That horse was dangerous!
Beth: Oh dear! Well, you can go climbing and I'll try horse riding. We can tell each other about it later!

Language tip → G 3, p. 152
I hurt myself.

4 What is it?

a) Rugby, climbing or horse riding?

1. Mark thinks it's a tough sport. rugby
2. Beth is scared of heights so she won't try this. rock climbing
3. Mark hurt himself when he did this. horse riding

b) Which sports do Mark and Beth finally choose?

Mark: rock climbing
Beth: horse riding

5 Find the words. → M Bus stop, p. 166

a) Find the opposites. → ○ p. 114

1. big ✔ small
2. slow quick
3. tough easy
4. friendly unfriendly
5. strong weak
6. dangerous safe
7. wet dry
8. quiet loud

weak	unfriendly
dry	small ✔
easy	loud
safe	quick

b) Finish the sentences. → V Adjectives for sportspeople, p. 181

1. She can wait. She's very patient.
2. He's very tired. He's exhausted.
3. She has won lots of prizes. She's very successful.
4. He's going to be a star. He's young and talented.

| talented | patient |
| exhausted | successful |

6 (WRITING) Copy the text. Add the adjectives from the box. → M Peer correction, p. 169

21/3

Rafting is an interesting (1) sport for people from 12 to 99.
great – friendly Spend a —— (2) day on the river. Meet our —— (3) instructors
nice – easy and other —— (4) people. Rafting is —— (5) to learn but you
dry – exciting won't stay —— (6). You'll love our —— (7) trips.

great	dry
interesting ✔	nice
exciting	easy
friendly	

WRITING SKILLS

Adjektive machen einen Text interessanter.
Wenn du einen Entwurf schreibst, überlege:

Wo kannst du Adjektive ergänzen, um Personen
oder Gegenstände zu beschreiben?

7 (SOUNDS) Listen, read and say.

1,15

Make a chart. Put the words into groups.

| popular ✔ | canoeing | adventure | difficult |
| equipment | interesting | instructor | horse riding |

Ooo	oOo
popular	canoeing
difficult	adventure
interesting	equipment
horse riding	instructor

Language detectives → G4, p. 153

Rugby is a <u>popular</u> <u>sport</u>.
You can <u>learn</u> the rules <u>quickly</u>.
We <u>go</u> <u>slowly</u> down the river.

Wann brauchst du die Endung <u>-ly</u>?

8 How did they do it? Complete the sentences.

22/4

1. I climbed the wall <u>slowly</u>. (slow)
2. We arrived —— . (safe) safely
3. The instructor called to us —— . (loud) loudly
4. The rugby player ran —— . (quick) quickly
5. The team won the game —— . (easy) easily
6. We rode our bikes —— . (careful) carefully
7. They talked to each other —— . (quiet) quietly

Sei vorsichtig bei Wörtern wie
careful und easy!
carefully
easily

9 Complete the report.

22/5-6
23/7

a) Make adverbs. Add them to the text. → ◯ p. 114

good	excited	fast	slow	heavy ✓	hungry

Last month <u>Class</u> 9G went on a <u>camping</u> trip to
Snowdonia. It started to rain <u>heavily</u> (1) so we had to
walk —— (2). At lunchtime we ate our picnics —— (3).
slowly – hungrily
excitedly   On Sunday we went canoeing —— (4). We went down
fast – well the river —— (5). Everything went —— (6) and no one
got wet. Phew! We had lots of fun.

GRAMMAR → G4, p. 153

A <u>fast</u> game - she runs <u>fast</u>
A <u>hard</u> day - he works <u>hard</u>
A <u>good</u> song - they sing <u>well</u>

b) What does the coach tell the rugby team before the match? Make sentences. Use adverbs.

You have to play
the ball quickly.
You have to …

play	be	win	think
run	…		

quick	good	clever
careful	fast	hard	…

You have to run fast.
You have to play carefully.
You have to think quickly.
You have to win cleverly.

10 (WRITING) Adjective or adverb?

23/8

a) Complete the dialogue. → ○ p. 115

Mark: Beth, how was horse riding today?
Beth: It was **awful**/~~awfully~~ (1). It was **wet**/~~wetly~~ (2) and rained ~~terrible~~/**terribly** (3).
Mark: So you had to ride ~~careful~~/**carefully** (4)?
Beth: Yes, and there were lots of **crazy**/~~crazily~~ (5) people on bikes too. Some of them rode ~~dangerous~~/**dangerously** (6).
Mark: Was your horse **nervous**/~~nervously~~ (7) because of them?
Beth: No, it wasn't. Look, here's a photo…

b) Write a text about a sports star. Use adjectives and adverbs.
Now read your text to a partner. Can he or she guess who it is?

small   English
plays football well
runs fast   …

11 (YOUR TURN) A poster about your favourite activity or sport → V Sports and activities, p. 186

→ M Gallery walk, p. 168

a) Make a poster about your favourite sport or activity. Make notes. Find more information. Add pictures.

– What's the sport like?
– What do you do?
– What must you be like?
– What equipment do you need?

b) Present your poster.

Skiing – my favourite sport

It is:
• exciting
• popular
• fun
• fit
• careful
• not scared

Equipment ⇑

Skiing is an exciting sport.
It's easy. You can ski fast on beautiful mountains.
You must be fit and careful.
You can borrow equipment and special clothes.

Ich kann Informationen über eine Sportart präsentieren. ✔

Emergency on the beach

1 What do you do if you need help? Which number do you call?

You can call for help or ask people to help you. You call 999 or 112.

2 (READING) Read the dialogue.

1,16

1 **Operator:** Hello, Emergency Services, which service?

Dylan: Hello, it's an emergency. I need an ambulance now! Please hurry!

5 **Operator:** OK, please wait a moment.

Janet: Hi, this is Janet from North Wales Ambulance Service. What's the problem?

Dylan: There's a man on the beach. His head is bleeding badly and his leg is too.

10 **Janet:** Tell me slowly what has happened.

Dylan: He has just had an accident. Maybe he fell over on the rocks. I think he has broken a leg.

Janet: OK, where are you? [læn'dɪdnəʊ]

Dylan: I'm on the north beach in Llandudno. 15

Janet: Good, the ambulance is coming. Is the man awake?

Dylan: Yes, he is.

Janet: Can you give me your name and your phone number, please? 20

Dylan: Dylan Adams. 07810 460 228.

Janet: Listen, Dylan. Stay with the man. The ambulance should arrive very soon. You've done the right thing.

Dylan: Thanks. Bye. 25

3 Right or wrong?

1. Dylan needs the police.
   That's wrong.
2. The man has hurt his head. right
3. He has a problem with his leg too. right
4. Dylan is on the south beach. wrong (north)
5. Dylan's family name is Thomas. wrong (Adams)
6. Dylan should stay with the man. right

4 (LISTENING) Look at the list and listen.

1,17

Which of these things does the caller *not* say?

A good emergency call

1. Say which service you need. ✔
2. Say what has happened. ☐
3. Say where you are. ☐
4. Give your name and phone number. ☐

4. Give your name and phone number.

CULTURE

In Großbritannien ist die Notrufnummer (Polizei, Feuerwehr, Krankenwagen oder Küstenwache) die 999. Man kann aber auch immer die 112 anrufen. Welche Nummer wählst du im Notfall in Deutschland?

5 (WRITING) **Match the sentences. Look at the pictures for help.**

24/1-2

 1. I've <u>cut</u> my <u>finger</u>. ✔

 2. My <u>tooth</u> hurts.

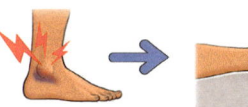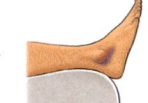 3. You've <u>broken</u> your arm.

4. I've twisted my <u>knee</u>.

5. She's <u>burnt</u> her finger.

6. He's <u>sprained</u> his ankle.

A You need a <u>cast</u>. 3   B I'll put a <u>bandage</u> on it. 4   C <u>Cool</u> it with <u>water</u>. 5

D <u>Take this tablet</u>. 2   E Don't <u>move</u> it. 6   F Here's a <u>plaster</u>. ✔ 1

24/3 **6** (SPEAKING) **Find excuses. Why can't you do PE?**

a) Make sentences. → ○ p. 115

I'm so sorry. I can't do PE today. My head hurts
terribly. I have a sore throat too. I've also
twisted my knee. …

I have cut …   I have burnt …

I have broken …   My … is bleeding

…

SPEAKING SKILLS

Wenn du sprichst, kannst du deine Stimme, dein Gesicht
und deine Hände benutzen. Das kann dir helfen, dich
besser verständlich zu machen.

b) What do you need? Add more sentences. → **V** Health and medicine, p. 182

I'm so ill. I think I need … / Please bring me …

some sleep   some medicine   a cuddly toy   an injection   an operation

→ KV 10, 11

Language → **G5**, p. 154

He <u>has had</u> an accident.
He <u>has broken</u> his leg.
You've <u>done</u> the right thing.
What <u>has happened</u>?

Do you remember?

Welche Zeitform ist das?
Wie bildest du sie?
Wie und wann benutzt du sie?

7 **What has happened? Make sentences.**

25/4

1. burn • <u>hand</u>

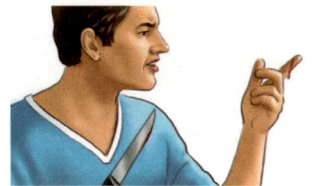

2. cut • finger

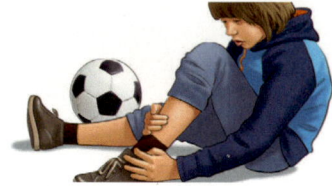

3. twist • ankle

4. break • leg

5. hit • head

6. have • accident

1. He <u>has burnt</u> his hand.

2. He has cut his finger. 3. He has twisted his ankle. 4. She has broken her leg. 5. He has hit his head. 6. They have had an accident.

25/5 **8** (WRITING) **What has Megan already done? What hasn't she done yet?**

a) Make sentences. → ○ p. 115

What she has already done:
Put on her uniform
Open the door
Have lunch
Write a message

What she hasn't done yet:
Collect the bandages
Drink tea
Call the hospital

8 a) She has already opened the door. She has already had her lunch. She has already written a message.
She hasn't collected the bandages yet. She hasn't drunk her tea yet. She hasn't called the hospital yet.

Megan <u>has</u> already <u>put on</u> her uniform.

b) Look at the picture again. Make more sentences.
Use <u>already</u> and <u>not yet</u> and the words from the box.

put on boots • close the window •
put on the helmet • get a torch

8 b) She hasn't put on her boots yet. She hasn't closed the window yet. She has already put on her helmet. She has already got a torch.

9 (SPEAKING) Make dialogues.

a) Complete the dialogue with a partner. → ○ p. 116

26/6

Kim: Hey, I —1.— your brother at football <u>training</u> last Monday. (not see) What's wrong with him?
Jamie: He —2.— in hospital last week. (be)
Kim: Oh, I'm sorry. He —3.— already —4.— his leg this year, right? (hurt)
Jamie: Yes, last time he and his friend —5.— to try some new cool <u>skateboard</u> <u>tricks</u>. (want)
Kim: When —6.— he —7.— home? (come)
Jamie: My parents —8.— just —9.— him <u>back</u> from the hospital. (bring)
Kim: That's great. —10.— his friend already —11.— the good news? (hear)
Jamie: No, I —12.— him yet. (not call)
Kim: OK, I'll have to go. See you.

Du musst dich hier zwischen dem simple past und dem present perfect entscheiden.
Die Signalwörter können dir helfen.

choose!

1. didn't see
2. was
3. + 4. has – hurt
5. wanted
6. + 7. did – come
8. + 9. have – brought
10. + 11. Has – heard
12. haven't called

b) Talk to a partner.

26/7-8

Partner A:
Have you ever been in hospital?
Have you ever had an operation?
Have you ever had a cast?
When did it happen?
What happened? Where did it happen?
What was the problem?

Partner B:
Yes, I have been in hospital. / No, I haven't …
It happened in May/August/… .
It was on Monday/Tuesday/… .
It was on 23rd June.
…

10 (YOUR TURN) A role play: Emergency! → V Emergency, p. 187

27/1-2

1. Work with a partner. Write a list like this. Add your own ideas.
2. Exchange your list with another pair.
3. Practice the emergency call. Look at the checklist for help.
4. Act the role play.
5. Give feedback to the other pairs.
   → M Tip top, p. 171

Who? Lena
Where? In the swimming pool
How? fallen over
What's the problem? Arm

Ich kann den Rettungsdienst informieren.

A trip to a Caldicot Castle

1 Have you ever been to a castle? What castles do you know?

2 (READING) Read the report.

1,18

YEAR 9 AT CALDICOT CASTLE

Story by school <u>reporter</u> Richard 'the Lionheart' Smith.

1 **Castle of history**

On a sunny Tuesday morning Year 9 visited
Caldicot Castle in Wales. When we arrived, we
saw that Caldicot Castle is a big building. It is
5 a stone castle and it is over 900 years old.
I said, "Wow, this castle is even older than

[ˈjeɪts] Mr Yeates, our History teacher!"
Everyone laughed. Mr Yeates didn't. ☹

Castle of adventure

We <u>jumped</u> when a big door opened   10
loudly. A <u>knight</u> came out of a <u>cloud</u> of
smoke!   [ˈlɑːnsəlɒt]
He said, "I am Lancelot, a knight of this
castle. I travelled in time to tell you
kids about the castle." The castle had   15
dark <u>corridors</u> and tall towers. It was a
real adventure.
(I don't think Lancelot really was a
knight from the past - I saw him with a
mobile phone!)   20

3 Find the information.

1. Who went on the trip?
2. When did they go?
3. Where did they go?

4. Who told them about the castle?
5. What did knights learn at 'knight schools'?
6. What did they do in the end?

1. Year 9 with Mr Yeates
2. on a sunny Tuesday morning
3. to Caldicot Castle in Wales

4. Lancelot, a knight of the castle
5. They learned how to joust.
6. They took a photo as a souvenir.

Bevor du anfängst zu lesen, schaue dir die zwei Seiten an und überlege. Was für eine Art Text ist es? Wer könnte den Text geschrieben haben?

Für wen könnte der Text geschrieben worden sein? Können dir die Fotos helfen, den Text zu verstehen?

How to joust [dʒaʊst]

[ˈsɔːd]

Lancelot showed us how to put on armour and hold a sword (not a real one but still very heavy!). It made you feel like a real knight. It was the best!
The jousting was super cool and we all tried it. Even Ellie 25
could do it in her wheelchair. In the old days there was a 'knight school' at the castle, and the knights learned how to joust there. When they were naughty, the knights had to go to the stocks!
We saw some real jousting. That was cool! 30

Lancelot goes back to the past

In the late afternoon we'd seen everything in the castle.
Lancelot said it was time for him to return to the past (I hope he remembered to take his phone!)
Before we left, Mr Yeates wanted to see the stocks. Why did he want to see them? Did he 35
want something like that at our school?

No, of course he didn't. But we tried them out for fun and we took this photo as a souvenir.
We all loved the trip and learned lots about Caldicot Castle! 40

4 Choose one of these tasks.

28/1
29/2-4

a) Make a sound diary for the castle trip. Collect, make and record the sounds.

Play the recording to your class - can they guess the sounds?

 OR

b) Draw a plan of a castle you know. Label it in English and add some information (how old?, who lived there, … ?)

Ich kann einen Bericht auf einer Schulwebsite verstehen. ✔

The ride of your life!

Dos and Don'ts at Zip World

1   Zip World in Snowdonia has the fastest zip line in the world and the longest in Europe. And YOU can ride it! Get ready for the ride of your life!

     DO wear the equipment we give you. It keeps you safe. The
5 helmet and goggles protect your head and eyes, and the red suit protects your skin, but also makes you travel more quickly!

     DO listen to what your instructor says. You will get important information.

     DO wear warm clothes and bring some gloves. Even if the weather is sunny, you will feel very
10 cold on the zip line.

     DO check the website before you come. If the weather is bad (for example if it is raining heavily or is very windy), the zip line may not be safe and we may close it. You will get your money back.

     DO book a place. If you don't, you may have to wait a long time.

15 DON'T wear sandals or flip flops. If you lose a shoe, we will not find it for you!

     DON'T be afraid if you change your mind. We want you to have fun, and if you change your mind and don't want to ride, just let us know.

1 Beantworte die Fragen.

30/1-2

1. Welche Sicherheitsausrüstung gibt es? Helme, Schutzbrillen, rote Anzüge
2. Welche Kleidung solltest du tragen? warme Kleidung, Handschuhe
3. Was passiert bei schlechtem Wetter? Die Zip Line ist bei schlechtem Wetter geschlossen.
4. Was passiert, wenn du doch nicht mehr damit fahren willst? Man kann Bescheid sagen.

2 Would you like to try an activity like this?

Would you like to try it? Say why or why not.
Have you ever done an activity like this (hot air balloon? roller coaster?) Talk about it.

Ich kann Informationen über eine Freizeitaktivität weitergeben. ✔

The <u>briefcase</u>

Maybe they are on holiday.
Maybe it's in winter because the girls are wearing coats and hats.
Maybe they found the briefcase on the beach.
Maybe there's money in the briefcase.

1 Look at the photo and guess.

[əˈlɪʃə]

Why are Laura and Alicia at the beach?
What time of the year is it?
Why is there a briefcase?
What's in it?

Now watch the film and check. Were you right?

2 (VIEWING) Watch the film. Right or wrong?

4

1. After the girls and Mr Becket had lunch, the girls go shopping.
2. A man <u>answers his phone</u> and then leaves his briefcase on the beach.
3. The girls <u>cannot</u> open the briefcase.
4. The man from the beach runs after the girls.
5. The girls find out that the briefcase is only a <u>prop</u> for a film.

CULTURE

Es gibt unterschiedliche Strände in Wales – wenn du Surfer bist, findest du im Westen perfekte Bedingungen. Aber es gibt auch Strände, wo du Seehunde und sogar Delfine beobachten kannst! Würdest du gerne an einen dieser Strände fahren?

2 1. Wrong, they go to the beach. 2. That's right.
3. Wrong, they can open it. 4. That's wrong. It's another man. 5. That's right.

3 (SPEAKING) Talk about the film.

Watch the last part of the film again (from 2:56). Do you like the ending? Give reasons.

☺	☹
I like the <u>ending</u> because it's funny/... . I <u>expected</u> ... . I thought	I don't like the ending because it's boring ... . I expected something different. I thought ... .

VIEWING SKILLS

In jedem guten Film gibt es einen Wendepunkt.
Das ist der Moment, in dem sich die Handlung plötzlich ändert.
Was ist der Wendepunkt in diesem Film?

The turning point of the film is when the girls find out that the briefcase is just a prop for a film.

Ich kann einen Film über ein Abenteuer in Wales verstehen. ✔

Checklist

Ich kann Informationen über Freizeitaktivitäten in Wales verstehen. ✔

31

Ich kann Informationen über eine Sportart präsentieren. ✔

... is an exciting sport. • It's quite easy. • You can learn the rules quickly. • You must wear a helmet.

31

Ich kann den Rettungs- dienst informieren. ✔

It's an emergency! • I need an ambulance. • I think he has broken a his leg. • His head is bleeding. • She's burnt her hand.

32

Ich kann einen Bericht auf einer Schulwebsite verstehen. ✔

32

Ich kann Informationen über eine Freizeitaktivität weitergeben. ✔

33

Ich kann einen Film über ein Abenteuer in Wales verstehen. ✔

❋ (TASK) A photo story

Work in groups of three or four students. Each group makes a photo story. The groups can use the computer to make their stories as posters. Each group presents its story and gets feedback from the other groups.

Step 1

Find a good story.

Collect ideas and pictures. Your story can be about:
– a sport
– an emergency
– a trip
– ...

Your pictures should have the same style. Don't mix comics with real life pictures. (You can also take your own photos.)

STUDY SKILLS

Wenn du mit einem Computer arbeitest, speichere deine Dateien in einen Ordner. Benenne die Dateien und den Ordner sinnvoll.

Step 2

Make a plan.

Put the pictures in a good order.
Remember:
Your story must have a beginning,
a middle and an ending.

> **STUDY SKILLS**
>
> Es gibt spezielle Computerprogramme,
> die dir helfen können, deine Fotos zu einer
> Geschichte zusammenzusetzen. Frage
> deinen Informatiklehrer, wenn du Hilfe
> brauchst.

Step 3

Add texts to your pictures.

You can have speech bubbles and / or captions.

The next day …

Hey! That's so cool!

Step 4

Check your draft. → M Peer correction, p. 169

Does it have all the important information? Check the spelling.
Ask a friend to read the story. What advice can he or she give you?

Step 5

Write the clean copy of your draft.

The clean copy should have no mistakes. Write or type as carefully as you can!

Step 6

Present your story to the other groups and get feedback. → M Tip top, p. 171

Which story was the best and why?

Extra practice

1 What's the word? (nach 34/1)

1. Cardiff is the … city of Wales. capital ✔
2. These are water sports. a)
3. You read them when you are in a car. g)
4. These can help people at sea. e)
5. A tough sport which is popular in Wales h)
6. You must know them when you play a game. i)
7. They don't get money for their work. d)
8. Not indoor f)
9. Not a good sport for you when you're scared of heights c)

a) canoeing, rafting
b) capital ✔
c) rock climbing
d) volunteers
e) lifeboats
f) outdoor
g) road signs
h) rugby
i) rules

2 What did the rock climbing instructor say? Adjective or adverb? (nach 37/10)

Good morning everybody! Now listen ~~careful~~ • carefully (1), please. Mark, if you talk ~~loud~~ • loudly (2), no one can hear me! The weather is good • ~~well~~ (3) for climbing today. We'll work hard • ~~hardly~~ (4) in the morning. Then we'll do some easy • ~~easily~~ (5) rock climbing in the afternoon. But please remember the rules: Always climb ~~slow~~ • slowly (6). You must be careful • ~~carefully~~ (7) if the rock is wet • ~~wetly~~ (8). I'm sure we'll have fun and you'll be tired • ~~tiredly~~ (9) this evening!

3 Match the parts of the dialogue. (nach 38/4)

1. Hello, Emergency Services, which service? F
2. Hello, this is Sarah from Cardiff Ambulance Service. What's the problem? E
3. Tell me slowly what has happened. D
4. OK, where are you? B
5. Right, the ambulance is coming. A
6. Can you give me your name and phone number, please? G
7. Listen, Pete. Stay with the girl. The ambulance should arrive soon. C

A Great.
B I'm in East Street, near the bus stop.
C Of course. I'll wait here.
D She's just had an accident. She's fallen off her bike.
E There is a girl on the road. She's bleeding and …
F This is an emergency. I need an ambulance!
G Pete Brown. 077 386 941 23.

4 Write about accidents. (nach 39/5)

a) First write the words.

1. have an a ——
   have an <u>accident</u>
2. break my arm
3. cut my finger

4. twist my knee
5. burn my finger
6. sprain my ankle

b) Make sentences.

1. <u>I've had</u> an accident.
2. I've … .

2. I've broken my arm.
3. I've cut my finger.
4. I've twisted my knee.
5. I've burnt my finger.
6. I've sprained my ankle.

5 What have the people done? What haven't they done yet? (nach 40/8)

buy some tablets
not take them

burn his hand
not cool it

twist her knee
not put a bandage on
it

go to the doctor
not see the doctor

1. Claire <u>has bought</u> some tablets. She <u>hasn't taken</u> them yet.
2. Nick … .   3. Molly … .   4. Joe … .

5 2. Nick has burnt his hand. He hasn't cooled it yet.
3. Molly has twisted her knee. She hasn't put a bandage on it yet.
4. Joe has gone to the doctor. He hasn't seen the doctor yet.

6 Complete the text. (nach 41/9)

Megan loves outdoor activities and sports. She <u>has already tried</u> many things (1 already / try). She —— (2 start) to play tennis when she —— (3 be) ten years old. Two years ago she —— (4 ride) her bike up Mount Snowdon. But canoeing is her favourite and she —— (5 already / win) lots of prizes. Last year she —— (6 have) an accident and —— (7 break) her arm. But it —— (8 get) better quickly and she —— (9 already / be) on the river again this year. —— (10 you / ever / go) canoeing?

6 2. started 3. was 4. rode 5. has already won 6. had 7. broke 8. got 9. has already been 10. Have you ever gone

1,19

The Baker – an interesting film?

[rɪ'vju:]
Review 1 ★★★★☆

I really enjoyed *The Baker*. → 1. Introduction

This comedy has an interesting story about a murderer who runs away from London. He goes to Wales to hide when he has some problems. He becomes the town's new baker so he quickly has to learn how to make cakes and bread. No one knows his secret until his enemy arrives. The film finishes with a big, funny fight. → 2. Content

The stars are brilliant. The actors who play the Welsh people in the town are really funny. The location is very beautiful. There is also a great love story in the film. → 3. The writer's opinion

Go and see this film! I give it four stars. → 4. Conclusion

Review 2 ★☆☆☆☆

The Baker is one of the worst films I have ever seen.

It is the story of a murderer who gets a job wrong, so he moves to a small town in Wales and becomes a baker. Of course, he falls in love with a beautiful Welsh woman and doesn't want to be a murderer again, but the other people in the town find out his secret.

It is a really boring story and the film is very slow. The actors aren't very good and the ending is awful. It is a comedy, but it is more silly than funny.

Give this film a miss! I only give it one star.

Giving your opinion:

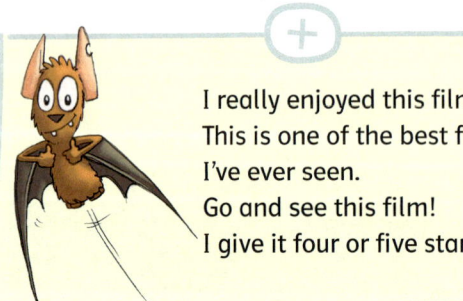

(+)

I really enjoyed this film.
This is one of the best films
I've ever seen.
Go and see this film!
I give it four or five stars.

(–)

I didn't enjoy this film.
This is one of the worst
films I've ever seen.
Give this film a miss!
I give it one or two stars.

1 Look at the first review.

1. Match these sentences with the parts of the review.

A The writer <u>gives reasons</u> why he or she likes the film. **3**

B The writer <u>rates</u> the film and gives <u>advice</u>. **4**

C The writer talks about the story of the film. **2**

D The writer says which film he or she is writing about. **1**

> Filmkritiken geben die persönliche Meinung des Verfassers wieder. Die Kritiken folgen stets demselben Aufbau. Sieh dir dazu das Beispiel an.

2 Read the second review.

2 1. The writer of review 2 doesn't like the film. He or she thinks it's silly, the actors aren't very good, the story is really boring and the ending is awful.

1. Does the writer like the film or not? Why?

2. Find the parts of the structure in review 2.

> Um herauszufinden, wie die Meinung des Verfassers ist, sieh dir die Bewertungen an und achte auf die Wortwahl.

36/1-2

37/3

3 Write a film review.

2 2. introduction: line 1; content: lines 2 – 6; the writer's opinion: lines 7–9; conclusion: line 10

a) Think about the last film you saw. Make notes about the story, actors and location.

The actors are … . The stars are … .
This film is a comedy / <u>drama</u> / <u>romance</u>.
The story / location / <u>start</u> / ending is … .

> Erstelle zuerst eine Stichwortsammlung zu allem, was dir zu diesem Film einfällt.

b) Write a draft of the review. Give the film a star rating.

> Wenn du deinen ersten Entwurf schreibst, beachte die richtige Reihenfolge. Eine Checkliste kann dir dabei helfen. Denke an das simple present.

c) Look at the review again. Where can you add some adjectives?

> Mache deine Kritik interessanter und benutze Adjektive, die deine Meinung unterstützen.

d) Write a clean copy of the review.

e) Read a partner's review and give feedback. Would you like to see the film he or she has written about?

> Wenn du die Filmkritik deines Partners oder deiner Partnerin gelesen hast, gib ihm oder ihr Feedback. War der Aufbau der Kritik in Ordnung? Hat die Kritik den Film gut erklärt? Ist die Meinung zu dem Film deutlich herausgekommen?

→ KV 1, 2

🌐 Find more online:
fe76m3

5 🎞 1,20 ☞

Unit 3

Made in Scotland

['edinbrə]

The capital of Scotland is Edinburgh. It is a very old city. Lots of inventors were born and worked in Edinburgh.

Helpful words:
statue
knight's armour
battleaxe

Robert the Bruce was born in 1274. Robert often fought against the English. Today Scotland is a part of the United Kingdom, but in the past it had its own king or queen.

1 What do you know?

a) Before you read, look at the pictures. What can you see? Talk to a partner.

I can see … / There is … / There are …

b) Read the texts. What else can you find out?

people	clothes	music
weather	food	

2 Right or wrong?

40/1-2

1. Many inventors were born in Edinburgh. **That's right.**
2. Robert the Bruce was born in 1375. wrong (1274)
3. Scotland had a king or queen. right
4. Scotland isn't a windy place. wrong
5. Tourists can't stay in cottages. wrong
6. A kilt is a skirt for men. right

3

Scotland doesn't have much sun but it is a windy place. Now Scotland gets lots of clean electricity from wind farms.

4

Scotland has some beautiful mountains and lakes. Tourists can stay in modern cottages and enjoy the countryside.

5

There are lots of Scottish traditions, like the bagpipes and the kilt, a skirt for men. Scots often eat porridge for breakfast, a warm dish with oats and milk.

🔊 **3** (LISTENING) **Listen to the interview at Whitelee Wind Farm.**

1,21 💿

Finish the sentences.

1. We're one of the —— wind farms in the UK. largest
2. Some turbines are 110 metres, others are 140 metres tall.
3. Wind farms are important because they make —— electricity. clean
4. Are the turbines dangerous for birds?
5. We have a special plan to protect them.

> (wind) turbine ['tɜːbaɪn] – Windrad
> to protect [prə'tekt] – schützen
> nature ['neɪtʃə] – Natur
> dangerous ['deɪndʒrəs] – gefährlich

Ich kann Informationen über Schottland herausfinden. ✔

A Scot <u>who</u> <u>changed</u> the world

1 (READING) **Read the biography.**

1,22
41/1

1 Alexander Graham Bell was born in Edinburgh in 1847.
He is the man who <u>invented</u> the <u>telephone</u>. Bell <u>grew up</u>
in Edinburgh and went to school there and in London.
When he was older he became a teacher.

5 His mother and his wife were both <u>deaf</u>, and Bell was very
interested in <u>speech</u>. He wanted to make a machine <u>which</u>
could change the <u>sounds</u> of speech to electricity.
Bell moved to <u>Canada</u> when he was 23. In 1871 he went to
Boston in the <u>USA</u>. He opened a school there for people

10 who couldn't hear well. He also worked on his <u>invention</u>
every night.
Bell invented the telephone in 1876. It <u>wasn't made of</u>
<u>plastic</u> like the phones which we use today. It was big
and heavy because it was made of <u>metal</u> and <u>wood</u>.

15 The invention was a <u>success</u> and Bell became <u>rich</u>.
Bell died in Canada in 1922. He was a man <u>whose</u>
invention changed the world forever.

1876   1920   1960   1970   1980   2000   2010

2 Find the information.

a) Correct the sentences. → ○ p. 116

> 2. wrong (teacher) 3. wrong (He moved to Canada when he was 23.)
> 4. wrong (It was made of metal and wood.) 5. wrong (He became rich.)
> 6. wrong (He died in Canada in 1922.)

1. Bell invented the car.
    That's wrong. Bell invented the telephone.
2. Bell was a builder.
3. Bell moved to England when he was 23.

4. Bell's telephone was made of plastic.
5. Bell didn't become a rich man.
6. Bell died in Canada in 1822.

b) Find out more details.

1. Which countries did Bell live in?
2. How old was Bell when he died?

> 1. He lived in Scotland, England, Canada and the USA.
> 2. Bell was 75 years old when he died.

READING SKILLS

Eine Biografie erzählt die Lebensgeschichte
einer Person. Finde Wortgruppen, wie *was born*,
mit denen du über das Leben dieser Person
berichten kannst. Sie helfen dir, den Text
schneller zu verstehen.

3 Put the phrases in the right order for Bell's life.

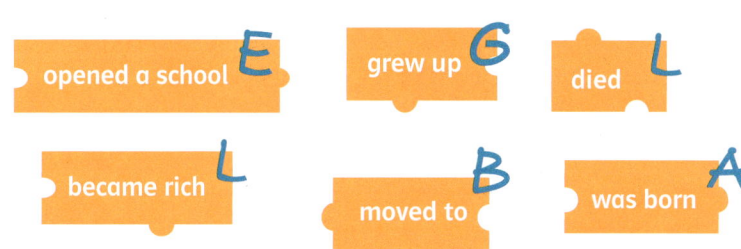

opened a school **E**   grew up **G**   died **L**

became rich **L**   moved to **B**   was born **A**

A – G – B – E – L (became rich) – L (died) → A. G. Bell

Wenn du die Wortgruppen in die richtige Reihenfolge bringst, ergibt sich ein Lösungswort.

1,23 **4** (LISTENING) Listen to John Dunlop's biography.
['dʌnlɒp]

a) Listen to the short profile. Choose the right answers. → ○ p. 117

John Dunlop
- born in a) 1850 • b) 1840
- moved to a) Ireland • b) Germany
- started his company in a) 1876 • b) 1889
- died in a) 1912 • b) 1921

b) Listen again. Which of these two is Dunlop's invention?

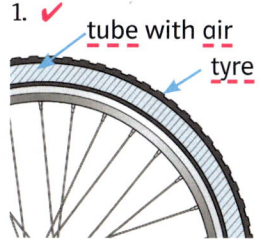

1. ✔ tube with air tyre

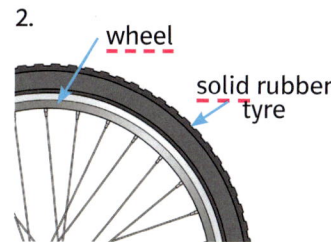

2. wheel solid rubber tyre

5 Things and materials.

41/2 a) Match the things with the materials. → ○ p. 117

1. T-shirts
2. Bike tyres
3. Phones
4. Tables
5. Shoes
6. Books

are usually made of

leather. 5
paper. 6
plastic. 3
wood. 4
cotton. 1
rubber. 2

41/3 b) Find things which are made of these materials. → **V** Materials, p. 189

A bridge is made of steel. …

[ˌæljəˈmɪniəm]

steel   cardboard   silk   wool   aluminium
boxes   blouses   scarves   bikes

6 (SOUNDS) Say the words. Then listen and check your answers.

1,24
1. [ˈtelɪfəʊn] telephone
2. [ɪnˈventə] inventor
3. [ɪn ˌədɪnbrə] in Edinburgh
4. [ə ˌkɒtn ˈʃɜːt] a cotton shirt
5. [ˌhevi ˈmetl] heavy metal
6. [ə ˌleθə ˈtʃeə] a leather chair

Language detectives → G6, p. 155

Bell is the man who invented the telephone.
The school was for people who couldn't hear well.
He wanted to make a machine which could change the sounds of speech.
His telephone wasn't like the phones which we use today

Wann benutzt du who, wann benutzt du which?

7 Match the sentence parts. Describe people and things.

42/4

1. T-shirts and jeans are clothes
2. An inventor is a person
3. Dunlop was an inventor
4. A machine is something
5. Scots are people
6. Scotland is a country
7. Cars and bikes have tyres

+ which / who +

has had a lot of inventors. 6 – which
are made of rubber. 7 – which
made a tyre with air in it. 3 – who
come from Scotland. 5 – who
are usually made of cotton.
helps people with their work. 4 – which
has ideas and makes new things. 2 – who

8 (SPEAKING) Talk about people and things. → M Bus stop, p. 166

42/5

a) Ask your partner. Can he or she find the person or thing? → ○ p. 118

which/that 1. It's a thing —— goes on the wheel of a bike or car. tyre?
who/that 2. It's a person —— feeds animals at the zoo. zookeeper?
who/that 3. It's a person —— is the first player in a team. captain?
which/that 4. It's a thing —— tells you the time. clock?
who/that 5. It's a person —— works with machines. engineer?
which/that 6. It's a thing —— you use to cut food. knife?

Du kannst *that* in Sätzen wie diesen benutzen:
It's a thing that … .
It's a person that … .

1. A: It's a thing which goes on the wheel of a bike or car.
   B: Is it a tyre?
   A: That's right!

b) Choose one of these pictures. Describe it. Can your partner guess what or who you are thinking of?

teacher

Greetings from Sunny Beach
postcard

friend

pencil

hairdresser

biscuit

It's a person … / It's a thing …

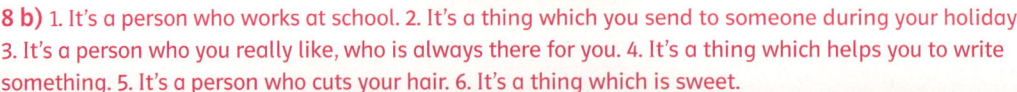
8 b) 1. It's a person who works at school. 2. It's a thing which you send to someone during your holiday. 3. It's a person who you really like, who is always there for you. 4. It's a thing which helps you to write something. 5. It's a person who cuts your hair. 6. It's a thing which is sweet.

9 Make sentences about Bell and Dunlop.

a) Use <u>whose</u> to make one sentence out of two. → ○ p. 118

43/6

1. Dunlop was an inventor.
   His invention made the bike better.
2. Bell was a teacher.
   His mother and wife were both deaf.
3. He was one of many Scottish inventors.
   Their work made Scotland famous.

> **GRAMMAR** → **G6**, p. 155
>
> Dunlop was an inventor <u>whose invention</u> made the bike better.

1. Dunlop was an inventor whose invention …
2. Bell was a teacher whose mother and wife …
3. He was one of many Scottish inventors whose work …

b) Choose <u>who</u> or <u>whose</u>?

43/7

1. People —— inventions are successful often become rich.   whose
2. There are lots of Scots —— don't live in Scotland.   who

✳10 (YOUR TURN) A short biography → **V** Inventors and inventions, p. 193

a) Here are three inventions. Choose one. Find information in the library or on the internet.
Write a short biography of its inventor. Add photos. → **M** Writers' conference, p. 171

43/8

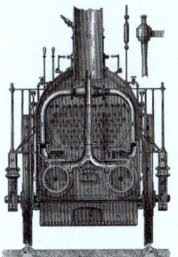

1 <u>steam engine</u>

2 blue jeans

3 <u>light bulb</u>

These phrases can help you to write your biography:

He / She was born in (place) in (year).
He / She is the person who invented … .
It is a thing which … . It is / was made of … .

He / She grew up in … .
He / She died in (place) in (year).

> **WRITING SKILLS**
>
> Eine kurze Biografie behandelt die wichtigsten Fakten aus dem Leben einer Person.
> Schreibe sie in chronologischer Reihenfolge auf. Sage auch, was an diesem Menschen
> besonders ist. Benutze das simple past.

b) Present your biographies. What information did you find interesting?
→ **M** 1-minute-presentation, p. 166

> Ich kann Informationen über einen Erfinder präsentieren.   ✔

Hier lerne ich, mich über Ausflugsmöglichkeiten zu unterhalten.

Where can we stay?

1 (READING) **Read the dialogue.**

1,25

1 **Mum:** Katie, Jake, Harry. It's time to plan our trip to the Highlands. We'll have to decide where we want to stay. I'd love to stay in a cosy B & B in Inverness. [ˌɪnvəˈnes]
Dad: Abby, I thought we could go camping. You know
5 I love hiking. It's a simple and cheap way to spend our holidays. If we stay at a campsite, we'll be outside all day.
Jake: Dad! No way! We'll freeze if we go camping. And there'll be insects too.
Katie: Are you serious, Dad? I agree with Jake. No
10 camping! If we go to a hotel, there won't be any insects. And we'll have our own bathroom. [ˈbʊfeɪz]
Jake: Katie is right. A hotel is great. And the buffets are fantastic. If we don't stay in a hotel, we won't get nice food!
15 **Mum:** I don't want to go camping either but I'm sorry, it won't be a hotel, kids. That's too expensive. We could rent a holiday cottage but spending a few days at a B & B is a better idea. Maybe we can get some tips about local food.
20 **Dad:** Yes, I think so too. If nobody wants to go camping, that's fine. But let's go to Loch Ness. Maybe we'll see Nessie, the Loch Ness monster …

> I don't want to go camping!

> Dad! No way! If we go camping …

> If nobody wants …

2 **Find the most important information.** → **M** Bus stop, p. 166

44/1

a) Copy and complete the table.

Who?	Where?	Why?
Abby (Mum)	B & B	not too expensive, tips about local food
Harry (Dad)	campsite	cheap, they can go hiking, they're outside all day
Katie	hotel	no insects, own bathroom
Jake	hotel	fantastic buffets/nice food

Language tip → **G 7**, p. 156
I love **hiking**.
Spending a few days in a B & B is a good idea.

b) Where would you like to stay? Why?

CULTURE

Briten übernachten oft in einem B & B (bed and breakfast). Das sind Gästezimmer, die privat vermietet werden. Würdest du gerne in einem B & B übernachten? Weshalb?

3 Where do people stay on their holidays?

a) Match the words with the definitions. → ○ p. 118

44/2-
3a)

1. hotel C
2. campsite A
3. bed and breakfast D
4. hostel E
5. caravan B

A It's a place where you go camping.
B It's a small home. Cars can take small ones from place to place.
C It's a big building which has a swimming pool and large buffets.
D It's a place that's almost like home.
E It's usually a place where young people stay. There's often a kitchen for everyone too.

b) Put the steps in the right order. → **V** Going on holiday, p. 190

44/3b)

4	1	5	2	3
check out	ask about prices	pay the bill	make a reservation	check in

1,26
45/4

4 (LISTENING) Which picture is it?

a) Listen to Jim and Dianne. Look at the pictures. Where did they stay? → ○ p. 119

hotel

bed and breakfast ✔

hostel

b) Why did you choose the picture? Give reasons.

I chose picture X because the … . And … .

> **LISTENING SKILLS**
>
> Bevor du den Text hörst, sieh dir die Bilder an.
> Welche Wörter fallen dir dazu ein? Achte beim Hören auf diese Wörter.

Language detectives → **G8**, p. 157 → **G9**, p. 158

We'll freeze if we go camping.
If we go to a hotel, there won't be any insects.
If we don't stay in a hotel, we won't get nice food!

Welche Satzhälfte steht für eine Bedingung?
Welche für eine Konsequenz?
Welche Zeiten werden in den Satzteilen verwendet?

5 **Complete the sentences.**

45/5

1. If Jake goes to Edinburgh, he —— (go) shopping.
   If Jake goes to Edinburgh, he'll go shopping.
2. If Dad has time, he —— (visit) the castle. 'll visit
3. If I see a nice souvenir, I —— (buy) it. 'll buy
4. If we stay at a campsite, maybe we —— (get) cold. 'll get
5. If I see the Loch Ness monster, I —— (take) a photo. 'll take
6. If we find Nessie, we —— (become) famous. 'll become

46/7 **6** **Make sentences about a holiday in a hotel.**

 a) Complete the sentences. → ○ p. 119

45/6

1. If everyone —— (agree), we'll stay in a hotel.
   If everyone agrees, we'll stay in a hotel.
2. If we —— (stay) in a hotel, we'll have a TV. stay
3. If I —— (have) a TV, it won't be boring. have
4. If the son —— (watch) TV all day, he won't meet other kids. watches
5. If we —— (go) to a good hotel, I'll have internet too. go
6. If we —— (not find) anything interesting online, we'll ask at the tourist information. don't find

b) Make sentences.

1. get up early • go swimming before breakfast
   If I get up early, I'll go swimming before breakfast.

2. be hungry • eat at hotel restaurant
3. not rain • go horse riding
4. try haggis • like it
5. visit museum • be open on Tuesdays
6. not get cold • wear a jacket

Pass auf! Welcher Satzteil sollte das if haben?

6 b) 2. If I'm hungry, I'll eat at the hotel restaurant. 3. If it doesn't rain, I'll go horse riding. 4. If I try haggis, I'll like it. 5. I'll visit the museum if it's open on Tuesdays. 6. I won't get cold if I wear a jacket.

7 What will we do if ... ?

1. ... if the weather is nice. 2. ... we'll pay fifty pounds. 3. ... we'll have a barbecue. 4. ... we'll take a photo. 5. ... if we stay in a tent. 6. ... if there's no swimming pool.

a) Look at the pictures. Make sentences. → ○ p. 120

46/8a)

1. We'll go hiking in the mountains if ... . (the weather / nice)

2. If we leave the hostel after ten o'clock, ... (pay)

3. If there's a party at the campsite, ... (have / barbecue)

4. If we go to the Highlands, ... (take / photo)

5. We'll have a problem with insects if ... . (stay / tent)

6. We won't stay in that hotel if ... . (no swimming pool)

b) What will happen if ...?

46/8b)

1. If we have a party at the hostel, we'll go to bed late. If we go to bed late, ...

8 (SPEAKING) Play a game with wishes. → M Round robin, p. 170

Write a wish on a card. Put the cards in a box and take a wish. What will you do if it comes true?

| meet ... | find a ... |
| become rich | ... |

A: If I get a phone for my birthday, I'll ... .   B: If I meet ... , I'll ... .

9 (YOUR TURN) A role play → V Places to stay, p. 194

47/1-2

Act a role play with two others. Where can you go and stay? Use the cards and the phrases.

[mə'gəʊən]
MacGowan Hotel *A*
Place: Glasgow
Activities: museums, food, theatre, shopping
Price: £275 for 2 people for 2 nights

Nessie's Nest (B & B) *B*
Place: Inverness
Activities: walking, canoeing, cycling, Loch Ness
Price: £420 for 4 people for 3 nights

No Tree Hostel *C*
Place: Isle of Skye [ˌaɪlˌəvˈskaɪ]
Activities: bird watching, boat trips, beach walks
Price: £25 for 1 person for 1 night

... is cheaper / more expensive.   I would like to ... .
If you like ..., you will/won't like ... .   I think so too. / I agree / disagree.

Ich kann mich über Ausflugsmöglichkeiten unterhalten.

Robert the Bruce

1 What do you know about Robert the Bruce and the history of Scotland and England?

2 (READING) Read the comic strip.

1,27

1 Welcome to the 14th century! At this time there are lots of battles between Scotland and England.

2 In 1306 …

3 Edward I, King of England, has a strong <u>army</u> …

4 After the sixth battle …

READING SKILLS

Wenn du ein Wort nicht weißt, sieh dir die Bilder an. Sie können dir helfen, die Geschichte besser zu verstehen. Wer spricht? Wie ist die Situation? Was kannst du aus dem Gesicht einer Person ablesen? Du musst aber nicht jedes Wort kennen.

5 Robert the Bruce sees something in the cave.

6 A few days later …

The spider is amazing. It falls, then climbs, it falls, then climbs. It still tries to make its web. It never gives up. So I must never give up!

We must stay together and be brave! We must not give up! We can beat the English!

7 The Scots and the English fight a lot in the years after this. Robert the Bruce loses some battles, but he also wins some. Edward I, the English king, is angry …

This is crazy! Our king is too old and too ill …

I'm going to invade Scotland myself!

8 On the way to one battle Edward I dies.

9 In 1314, at Bannockburn, near Stirling …

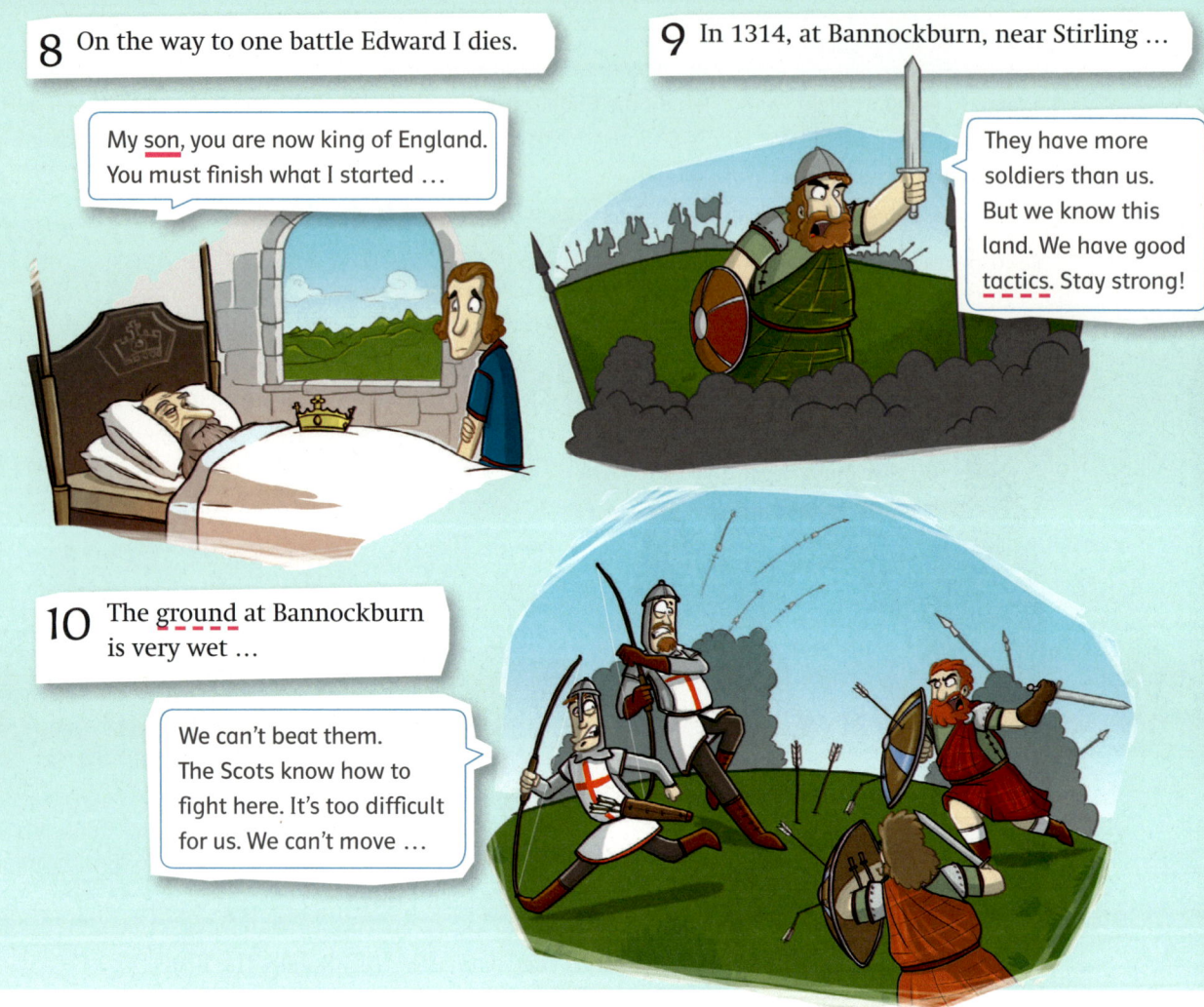

> My son, you are now king of England. You must finish what I started …

> They have more soldiers than us. But we know this land. We have good tactics. Stay strong!

10 The ground at Bannockburn is very wet …

> We can't beat them. The Scots know how to fight here. It's too difficult for us. We can't move …

3 Talk about the story.

Did you like the story? Talk about it with a partner and say why (or why not).

4 Answer the questions.

1. When did the story happen?
   in the 13th century • in the 14th century
2. Who is the hero of the story?
   Robert the Bruce • Edward II

3. Where did the Scottish win?
   at Culloden • at Bannockburn
4. What happened to the English?
   They ran away. • They stayed.

3

11 After two days …

Look, men! They're running away. We've won!

HOORAY!

HOORAY!

Under Robert the Bruce there was peace in Scotland and it was a free country. He was a brave man and a great leader. He was Scotland's most successful king.

12 In the years after this Robert is a good king and the Scots are proud.

WE LOVE you!

I ♥ U   WE ♥ KING ROBERT

Hooray! The English are beaten!

We love you! Thank you!

13 In 1329 …

This is a sad day for Scotland!

---

5 **Choose one of these tasks.**

48/1
49/2-3

a) A short biography of Robert the Bruce.

Search the internet about the life of Robert the Bruce. Then write a short biography. Add pictures.
→ **M** Peer correction, p. 169

 **OR**

b) Make a poster about the battle of Bannockburn.

Search the internet. Find pictures. Add some information.

> **STUDY SKILLS**
>
> Wenn du im Internet Informationen zu einer Person suchst, suche nur nach den wichtigsten Daten und Fakten. Schreibe dir diese als Stichpunkte auf. Benutze sie dann, um die Biografie zu schreiben.

Ich kann einen Comic über eine Schlacht verstehen. ✔

Some Scottish and German dishes

Deep fried chocolate

If you like chocolate, you'll love this snack! A fish and chip shop in Scotland put a bar of chocolate in the same batter it used to cover the fish and then fried it in hot oil. Lots of people thought that this gooey, sticky treat that is crisp on the outside was fun to eat.

['guːi]

Kirschmichel

Kirschmichel ist eine traditionelle Süßspeise, die vor allem im Süden Deutschlands serviert wird. Älteres Brot oder Brötchen werden mit Butter, Eiern, Milch und Zucker vermengt. Dazu kommen Kirschen. Alles wird im Ofen gebacken und noch warm serviert.

Haggis

Haggis is a famous Scottish dish. It's a kind of meat pudding which can include the heart, liver and lungs of a sheep, together with onions and oatmeal. Sometimes it's even served in the sheep's stomach.

Himmel und Erde

Himmel und Erde ist ein beliebtes Gericht in einigen Teilen von Deutschland, z. B. im Rheinland. Kartoffeln und Äpfel werden gekocht, gestampft und miteinander vermischt. Dazu wird Bratwurst oder traditionell Blutwurst serviert.

1 Beantworte die Fragen.

50/1

Eine Deutsche und ein Schotte haben diese Texte gesehen, aber sie verstehen sie nicht ganz. Beantworte ihre Fragen in der jeweiligen Sprache.

1. Schokolade gibt es bei uns auch. Was ist da so besonders?
2. Ich bin Vegetarierin. Kann ich das traditionelle Haggis essen?
3. What's 'Kirschmichel'? I can see the word 'Brot'. Is it a kind of sandwich?
4. 'Äpfel' means 'apple', doesn't it? Is 'Himmel und Erde' a cake with apples?

3. No, it's a German dessert. You mix bread with butter, eggs, milk and sugar and add cherries. Finally you put it in the oven to bake. 4. No, it made of mashed apples and potatoes. It usually comes with sausage

2 What do you think?

Do you like trying different types of food? What's a typical German dish for you?

Ich kann Informationen über Gerichte weitergeben.

The old phone

1 Talk about old phones.

Have you ever seen or used a phone like this?
Can you send messages with it?
What's a <u>pay phone</u>? Where can you find them?
You can find some pay phones in town. You must pay
to use the phone.

2 (VIEWING) Watch the film.

6 🎬

a) Which summary is correct?

1. Alicia helps her grandmother with the shopping and
   her <u>video chat</u>. After that, her <u>neighbour</u> Alva gives her
   an old TV.
2. Marley gets an old phone from Alicia. She <u>repairs</u> it and
   her friends are proud of her.
✔ 3. Alicia helps her neighbour, who gives her an old phone.
   Marley knows how to use it as a <u>radio</u>.

b) Who says it?

1. "I've never had a video chat before." That's Alva.
2. "I have an idea!" That's Marley.
3. "I want to see what you're <u>up to</u>!" That's Alicia.
4. "Wow! It looks interesting! What is it?" That's Laura.
5. "It's amazing what you can do with an old telephone!" That's Laura.

3 (WRITING) Write about the film.

Watch the last part of the film again (from 3:20).
Describe what happens. Use the words for help.

| attach | pipe | antenna |
| connect | signal |

You can start like this:
Marley took an old phone. Laura and Alicia wanted ... .
Marley ... . They heard ... . It was ... .
to see – attached a pipe and connected the antenna – a radio signal – cool

Ich kann einen Film über ein Experiment verstehen. ✔

Checklist

Ich kann Informationen über Schottland verstehen.	✔

51 🗗

Ich kann Informationen über einen Erfinder präsentieren.	✔

… was born in (place) in (year). • He / She is a person who … . • … grew up • … invented the first … in … . • It was a … which … . • … died in (place) in (year).

51 🗗

Ich kann mich über Ausflugsmöglichkeiten unterhalten.	✔

Let's go to … . • … is cheaper / more expensive. • I like / don't like … , so … is better for me. • If you like / don't like … , you will / won't like … .

52 🗗

Ich kann einen Comic über eine Schlacht verstehen.	✔

52 🗗

Ich kann Informationen über Gerichte weitergeben.	✔

53 🗗

Ich kann einen Film über ein Experiment verstehen.	✔

❀ (TASK) An advert

Work in groups of three or four students. Each group thinks of a product and makes an advert (ad) for it. Each group presents the ad and gets feedback from the other groups.

Step 1

Look at the ads.

Do you like them? Discuss.

1

A holiday you'll **never** forget in a magical tree house in the **beautiful** Scottish mountains!

From only **£595** for three wonderful nights! Other locations and offers available.

Book NOW at
www.holidaytreehouse.co.uk

2

FULL SERVICE
Mechanic On Duty!
GARAGE
Since 1960
TYRES • PETROLS • OILS
Free Coffee!

interesting   boring   funny   exciting
nice photos   lots of information   …

Step 2

What makes a good ad? → M Think–pair–share, p. 171

Look at the examples in Step 1 for help.
Look at the language, the photos and the information.

Step 3

Make and design your ad.

1. Choose your product.
2. Think: What is good about the product?
   What kind of people should buy the product?
3. Choose pictures or photos.
4. Write the text.
5. Make a draft of the ad. You can use a computer
   or a large piece of paper.

> **STUDY SKILLS**
>
> Wähle ein interessantes oder ungewöhnliches
> Produkt. Entscheide, für wen deine Werbung
> sein soll. Wähle ein Foto, das für sich selbst
> spricht. Der Text sollte einfach und klar sein und
> die Leser ansprechen. Benutze daher Fragen
> und Aufforderungen.

Step 4

Check your draft.

Does it have all the important information? Check the spelling too.

Step 5

Make your ad and show it to the other groups. → M Gallery walk, p. 168

Step 6

Get feedback from the other groups. → M Tip top, p. 171

What was good/not so good? Which ad was the best and why? Think about:

the text   the design   the message   the photo(s)   who the ad is for   . . .

Extra practice

1 Match the sentence parts. (nach 53/3)

1. Scottish men
2. Tourists can   F
3. Edinburgh is   G
4. Robert the Bruce   B
5. Porridge is   H
6. In the past Scotland   E
7. A lot of inventors   D
8. Wind farms make   A

A clean electricity for Scotland.
B often fought against the English.
C sometimes wear a kilt.
D were born in Scotland.
E had its own king or queen.
F stay in a cottage.
G the capital of Scotland.
H a Scottish breakfast dish.

2 What's the material? (nach 55/5)

rubber   wood   leather   metal   plastic   paper   cotton

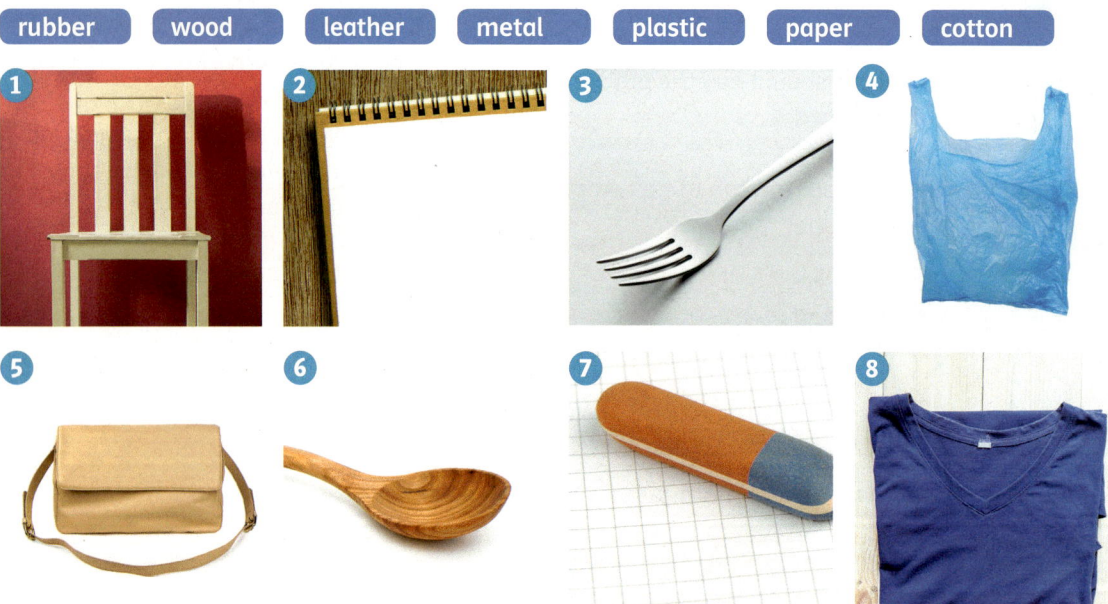

1. This chair is made of wood.

2. This notebook is made of paper. 3. This fork is made of metal. 4. This bag is made of plastic. 5. This bag is made of leather. 6. This spoon is made of wood. 7. This eraser is made of rubber. 8. This T-shirt is made of cottton.

3 Make sentences. (nach 56/8)

1. A kilt is a skirt
2. Robert the Bruce was a king
3. Edinburgh is a Scottish city
4. Porridge is a dish
5. Scotland is a country
6. A cottage is a house
7. An inventor is a person

who
which

is for men.
fought against the English. 2 – who
is very old. 3 – which
has oats in it. 4 – which
doesn't have much sun. 5 – which
is small and often in the country. 6 – which
invents machines and other things. 7 – who

4 Use <u>whose</u> to make one sentence out of two. (nach 57/9)

1. Inventors are important persons. Their ideas make life easier.
   Inventors are important persons whose ideas … .
2. Bell was a famous inventor. His wife and his mother were both deaf.
3. Bell was a teacher. His wish was to help people who couldn't hear well.
4. Bell became a famous man. His invention changed the world forever.

> 2. Bell was a famous inventor whose wife …
> 3. Bell was a teacher whose wish …
> 4. Bell became a famous man whose invention …

5 Complete the sentences. (nach 60/6)

1. If we ⸺ (not want) to pay much, we ⸺ (stay) at a campsite. don't want – 'll stay
2. We ⸺ (freeze) if we ⸺ (stay) at a campsite. 'll freeze – stay
3. There ⸺ (not be) any insects if we ⸺ (go) to a cosy B&B. won't be – go
4. If we ⸺ (be) in a hotel, we ⸺ (have) our own bathroom. are – 'll have
5. We ⸺ (not get) nice food if we ⸺ (stay) at a campsite. won't get – stay
6. If we ⸺ (choose) a hotel, we ⸺ (not have) money for anything else. choose – won't have
7. We ⸺ (take) a cottage if a hotel room ⸺ (be) too expensive. 'll take – is
8. If we ⸺ (see) the Loch Ness monster, everyone ⸺ (be) happy. see – will be

6 Make sentences. (nach 61/8)

1. go …/visit Edinburgh   2. see …/take a photo   3. have …/go shopping

4. stay in a B&B/eat …   5. wet tomorrow/not go …   6. go …/learn about history

1. If I <u>go</u> to Scotland, I <u>will visit</u> Edinburgh.
2. If I see Nessie, I'll take a photo.
3. If I have money, I'll go shopping.
4. If I stay in a B&B, I'll eat porridge.
5. If it's wet tomorrow, I won't go to the mountains.
6. If I go to the museum, I'll learn about history.

Hier kannst du lernen, wie du Wörter in einem Wörterbuch nachschlägst.

1,28

On Ben Nevis

Avalanche hits rock climbers

10:35 published Monday 8th January

Four rock climbers who set off an avalanche in the Scottish highlands on Sunday 7th January were very lucky to escape with their lives.

The four young men, all from London, were climbing Ben Nevis, the highest mountain in the UK. At about 2 p.m. a huge wave of snow swept them 300 metres down the mountain.

In an interview later that day one of the men said, "I fell for a very long time. I didn't believe that I would survive. My friends and I, we all had safety equipment like red coats and red helmets. But still, we were really lucky to walk out. It was a very scary adventure. The rescue helicopter had already started to look for us. It took us to hospital, but we were all OK. Only one of my friends had a twisted ankle."

Next year, the climbers will climb the highest mountain in Europe, Mont Blanc.

1 Look at the dictionary entry.

Use the entry for 'hit' to find the right German word(s) in these sentences:

1. The avalanche hit the climbers.
2. The car hit a tree.
3. The musical *Cats* is a real hit.
4. The boy hit the ball very hard.
5. There were 143 hits for this search.

1. treffen
2. gegen etw. stoßen
3. der Hit
4. schlagen
5. der Treffer

hit hɪt] I. *n* ❶ Schlag *m* ❷ *(shot)* Treffer *m;* **to suffer a direct** ~ direkt getroffen werden ❸ *(success)* Hit *m;* **to be a** [**big**] ~ **with sb** bei jdm gut ankommen ❹ INET Besuch *m* einer Webseite ❺ COMPUT *(match)* Treffer *m* II. *vt* <-tt-, hit, hit> ❶ schlagen ❷ *button* drücken ❸ *(collide)* **to** ~ **sth** gegen etw *akk* stoßen; *car* gegen etw *akk* krachen *fam* ❹ *(shoot)* **to be** ~ getroffen werden ❺ *(occur)* **to** ~ **sb** jdm auffallen III. *vi* ❶ **to** ~ **hard** kräftig zuschlagen; **to** ~ **at sb** nach jdm schlagen ❷ *(attack)* **to** ~ **at sb** jdn attackieren *a. fig*
◆ **hit back** *vi* zurückschlagen; **to** ~ **back at sb** jdm Kontra geben
◆ **hit off** *vt* **to** ~ **it off** [**with sb**] *(fam)* sich prächtig [mit jdm] verstehen

Wenn Wörter in einem Wörterbuch aufgelistet werden, nennt man sie „Einträge". Jedes Wort wird in seiner Grundform angegeben. Suche zuerst immer danach.

Hier wird dir angezeigt, wie das Wort ausgesprochen wird.

Hier siehst du, ob das Wort ein Verb oder ein Substantiv ist.

Nützliche Redewendungen stehen unter dem Grundwort.

Viele Wörter haben mehr als eine Bedeutung. Es gibt jeweils eine Nummer für jede Bedeutung.

Diese Wörter helfen dir, die richtige Bedeutung zu finden.

56/1
57/2-4

2 Work with a dictionary.

a) Find the right German meaning for the underlined words in the text. Use an English-German dictionary.

b) What do the same words mean here?

1. The man waved wildly from the window.
2. A tornado swept through the town.
3. Can I have a look at that magazine?
4. The man escaped from prison in the night.
5. The plane went into a steep climb.

2 a) 1. to escape (with their lives) = (mit dem Leben) davonkommen 2. to climb sth. = (hinauf)steigen, ersteigen, (hoch)klettern, erklimmen 3. a wave (of snow) = eine (Schnee-) Welle 4. to sweep sb./sth. down = etw./jmd. mitreißen 5. to look for sb./sth. = nach jmd./etw. suchen 6. the climbers = Bergsteiger/Bergsteigerin, Kletterer/Kletterin

Du kannst auch Online-Wörterbücher benutzen. Pass aber auf. Nimm nicht gleich die erstbeste Bedeutung. Lies erst den gesamten Eintrag. Du kannst auch die Bedeutung in einem Deutsch-Englisch Wörterbuch gegenprüfen.

2 b) 1. jdm (nach)winken 2. (hin)wegfegen 3. sich etw. ansehen 4. ausbrechen 5. Steigflug

♕ Find more online:
fe76m3

7 🗐 2,1 ☞

Unit 4

In Northern Ireland

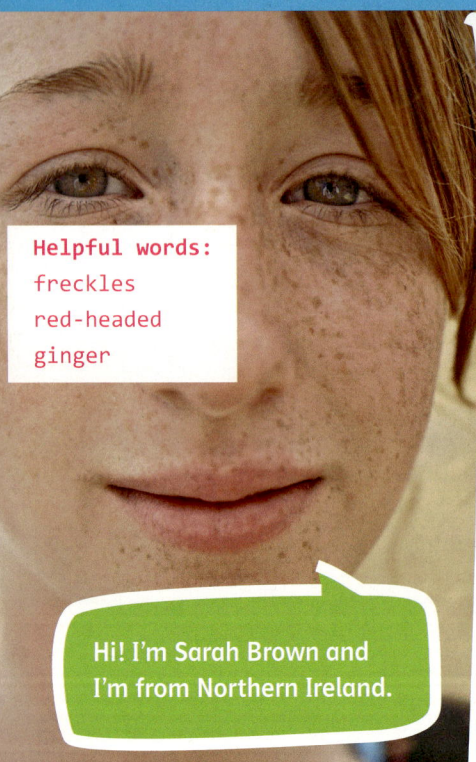

Helpful words:
freckles
red-headed
ginger

Hi! I'm Sarah Brown and I'm from Northern Ireland.

1

Belfast is the capital of Northern Ireland. You can see a lot of murals on the buildings. They are from the time of 'The Troubles', when there were problems between Protestants and Catholics. [ˈkæθlɪkz]

2

My friend Julie and I visited the Giant's Causeway in the summer. That's on the coast of Northern Ireland. It was great!

◖ **1** **Match the headings with the photos or texts.**

A   A lucky day for George 5
B   A new town and job 3
C   A small town shop 4
D   Pictures on walls 1
E   A great summer trip 2

◖ **2** **Answer the questions.**

58/1 ☷

1. What can visitors see on the buildings in Belfast?
2. Where is the Giant's Causeway?
3. Why are Sarah's parents busy?
4. What is there in Randalstown?
5. Which ship was built in Belfast?

1. murals 2. on the coast of Northern Ireland
3. They run a B & B. 4. aunt Maggie's shop
5. the Titanic

3

My dad lost his job in Belfast so we have just moved near Lough Neagh. My parents run a bed and breakfast there now.
They are very busy!

[ˌlɒx ˈneɪ]

4

My aunt Maggie runs a shop in Randalstown, a small town northwest of Belfast. You can buy a lot of things there. And I always get free sweets!

5

Belfast was famous for ships. The Titanic was built here in 1912. My grandad's uncle George got a job as a waiter on it. He was sick on the day it left, so he didn't travel. Phew!

---

3 (LISTENING) **Right or wrong?**

2,2
58/2

1. The man would like some information about Belfast.
   That's wrong. He would like . . . .
2. Buses go every 20 minutes.
3. The visitor centre tells the story of Mike O'Donnell.
4. An adult ticket costs £7.50.
5. A family ticket is £22.

1. some information about the Giant's Causeway.
2. That's right. 3. That's wrong. It tells the story of Finn McCool. 4. That's wrong. It's £9. 5. That's right.

outside [ˌaʊtˈsaɪd] – draußen
visitor centre [ˈvɪzɪtə ˌsentə] –
   Besucherzentrum
giant [dʒaɪənt] – Riese
to cost [kɒst] – kosten
adult [ˈædʌlt] – Erwachsene/r
probably [ˈprɒbəbli] –
   wahrscheinlich

Ich kann Informationen über Nordirland herausfinden.

I'm really fed up!

1 (READING) **Read the e-mails.**

2,3
59/1

E-MAIL

1 Hi Julie,
I need your advice. I'm really <u>fed up</u>.
Mum and Dad <u>never</u> have any time for me <u>any more</u>. They're busy with their new B & B.
5 They work hard all day. And <u>in the evenings</u> they're tired. We had so much fun together when we lived in Belfast. But now?
At the weekends Mum always <u>nags</u> me to tidy up the dining room. But Ashley helps me a lot!
10 Sometimes little brothers can be <u>useful</u>. ☺
I don't like the B & B. We have new guests every day and they always ask the same questions. "Blah blah blah … ." It <u>drives me crazy</u>! I miss you <u>so much</u>!
15 If you were here, I wouldn't be so <u>lonely</u>.
See you,
Sarah ☹

E-MAIL

1 Hi Sarah,
I miss you too. It's so boring here <u>without</u> you. Can't you talk to your parents? I think they would understand if you told them how you
5 feel. If I were you, I would speak to your dad first. He will listen.
If I lived in a B & B, I'd probably <u>hate</u> it too. But think <u>positive</u>! Maybe your guests can tell you interesting stories?
10 If I visited you in our next holidays, you could show me Lough Neagh. I would probably ask the same <u>silly</u> questions as the tourists. But I have to go to Dublin with my family.
Come to Belfast soon! If you were here now,
15 I would take you to the cool new <u>milkshake</u> place in town.
I'll call you tomorrow.
Julie XOX

2 Find the answers.

1. Does Sarah like the new place?
2. What are Sarah's problems?
3. Which advice does Julie give?

| She says … | She doesn't like … | There are … |

| She feels … | She can … | She could … |

3 (SPEAKING) **What do you think?**

a) Talk about these questions. → ○ p. 120
→ M Think-pair-share, p. 171

1. Can you understand how Sarah feels? Why? Why not?
2. Is Julie's advice OK? Why? Why not?

I think it's OK • a problem • not so easy because …

b) Make questions.

Which questions may the guests at the B & B have?

3b) Where is the next shopping centre? Where can we buy …? When do the shops open/close? How long does it take to go to …? How much is …? Is there a café/restaurant …?

4 (LISTENING) **Listen to the phone call. Choose the right answer.**

2,4

1. Who called Sarah?
   ~~Ashley~~ • Julie

2. When was Sarah fed up?
   Yesterday • ~~Two days ago~~

3. Who will Sarah talk to later that week?
   Her dad • ~~Her mum~~

4. When will the girls talk again?
   ~~Tomorrow morning~~ • Tomorrow afternoon

5 Work with adjectives.

a) **Make a chart. Sort the adjectives.** → ○ p. 121 → M Bus stop, p. 166

59/2

sad ✔   furious   smart   confident   horrible   optimistic

☺	☹
smart confident optimistic	sad furious horrible

Du brauchst für einige dieser Wörter ein Wörterbuch. Auf Seite 73 findest du Tipps, wie du mit einem Wörterbuch arbeitest.

b) **Find words with the same meaning. Match the new words with the words from a).**

59/3   → **V** Adjectives for feelings, p. 195

1. down – sad
2. dreadful – horrible
3. hopeful – optimistic
4. intelligent – smart
5. sure of oneself – confident
6. very annoyed – furious

 6 (WRITING) **Describe an important person in your life.** → M Peer correction, p. 169

60/4

Choose a person (family or friend) and write a short text.

What's good and not so good about him or her?

Use the example for help.
You can use the adjectives from Ex. 5 too.

> My best friend always listens to me. He's smart and knows a lot of things. He also … . But he's often late. That really makes me furious. Sometimes he … .

 7 (SONG) **Let your tears fall**

2,5

Listen to the song. What advice does the singer give?

1 Watch your tears fall, let them fall, falling now,
Make the seas calm, take you in my arms, you
cry. (Let your tears fall …)
It's not a crime to fall apart sometimes,
5 It's not a crime to ask why, to ask why, you cry.
(Let your tears fall …)
I will come, no, I won't run,
I'm not scared, to care.

Come to me when you're in need,
10 Set it free, let the truth breathe.
(Chorus): Tell me all your secrets,
   tell me your fears,
I'm gonna push you away,
   then I'll pull you near,
15 No, I won't judge you, I'm gonna help
   you through.

Language detectives → G10, p. 159

If I lived in a B&B, I would hate it too.
If you were here, we'd go to the new place.
They would understand if you told them how you feel.

Sieh dir die Verben an. Was ist anders als in den if-Sätzen Typ I,
die du bereits kennst?

8 (WRITING) Complete the sentences.

60/5-6

If Sarah was 10 years older, …

| visit | work | live | move ✓ | meet | find |

1. she would move to Belfast.
2. … a job. she would find
3. … in an office. she would work

4. … in a flat. she would live
5. … with Julie. she would meet
6. … her parents often. she would visit

9 What would happen?

a) Put in the verbs. → ○ p. 121 → M Peer correction, p. 169

61/7

1. If Sarah —— (go) to a sports club, she would make new friends.
   If Sarah went to a sports club, she would make new friends.
2. If Sarah —— (speak) to her parents about her problems, they would understand her better. spoke
3. If Sarah and her friend Julie —— (meet) each other more often, they would be happier. met
4. If Julie —— (not live) in Belfast, Sarah would see her best friend more often. didn't live
5. Sarah would spend more time in his room if Ashley —— (not listen) to that awful music. didn't listen
6. Mum and dad wouldn't be so tired if they —— (not work) so hard. didn't work

b) Finish these sentences with your own ideas.

1. If Sarah invited —— (invite) a new friend home, her parents would … .
2. If Sarah's parents —— (not listen) to her, … . didn't listen
3. If Sarah's brother was —— (be) older, … .
4. If her parents —— (not work) in a B&B, … . didn't work

10 (SPEAKING) What would you do in this situation?

61/8

a) Make questions and answer them. Work with a partner. → ○ p. 121   → M Double circle, p. 167

Here are some ideas:

- you lose your phone   → ask friend / call my number
- you find a dog near your house   → take … home
- you meet your favourite singer   → take a photo
- you get a plane ticket to another country   → go to …
- you have a year without school   → …

10a)
… if you found …
… if you met …
… if you got …
… if you had …

A: What <u>would you do</u> if you <u>lost</u> your mobile phone?
B: I <u>would ask</u> a friend: "Can you call my number, please?"

61/9

b) Read the headlines. What would you do in each situation?

School boy finds 200 year old <u>coins</u> in garden!   Woman wins big prize in art <u>competition</u>!

Engineer invents <u>time travel</u> machine!

�֍ 11 (YOUR TURN) An e-mail with advice → V Giving advice, p. 199

a) Read the e-mail. What is Steve's problem?

E-MAIL

Hi Julie,

I've got a big problem. 'Tigerboy III' is in cinemas now. My mum hates these movies. But I really wanted
to see it. Yesterday I told her: "I have to do homework together with Seb tonight." But Seb, Carol and I
went to watch the movie. And what happened? We walked into the building and my mum's best friend
was there. Of course she saw me.
What should I do now? Mum will be furious …
Please help me!
See you,
Steve

b) Write an e-mail to Steve and give advice. These phrases can help:

That sounds awful. / That's bad news.
Think positive. / I have a good idea. /
Why don't you …
If I were you, … / If you told your mum, … /
If you talked to your mum's friend, …
Call me later. / Let's speak soon. / …
→ M Writers' conference, p. 171

WRITING SKILLS

Folge diesen Schritten:
- Denke an eine Anrede und einen Schluss.
- Zeige, dass du das Problem verstanden hast.
- Gib zwei Tipps.

Ich kann einem Freund oder einer Freundin einen Ratschlag geben.   ✔

Hier lerne ich, in einem Geschäft ein Gespräch zu führen und dort etwas einzukaufen.

Buy one, get one free

1 (READING) Read the dialogue in Maggie's shop in Randalstown.

2,6
62/1a)

1 **Maggie:** Hello! You're Ian Thompson's son, aren't you? How are you today?

Dan: Yes, that's right! I'm fine, thanks. I have to buy some things for my dad.

5 **Maggie:** What would you like?

Dan: I'd like some raspberry jam, please.

Maggie: Oh dear, we don't have any raspberry jam. But we have strawberry jam. Look, this one is the cheapest, but it's as tasty as the

10 others. There's a special offer. Buy one, get one free!

Dan: Strawberry is fine. I'll have two jars then. Do you have any brown bread?

Maggie: Yes, we do. There's some sliced bread

15 over there, and we have special farmer's bread. Our customers love it. But it's a little more expensive than the other one.

Dan: How much is a loaf?

Maggie: It's £1.20.

20 **Dan:** I'd like one loaf of farmer's bread, please. I have to post a letter for my dad too. Can I have four stamps, please?

Maggie: Of course. Where is the letter for? Oh, Ballyronan? That's where my niece lives.

25 **Dan:** Really?

Maggie: Yes. Her family moved there from Belfast. They have a B & B there now. Of course, Ballyronan isn't as big as Belfast,

and it's less exciting than the big city too. Well, that's £2.52 for the stamps. Anything 30 else?

Dan: I think I have everything. Thanks.

Maggie: OK. That will be £5.27, please.

Dan: Sorry, can you repeat that, please? I didn't get that. 35

Maggie: Yes, of course. £5.27, please.

Dan: Sorry, I've only got a twenty pound note.

Maggie: That's OK. So that's £14.73 change. Here you are. 40

Dan: Thanks. Bye now.

Maggie: You're welcome. Bye!

2 Find out about the shopping trip.

a) Which is Dan's shopping list?

A raspberry jam	B strawberry jam	C raspberry jam
bread	bread	bread
one stamp for letter	four stamps	four stamps ✔

b) How much does the jam cost?

The jam costs £1.55.

3 Find the phrases in the dialogue.

What can you say …

1. to <u>check</u> that a person is OK?
2. when you don't hear or understand?
3. when you give something to a person?
4. when a person says thank you?

1. How are you? 2. Can you repeat that, please? I didn't get that. 3. Here you are. 4. You're welcome.

4 Work with shopping phrases.

a) Put the phrases in A in the right order. The phrases in B can help you. → ○ p. 122
62/1b) → M Peer correction, p. 169

Shop assistant:
A That will be £3.63.
B Goodbye!
C That's £1.37 change.
D Anything else?
E Hi!
F What would you like?

Customer:
1. Hello!   E
2. I'd like … .   F
3. Yes, … . / No, thanks.   D
4. Here you are.   A
5. Thank you.   C
6. See you.   B

b) Who can say these phrases, the customer or the shop assistant?
62/1c)

¹   ²

² Sorry, we've <u>run out</u> of that.   ¹ Do you have another <u>brand</u>?   ² I can <u>order</u> some for you.

² Do you have the <u>exact change</u>?   ¹ Sorry, I've <u>changed my mind</u>.

5 (LISTENING) Listen to two more customers in Maggie's shop.

2,7
62/2
a) Look at the things and listen. Who buys which thing(s)?

Customer 1 buys tissues.
Customer 2 buys peanut butter.

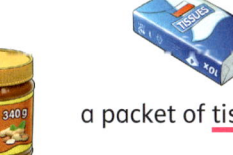
 a packet of <u>tissues</u>

b) Listen again. How many do the customers buy? How much is it?
Customer 1 buys two packets of tissues. They're 25p for a packet. a jar of <u>peanut butter</u>
Customer 2 buys three jars of peanut butter. It's £4.26 for three jars.

a bottle of
<u>mineral water</u>

6 (PUZZLE) Which is more money, A or B?
A is more money. A is £10.72. B is £10.66.

CULTURE

Alle britischen Münzen und Banknoten haben auf einer Seite das Bild des Königs oder der Königin. Welche Menschen oder Dinge sind auf eurem Geld zu sehen?

Language → G 11, p. 160

Ballyronan isn't <u>as</u> <u>big</u> <u>as</u> Belfast.
It's <u>less</u> exciting <u>than</u> the big city.
This one is the <u>cheapest</u>.
It's <u>more</u> expensive <u>than</u> the other one.

Wie sagen wir, dass zwei Dinge gleich sind?
Wann benutzen wir <u>more</u> / <u>most</u> und wann benutzen wir <u>-er</u> / <u>-est</u>?
Was bedeutet das Wort <u>than</u>?

Erinnerst du dich, wie du Dinge auf Englisch vergleichst?

7 Compare the things on the shelf.

63/3-4a)

1. The loaf of sliced bread is <u>bigger than</u> the brown loaf. (big)
2. The brown box of tea is —— the red one. (cheap) cheaper
3. The raspberry jam is —— the peanut butter. (expensive) more expensive than
4. The jar of jam is —— the jar of peanut butter. (big) as big as
5. The tissues in the green packet are not —— the tissues in the blue packet. (cheap) not as cheap as
6. The mineral water from Northern Ireland is —— the Scottish water. (expensive) less expensive than

8 (SPEAKING) What do you think? Talk with a partner.

63/4b)

a) Compare the things. → ○ p. 122

1. chocolate or strawberry? (tasty)
   A: I think chocolate is <u>tastier than</u> strawberry. Do you agree?
   B: Yes, I think you're right.
2. winter or summer? (good)
3. picnic or restaurant? (cheap)
4. speaking any language or talking to animals? (interesting)
5. doing homework or tidying your room? (exciting)
6. having a <u>camel</u> or being a camel? (funny)

| as ... as | not as ... as | -er than | more ... than | less ... than |

b) Compare these things. Do you agree?

dogs or cats?   football or tennis?   small shops or big shops?

8a) 2. I think winter is not as good as summer. 3. A picnic is cheaper than going to a restaurant. 4. Speaking any language is as interesting as talking to animals. 5. Doing homework is more exciting than tidying your room. 6. Being a camel is funnier than having a camel.

4

Language detectives → G 12, p. 161

I have to buy <u>some</u> things for my dad.
Oh dear, we don't have <u>any</u> raspberry jam.
Do you have <u>any</u> brown bread?

Wann benutzen wir <u>some</u> und wann benutzen wir <u>any</u>?
Finde weitere Beispiele im Text auf Seite 80.

64/5 **9** <u>Some</u> or <u>any</u>?

a) Put in <u>some</u> or any. → ⭕ p. 122

1. I'd like to buy <u>some</u> comics.
2. Sorry, we don't have —— tissues. *any*
3. Do you have —— sweets in your bag? *any*

4. Oh dear! We don't have —— change! *any*
5. Let's eat —— cake! *some*
6. Sorry, I didn't buy —— orange juice. I forgot! *any*

b) Make the second sentence. Use the ideas on the right.

1. I can't go out today. I have to do <u>some</u> homework.
2. Oh dear, my nose! …
3. I'm very hungry. …
4. Are you thirsty? …

be / sandwiches in the kitchen ?

have / tissues ?   have / homework + ✔

give you / mineral water +

2. Do you have any tissues? 3. Are there any sandwiches in the kitchen? 4. I can give you some mineral water.

10 (YOUR TURN) **A shopping dialogue** → V Shopping, p. 200

64/6-7
65/1

a) Write notes for a shopping dialogue with a partner. You can use the phrases from Ex. 4 on page 81. Here are some more ideas:

Assistant:
Ask friendly questions. (How are you? / …?)
Say what is cheaper, more/less …
Say that there is a special offer.
Say that you have some new/cool/…

Customer:
Answer the assistant's questions. (Be friendly!)
Say that you need some … and why.
Ask: "Do you have any …?"
Say: "No thanks, I don't need any …"

SPEAKING SKILLS

Höre deinem Gegenüber zu, wenn er oder sie mit dir spricht. Zeige Interesse an dem, was er oder sie sagt. Wenn du etwas nicht verstehst, sage: „Sorry, can you repeat that, please?" Versuche zu helfen, wenn jemand stecken bleibt.

b) Practise and act the dialogue. → M Read and look up, p. 170

Ich kann in einem Geschäft ein Gespräch führen und dort etwas einkaufen. ✔

The Titanic disaster

1 What do you already know about the Titanic? → M Think-pair-share, p. 171

2 (READING) Read the newspaper report.

2,8

The Belfast News
Wednesday, 17th April 1912

Titanic hits iceberg and sinks

TWO DAYS AFTER – MORE FACTS
The Titanic, was built here in Belfast's shipyard. It hit an iceberg shortly before midnight on 14th April. A few hours later it sank. It was on its way from Southampton to New York on its first voyage. There were more than 2,200 passengers and crew on board. Only about 700 people survived the accident.

WORLD'S LARGEST SHIP
The Titanic was the largest and most expensive ship in the world. It had a swimming pool, a gymnasium and two libraries. The ship's builders, The White Star Line, said that their ship was safe. So it only had 20 lifeboats. That was only enough for half of the people on board.

3 Talk about the report.

Was there anything new to you? What did you find most interesting?

4 Find the facts.

1. time and date of accident?
2. from where to where?
3. number of people on board?
4. number of people who survived?
5. number of lifeboats?
6. number of crew members from Northern Ireland?

1. shortly before midnight on 14th April 1912 2. from Southampton to New York
3. more than 2,200 people 4. about 700 people 5. twenty lifeboats 6. twenty

READING SKILLS

Auf die Bedeutung mancher englischer Wörter kannst du selbst kommen, weil du sie so ähnlich schon im Deutschen kennst, wie etwa iceberg, optimistic und passenger. Findest du weitere Beispiele im Text?

LOCAL MEN DIE AT SEA
Twenty of the crew were from Northern Ireland. The ship's doctor, Dr John Simpson, 37, was born in Belfast. His mother was optimistic when a letter from him arrived at her home yesterday. However, we now know that Dr Simpson did not survive.

Dr John Simpson

DOG SAVES LIVES
Some of the dogs on board were lucky. One of the dogs on board saved the lives of the people in one of the lifeboats. A ship only found the lifeboat because they heard the dog.

HOW COULD IT HAPPEN?
Why did no one see the iceberg? Why were there only 20 lifeboats for the 2,200 people on board? And how can we make sure that something like will never happen again?

Some ships today have over 6,500 passengers and crew. All ships must have one lifeboat place for every person on board.
Dr Simpson's last letter to his mother is now in the Belfast Titanic museum.

5 Choose one of these tasks.

66/1
67/2-4

a) A letter

Imagine you are on board the Titanic when it leaves Southampton. Write a letter for 13th April 1912 (100 words). Think about these questions:

 OR

> **How do you feel?**

> **What is it like on board?**

> **What can you do there?**   **. . .**

b) A diary entry

Imagine you survived the disaster. Write the diary entry for 15th April 1912 (100 words). Think about these questions:

> **Where are you now?**

> **How do you feel?**

> **What was it like on the lifeboat?**

> **. . .**

Ich kann einen Zeitungsartikel über eine Katastrophe verstehen. ✔

At a bed and breakfast

1 Beantworte die Fragen.

68/1-2

Du übernachtest mit deiner Familie im „Browns Bed & Breakfast" in der Nähe von Lough Neagh. Dort siehst du diese Schilder.

1. Wer darf hier parken? Was passiert mit Falschparkern?
2. Wann soll man die Klingel betätigen? Was meinst du, warum wurde der Text auf dem Schild geändert?
3. Bekommen die Gäste im B & B wirklich Frühstück ans Bett?
4. Was müssen die Gäste bei der Ankunft machen?
5. Was machst du mit den nassen Handtüchern, wenn du dieses Schild im Bad siehst?
6. Was bedeutet dieses Schild?

> **CULTURE**
>
> In britischen B & B gibt es oft lustige Schilder. Was ist das lustigste Schild, das du jemals gesehen hast?

2 What rules would you have?

If you ran a B & B, what rules would you have? Make signs for two of them.

> **Ich kann Informationen über ein B & B weitergeben.**

The cousin from Northern Ireland

1 Talk about the photos.

['neɪθn] [ʃɔːn]

Nathan and Laura are with their cousin, Sean. Look at the photos from the film.
What do you think is happening?

A

B

C

2 (VIEWING) Watch the film.

8

a) Right or wrong? Correct the wrong sentences.

That's wrong. 1. Sean is very good at sport.
That's right. 2. There are some good basketball teams in Northern Ireland.
That's right. 3. Nathan is not very good at computers.
That's wrong. 4. Sean can't help Nathan with his computer problems.
That's right. 5. The boys want to cook a meal together.

b) Watch for details.

1. What colour is Sean's shirt? blue
2. What's behind the basketball court? a playground
3. How many bottles of water are there? four
4. What colour is the bench that they sit on? green/brown

> **CULTURE**
>
> Viele (Nord)Iren sind in der Vergangenheit ins Vereinigte Königreich gezogen. Heute haben etwa sechs Millionen Menschen im Vereinigten Königreich zumindest einen (nord)irischen Vorfahren. Hast du Familienmitglieder, die in anderen Ländern wohnen?

3 (SPEAKING) Talk about the film.

Watch the film again from the start to 1:00.
How do the kids feel? Match the feelings with the names and tell your partner.

Sean **Nathan** **Laura** **Marley**   angry   proud   unhappy   sorry   ...
unhappy   proud   sorry   angry

> **VIEWING SKILLS**
>
> An einem Filmdreh sind viele Personen beteiligt, z. B. ein Drehbuchautor, ein Regisseur, ein Kameramann oder Make-up artists. Würdest du gerne bei einer Filmproduktion mitmachen?

> **Ich kann einen Film über eine Auseinandersetzung verstehen.** ✔

Checklist

Ich kann Informationen über Nordirland verstehen. ✔️

69 ↗

Ich kann einem Freund oder einer Freundin einen Ratschlag geben. ✔️

Think positive. • I have a good idea. • If I were you, … • If you told …, …

69 ↗

Ich kann in einem Geschäft ein Gespräch führen und dort etwas einkaufen. ✔️

How are you today? • I'd like … . • This … is less expensive than that one. • Here's your change.

70 ↗

Ich kann einen Zeitungsartikel über eine Katastrophe verstehen. ✔️

70 ↗

Ich kann Informationen über ein B & B weitergeben. ✔️

71 ↗

Ich kann einen Film über eine Auseinandersetzung verstehen. ✔️

✳️ (TASK) A newspaper report

Work in groups of three or four students. Each group thinks about an interesting, fun, or scary event during their last school year. Each group writes a report about it.

Step 1

Collect ideas.

Choose an event. Collect ideas. Make a mind map.

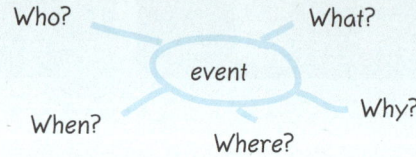

Who? What? event When? Where? Why?

Step 2

Look at the example.

It shows the most important features of a newspaper report.

1 Headline
2 Date, author
3 Introduction
4 Main part
5 Ending

1 Film crew visits local school

2 7th April 2016, by Jamie Smith

3 A film crew was at Hollywell School on Saturday. But nobody knows what the film will be!

4 Students heard the news yesterday from the headteacher, Lucy Green. Mrs Green told us: "A film company came to the school on Saturday and they filmed in the morning and the afternoon. We are all very excited, but we don't know the name of the film yet."

"No children or teachers were at the school. The caretaker opened the doors at 9 o'clock but left after that," she added.

5 Film companies often work in Northern Ireland, of course, but Hollywell School has never been in a film before.

Hollywell School

Step 3

Write the introduction, the main part and the ending.

a) Introduction:
Write one or two sentences.
Answer the Wh-questions.

It took place in … on … . • … were there. •
… because … .

b) Main part:
Write more details about the event.

First … •
Then … . • After that … . • …

c) Ending:
Write one or two sentences to finish your report.

In the end … . • Finally … . • …

Step 4

Find one or two photos.

Write captions for the photos.
Find a headline.
Headlines are always very short.
Only use about five words.
Say who wrote the report and when.

Step 5

Check your report.   → **M** Writers' conference, p. 171

Are there any spelling mistakes?
Did you write clearly?
Do you have a headline?
Did you add a date?
…

WRITING SKILLS

Wenn du einen Computer benutzt, kann dir die
Rechtschreibprüfung helfen, Fehler zu vermeiden.
Damit sich dein Text flüssiger liest, verwende
Bindewörter (but, and, after that). Ergänze Adjektive.

Step 6

Present your report. Give feedback to other groups. → **M** Tip top, p. 171

Extra practice

1 Find the places. (nach 75/5)

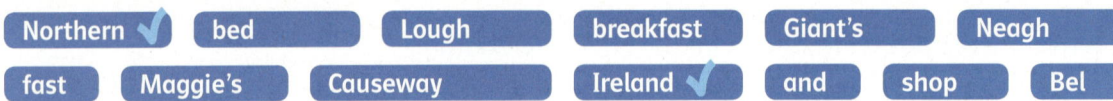

| Northern ✓ | bed | Lough | breakfast | Giant's | Neagh |
| fast | Maggie's | Causeway | Ireland ✓ | and | shop | Bel |

1. Northern Ireland   2. bed and breakfast   3. Lough Neagh   4. Giant's Causeway
5. Belfast   6. Maggie's shop

2 Find the adjectives and make a word. (nach 77/5)

| sad | furious | smart | confident | horrible | optimistic | fed up |

1. smarT
2. cOnfident
3. fed Up
4. fuRious
5. horrIble
6. Sad
7. opTimistic
8. TOURIST

1. It means clever. (fifth letter)
2. You are … when you know that you are good at something. (second letter)
3. Sarah was really … . (first letter of second word)
4. It means very angry. (third letter)
5. It means very bad. (fifth letter)
6. It's the opposite of happy. (first letter)
7. It means that you feel good about the future. (third letter)
8. The new word is … .

Aus den Hinweisen in den Klammern ergibt sich ein neues Wort.

3 What would they do? (nach 78/9)

1. If Julie —— (live) in a B & B, she would talk to the tourists.
   If Julie lived in a B & B, she would talk to the tourists.
2. If Sarah's parents had more time, it —— (be) more fun.   would be
3. If Sarah's mum didn't nag her, Sarah —— (feel) better.   would feel
4. If Ashley —— (not help) Sarah, it would be horrible.   didn't help
5. If Julie —— (live) nearer, Sarah —— (not miss) her.   lived – wouldn't miss
6. If Julie —— (visit) Sarah, she —— (ask) silly questions.   visited – would ask
7. If Sarah and her family —— (live) in Belfast, Sarah —— (see) her friend more often.   lived – would s|

4 Complete the shopping dialogue. (nach 81/4)

1. Shop assistant: Hello. What would you —— ?   like
2. Customer: Hi. I'd like a —— of strawberry jam and a bottle of mineral water, please.   jar
3. Shop assistant: That will be £3.30. Anything —— ?   else
4. Customer: No, thanks. Here you —— .   are
5. Shop assistant: Here's 70p —— . Bye now.   change
6. Customer: See —— .   you

5 Write a shopping list. (nach 81/5)

– two bottles of orange juice, two loaves of bread, a jar of strawberry jam, a bottle of mineral water, a jar of peanut butter, a packet of tissues

6 Compare the things. (nach 82/8)

| is as … as | isn't as … as | is -er/more … than |

1. Northern Ireland 13,843 km² – Scotland 78,387 km² (big)
   Northern Ireland isn't as big as Scotland.
2. the train: takes an hour – the car: takes 75 mins (fast)
3. rice: ✔ – pasta: ✔ (good)
4. rugby: ☺ ☺ – football: ☺ ☺ ☺ (popular in Northern Ireland)
5. Belfast: 19°C – Berlin: 22°C (warm today)
6. orange juice: 1L, £2.75 – mineral water: 1L, £1.85 – (expensive)

> 2. The train is faster than the car.
> 3. Rice is as good as pasta.
> 4. Rugby isn't as popular as football in Northern Ireland.
> 5. Belfast isn't as warm as Berlin today.
> 6. Orange juice is more expensive than mineral water.

74/1-2
75/3-4

7 Complete the dialogue in the supermarket. (nach 83/9)

Some or any?
1. Customer 1: I can't see any peanut butter. Can you?
2. Customer 2: Yes, it's here. They have —— jars on special offer. some
3. Customer 1: Tissues are on our list too. There are —— over there. some
4. Customer 2: Great. Can you see —— brown bread? any
5. Customer 1: No, but they have —— white bread. It looks very nice. some
6. Customer 2: Oh! There aren't —— more cakes. Maybe they've sold them all! any
7. Customer 1: I haven't eaten —— chocolate today. any
8. Customer 2: Really? Let's buy —— now! some

A day in Lisburn

in the upper left corner

in the background

in the upper right corner

in the middle

on the right (side)

on the left (side)

in the lower left corner

in the foreground

in the lower right corner

1 What, who, where?

Answer the questions about the picture.

1. What can you see? I can see a city/a city centre.
2. Who can you see? There are lots of people.
3. Where is it? It's the city centre./It's in Lisburn.

> Bevor du anfängst, sieh dir das Bild genau an. Sage zuerst sehr allgemein, was du siehst. Beantworte dazu kurz die drei Fragen.

2 Describe the picture.

a) Add more details.

In the upper left corner there is a plane.
On the left (side) I can see a book shop.
In the lower left corner there are a band, a man and a woman with a bike.
In the background I can see a museum.
In the middle there is a café.

> Halte eine von dir vorher festgelegte Reihenfolge ein. Beginne z. B. von links oben und gehe dann nach rechts unten.

b) Look at the picture again.
Where are the people or the things?

In front of the ice cream van there are ... a woman, her son and a dog.
Next to the book shop there is a café.

> Sage, wo sich die Personen aufhalten oder wo sich Gegenstände befinden. Nutze dazu folgende Präpositionen: next to, between, behind, over, in, on, in front of, under.

3 What are the people doing?

Look at the people and say what they are doing. The man in the wheelchair is listening to the band. The two girls in the lower right corner are meeting.
In front of the café some people are having lunch.
The dog is eating the boy's ice cream.

> Ergänze, was die Personen tun. Benutze das present progressive.

4 Describe your own picture.

74/1-2
75/3-4

Choose a picture or photo and describe it.

→ KV 1, 2

Find more online:
fe76m3

9 2,9

Unit 5
Welcome to Ireland

The green republic

Helpful words:
lighthouse
coast
rocks

1

Welcome to Ireland! The Republic of Ireland is in the European Union and it uses the euro. But it isn't part of the United Kingdom.

Helpful words:
violin/
fiddle
(Irish) flute

2

There are lots of famous Irish bands, and people often pl[a] music in pubs. Many cities have a youth orchestra too. Orchestras from other countries often come to play conce[rt]

---

1 Choose one picture. Describe it to a partner.

78/1-2

You can use these phrases:

- In the foreground there is …
- In the middle there are …
- In the background I can see …
- …

You can also look for help on the skills pages 92–93.

2 Right or wrong?

1. The Irish use the pound to pay.
2. There are many youth orchestras in Ireland.
3. Keith Hanley won in a competition for singers.
4. The arts programmes in Dublin have courses in sports like tennis and football.
5. The Irish colour is blue.

2 1. Wrong, they use the euro. 2. That's right. 3. That's right. 4. Wrong, they have courses in music, acting, dancing and filmmaking. 5. Wrong, the Irish colour is green.

3

Keith Hanley is an Irish singer from a small town near Cork. He is a winner of 'The Voice of Ireland' competition. Keith's favourite musical style is hip hop.

Helpful words:
shamrock
beard

5

4

Dublin, the capital of Ireland, has lots of arts programmes for young people. There are courses in music and acting, dancing and making films.

Every year on 17th March the Irish celebrate St Patrick's Day. The people wear green, the Irish colour. There are many parties.

---

3 (LISTENING) **Which statement about Keith Hanley is right? A or B?**

2,10

A
- 19 years old
- cares for animals
- hobbies: singing, dancing and playing the saxophone

B
- 19 years old
- cares for children with special needs
- hobbies: singing, dancing and playing the guitar

B is right.

to care for [tə ˈkeə ˌfɔː] – sich kümmern um
sign language [ˈsaɪn ˌlæŋgwɪdʒ] – Zeichensprache
with special needs [wɪθ ˈspeʃl ˌniːdz] – mit Behinderung
guitar [giˈtɑː] – Gitarre

Ich kann Informationen über Irland herausfinden. ✔

At home with the O'Brians

🔵 **1** (READING) **Read the dialogue.** → **M** Dramatic reading, p. 167

2,11

1

1 **Conor:** Here we are. I'll show you the house. Just leave your bags here. You don't have to <u>take off</u> your shoes. … Here's the kitchen. There's the <u>fridge</u>. Just <u>help yourself</u>. We don't
5 usually have breakfast together during the week but we all meet for dinner <u>around</u> 6:30.
Leo: Could we have an Irish breakfast one day, please?
Conor: No problem. We can have it at the
10 weekend. But <u>on weekdays</u> I often just have <u>cereal</u>.
Leo: That's fine with me. Some people have bread with ham or cheese. But I prefer a <u>sweet</u> breakfast.

3

15 **Conor:** That's Maddy's bedroom. That's Jamie's. OK. Just make yourself at home. Are you hungry? Would you like some tea?
Leo: No, thanks. I don't drink tea.
Conor: Ha. I don't mean the drink but the
20 meal. Mum is <u>preparing</u> a snack in the kitchen now. Just come down when you're ready and <u>join</u> us.
Leo: Thanks a lot.

2

Conor: This is the bathroom. Mum put some <u>towels</u> for you over there. You can use all 25
the <u>shampoo</u>, <u>except</u> Maddy's. She hates to <u>share</u> hers with others. Maddy isn't at home at the moment. She's <u>practising</u> with her school band. Are you nervous about your own concert? It'll be great. You can put your 30
<u>toothbrush</u> and other things over here. Did you bring an <u>adaptor</u>?
Leo: Err, I think I didn't.
Conor: Don't worry, we often have guests from other countries. We always have one at 35
home. You can use <u>ours</u>.
Leo: Great. Thanks.
Conor: Oh, the phone is ringing. Just a second.

Leo Kurz (14), from Hanau in Germany

Conor O'Brian (14), from Cork in Ireland

🔵 **2** **Answer the questions.**

1. Which rooms does Conor show Leo?
2. When does the family meet for dinner?
3. What would Leo like to try for breakfast?
4. What doesn't Maddy like to do?
5. Why does Conor's family have an adaptor?
6. What does Conor mean when he says "Would you like some tea"?

CULTURE BOX

Die meisten Briten und Iren essen abends warm. Einige nennen das 'tea', andere 'dinner'. Esst ihr abends warm? Wann esst ihr Abendbrot?

1. the kitchen, the bathroom, Maddy's and Jamie's bedrooms
2. around 6:30
3. an Irish breakfast
4. She doesn't like to share her shampoo.
5. Because they often have guests from other countries.
6. He means something to eat.

3 (LISTENING) Complete Leo's and Mrs O'Brian's sentences.

2,12

1. Do you have —— you need? everything
2. I couldn't find out how to —— the window. close
3. Would you like some —— and sausages for dinner? chips
4. I'm sorry. I thought of —— . crisps
5. Would you please get the —— ? plates and glasses
6. I brought some —— for you. presents

4 (WRITING) Make a mind map with things for a trip. → M Think-pair-share, p. 171

79/1

towel — things for the bathroom — shampoo
comb

raincoat

charger

things for a trip

ID

personal things

mobile

books

clothes
pullover — T-shirts
socks

things for information
map ? dictionary

5 What would you take on a trip?

a) Match the things for a trip with the words. Add them to your mind map. → ○ p. 123

79/2

['neɪl ˌsɪzəz] 1. nail scissors   C
['kəʊm] 2. comb   B
3. toothpaste   E
4. hairdryer   A
['ʃaʊə ˌdʒel] 5. shower gel   D
6. body lotion   F

5 b) 2. You need soap when your hands are dirty.
3. You need perfume when you want to smell nice.
4. You need a mirror when you want to see yourself.
5. You need a hairbrush when your hair is a mess.

b) When do you need …? → V In the bathroom, p. 201

79/3

hair gel   soap   perfume   mirror   hairbrush

1. You need hair gel when you hair is a mess.

6 (SPEAKING) Play the game: I'm going to take …

80/4

A: I'm going to take a toothbrush.
B: I'm going to take a toothbrush and an umbrella.
C: I'm going to take a toothbrush, an umbrella and … .

SPEAKING SKILLS

Wenn dir ein Wort nicht so schnell einfällt, benutze Pausenfüller, z. B. Well … / I think … / Uhm … .

Language detectives → **G13**, p. 162

We <u>usually</u> <u>have</u> breakfast together.
Mum <u>is preparing</u> a snack in the kitchen <u>now</u>.

Was ist der Unterschied zwischen den beiden Situationen?

Die Signalwörter helfen dir, die richtige Zeitform zu finden.

7 Choose the right form. → M Peer correction, p. 169

80/5-6
81/7

1. Conor: Hi Leo, what ~~do you do~~ • **are you doing** <u>right now?</u>
2. Leo: ~~I listen~~ • **I'm listening** to some new songs.
3. Conor: I usually **listen** • ~~am listening~~ to rock music. What do you like?
4. Leo: I always **enjoy** • ~~am enjoying~~ hip hop music a lot. This is Torch OneTwo, a new <u>German rapper</u>. **He** usually **writes** • ~~is writing~~ about his life.
5. Conor: The music sounds OK. What ~~does he talk~~ • **is he talking** about now?
6. Leo: **He** ~~sings~~ • **is singing** about his city, Heidelberg.
7. Conor: **We** never **hear** • ~~are hearing~~ about German hip hop <u>artists.</u>

8 Complete the text messages.

a) Simple present or present progressive? → ○ p. 123

81/8

1 **Leo Germanguy**
I'm in the bathroom right now and I —— (look for / towels). Where are they?
'm looking for the towels

2 **Conor O'Brian**
We always —— (put / in <u>cupboard</u>). Let me know if you can't find them there.
put them in the cupboard

3 **Conor O'Brian**
I'm going to be home late. I am at school and I —— (finish / Art <u>project</u>). Will u tell mum?
'm finishing my Art project

4 **Mad O'Brian**
I'll tell her. But she —— (hate / it) when you're late.
hates it

5 **Mad O'Brian**
I'm here and I —— (<u>wash</u> / <u>hair</u>). And now my shampoo isn't here. Grrrrrh!!! M
'm washing my hair

6 **Conor O'Brian**
Boy, Maddy is angry. She never —— (share / shampoo). Did you take it???
shares her shampoo

b) Write Leo's text messages for these situations:
- You wait at bus stop. There's no school bus.
- You have dinner with the family. You like the food.

81/9 **9** Rewrite the sentences.

a) Rewrite the sentences. Use possessive pronouns. → ○ p. 124

1. It's Dad's chocolate pudding. – It's <u>his</u>.
2. It's Maddy's tea cup. – It's hers.
3. It's my rain coat. – It's mine.
4. It's Mum's and Dad's room. – It's theirs.
5. It's your shirt. – It's yours.
6. It's our cat. – It's ours.
7. It's Conor's bike. – It's his.

GRAMMAR	→ **G14**, p. 163
my – <u>mine</u>	your – <u>yours</u>
his – <u>his</u>	her – <u>hers</u>
our – <u>ours</u>	their – <u>theirs</u>

b) Leo has forgotten many things. Who can he borrow things from?

Mr O'Brian   soap 1
Conor   shampoo 2
Mr and Mrs O'Brian   hairdryer 3
Jamie   adaptor 4
Maddy   toothpaste 5

9 b) 1. I can borrow his.
2. I can borrow his.
3. I can borrow theirs.
4. I can borrow his.
5. I can borrow hers.

✱**10** (YOUR TURN) **A text message dialogue** → **V** Things for a trip, p. 206

You are staying with a host family: Your <u>partner</u> is in town and you are at home. Write a text message dialogue.

A

(at home)
1. Say hi. Ask what your partner is doing and where he or she is.

3. Answer. Say that you have forgotten … / you can't find … / you would like to borrow ….

5. Answer: It's a good / bad idea because ….

B

(in town)
2. Answer your partner. Ask: Is he or she OK?

4. Answer your partner. Ask: Can he or she meet for an ice cream (where, when)?

6. Finish the dialogue.

WRITING SKILLS

Wenn du Wörter in einer Textnachricht in Großbuchstaben schreibst, „schreist" du dein Gegenüber an. Bleib höflich.

Ich kann mich mit meiner Gastfamilie unterhalten. ✔

Hier lerne ich, eine Reise mit öffentlichen Verkehrsmitteln zu planen.

Getting around in Dublin

1 (READING) **Read the flyer and the dialogue.** → M Read and look up, p. 170

2,13
82/1

1 **Jamie:** I can't wait to go to the Striking Moves workshop tomorrow. I'm sure they'll teach us some new moves there.
Lisa: I think so too. We should plan our journey.
Jamie: Where is the workshop?
5 **Lisa:** It's in Sackville Place. It's not far from The Spire on O'Connell Street.
Jamie: How do we get there? I don't use public transport very often!
Lisa: Here, I've brought the timetables. All right, let's see
10 what we can find out. We can take the number 9 bus to Goldenbridge. We must get off the bus there and change to the tram. Then it's ten stops on the Red Line to Abbey Street.
Jamie: How long does the journey take?
Lisa: About an hour. Maybe longer. The bus may not be on
15 time. It usually isn't.
Jamie: Well, the workshop starts at 10, so we must leave by 8:30. We really mustn't be late. Why don't we meet at the bus stop near my house? There's a bus at 8:25.
Lisa: That sounds good to me.
20 **Jamie:** OK. How much is the fare?
Lisa: We can get tickets that are valid all day for three fifty each. But we needn't spend that much money. A single ticket costs one forty each. And then it's the same for the way back.
Jamie: Great. See you tomorrow, then I won't be late …

The Spire
[ðə ˈspaɪə] large, pin-like
monument on O'Connell
Street in Dublin

STRIKING MOVES
Dance and drumming workshop

Take part in our exciting project!
Learn the coolest moves!

Saturdays 21st, 28th June and 5th, 12th July
10 a.m. – 5 p.m.

14 Sackville Place, Dublin

For ages 15–35

2 **Answer the questions.**

a) Find the information.
  to the Striking Moves workshop in Sackville Place
  1. Where do Lisa and Jamie want to go?
  2. Which tram do they take? the Red Line
  3. How many stops are there to Abbey Street? ten
  4. What's special about the buses? They are often late.
  5. How long is the workshop? seven hours
  6. Who can take part in the workshop? people between 15 and 35

b) When would you choose a day ticket and when single tickets?
  I would use a day ticket if I wanted to go to more than one place during one day. I would take single tickets if I already knew I only needed two rides.

CULTURE

Du kannst in Dublin mit dem Bus und / oder der Straßenbahn fahren. Es gibt zwei verschiedene Systeme und zwei getrennte Pläne. Welche öffentlichen Verkehrsmittel gibt es da, wo du wohnst?

3 Find the odd one out.

a) Which word doesn't go with the others? Why? → ○ p. 124

82/2

1. train • bus • ~~ticket~~
2. fare • receipt • ~~present~~
3. stop • line • ~~museum~~

4. on time • ~~sure~~ • late
5. date • timetable • ~~map~~
6. ~~plan~~ • change • get off

b) What are these tickets valid for? → **V** Public transport, p. 203

82/3

| daily | weekly | monthly | single | return |

A daily ticket is valid for one day.

A weekly ticket is valid for one week/seven days.
A monthly ticket is valid for one month.
A single ticket is valid for one way of the journey.
A return ticket is valid for the journey there and back.

83/4 **4** (SPEAKING) **Find the way.** → **M** Milling around, p. 168

a) Look at the map and find the best way to get from James's to … → ○ p. 124

- George's Dock
- Connolly train **station**
- Milltown

To get from James's to George's Dock, take the Red Line. It's eight stops. Get off the tram and you're there.

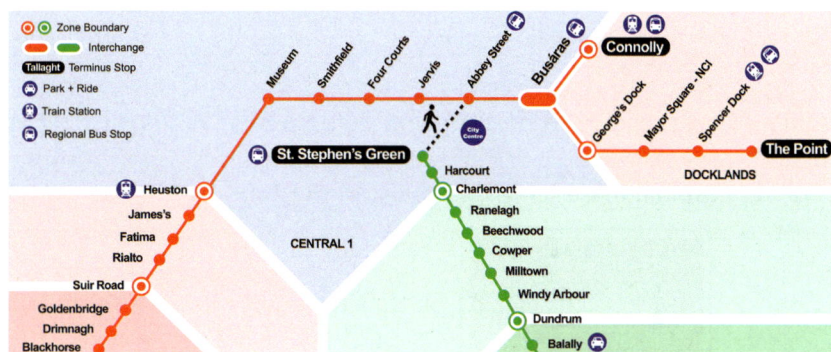

b) Make a list with three places. Partner A's list are the starting points and partner B's list is where you want to go. Give each other directions.

5 (SONG) Luminous

2,14

Listen to the song by the Irish group, Jedward: What will the singer always know, and why?

['dʒedwəd]

1 We see the day, tryin' to fight it.
It's all in vain, 'cause we know the night wins,
But we don't care,
We're lighting up like a flare.

5 It's so unreal,
The light that you're shining.
You make me feel like
The darkness won't matter,

'Cause you and I,
10 Don't care where the day has gone.
We don't need the break of dawn,
We don't need the break of dawn.

(Chorus): And I will always know where you are,
15 'Cause I can see you glow in the dark.
We got the stars, and moon in us,
We're always gonna be luminous.

Language detectives → **G15**, p. 164

We <u>must</u> get off the bus.
We <u>needn't</u> buy tickets for the journey back.
We <u>mustn't</u> be late.
We <u>can</u> take the number 9 bus.
The bus <u>may not</u> be on time.

<u>Must</u>, <u>mustn't</u>, <u>needn't</u>, <u>can</u> und <u>may</u>, <u>may not</u> sind besondere Verben. In welchen Situationen benutzt du sie?

6 What <u>can</u> kids do at a dance workshop? What <u>mustn't</u> they do?

83/5

1. They ~~can~~ • **mustn't** be late.
2. They ~~can~~ • **mustn't** eat during the dance <u>classes</u>.
3. They **can** • ~~mustn't~~ stop dancing when they need a break.
4. They ~~can~~ • **mustn't** talk when the teachers dance.
5. They **can** • ~~mustn't~~ drink water when they are thirsty.
6. They **can** • ~~mustn't~~ learn new dance <u>steps</u>.

7 (SPEAKING) What <u>must</u> you do on a bus? What <u>mustn't</u> you do?

84/6a)

a) Explain these school bus rules. → ○ p.125

FOLLOW THE SCHOOL BUS RULES

You read:
1. Talk quietly.
2. Don't eat ice cream.
3. Don't talk to the <u>driver</u>.
4. Don't bring pets.
5. Keep your head, hands and feet inside.
6. Don't <u>push</u> other students.

You say:
1. You must talk quietly.
2. You mustn't eat ice cream.
3. You mustn't talk to the driver.
4. You mustn't bring pets.
5. You must keep your head, hands and feet in the bus.
6. You mustn't push other students.

b) Think of other bus rules. Then talk with a partner. Are your partner's rules OK?

84/6b

You mustn't listen to loud music on the bus.   You mustn't put your feet on the seat.   You mustn't eat chewing gum on the b

8   Make sentences. Choose <u>must</u> or <u>needn't</u>. → M Peer correction, p. 169

84/7

1. <u>I have two tickets. So you</u>
2. Do you really think we
3. It's already four o'clock! We
4. Alan is at the workshop. So we
5. I can hear you very well. You
6. Do you know where Kate is? We

must

needn't

<u>buy one. You can have one of mine.</u>
take our coats? It's a warm day!   2 – must
go now or we won't get our bus.   3 – must
wait for him at the bus stop. Let's go.   4 –
                                          needn't
talk loudly.   5 – needn't
call her. We can meet her at the station.
                                          6 – needn't

9   (WRITING) <u>Must</u>, <u>needn't</u> or <u>mustn't</u>?

a)   Put in the right verb. → ○ p. 125

84/8

needn't   1. Dogs <u>travel</u> free. You —— buy an extra ticket.
must   2. Your dog —— be with you all the time.
mustn't   3. Your dog —— hurt people.
must   4. It —— be nice to other people.
needn't   5. You —— <u>carry</u> a small dog in a bag. It's OK to hold it.
mustn't   6. You —— play with your dog when you're on the bus.

b)   Find rules for a pet at home. Write a list.

| sleep | eat | play | go out | sit |

❋10   (YOUR TURN) A journey by public transport → V Public transport, p. 207

P

85/1

a)   Find out how to get from the airport or train station to your house on public transport.

b)   Write an e-mail to a friend from another country. Give him or her advice how to get to your house from the airport or train station.

You should take ... .
Then ... .
It's ... stops.
The journey takes ... .
You must buy ... .
You needn't ... .
It costs ... .

E-MAIL

Hi Helen,

Let me tell you how to get to my house from the airport. You should take the train ...
Best wishes,
...

A different kind of gold

1 Have you ever moved to another place? How did you feel?

2 (READING) Read the story.

2,15

1   It was St Patrick's Day yesterday. And I
    wished I was back home in Ireland. My Dad
    and I moved here two months ago and I
    still miss my Irish friends and our nice little
5   home in Donegal. [ˌdɒnɪˈgɔːl]

[niːv]   Oh, I should introduce myself to you.
    My name is Niamh. That's an old Irish girl's
    name. You say it 'neve', like 'leave'.
    I always have to explain it to people here in
10 Northampton in England. That's where we
    moved. Dad worked in a factory in Donegal
    until it closed last year. He tried to find
    another job in the area, but lots of other
    factories were closing too. He finally found a
15 job but that meant that we had to move
    to England.

So yesterday it was my favourite holiday,
St Patrick's Day. Back home there are lots of
parades and parties. Everyone wears green
20 clothes. In fact the whole city is green.
We send cards with shamrocks and rainbows
on and give each other sweets in gold paper.
The shamrock is our national flower. The
rainbows and the sweets are from an old
25 Irish story. It says there's a pot of gold at
the end of the rainbow.

There were parties here in Northampton too.
It almost felt like being home, but I still don't
know a lot of people and places. So I stayed
30 at home. That's why the day just made me
feel very lonely and homesick. I got even
sadder because the netball girls Sonya, Billy
and Nisha, who I really like, didn't answer
any of my calls.

3 Talk about feelings.

a)   Make a list of adjectives and verbs that describe how Niamh feels. Compare with a partner.
     to miss, lonely, homesick, sad, miserable
b)   How does Niamh's feelings change in the last paragraph? Give reasons.

| First Niamh feels / is … because … | Then she feels … because … | She is … |

4 Talk about St Patrick's Day.

Look at the third paragraph (lines 16 to 25). What did you learn about St Patrick's Day that you
didn't know before?

> **3 b)** First Niamh feels lonely and homesick because she misses her
> friends in Ireland and her old home.
> Then she feels more hopeful and more at home because her new friends
> visit her and take her out to a St Patrick's Day party.

READING SKILLS

In manchen Geschichten muss man auf die Hinweise achten, wie sich Menschen fühlen oder was passiert ist. Man nennt das „zwischen den Zeilen lesen".

35 When Dad came home from work that afternoon, I was just sitting at the window. "Are you OK, Niamh?" he asked me. "Yes," I said.
But Dad didn't believe me. So he tried to
40 cheer me up with this old poem (don't ask me where he got that one from):

At the end of the rainbow is a pot of gold,
My dad would say to me.
We packed our bags, our house was sold,
45 *We crossed the Irish Sea.*
But until the fable once foretold
Actually comes to be,
The wealth of friends and family old
Is gold enough for me.

50 He wasn't very successful. I still felt miserable and just wanted to feel sorry for myself. Do you know what I mean?

Later that day, in the late afternoon, our doorbell rang. Dad said: "You can go to the
55 door." When I opened it I couldn't believe my eyes. The netball girls. All three dressed in green clothes and big green party hats on. I couldn't help but laugh. "Surprise!" they said. "Your dad says it's OK to take you to a
60 St Patrick's Day party at our youth centre. Do you want to join us?" I rushed into my room and grabbed my Paddy's Day outfit as fast as I could. Maybe this was the beginning of something wonderful.

5 Choose one of these tasks.

a) Some singers and bands have left Ireland to become successful in Britain or the USA. Others come from a family which moved to these countries a long time ago.

Find information and photos on the internet for a short presentation about one of them.
→ M 1-minute-presentation, p. 166

86/1
87/2-4

 OR

b) Write your own poem. Choose one of these titles:

Friends   **Leaving home**

1. Make a list of words that match the title.
2. Make an outline of an object or shape. It should be big enough to write ten words into it.
3. Write them into the shape. Share your poems with the class.

Ich kann eine Geschichte über einen Umzug in ein anderes Land verstehen. ✔

A German star

Emilia Schüle

Emilia Schüle

1 Die Schauspielerin Emilia Schüle kam als Ein-
jährige 1993 aus Russland nach Deutschland.
Bereits mit acht Jahren begann sie, Ballett-
stunden und Unterricht in Hip-Hop und Street
5 Dance zu nehmen. Mit 13 Jahren nahm sie am
Theaterworkshop „Talents Getting Started" teil
und beeindruckte die Jury mit ihrem Können.
Danach erhielt sie erste Rollen als Schauspielerin
und spielte auch in einigen Werbefilmen mit.

10 Ihre erste Hauptrolle hatte sie 2007 in dem Film
„Manatu – Nur die Wahrheit rettet dich", in dem
es um ein magisches Brettspiel geht. Auch in der
bekannten Serie „Tatort" spielte sie schon mit.
Bekannt wurde sie schließlich durch die beiden
15 Filme „Freche Mädchen" und Freche Mädchen 2",
in denen sich alles um Teenagerfreundschaften
und erste Liebesprobleme dreht.

Emilia hat in dieser kurzen Zeit ihrer Schauspieler-
karriere schon einige Preise verliehen bekommen:
Im Jahr 2014 erhielt sie die „Goldene Kamera" 20
und den „Deutschen Schauspielerpreis" in der
Kategorie „Beste Schauspielerin Nachwuchs".
Trotz dieser frühen Erfolge war es ihr sehr wichtig,
die Schule abzuschließen. Während des letzten
Schuljahres arbeitete sie sogar nebenher als 25
Schauspielerin.

1 Talk about Emilia Schüle.

88/1-2

You are on an exchange visit in Ireland. Your exchange partner sees the article
and is interested in acting. Tell her about Emilia Schüle. Say:

1. who she is
2. how she became an actor
3. what TV and film work she has done

1. Emilia Schüle is a German actor.
2. She was in the 'Talents Getting Started' competition and
did well. She got her first job as an actor after that.
3. She was in 'Manatu – Nur die Wahrheit rettet dich', 'Tatort',
'Freche Mädchen' and 'Freche Mädchen 2'.

2 And you?

Would you like to be an actor? Say why or why not.

Ich kann Informationen über eine Schauspielerin weitergeben.

The guitar lesson

1 **Talk about music.** → M Think-pair-share, p. 171

What is music good for? What can you do with music? Collect words.

dance
impress
music
listen to
…

CULTURE

Musik spielt im Leben vieler Menschen überall auf der Welt eine große Rolle. Die meisten Länder haben besondere Instrumente. Einige der traditionellen irischen Instrumente sind die Harfe und das Bodhran (eine Art Trommel). Kennst du traditionelle Instrumente in anderen Ländern?

2 (VIEWING) **Watch the film.**

xx a) Watch the film from the beginning to 1:45. Find the right answer.
1. Where does Ciara (the music teacher) ['kiərə] want to go?
   ~~a) Victoria Station~~ • b) Greenwich
2. Where did Hayley work?
   a) in a café and on a pineapple farm • ~~b) at a restaurant and on a wind farm~~
3. What does Hayley mean when she says, "I go wherever the wind takes me."
   ~~a) She'll go to a very windy place next.~~ • b) She doesn't know where she'll go next.

b) Watch the film from 1:45 to the ending.

1. Where does Marley find out about the guitar lessons? on a piece of paper, on a tree
2. What does Alicia think about Marley's idea at the end? She thinks it's OK.
3. Why does Marley want to have guitar lessons? Because he likes Alicia. He wants to impress her.

3 (SPEAKING) **Talk about the film.**

a) Which places are not in the film?

bus station   café   supermarket
streets in Greenwich   music school
café, supermarket

b) What do you think: why did the filmmakers choose the places to shoot the film?

VIEWING SKILLS

Es ist schwierig, einen Film im Freien zu drehen. Wenn man in einer belebten Straße dreht, können fremde Personen durchs Bild laufen oder die Hintergrundgeräusche stören. In geschlossenen Räumen zu drehen ist aber auch nicht einfach. Das Team braucht viel Platz für Kameras und Mikrofone. Daher drehen viele Produktionsfirmen im Studio.

Ich kann einen Film über Musikunterricht verstehen. ✔

Checklist

Ich kann Informationen über Irland verstehen. ✔

 89

Ich kann mich mit meiner Gastfamilie unterhalten. ✔

I didn't pack any … . • You can put your … here. • We usually eat at half past six.

 89

Ich kann eine Reise mit öffentlichen Verkehrsmitteln planen. ✔

You can take a number 9 bus to … . • You must change at … . • The journey takes … minutes. • The tickets cost … .

 90

Ich kann eine Geschichte über einen Umzug in ein anderes Land verstehen. ✔

90

Ich kann Informationen über eine Schauspielerin verstehen. ✔

 91

Ich kann einen Film über Musikunterricht verstehen. ✔

✳ (TASK) A quiz

Work in groups and write questions for a quiz about the five countries of the British Isles. Each group writes eight questions for one country. The groups are the teams when you do the quiz.

Step 1

Collect ideas and decide on your questions.

a) Collect ideas for questions about your country.

| England | Northern Ireland | Wales | Scotland | The Republic of Ireland |

Here are some ideas for questions (you can ask about things that were in the units in this book):
- food?
- sport?
- town?
- famous person?
- flag?
- transport?
- …

CULTURE

 Diese Flagge wird normalerweise mit Nordirland in Verbindung gebracht. Man nennt sie St Patrick's Cross. (Offiziell hat Nordirland keine eigene Flagge. Man benutzt die Flagge Großbritanniens.)

b) Make a long list with everyone's ideas. Then look at all the ideas together and agree on a short list.
→ M Placemat, p. 169

STUDY SKILLS

Hört euch alle Ideen gut an. Gebt allen eine Chance, zu erklären, was er oder sie gemeint hat. Einigt euch auf eure Ideen für die Fragen.

Step 2

Write your questions and check the answers.

a) Each student writes a card with one question and the answer on the back.

b) Another student checks the English. A third student checks that the answer is correct.

c) Each student in the team has to read one or more questions. Decide on the order of the questions and practise before you do the quiz.

Step 3

Get ready for the quiz.

1. When can you do the quiz?
2. Who can be the umpire and start/finish the quiz?
3. Which team reads its questions first?

Jedes Team kann eine Flagge vorbereiten. Ihr könnt auch ein Maskottchen mitbringen. Viel Glück!

Step 4

Do the quiz.

Each team reads its questions. The other teams write the answers.

SPEAKING SKILLS

Lest die Fragen laut und deutlich vor. Seht die anderen Teams an, wenn ihr eure Fragen vorlest. Wenn ihr eine Frage nicht versteht, fragt höflich nach. (Wenn ihr die Antwort wisst, behaltet sie zunächst für euch).

Can you say that again please?

Sorry, I didn't understand that!

Can you speak louder, please?

One student from each team checks the answers at the end and gives the results to the umpire. The umpire says who the winner is.

Step 5

Talk about the quiz. → M Round robin, p. 170

Did you enjoy the quiz? What was good/not so good about it?

Extra practice

1 Find the words. (nach 95/3)

1. There is a —— for singers in Ireland every year. competition
2. —— is on 17th March. Everybody wears —— clothes. St Patrick's Day – green
3. People often play music in —— in Ireland. pubs
4. Teenagers can learn how to —— at special —— in Dublin. dance – courses
5. Ireland isn't part of the United Kingdom, but it is in the ——. EU (European Union)
6. Many Irish cities have a youth ——. orchestra

2 What is it? (nach 97/5)

1. You put it on a toothbrush. toothpaste
2. This is where you have breakfast. kitchen
3. This is where you sleep in. bed
4. It's a cold place for milk or cheese. fridge
5. You need it when your hair is dirty. shampoo
6. It's a hot drink and a meal. tea
7. It's for when your hair is wet. It needs electricity. hairdryer

3 Put in the right forms. Simple present or present progressive? (nach 98/8)

1. I can't talk now. I —— (do) my homework.
   I can't talk now. I'm doing my homework.
2. Conor sometimes —— (cook) for the family. cooks
3. We usually —— (have) breakfast at eight o'clock. And you? have
4. Maddy —— (practise) with the school band at the moment. 's practising
5. Look at that woman! She —— (wear) the same T-shirt as me. 's wearing
6. Conor often —— (use) Maddy's shampoo. uses
7. What's that noise? Oh, it's Leo. He —— (shout) at his sister. 's shouting
8. You'll need an umbrella in Ireland. It often —— (rain) there. rains

5

4 Match and make sentences. (nach 100/2)

a) Match the words.

get   public   bus

get off
public transport
bus timetable
pay the fare

the journey ✔   the fare   timetable

plan ✔   pay

transport   off

b) Put in the words from a).

1. The workshop is tomorrow. We must plan the journey.
2. Don't —— here – this isn't our stop.   get off
3. You must —— when you travel on a bus or a train.   pay the fare
4. The —— tells you when the bus leaves and arrives.   bus timetable
5. I don't understand buses. I don't use —— very often.   public transport

5 Concert rules. Must or mustn't? (nach 102/7)

1. You —— bring glass bottles.   mustn't
2. You —— buy a ticket.   must
3. You —— make films with your mobile.   mustn't
4. You —— push other people.   mustn't
5. You —— leave big bags outside.   must
6. You —— bring your own food.   mustn't
7. You —— sit on the stairs.   mustn't
8. You —— put rubbish on the floor.   mustn't

6 Put in the right words. (nach 103/9)

1. It's raining now. We —— take an umbrella.   must
2. Our tickets are valid. You —— worry.   needn't
3. That bus is always on time. We —— be late.   mustn't
4. Ssh, not so loud. We —— talk quietly.   must
5. I've heard that joke already. You —— tell me.   needn't
6. What's the next stop? I'll ask the driver.
   No, you —— talk to the driver.   mustn't
7. Look, here's a plan. You —— ask.   needn't
8. Come on. We —— get off here.   must

must (3x)

mustn't (2x)

needn't (3x)

Diff corner

Unit 1, p.13

○ **4** (WRITING) **Where can you buy these things?**

Complete the sentences.

card   clothes ✔   sports

shoe   baker's

A You can buy jeans at the <u>clothes</u> shop.
B You can buy bread at the <u>baker's</u>.
C You can buy a football at the … shop. sports
D You can buy a birthday card at the … shop. card
E You can buy shoes at the … shop. shoe

Unit 1, p.14

○ **8** (SPEAKING) **Interview your partner.** → **M** Double circle, p.167

Ask a partner questions. He or she gives short answers.

A:			B:
Do you		go to the cinema?	Yes, I do.
Do your friends	sometimes	do your homework?	No, I don't.
Does your dad	often	play football?	Yes, he/she does.
Do they	usually	watch TV?	No, he/she doesn't.
Does he		go shopping?	Yes, they do.
			No, they don't.

Do you often go shopping?   Yes, I do. / No, I don't.

Unit 1, p.15

○ **9** (WRITING) **Make questions and answers.**

Match the questions and answers.

1. <u>Do you know where the football stadium is?</u>
2. Does it take long to get there? F
3. Where is the nearest bus stop? E
4. When do the buses leave? B
5. Are bus tickets expensive? D
6. Where can I buy a ticket? A

A On the bus.
B I think it's every five minutes.
C <u>Yes, I do.</u>
D No, they aren't. Just 90p.
E It's just five minutes down that road.
F Yes, it does. But there's a bus.

Unit 1, p.17

○ **3 Sort the words into groups.** → **M** Peer correction, p. 169

Copy the table. Put the words and phrases into the right groups.

words for the size **1**	where **2**	sorts of places **3**

2 in the centre of . . .   **3** village   **2** . . . miles away from   **1** small

2 near . . .   **2** in the north/south/east/west of   **3** town

1 large   **3** city   **2** in the mountains   **1** big

Unit 1, p.18

○ **6 Make Tom's story.**

Complete the sentences.

went   wasn't   fell   got up   wanted   heard   was   had   saw

1. Last Saturday morning things <u>went</u> a little crazy on our farm. (go)
2. I —— a noise in the garden (hear) and I —— . (get up)   heard – got up
3. I —— my dad in the garden. (see)   saw
4. He —— to put Bert and Daisy, our goats, in his tractor. (want)   wanted
5. Suddenly he —— in the mud, head first. (fall)   fell
6. It —— so funny. (be) I just —— to laugh. (have)   was – had
7. Dad —— very happy. (not be)   wasn't

Unit 1, p.18

○ **7** (WRITING) **What didn't Hannah and Kilkenny do on Saturday?**

Make sentences with <u>didn't</u>, <u>wasn't</u> or <u>weren't</u>.

1. Hannah <u>didn't walk</u> to the baker's in the morning.
2. Hannah —— (not be) in the living room at two o'clock.
   wasn't
3. Hannah —— (not do) her homework in the afternoon.
   didn't do

p.113

4. She and her sister —— (not make) jewellery at five o'clock.   didn't make

5. Later she —— (not write) a text message.   didn't write

6. Hannah and her sister —— (not be) at the cinema.   weren't

---

Unit 2, p. 35

○ **5 Find the words.** → M Bus stop, p. 166

Find the opposites.

1. big – small
2. slow – quick
3. tough – easy
4. friendly – unfriendly
5. strong – weak
6. dangerous – safe
7. wet – dry
8. quiet – loud

weak	unfriendly	dry
small ✓	easy	loud
safe	quick	

Unit 2, p. 36

○ **9 Complete the report.**

Add these words to the text.

well | excitedly | fast | slowly | heavily | hungrily

2 fast
3 hungrily
4 excitedly
5 slowly – 6 well

Last month Class 9G went on a camping trip to Snowdonia. It started to rain heavily (1) so we had to walk —— (2). At lunchtime we ate our picnics —— (3). On Sunday we went canoeing —— (4). We went down the river —— (5). Everything went —— (6) and no one got wet. Phew! We had lots of fun.

> **GRAMMAR** → G4, p. 153
>
> A fast game – she runs fast
> A hard day – he works hard
> A good song – they sing well

Unit 2, p. 37

○ **10** (WRITING) **Adjective or adverb?**

Complete the dialogue.

*Nach den Formen von „to be"
(„was", „were") benutzt du
immer nur Adjektive!*

Mark: Beth, how was horse riding today?
Beth: It was <u>awful</u>/~~awfully~~ (1). It was wet/~~wetly~~ (2)
and rained ~~terrible~~/terribly (3).
Mark: So you had to ride ~~careful~~/carefully (4)?
Beth: Yes, and there were lots of crazy/~~crazily~~ (5) people on
bikes too. Some of them rode ~~dangerous~~/dangerously (6).
Mark: Was your horse nervous/~~nervously~~ (7) because of them?
Beth: No, it wasn't. Look, here's a photo of us …

Unit 2, p. 39

○ **6** (SPEAKING) **Find excuses. Why can't you do PE?**

Make sentences. Use the words in the box.

Dear teacher,
I'm so sorry. I can't do PE today.
My head hurts terribly. I have a sore
throat too. I've also twisted my knee.
… I just don't feel well. ☹

> I have cut my finger / hand / … .
> I have burnt my finger / hand / arm / … .
> I have broken my finger / hand / arm / foot / leg …
> My … is bleeding …

Unit 2, p. 40

○ **8** (WRITING) **What has Megan already done? What hasn't she done yet?**

Make sentences.

What she has already done:
Put on her uniform
Opened the door
Had lunch
Written a message

What she hasn't done yet:
Collected the bandages
Drunk tea
Called the hospital

Megan <u>has</u> already <u>put</u> on her uniform. Megan <u>hasn't collected</u> … <u>yet.</u>   the bandages

She has already opened the door.   She hasn't drunk her tea yet.   She has already had
her lunch.   She hasn't called the hospital yet.   She has already written a message.

Unit 2, p. 41

○ **9** (SPEAKING) **Make a dialogue.**

Complete the dialogue. Use the simple past (<u>last</u>) or the present perfect (<u>already</u>, <u>yet</u>, <u>just</u>).

didn't see **Kim:** Hey, I —— your brother at football training <u>last</u> Monday. (not see) What's wrong with him?

was **Jamie:** He —— in hospital <u>last</u> week. (be)

has – hurt **Kim:** Oh, I'm sorry. He —— <u>already</u> —— his leg this year, right? (hurt)

wanted **Jamie:** Yes, <u>last</u> time, he and his friend —— to try some new cool skateboard tricks. (want)

did – come **Kim:** When —— he —— home? (come)

have – brought **Jamie:** My parents —— <u>just</u> —— him back from the hospital. (bring)

Has – heard **Kim:** That's great. —— his friend <u>already</u> —— the good news? (hear)

haven't called **Jamie:** No, I —— him <u>yet</u>. (not call)

Kim: OK, I'll have to go. See you.

Unit 3, p. 54

○ **2** (READING) **Find the information.**

1 Alexander Graham Bell was born in Edinburgh in 1847. He is the man who invented the <u>telephone</u>. Bell grew up in Edinburgh and went to school there and in London. When he was older, he became a <u>teacher</u>.

5 His mother and his wife were both deaf, and Bell was very interested in speech. He wanted to make a machine which could change the sounds of speech to electricity. Bell moved to <u>Canada</u> when he was 23. In 1871 he went to Boston in the USA. He opened a school there for people

10 who couldn't hear well. He also worked on his invention every night. Bell invented the telephone in 1876. It wasn't made of plastic like the phones which we use today. It was big and heavy because it was made of <u>metal and wood</u>.

15 The invention was a success and Bell became rich. Bell died in Canada in <u>1922</u>. He was a man whose invention changed the world forever.

Correct the sentences.

1. Bell invented the car.
   That's wrong. Bell invented the telephone.
2. Bell was a builder.
3. Bell moved to England when he was 23.

4. Bell's telephone was made of plastic.
5. Bell didn't become a rich man.
6. Bell died in Canada in 1822.

2. Wrong, he was a teacher. 3. Wrong, Bell moved to Canada when he was 23. 4. Wrong, it was made of metal and wood. 5. Wrong, he became a rich man. 6. Wrong, he died in Canada in 1922.

Unit 3, p. 55

4 (LISTENING) Listen to John Dunlop's biography.

1,23

Listen to the profile. Choose the right answer.

1 John Dunlop was born in Ayrshire on the west of Scotland in 1840.
He went to school there and in 1859 he started work as a vet in Edinburgh.
5 In 1867 he moved to Ireland and worked as a vet there. Dunlop often had to go to farms. This was difficult because the roads in Ireland were awful.
One day in 1887 he noticed that his young
10 son's tricycle was very uncomfortable. Its tyres were made of solid rubber. Dunlop took a garden hose and used it as a kind of tube. He put air in it and put it around the wheels. Riding the tricycle was much nicer with air
15 in the tyres.

Dunlop wasn't the first person to invent a tyre like this. Another Scot, Robert Thomson, had the same idea in 1845. But Dunlop's tyres were cheaper. In 1889 he started the Dunlop Rubber Company. The 20
company was a success, but Dunlop didn't really get rich. He sold his part of the company in 1896. After that the Dunlop Rubber Company made tyres for the new cars, and Dunlop's name became famous all 25
around the world. Dunlop lived quietly in Ireland and bought part of a clothes company. He died in 1921.

John Dunlop
– born in a) 1850 · b) 1840
– moved to a) Ireland · b) Germany
– started his company in a) 1876 · b) 1889
– died in a) 1912 · b) 1921

Unit 3, p. 55

5 Things and materials.

What is the right material?

1. T-shirts are usually made of cotton · wood.
2. Bike tyres are usually made of paper · rubber.
3. Mobile phones are usually made of wood · plastic.
4. Tables are usually made of wood · cotton.
5. Shoes are usually made of leather · paper.
6. Books are usually made of metal · paper.

Unit 3, p. 56

○ 8 (SPEAKING) Talk about people and things. → M Bus stop, p. 166

Ask your partner. Can he or she find the person or thing?

1. It's a thing —— goes on the wheel of a bike or car. which
2. It's a person —— feeds animals at the zoo. who
3. It's a person —— is the first player in a team. who
4. It's a thing —— tells you the time. which
5. It's a person —— works with machines. who
6. It's a thing —— you use to cut food. which

clock 4   tyre 1 ✓   engineer 5
captain 3   knife 6   zookeeper 2

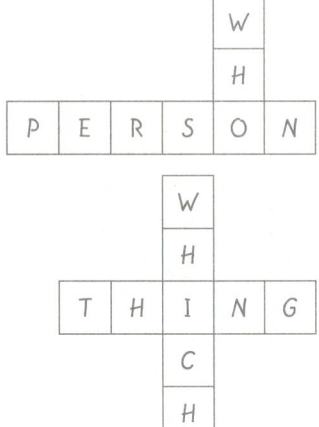

1. A: It's a thing which goes on the wheel of a bike or car.
   B: Is it a tyre?
   A: That's right!

Unit 3, p. 57

○ 9 Make sentences about Bell and Dunlop.

Use whose to make one sentence out of two.

whose 1. Dunlop was an inventor —— . His invention made the bike better.
whose 2. Bell was a teacher —— . His mother and wife were both deaf.
whose 3. He was one of many Scottish inventors —— . Their work made Scotland famous.

Unit 3, p. 59

○ 3 Where do people stay on their holidays?

Match the words with their definitions.

A It's a place where you go camping.   2
B It's a small home. Cars can take small ones from place to place.   5
C It's a big building which has a swimming pool and large buffets.   1
D It's a place that's almost like home.   3
E It's usually a place where young people stay.
There's often a kitchen for everyone too.   4

p. 119

1. hotel   2. campsite   3. bed & breakfast   4. hostel   5. caravan

Unit 3, p. 59

4 (LISTENING) Which picture is it?

1,26

Listen to Jim and Dianne. Look at the pictures. Where did they stay?

Look at the windows, chairs, shelves, pictures and lamps.

hotel   bed and breakfast ✔   hostel

Unit 3, p. 60

6 Make sentences about a holiday in a hotel.

"he", "she", "it" – das "s" muss mit.

Complete the sentences.

1. If everyone —— (agree), we'll stay in a hotel.
   If everyone agrees, we'll stay in a hotel.
2. If we —— (stay) in a hotel, we'll have a TV. stay
3. If I —— (have) a TV, it won't be boring. have
4. If the son —— (watch) TV all day, he won't meet other kids. watches
5. If we —— (go) to a good hotel, I'll have internet too. go
6. If we —— (not find) anything interesting online, we'll ask at the tourist information. don't find

Unit 3, p. 61

○ **7 What will we do if ...?**

Look at the pictures. Make sentences.

1. We'll go hiking in the mountains if ... .

2. If we leave the hostel after ten o'clock, ...

3. If there's a party at the campsite, ...

4. If we go to the Highlands, ...

5. We'll have a problem with insects if ... .

6. We won't stay in that hotel if ... .

3 we'll have a barbecue	4 we'll take a photo	5 stay in a tent
2 we'll pay fifty pounds	6 there's no swimming pool	1 the weather is nice

Unit 4, p. 76

○ **3 (SPEAKING) What do you think?** → M Think-pair-share, p. 171

Talk about these questions.

1. Can you understand how Sarah feels? Why? Why not?

I can understand how she feels		her parents don't have time for her.
	because	she's new.
		she doesn't know a lot of people.
I can't understand how she feels		she moved to an interesting place.
		she will meet new people.
		…

2. Is Julie's advice OK? Why? Why not?

I think it's OK		Sarah's dad is OK.
	because	Sarah will learn a lot from the guests.
		…
I think it's a problem / not so easy		her parents are very busy.
		there are new guests every day.
		…

Unit 4, p. 77

○ **5 Work with adjectives.** → **M** Bus stop, p. 166

Make a chart. Sort the adjectives.

| sad ✔ | furious | smart | confident | horrible | optimistic |

☺	☹
smart	sad
confident	furious
optimistic	horrible

Du brauchst für einige dieser Wörter ein Wörterbuch. Auf Seite 73 findest du Tipps, wie du mit einem Wörterbuch arbeitest.

Unit 4, p. 78

○ **9 What would happen?** → **M** Peer correction, p. 169

Put in the verbs.

| didn't work | spoke | didn't live | went | didn't listen | met |

1. If Sarah ——— (go) to a sports club, she would make new friends.
   If Sarah <u>went</u> to a sports club, she would make new friends.
2. *spoke* If Sarah ——— (speak) to her parents about her problems, they would understand her better.
3. *met* If Sarah and her friend Julie ——— (meet) each other more often, they would be happier.
4. *didn't live* If Julie ——— (not live) in Belfast, Sarah would see her best friend more often.
5. *didn't listen* Sarah would spend more time in his room if Ashley ——— (not listen) to that awful music.
6. *didn't work* Mum and dad wouldn't be so tired if they ——— (not work) so hard.

Unit 4, p. 79

○ **10** (SPEAKING) **What would you do in this situation?** → **M** Double circle, p. 167

Make questions and answer them. Work with a partner.

What would you do if …
– you lost your phone
– you found a dog near your house
– you met your favourite singer
– you got a plane ticket to another country
– you had a year without school

I would …
→ ask friend / call my number
→ take / home
→ take / photo
→ go to / …
→ …

A: What <u>would you do</u> if you <u>lost</u> your phone?
B: <u>I would ask</u> a friend to call my number.

Unit 4, p. 81

○ **4 Work with shopping phrases.** → M Peer correction, p. 169

Complete the dialogue.

| ² What would you like? | ⁴ That will be £3.63. | ⁶ Goodbye! |

A
1. Hi!
2. …
3. Anything else?
4. …
5. That's £1.37 change.
6. …

B
1. Hello!
2. I'd like … .
3. Yes, … . / No thanks.
4. Here you are.
5. Thank you.
6. See you.

Unit 4, p. 82

○ **8 (SPEAKING) What do you think? Talk with a partner.**

Compare the things with a partner.

1. chocolate or strawberry? (tasty)
   A: I think chocolate is tastier than strawberry. Do you agree?
   B: Yes, I think you're right.
2. winter or summer? (better)
3. picnic or restaurant? (cheaper)

4. speaking any language or talking to animals? (more interesting)
5. doing homework or tidying your room? (more exciting)
6. having a camel or being a camel? (funnier)

| as … as | not as … as | -er than | more … than | less … than |

Unit 4, p. 83

8 2. I think winter is better than summer. 3. I think a picnic is cheaper than going to a restaurant. 4. I think speaking any language is more interesting than talking to animals. 5. I think doing homework is more exciting than tidying your room. 6. I think being a camel is funnier than having a camel.

○ **9 Some or any?**

Put in some or any.

1. I'd like to buy some comics.
2. Sorry, we don't have — tissues.   any
3. Do you have — sweets in your bag?   any
4. Oh dear! We don't have — change!   any
5. Let's eat — cake!   some
6. Sorry, I didn't buy — orange juice. I forgot!   any

In verneinten Aussagen und Fragen steht „any"!

Unit 5, p. 97

○ 5 What would you take on a trip?

Match the things.

1. nail scissors
2. comb
3. toothpaste
4. hairdryer
5. shower gel
6. body lotion

Unit 5, p. 98

○ 8 Finish their text messages.

Simple present or present progressive?

1 Leo Germanguy
I'm in the bathroom right now and I … (~~look for~~ / am looking for) towels. Where are they?

2 Conor O'Brian
We always … (put / ~~are always putting~~) them in the cupboard. Let me know if you can't find them there.

3 Conor O'Brian
I'm going to be home late. I am at school and I … (~~finish~~ / am finishing) my Art project. Will u tell mum?

4 Mad O'Brian
I'll tell her. But she (hates / ~~is hating~~) it when you're late.

5 Mad O'Brian
I'm here and I … (~~wash~~ / am washing) my hair. And now my shampoo isn't here. Grrrrrh!!! M

6 Conor O'Brian
Boy, Maddy is angry. She never … (shares / ~~is never sharing~~) her shampoo. Did you take it???

Unit 5, p. 99

○ **9** **Rewrite the sentences.**

Rewrite the sentences. Use possessive pronouns.

1. It's **Dad's** chocolate pudding. – It's <u>his</u>.
2. It's **Maddy's** tea cup. – It's hers.
3. It's **my** rain coat. – It's mine.
4. It's **Mum's** and **Dad's** room. – It's theirs.
5. It's **your** shirt. – It's yours.
6. It's **our** cat. – It's ours.
7. It's **Conor's** bike. – It's his.

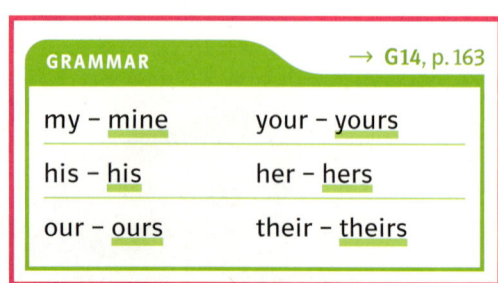

GRAMMAR	→ G14, p. 163
my – <u>mine</u>	your – <u>yours</u>
his – <u>his</u>	her – <u>hers</u>
our – <u>ours</u>	their – <u>theirs</u>

Unit 5, p. 101

○ **3** **Find the odd one out.**

Which word doesn't go with the others? Why?

Think of times, prices, transportation, verbs.

1. train • bus • ~~ticket~~
2. fare • receipt • ~~present~~
3. stop • line • ~~museum~~
4. on time • ~~sure~~ • late
5. date • timetable • ~~map~~
6. ~~plan~~ • change • get off

Unit 5, p. 101

○ **4** (SPEAKING) **Find the way.** → M Milling around, p. 168

Look at the map and find the best way to get from James's to …

– George's Dock
– Connolly train station
– Milltown

To get from James's to George's Dock, take the Red Line. It's eight stops. Get off the tram and you're there.

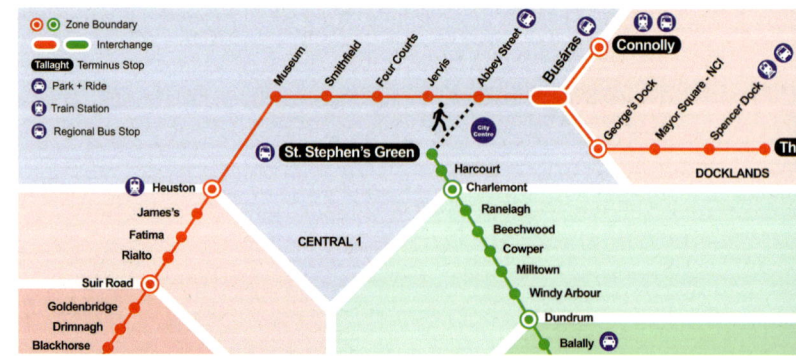

Stay on the tram for … stops.   Take the Green Line.

Take the Red Line to … .   Change at … and walk to … .   …

4 a) 2. To get from James's to Connolly train station, take the Red Line to Busáras. It's seven stops. Change there and take the Red Line to Connolly train station. It's one stop. To get from James's to Milltown, take the Red Line to Abbey Street. It's six stops. Get off there, walk to St. Stephen's Green and take the Green Line to Milltown. It's six stops.

Unit 5, p.102

○ **7** (SPEAKING) **What <u>must</u> you do on a bus? What <u>mustn't</u> you do?**

Explain these school bus rules.

FOLLOW THE SCHOOL BUS RULES

You read:

1. Talk quietly.
2. Don't eat ice cream.
3. Don't talk to the driver.
4. Don't bring pets.
5. Take your rubbish with you.
6. Keep your head, hands and feet inside.
7. Don't push other students.

You say:

1. You must talk quietly.
2. You mustn't eat ice cream.
3. You mustn't talk to the driver.
4. You mustn't bring pets.
5. You must take your rubbish with you.
6. You must keep your head, hands and feet inside.
7. You mustn't push other students.

Unit 5, p.103

○ **9** (WRITING) **<u>Must</u>, <u>needn't</u> or <u>mustn't</u>?**

Put in the right verb.

needn't 1. Dogs travel free. You —— buy an extra ticket.
must 2. Your dog —— be with you all the time.
mustn't 3. Your dog —— hurt other people.
must 4. It —— be nice to other people.
needn't 5. You —— carry a small dog in a bag. It's OK to hold it.
mustn't 6. You —— play with your dog when you're on the bus.

must = müssen
needn't = nicht müssen
mustn't = nicht dürfen

Unit 1, More about . . .

The Norman conquest

2,16

I want to be king of England!

1

The old king of England, Edward, died in 1066. He had no children and both his Anglo-Saxon brother-in-law, Harold, and his French cousin, William, Duke of Normandy, wanted to be the next king of England. Harold made himself king, and William was very angry. So what did he do next? He sailed to England with his army . . .

2 Harold and William fought the battle on Senlac Hill, near Hastings. William's men were knights and they were better trained. They fought on horses and were good archers. Harold's men fought on foot and they were already tired from an earlier battle at Stamford Bridge, 200 miles away in the north of England. (Yes, they had to walk those 200 miles!)

conquest – *Eroberung*	army – *Heer; Armee*
the Anglo-Saxons – *die Angelsachsen*	knight – *Ritter*
(das Volk, das schon vor 1066 in England lebte)	archer – *Bogenschütze; Bogenschützin*
brother-in-law – *Schwager*	tapestry – *Wandteppich*
duke – *Herzog*	surname – *Nachname; Familienname*

3

How do we know what happened during the battle? Well, we have the 70-metre long Bayeux Tapestry to tell us! The tapestry is like a comic and it tells the story of the battle. It tells us that Harold died when he got an arrow in his eye, but we don't know if this really happened.

4

William became king of England on Christmas Day 1066. He was a big castle fan and built lots of them in England, including part of the Tower of London. He also took land from the Anglo-Saxons and gave it to his Norman friends.

5

Did the Normans change England? Yes, of course they did! For example, they brought many new words to the English language. Words like 'pork' and 'garden' come from this time. Guess what? There are still many English people who have Norman surnames, like Archer or Darcy. Before the Normans came to England, most people didn't even have surnames. They lived in small villages, so a first name or a nickname was often enough.

1 **What did you find most interesting in the text? Talk about it with a partner.**

Unit 2, More about . . .

The RNLI: Volunteers on the coast

Did you know?

- The RNLI is the Royal National Lifeboat Institution. It's a charity and it saves lives at sea.
- The RNLI has 237 lifeboat stations and about 4,600 crew members in the UK and Ireland.
- The RNLI rescues about 8,000 people per year.
- The RNLI has saved about 140,000 lives since 1824.
- Many of the lifeboat crew members are volunteers.
- The RNLI gets money from fundraising.

2,17 ☞ A rescue – boys in trouble

18th June 2016, by Simon Spade. **Yesterday the RNLI rescued two teenage boys who got into trouble when they were kayaking near Llandudno.**

The two 14-year-old boys went out too far in their kayaks and could not get back to the beach because of strong winds. A tourist spotted the boys and called the RNLI. The lifeboat crew got to the kayaks very quickly. Lifeboat helm Howard Link called the ambulance to meet them on the beach.

Both boys were very weak and seasick. They both spent the night in Llandudno hospital but are back home now.

Rules to remember

There are some rules to remember when you go to the beach:

S pot the dangers.

A lways go with a friend or adult.

F ind and follow the safety signs and flags.

E mergency – put up your hand and shout or call 999/112.

RNLI profiles

Most lifeboat crew members are volunteers. Let's meet some.

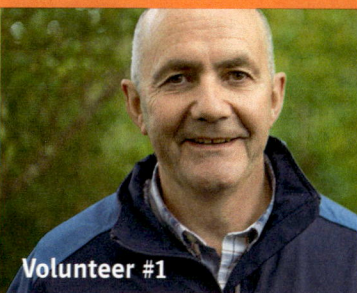

Volunteer #1

Name: Howard Link
Job: Postman

Lifeboat helm
I lead the rescue. It is my job to make sure that everyone on the boat stays safe while we are at sea.

Volunteer #2

Name: Susan Merchant
Job: Teacher

Lifeboat crew member
I grew up in Wales near the sea, so I have been in boats for many years. I help during the rescue and look after the rescued person.

Volunteer #3

Name: John Taylor
Job: Student

Lifeboat youth volunteer
I'm only 16 so I'm too young to join the lifeboat crew, but I work at the station. I look after the equipment and help at fundraising events.

Fundraising Calendar, Llandudno RNLI

January 25th:
10k run around Llandudno

March 17th:
Cake sale at the lifeboat station

April 4th:
Talent show at Llandudno High School

September 13th:
Fun boat race at West Beach

1 Talk about the RNLI.

1. Does Germany have a charity like the RNLI?
2. Would you join the RNLI? Why? Why not?

charity – *Wohltätigkeitsorganisation*	to rescue – *retten*
to save – *retten; bergen*	fundraising – *Spendenaktionen*
crew – *Crew; Besatzung*	to join – *Mitglied in / bei etwas werden*

The Highland Games

2,18

The winner will get a very good job.

History

Legend says that in the 11th century the Scottish king Malcolm III wanted to find the strongest and fastest men in the land. So he organized a competition. The winners became his bodyguards or they ran across the country with messages from the king. Later large families or 'clans' met every year to compete against each other.

Today

… people come from around the world every summer to watch the Highland Games. The Games take place in towns and villages all over Scotland. The 'heavy' events for the strongest and fittest people are the most popular, but there's also lots of music and dancing. There are also children's Highland Games for young people from 5–18.

Caber toss

The most famous 'heavy' event is the caber toss. A caber is a pole that is made from a tree. It's five metres long and very heavy (about 45 kg). People hold the caber at one end and throw it so that it lands on the other end. It's not important how far it goes.

Hammer throw

Competitors swing
a heavy ball which is on
the end of a long chain
around their heads.
Then they let go and throw
it as far as they can.

Stone put

There are two ways to
throw or 'put' the stone:
you can stand (then
you use a heavier stone)
or you can run with it
(then it's not so heavy).
In the first competitions,
men chose a stone from
a river.

Music and dance

No Highland Games
are complete without
the sounds of bagpipes
and Highland dancing.
One of the most famous
dances is the Sword Dance.

1 **Talk about the Highland Games.**

Would you like to go to the Highland Games?
Would you like to compete in the children's Highland Games?
Are there sports like this in your country?
Talk with a partner.

the Highlands – *Berge im Norden Schottlands*
bodyguard – *Leibwächter*
to compete (against) – *gegeneinander antreten*

pole – *Pfahl*
to let go – *loslassen*
complete – *vollständig*

Unit 4, More about . . .

2,19 🎧

The Troubles and after

Murals

If you go to Belfast, you'll see lots of large pictures on the sides of the buildings. These are called murals. They show events and people from the past which are important to people who live in the city. A lot of these murals are from the time that we call 'The Troubles'.

Different schools

Catholic and Protestant children in Northern Ireland often go to separate schools. Even in small towns there are often two schools – one for the children of each religion.

The background

Many Scottish and English Protestant people arrived and settled in what is now Northern Ireland about 400 years ago. Since then, there have often been problems between the Catholic and Protestant people who lived there. Some people (usually Protestants) want Northern Ireland to stay part of the UK. Others (usually Catholics) want it to be part of the Republic of Ireland. This disagreement has often caused fighting.

'The Troubles' (late 1960s–1998) were a very violent time in Northern Ireland's history. There was a lot of terrorism and more than 3,500 people died. When British soldiers came to help in 1969, people welcomed them, but many Catholics soon felt the soldiers were not on their side.

Belfast – then and now

During the Troubles, high walls separated Protestants and Catholics. These walls were called 'peace walls'. A lot has changed since then. Now everyone is working for a future without violence. Today Belfast is a very friendly city for tourists. Many of the walls are still there, but now you can walk from one side to the other. And you can write your own message on one of the 'peace walls'. More 'mixed' schools, for children from Protestant and Catholic families, open every year too.

New chances

Did you know that 30,000 people worked in Belfast's shipyards in the past? When we didn't need as many ships, many people lost their jobs. During the Troubles, not many businesses wanted to come to Northern Ireland and unemployment was high. This has changed and there are new jobs now in making films and TV series.

1 Talk about the text.

What did you find most surprising and interesting in the text? Talk about it with a partner.

to settle (in) – *besiedeln*	to separate – *trennen*
to cause – *verursachen*	peace – *Frieden*
violent – *gewalttätig; brutal*	business – *Unternehmen*
separate – *getrennt; verschieden*	unemployment – *Arbeitslosigkeit*

Highlights of Irish history

about 500 BC

I'm a Celt. The Celtic people are the early settlers of the island of Ireland.

9th century

I'm a Viking from Denmark. We invaded Ireland and our people lived here for about 300 years!

12th century

I'm Henry II, King of England. I invaded Ireland with a huge army.

16th century

I'm Henry VIII, King of England and Ireland. The English own 90% of Ireland now. Many Irish people don't like me.

Saint Patrick

Saint Patrick is the patron saint of Ireland. He lived about 1,500 years ago and brought Christianity to Ireland. There are many stories about his life. One of the most famous is that he drove all the snakes in Ireland into the sea where they drowned. St Patrick's Day is on 17th March every year.

settler – *Siedler, Siedlerin*
century – *Jahrhundert*
to own – *besitzen*
famine – *Hungersnot*
to emigrate – *auswandern*
to split – *teilen; spalten*
to sign – *unterschreiben; unterzeichnen*
patron saint – *Schutzheiliger, Schutzheilige*
to drive – *treiben*
economy – *Wirtschaft*
financial crisis – *Wirtschaftskrise*

1845

was the year of the Great Famine.
One million people died and one million emigrated.
I wanted to emigrate to America.

20th century

We split Ireland into Northern Ireland and the Republic of Ireland. There were many problems after this.

1998

I'm Bertie Ahern, prime minister of Ireland.
I signed an agreement which was a big step in the peace process.

2002

I'm the euro! Ireland began to use me in 2002. Ireland has been a member of the EU since 1973.

Celtic Tiger

When Ireland joined the EU in 1973, it was a poor country. Between 1995 and 2000, Ireland's economy grew very quickly and people said it was as strong as a tiger. Many companies moved their European offices to Ireland. After the European financial crisis in 2008, however, people said that the 'Celtic Tiger' was dead.

1 Talk about the text.

What did you find most surprising and interesting in the text about Ireland? Talk about it with a partner.

Extra

Be a better photographer[1].

1 **Do you take a lot of pictures? How many pictures do you take a day?**

Taking pictures is a fun hobby for many people. You probably take pictures almost every day with your phone too. Some people are professional photographers. They have very good cameras and know all the tricks. But even with your own phone you can get better results.

2 **Look at the pictures. Do you think they are OK? Why? Why not?**

☺ I like picture 1 because it is ... .
☺ I think picture 1 is great/OK because it has ... .
☹ I don't like picture 1 because it is ... .
☹ I think picture 1 isn't OK because ... .

nice colours • funny • interesting • great • ...
too light • too dark • blurred[2] • boring • ...

You have the perfect subject and the light couldn't be better. Just when you press the shutter[3], somebody jumps into the picture and makes a funny face. That's what's called a **photobomb**.

3 **Find funny photobombs on the internet and show them to the class. What's funny about them?**

---

1 photographer [fəˈtɒɡrəfə] – *Fotograf/Fotografin*; 2 blurred [blɜːd] – *unscharf*; 3 shutter [ˈʃʌtə] – *Auslöser*

Three simple tips for better pictures

1. Be creative. Change perspectives and angles[1]. Sometimes the world looks different then.

A front   B low angle   C birds-eye view

2. Always check the background. Sometimes the picture might be embarrassing[2] for someone.

That's wrong.   That's right.

3. Try to zoom with your camera. Or just move forward a foot or two. Sometimes details can be more interesting than the whole person or thing.

A Medium shot   B Close up   B Extreme close up

4 Choose an interesting subject and take three pictures. Use the tips.
Show your pictures to the class and discuss them.

1 angle [ˈæŋgl] – *Winkel;* 2 embarrassing [ɪmˈbærəsɪŋ] – *unangenehm*

How the heart works

1 Look at the sentences. Do you know any German sayings with the word 'heart'?

I know the words by heart.

I have a broken heart.

He has a heart of stone.

Follow your heart.

You're close to my heart.

2 Read the facts about the heart. What do you find most interesting?

The heart begins beating four weeks after conception[1] and does not stop until death[2].

Every day, the heart produces[3] enough energy to drive a truck 20 miles (about 32 km). In a lifetime, that is like driving to the moon[4] and back.

During an average[5] lifetime, the heart will pump nearly 1.5 million tons of blood[6] – enough to fill 200 wagons.

Take a tennis ball and squeeze[7] it tightly[8]: that's how hard the beating heart works to pump blood.

The heart beats 100,000 times a day.

The heart has its own electrical impulse[9]. It can beat even when it is outside of the body. But it must get enough oxygen[10].

3 What keeps your heart healthy?

A healthy heart is a happy heart. But what can you do to keep it happy? Make sentences.

1 conception [kən'sepʃn] – *Empfängnis*; 2 death [deθ] – *Tod*; 3 produce [prə'djuːs] – *erzeugen*; 4 moon [muːn] – *Mond*; 5 average ['ævrɪdʒ] – *durchschnittlich*; 6 blood [blʌd] – *Blut*; 7 squeeze [skwiːz] – *drücken*; 8 tight [taɪt] – *fest*; 9 impulse ['ɪmpʌls] – *Impuls*; 10 oxygen ['ɒksɪdʒən] – *Sauerstoff*

4 Read about the anatomy[1] of the heart

The heart is your strongest muscle. It's a little to the left in your chest[2] and about the size of your fist[3]. Your heart pumps blood through your body to provide you with oxygen and other useful things. Your blood moves through tubes (arteries[4] and veins[5]). Your heart has four different chambers[6] – two chambers in each side. The chambers on top are called atria[7], the ones on the bottom ventricles[8].

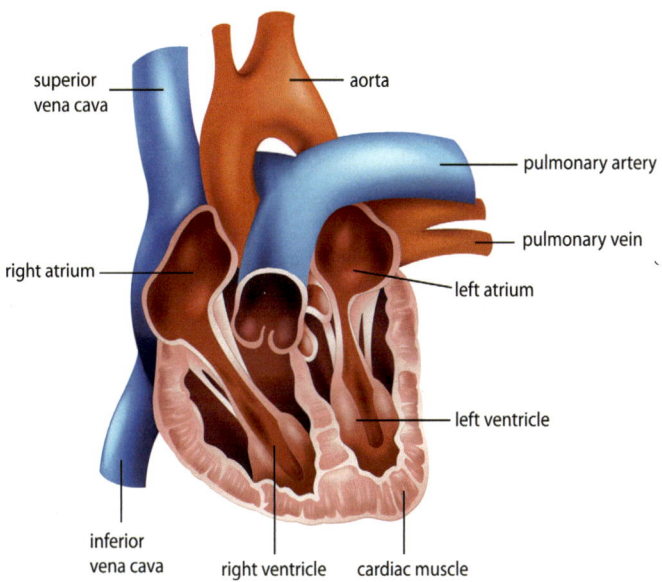

Anatomy of the Human Heart

superior vena cava

aorta

pulmonary artery

pulmonary vein

right atrium

left atrium

left ventricle

inferior vena cava

right ventricle

cardiac muscle

5 Find out your pulse[9].

Check your pulse in different situations.
Count the beats for one minute.

What's your pulse when you are sitting?
What's your pulse when you have just run for a minute?

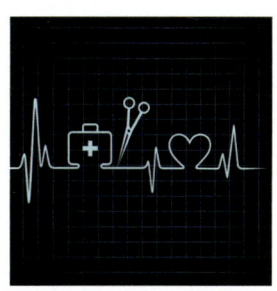

---

1 anatomy [ə'nætemi] – *Anatomie (Lehre vom Aufbau der Organismen)*; 2 chest [tʃest] – *Brust*; 3 fist [fɪst] – *Faust*;
4 artery ['ɑːtri] – *Arterie*; 5 vein [veɪn] – *Vene*; 6 chamber ['tʃeɪmbə] – *Kammer*; 7 atrium ['eɪtriəm] – *Vorhof (des Herzens)*;
8 ventricle ['ventrɪkl] – *Herzkammer*; 9 pulse [pʌls] – *Puls*

The London Eye Mystery by Siobhan Dowd (2007)

2,20

1 *My name is Ted. I live in London with my sister Kat and my parents. One day, my cousin*
Salim and his mum, my Aunt Gloria, come to stay. We go into town and we visit the
London Eye. I think it looks like a bike wheel up in the clouds. Salim rides on the London
Eye. Kat and I wait for him. But the pod1 comes down again and Salim isn't in it any
5 *more. What has happened to Salim?*

"Let's lie², ," said Kat. "About taking that ticket from a stranger³." She grabbed⁴
my arm.
"Lie," I repeated⁵. "Uhm. Lie."
"We could say Salim got lost in the crowds, say he …" She let my arm go. "Oh,
10 forget it," she said. "You can't lie."
We walked over to Aunt Gloria and Mum in the café.
We didn't say anything.
"There you are," Aunt Gloria said. "Have you got the tickets?"
Kat waited for me to say something.
15 I waited for Kat to say something.
"Where's Salim?" asked Mum. "Is he still in the queue?"
"Uhm," I said. "No."
"Where is he?"
"We don't know!" Kat said. "This man gave us his ticket. For free. He bought it,
20 but he didn't want to go on the ride."
"He had claustrophobia⁶," I said.
"That's right. And the queue was awful. So we took the ticket. And gave it to
Salim. And Salim went up alone. And he didn't come down."
Aunt Gloria looked up at the London Eye. "So he's still up there," she said.
25 Kat had a strange look on her face. "No," she said.
"He went up some time ago. Ted and I watched his pod. But when it came
down – he wasn't on it."

---

1 pod [pɒd] – *Gondel*; 2 lie [laɪ] – *lügen*; 3 stranger [ˈstreɪndʒə] – *Fremder*; 4 grab sth. [græb] – *nach etw. greifen*;
5 repeat [rɪˈpiːt] – *wiederholen*; 6 claustrophobia [ˌklɔːstrəˈfəʊbɪə] – *Platzangst*

Mum's face scrunched up[1], so I knew she was a) confused[2] or b) angry or c) both[3].
"What are you trying to say: He wasn't on it?!"
30 "He went up, Mum," I repeated. "But he didn't come down."
Mum's mouth became like an O.
"He went against the law of gravity[4], Mum. He went up but he didn't come down. Uhm."
Mum looked more angry than confused now. But Aunt Gloria looked calm[5].
35 "I think I know what happened," she said and smiled.
"I bet he went around one more time."
Yes, that's it, I thought.
"That's it," said Kat. "He just stayed on."
I looked at the big clock on the wall. "So … he'll land at … twelve thirty-two."
40 We went back to the Eye with Mum. Aunt Gloria stayed at the café so Salim would find her if he came back.
We watched a lot of pods open and close, but no Salim. 12:32 came and went. No Salim.
Mum asked a woman from customer services[6] but she couldn't help.
45 "Kat," Mum said, "It was wrong to take that ticket and let Salim go up alone."
Kat started crying[7]. "It's always my fault[8]. Never Ted's. Ted never does anything wrong."
"You're older, Kat. But really not much wiser." Mum stared[9] angrily at Kat and Kat stared back.
50 "Why don't we call his mobile?" I said.
"Of course! Ted," Mum said, "You're a genius. Why didn't we think of that before?"
We went back to Aunt Gloria in the café. There was no sign[10] of Salim.
2,21 "Call him on his mobile!" said Mum.
"OK," Aunt Gloria said. "Yes, maybe he's near us."
55 She called his number and put the phone to her ear with a smile. Then she looked confused.
"His phone isn't on." she whispered. "Why?"

1 scrunch up [ˈskrʌnʃˌʌp] – *verziehen*; 2 confused [kənˈfjuːzd] – *verwirrt*; 3 both [bəʊθ] – *beides*; 4 against the law of gravity [əˈgenst ðə lɔːˌəv ˈgrævəti] – *gegen das Gesetz der Schwerkraft*; 5 calm [kaːm] – *ruhig*; 6 customer service [ˌkʌstəmə ˈsɜːvɪs] – *Kundenservice*; 7 cry [kraɪ] – *weinen*; 8 fault [fɔːlt] – *Schuld*; 9 stare [ˈsteə] – *anstarren*; 10 sign [saɪn] – *Zeichen*

We called the police.

A police officer took our names and addresses. Could Salim find his way back to
our house? he asked. Yes, we said. Then he told us to do three things: a) keep[1]
trying his phone, b) go home and wait and c) try not to worry. And if Salim
wasn't home in a few hours, a police officer would visit us.

The officer said, "Children don't disappear[2]! He will be back soon."

So then we did b) and went home to wait. And Aunt Gloria did a): She called
Salim again and again. Mum and Kat tried to do c). Mum made tea. Kat brought
in a plate of my favourite biscuits, chocolate fingers. But no one ate any. We all
tried not to worry but it didn't really work.

I looked at Aunt Gloria.

"What are you staring at?" she cried out. "You wanted to go to the London Eye –
now this has happened! You and your silly bike wheel up in the clouds!" She sat
down on the sofa.

A bit later she said, "Oh, Ted. I'm sorry. I didn't mean[3] that."

"Gloria!" Mum said and sat down next to her. "Calm down, love."

She made a sign at me to say she didn't want me in the room.

So I went up to my room.

I got out my encyclopaedia[4] and sat on my bed, looking at some interesting
pages. The door opened and Kat came in. She sat on the bed next to me.

I looked up. "The dodo[5] disappeared, Kat," I said.

"What?"

"The dodo. It disappeared from the evolutionary path[6]."

"Right. The dodo. So?"

"Darwin would say it wasn't adaptable[7] enough to survive[8], so it didn't."

"I don't think Salim's disappeared from the evolutionary path, Ted."

"No, I know," I said, "But there's lots more about disappearing in my
encyclopaedia."

"Oh, yeah?" "There was Lord Lucan. People think he killed himself. Maybe he
did. But they never found his body, Kat. Maybe he wanted it to look that way,
but really disappeared … went away, say, to India and became a hippie."

---

1 keep trying sth. [kiːp ˈtraɪɪŋ] – *etwas immer wieder versuchen*; 2 disappear [ˌdɪsəˈpɪə] – *verschwinden*; 3 mean [miːn] – *meinen*;
4 encyclopaedia [ɪnˌsaɪkləˈpiːdɪə] – *Lexikon*; 5 dodo [ˈdəʊdəʊ] – *Dodo (ausgestorbener, großer, flugunfähiger Vogel)*; 6
evolutionary path [ˌiːvəˌuːʃnri ˈpɑːθ] – *Evolutionsgeschichte*; 7 adaptable [əˈdæptəbl] – *anpassungsfähig*; 8 survive [səˈvaɪv] –
überleben

"I don't see what that's got to do with –" There was a long silence[1].

90 "That's not very helpful, Ted."

"And there was the Mary Celeste, a big ship from New York. It turned up[2] near Gibraltar. Nobody was on board, like … like aliens beamed them up!"

"Ted, stop joking. It's not funny."

I closed my book and looked at Kat.

95 "OK," she said. "It wasn't a joke. I should know you never joke. So what do you mean?"

,22 I didn't really know what I meant. But Kat looked really sad and I wanted to say something nice.

"Kat," I said, "you and I are together in this. People disappear. And things. Most of 100 them reappear[3]."

Kat put her hand on mine and I saw the tears[4] on her face.

"Ted," she said, shaking[5] her head, "the Mary Celeste people never reappeared. Nor[6] the dodo. Nor Lord What's-His-Name. That police officer was right. People don't just disappear. Salim must be somewhere[7]. I have to find him. But I need your help. I 105 need your brain[8], Ted. No one is better at thinking than you."

That was Kat's first compliment to me ever. I put my hands into my jacket pockets[9] and went, "Uhm."

Then I felt something in one of the pockets – something surprising. I took it out and Kat and I stared at it.

110 "Salim's camera!"

How will the story go on? Will Salim return?

---

1 silence [ˈsaɪləns] – *Schweigen*; 2 turn up [ˌtɜːnˈʌp] – *erscheinen*; 3 reappear [ˌriːəˈpɪər] – *wieder auftauchen*; 4 tear [tɪə] – *Träne*; 5 shake [ʃeɪk] – *schütteln*; 6 nor [nɔː] – *und auch nicht*; 7 somewhere [ˈsʌmweə] – *irgendwo*; 8 brain [breɪn] – *Grips, Verstand*; 9 pocket [ˈpɒkɪt] – *(Jacken-)Tasche*

Ivanhoe

Characters:

Narrator
Rowena
Cedric
Athelstane
Rebecca
Isaac
Prince John
Three Norman knights
Five Anglo-Saxon knights
Ivanhoe (The Disinherited)
Crowd (5 – 8 people)
King Richard (The Black Knight)
Robin Hood
Robin's men (5 – 8 people)

2,23

Scene 1

1 NARRATOR: This is a story about brave[1] men and women. It is a story about hate[2] and about love. It is a story about power and great kindness[3]. Our story is old, but hate, love, power and kindness are still a big part of our lives today. The date is 1194. The place is England. But at this time the Normans ruled[4] England. The good King Richard is in another country. He was fighting in a

5 war[5], but now he is in prison far from his country. His awful brother, the Norman Prince John, now rules England and the Anglo-Saxons that live there are not happy.
(A trumpet[6] plays). Ah! Hear that. It is the start of the famous competition between Norman and Anglo-Saxon knights. Look, there sits Cedric, an Anglo-Saxon. He looks after the beautiful Rowena. Listen, they are having an argument.

10 *(Narrator leaves. Cedric and Rowena are sitting in the crowd – a semi-circle[7] of chairs are in front of the audience[8].)*
ROWENA: *(Angry)* No, I will not get married to him!
CEDRIC: But Rowena, Athelstane is an Anglo-Saxon and a good man! I am your father and I say you will get married to him!

15 ROWENA: *(Very angry)* You are not my father!
CEDRIC: But Rowena, I love you like my own child. I have looked after you.
ROWENA: Yes, it is true, you have. I had no mother or father, but you looked after me. But what about Ivanhoe, your real child?
CEDRIC: *(Angry now)* Today Ivanhoe is not my child! He went away to fight with the Normans

20 and King Richard. He is not a true Anglo-Saxon. Do not say his name again!

---

1 brave [breɪv] – *mutig;* 2 hate [heɪt] – *Hass;* 3 kindness ['kaɪndnəs] – *Güte;* 4 rule [ruːl] – *regieren;* 5 war [wɔː] – *Krieg;* 6 trumpet ['trʌmpɪt] – *Trompete;* 7 semi-circle ['semi 'sɜːkl] – *Halbkreis;* 8 audience ['ɔːdiəns] – *Zuschauer*

ROWENA: But I love Ivanhoe and I will only get married to HIM!

CEDRIC: *(angry)* Stop, girl!

(Rowena looks unhappy, but she doesn't say anything. She looks around. An old man and a young woman come on stage and sit near Rowena and Cedric).

25 **ROWENA:** *(To Cedric)* Who is that man and the beautiful woman over there?

CEDRIC: Ah, that is Isaac and his daughter Rebecca. Isaac is a great businessman[1]. He has a lot of money.

REBECCA: *(Speaks to her father)* Father, do you think the Anglo-Saxon knights will win the competition?

30 **ISAAC:** I'm not sure, Rebecca.

(The trumpet plays again; someone who is not on stage calls 'Prince John'. Prince John walks to his place and sits down. The crowd cheers[2].)

PRINCE JOHN: Let's start the competition!

(Trumpet plays again. Three knights on horses come from the right. They have a flag that says 'Normans'.
35 *Five knights on horses come from the left. They have a flag that says 'Anglo-Saxons'. All the knights have lances[3].)*

PRINCE JOHN: *(Stands up)* Let the first knights start!

(One Norman and one Anglo-Saxon knight attack[4] each other. The Norman hits the Anglo-Saxon with his lance and the Anglo-Saxon falls from his horse. Half the crowd cheer and half boo[5]. Prince John is laughing.
40 *Cedric, Rowena, Isaac and Rebecca look unhappy.*
The next Norman knight wins against the next Anglo-Saxon. The third Norman also wins. The knights who fall leave the stage. Two Anglo-Saxon knights are on stage.)

FIRST NORMAN KNIGHT: Who will fight us next?

(The two Anglo-Saxon knights are scared. Suddenly a new knight comes from the left. He holds a flag that
45 *says 'The Disinherited[6]'. This knight fights against the three Norman knights. He wins every time. He holds his flag up to Prince John.)*

PRINCE JOHN: Very good, brave knight. You call yourself the Disinherited. Do you have a real name?

IVANHOE: I am the Disinherited. My father does not want to call me his child. I fought with
50 your brother King Richard in the great war.

(Sounds of surprise from the crowd. Prince John looks very unhappy.)

PRINCE JOHN: All right, Disinherited. You are the winner of the first part of the competition. You can choose the woman who you believe is the most beautiful. She will be our competition queen.

55 *(Prince John puts a crown[7] on Ivanhoe's lance. Ivanhoe sees Rowena and gives the crown to her. She puts it on her head. The crowd cheers. Ivanhoe leaves the stage.)*

---

1 businessman ['bɪznɪsmæn] – *Geschäftsmann*; 2 cheer [tʃɪə] – *jubeln*; 3 lance [lɑːns] – *Lanze*; 4 attack [ə'tæk] – *angreifen*;
5 boo sb. [buː] – *jdn. ausbuhen*; 6 disinherited [ˌdɪsɪn'herɪtɪd] – *der Enterbte*; 7 crown [kraʊn] – *Krone*

Scene 2

1 *(Music is playing. The crowd is talking and laughing.)*
NARRATOR: *(On stage)* It is the second day of the competition. The knights fight with swords[1]. This is very dangerous. Some knights may get hurt. Look! The knights are coming. *(Trumpet plays. Narrator leaves.)*

5 *(Three Norman knights come from the right with a Norman flag. Two knights and Ivanhoe come from the left with an Anglo-Saxon flag. All the knights are on horses and have swords.)*
PRINCE JOHN: *(Stands up)* Let the second part of the competition start! *(Trumpet plays.)*
(There is a big fight: Ivanhoe is hit badly on his left side, but he still fights. The two Anglo-Saxon knights fall and cannot fight. Suddenly a new knight arrives from the side. This knight is wearing black. The crowd
10 *makes sounds of surprise. The Black Knight fights two of the Norman knights. Ivanhoe fights the last Norman knight. Ivanhoe and The Black Knight win against the Normans. They get off their horses and walk to each other.)*
IVANHOE: *(Whispers[2])* There is only one man in England who can fight like this. Is it really you?
KING RICHARD: *(Whispers back)* Yes, Ivanhoe. I am back. Meet me in the forest[3] in five days and
15 I will be King of England again. *(King Richard leaves the stage on his horse.)*
PRINCE JOHN: Disinherited! Come and get your prize. You are the winner! I give you this crown, but take off[4] your helmet.
(IVANHOE takes off his helmet. Sounds of surprise from the crowd)
PRINCE JOHN: Ah, it is you, Ivanhoe! The son of Cedric.
20 *(Prince John puts the crown on Ivanhoe's head. Ivanhoe falls. He is hurt badly.)*
ROWENA: *(Stands up)* We must help him! He is hurt. Come on!
CEDRIC: Sit down, Rowena! He is not part of my family. King Richard can help him.
ROWENA: King Richard is in prison in another country. He cannot help Ivanhoe. We must help him. He is your son and I love him. *(She starts to leave.)*
25 CEDRIC: *(Angry)* You will not help him!
ROWENA: But he was so brave and now he really needs our help. Please, Cedric, let's help him.
(Cedric pushes her back into her seat.)
REBECCA: *(Speaks to her father)* Father! We must help him. Come, father.
ISAAC: Wait, child, be careful! If we help him now, the Prince will hate us.
30 REBECCA: I don't care[5]! I will help him. (She looks at Isaac) Will you help me take that man home? *(Isaac nods[6]. He and Rebecca go to Ivanhoe. Rebecca talks to Ivanhoe.)* You are a brave man. I can help you. I will take you home and give you medicine[7].
IVANHOE: Thank you.
(Rebecca and Isaac carry Ivanhoe off stage.)

---

1 sword [sɔːd] – *Schwert*; 2 whisper [ˈwɪspə] – *flüstern*; 3 forest [ˈfɒrɪst] – *Wald*; 4 take off [ˌteɪkˈɒf] – *abnehmen*;
5 I don't care! [aɪ dəʊnt keə] – *Es ist mir egal!*; 6 nod [nɒd] – *nicken*; 7 medicine [ˈmedsn] – *Medizin*

Scene 3

1 *(In the forest. Robin's men are sitting around a fire. They are eating, drinking and laughing. King Richard is still wearing black. He is talking to Robin Hood.)*

ROBIN HOOD: Your plan is good, King Richard. We can fight Prince John and win.

KING RICHARD: When Cedric knows that the famous Robin Hood is fighting with me against
5 Prince John, he and the other Anglo-Saxons will join[1] us too.

ROBIN HOOD: Yes, I have sent one of my men to tell Cedric to meet us here. Listen! *(Robin's men stop talking and eating and listen carefully.)* I think I hear someone coming.

IVANHOE: *(Just his voice)* This must be the place, my friends.

(Isaac, Rebecca and Ivanhoe come on stage.)

10 IVANHOE: *(Very happy)* It is you, my King! *(Ivanhoe and King Richard hug.)*

KING RICHARD: It is good to see you too, my great friend. I escaped[2] from prison and now
I am back in England with my brave army [3]. Robin and I have a plan to chase[4] Prince John and
his men out of this country and I will rule England again. *(Robin's men cheer and start eating and
drinking again.)*

15 Who is this man and lovely woman with you? *(He looks at Isaac and Rebecca.)*

IVANHOE: This beautiful woman is Rebecca. She gave me medicine and made me well. And this
is her father.

ROBIN HOOD: Listen, I hear voices again.

CEDRIC: *(Just his voice)* Come! Robin Hood and his men must be here.

20 *(Cedric and Rowena come on stage.)*

ROWENA: *(Suddenly sees Ivanhoe)* Oh, Ivanhoe! *(She runs to Ivanhoe and they hug.)*

ROBIN HOOD: Cedric, this is King Richard. He was The Black Knight at the competition.

KING RICHARD: Your son, Ivanhoe, is a brave man, Cedric. He won the competition. I believe the
brave Ivanhoe and the lovely Rowena want to get married.

25 CEDRIC: *(Looks at his feet)* I … I thought Athelstane … *(Cedric doesn't know what to say. He looks at
Ivanhoe and Rowena and then at King Richard.)* You are right, King Richard. I have a brave son and
I am proud of him. He and Rowena WILL get married. *(Everyone cheers and Rowena and Ivanhoe hug
again.)*

ROBIN HOOD: Now let's use your plan; King Richard; and take action against[5] the awful Prince
30 John. Cedric, will you join us?

CEDRIC: Of course, Robin. Long live King Richard! *(Everyone says 'long live King Richard' together.)*

NARRATOR: *(Comes on stage)* Together, these brave men and women chased Prince John and his
men out of England. King Richard ruled England once more and the Anglo-Saxons were very
happy – so were Rowena and the great Ivanhoe. Long live King Richard!

---

1 join [dʒɔɪn] – *sich anschließen;* 2 escape [ɪˈskeɪp] – *entkommen;* 3 army [ˈɑːmi] – *Armee;* 4 chase [tʃeɪs] – *verfolgen;*
5 take action against sb. [teɪkˈækʃn əˈgenst] – *gegen jdn. vorgehen*

Grammar

G4

Mit **G** sind die Grammatikkapitel gekennzeichnet und der Reihe nach durchnummeriert. Eine Übersicht über alle Themen in diesem Band findest du auf der nächsten Seite.

Language tip   **G7**

Die Seiten kennzeichnen zusätzliche Grammatikkapitel. Du kannst dir die neuen Formen dort wie neue Vokabeln merken oder – wenn du es genau wissen willst – ein paar Regeln dazu lernen.

Hier stehen Besonderheiten und Tipps.

(TEST YOURSELF)

Hier kannst du üben.
Die Lösungen findest du auf S. 165.

(FÜR PROFIS)

Hier findest du knifflige Extras zum Thema.

R = Revision (Wiederholung)

Unit 1

G1 R: Die einfache Gegenwart

Revision: The simple present

Do you remember?

Wenn du einen Zustand beschreiben möchtest oder sagen willst, dass jemand etwas gewohnheitsmäßig tut oder dass etwas häufig oder regelmäßig geschieht, verwendest du das **simple present**.

Signalwörter	
every Monday	jeden Montag
always	immer
often	oft
usually	normalerweise
sometimes	manchmal
never	nie

I **like** computer games.	Ich mag Computerspiele.
He never **goes** to a fast food restaurant.	Er geht nie in ein Fastfood-Restaurant.
The new shop **sells** Indian food.	Der neue Laden verkauft indisches Essen.

 He, **she**, **it** – das **s** muss mit!

Mit **don't** oder **doesn't** (bei he, she, it) kannst du sagen, was man **nicht** macht.

I **don't know** where the best shops are.	Ich weiß nicht, wo die besten Geschäfte sind.
She **doesn't have** much time.	Sie hat nicht viel Zeit.

Und so kannst du fragen und kurz darauf antworten:

Do you sometimes **go** to the cinema?	Yes, I **do**.	No, I **don't**.
Does your brother **read** comics?	Yes, he **does**.	No, he **doesn't**.

Aussagen und Verneinungen mit **be** bildest du so:

I **am** (I'**m**)	I **am not** (I'**m not**)
you **are** (you'**re**)	you **are not** (you **aren't**)
he / she / it **is** (he'**s** / she'**s** / it'**s**)	he / she / it **is not** (he / she / it **isn't**)
we **are** (we'**re**)	we **are not** (we **aren't**)
they **are** (they'**re**)	they **are not** (they **aren't**)

Fragen und Kurzantworten mit **be** bildest du so:

Are you from York?	Yes, I **am**.	No, I'**m not**.
Is the park far away?	Yes, it **is**.	No, it **isn't**.

(TEST YOURSELF) **Put the verbs in the simple present.**

1. I sometimes —— (buy) clothes online.
2. She —— (do) her shopping every Friday.
3. The buses —— (not go) after 9 p.m.
4. —— you —— (go) to school by bus?
5. The girls —— (be) near the Viking Centre.
6. —— (be) Sam from Bristol?

Do you remember?

G2 R: Die einfache Vergangenheit

Revision: The simple past

Um über Dinge zu sprechen, die in der Vergangenheit passiert und vorbei sind, verwendest du die einfache Vergangenheit (**simple past**).

Das simple past bildest du so:
Hänge die Endung **-ed** an das Verb.
Achte auf unregelmäßige Verben, z. B. do → **did**; fall → **fell**; get → **got**; go → **went**; have → **had**; hear → **heard**; make → **made**; see → **saw**; write → **wrote**

Signalwörter	
yesterday	gestern
last month	letzten Monat
a week ago	vor einer Woche
in 2015	(im Jahr) 2015

Eine Liste der unregelmäßigen Verben findest du auf Seite 210.

| I **helped** my aunt last Sunday. | Letzten Sonntag half ich meiner Tante. |
| Hannah **bought** a coat yesterday. | Hannah kaufte gestern eine Jacke. |

Um zu sagen, was in der Vergangenheit nicht passiert ist, setzt du **didn't** (= did not) vor das Verb.

| I **didn't watch** TV yesterday. | Ich schaute gestern nicht fern. |
| Tom's parents **didn't like** Bramford. | Toms Eltern gefiel Bramford nicht. |

Und so kannst du im **simple past** Fragen stellen:

| **Did** you **have** a nice weekend? | Yes, I **did**. | No, I **didn't**. |
| When **did** your sister **visit** you? | At the weekend. | |

 Im Deutschen gibt es verschiedene Möglichkeiten, Vergangenes auszudrücken:

| Tim met Sarah. | Tim hat Sarah getroffen. / Tim traf Sarah. |

Aussagen und Verneinungen mit **be** bildest du so:

I **was** in York. I **wasn't** in London.	Ich war in York. Ich war nicht in London.
Sue **wasn't** at the zoo. She **was** at home.	Sue war nicht im Zoo. Sie war zu Hause.
The students **were** at the theatre. They **weren't** at the cinema.	Die Schüler waren im Theater. Sie waren nicht im Kino.

Fragen und Kurzantworten mit **be** bildest du so:

| **Were** you at home? | Yes, I **was**. | No, I **wasn't**. |
| **Was** it funny? | Yes, it **was**. | No, it **wasn't**. |

(TEST YOURSELF) **Put the verbs in the simple past.**

1. Hannah ―― (have) a great time.
2. I ―― (not hear) a noise.
3. ―― you ―― (have) a nice day?
4. What ―― you ―― (do) yesterday?
5. Last Friday Tom ―― (not be) at home.
6. ―― (be) you in Italy last summer?

Unit 2

G3 Reflexivpronomen und each other

Reflexive pronouns and each other

I have hurt myself.

Ich habe mich verletzt.

Im Englischen werden die Reflexivpronomen mit **-self** oder **-selves** gebildet. Im Deutschen werden sie meist mit „mir" oder „mich", „dir" oder „dich", „sich" usw. übersetzt.

I bought **myself** a new T-shirt.	Ich habe mir ein neues T-Shirt gekauft.
Can you see **yourself** in the window?	Kannst du dich im Fenster sehen?
He cut **himself** with a knife.	Er hat sich mit einem Messer geschnitten.
She asked **herself** why it happened.	Sie fragte sich, warum es passiert ist.
The cat hurt **itself**.	Die Katze hat sich verletzt.
We built **ourselves** a tree house.	Wir haben uns ein Baumhaus gebaut.
Help **yourselves**!	Bedient euch!
They hurt **themselves** during the sports lesson.	Sie haben sich beim Sportunterricht verletzt.

 Achtung: Beachte den Unterschied zwischen **themselves** und **each other**.

Ben and his sister are looking at **themselves**.	Ben und seine Schwester schauen sich an (= jeder sich selbst).
Ben and his sister are looking at **each other**. (= Ben looks at his sister and she looks at him.)	Ben und seine Schwester schauen sich gegenseitig an (= jeder den anderen).

(TEST YOURSELF) **Put in the correct word.**

1. I saw —— (myself / himself) in the newspaper.
2. Did you buy —— a present (itself / yourself)?
3. Grandma cut —— (herself / himself) with a knife.
4. We saw —— (yourselves / ourselves) on TV.
5. Sam and Ben always tell —— (each other / themselves) jokes.
6. The dog cut —— (itself / himself).

(FÜR PROFIS)

Du kannst mit den Reflexivpronomen auch betonen, dass jemand etwas selbst gemacht hat:

He made the cake **himself**.	Er hat den Kuchen selbst gebacken.

G4 Adjektive und Adverbien

Adjectives and adverbs

That was easy.
I won the race easily.

Das war leicht.
Ich hab' das Rennen leicht gewonnen.

Ein **Adjektiv** (Eigenschaftswort) beschreibt eine Person oder eine Sache.

Beth is a **good** student.	Beth ist eine gute Schülerin.
Climbing is a **dangerous** sport.	Klettern ist ein gefährlicher Sport.

Ein **Adverb** beschreibt, wie jemand etwas tut oder wie etwas geschieht. Im Englischen erkennt man Adverbien durch ein angehängtes **-ly**.

He ran **slowly**.	Er rannte langsam.
It happened **quickly**.	Es geschah schnell.

 Achtung Schreibweise: easy → eas**ily**; careful → careful**ly**

Es gibt aber auch unregelmäßige Adverbien:

That's a **good** song.	(Adjektiv)	Das ist ein gutes Lied.
She can sing **well**.	(Adverb)	Sie kann gut singen.

Manche Adverbien verändern sich nicht:

Rugby is a **fast** game.	(Adjektiv)	Rugby ist ein schnelles Spiel.
Look, the players are running **fast**.	(Adverb)	Schau, die Spieler rennen schnell.
This was a **hard** exercise.	(Adjektiv)	Das war eine schwierige Übung.
Mum works **hard** every day.	(Adverb)	Mama arbeitet jeden Tag schwer.

(TEST YOURSELF) **Use adjectives or adverbs.**

1. You must always ride —— (careful).
2. Max is a —— (good) tennis player.
3. Lucy speaks English —— (good).
4. Sherlock is a —— (clever) dog.
5. They walked home —— (slow).
6. Don't run so —— (fast).

Do you remember?

G5 R: Das Perfekt

Revision: The present perfect

Wenn eine Handlung in der Vergangenheit beginnt und in der Gegenwart zu einem Ergebnis führt, verwendest du das **present perfect**:
have / has + dritte Form des Verbs (past participle).

Signalwörter	
already	schon
just	gerade
not … yet	noch … nicht
ever (in Fragen)	jemals

Bei den meisten Verben hängst du für die dritte Form ein **-ed** an das Verb: help → help**ed**

I **have** just **played** football.	Ich habe gerade Fußball gespielt.
He **has** already **had** his lunch.	Er hat schon zu Mittag gegessen.

Achtung: Einige Verben haben unregelmäßige dritte Formen, z.B.:
break → broke → **broken**; do → did → **done**; be → was / were → **been**

Eine Liste der unregelmäßigen Verben findest du auf S. 210.

Um die Sätze zu verneinen, benutzt du **haven't** oder **hasn't** (bei he, she, it):

I **haven't called** the hospital yet.	Ich habe das Krankenhaus noch nicht angerufen.
She **hasn't been** to London yet.	Sie ist noch nicht in London gewesen.

Fragen und Kurzantworten bildest du so:

Have you ever **broken** your arm?	Yes, I **have**.	No, I **haven't**.
Has your brother ever **won** a prize?	Yes, he **has**.	No, he **hasn't**.
Have the girls **been** to the party?	Yes, they **have**.	No, they **haven't**.

Bei Fragen mit Fragewörtern stellst du das Fragewort an den Satzanfang.

What **has happened**?	Was ist passiert?
Where **have** you **been**?	Wo bist du gewesen?

(TEST YOURSELF) **Put the verbs in the present perfect.**

1. Where —— you —— (be), Dylan?
2. Sue —— already —— (do) her homework.
3. We —— just —— (have) an accident.
4. I —— (not ask) him yet.
5. —— you —— (forget) your mobile again?
6. Why —— she —— (not call) the ambulance yet?

G6 Relativsätze mit Relativpronomen

Relative clauses with relative pronouns

This is the coat which is best for tonight.

Das ist die Jacke, die für heute Abend am besten ist.

Wenn du eine Person oder eine Sache genauer beschreiben willst, verwendest du die Relativpronomen **who**, **which** oder **that**.

who   → Personen
which → Dinge
that   → Personen und Dinge

Bell was **the man who / that** invented the telephone.	Bell war der Mann, der das Telefon erfand.
He invented **machines which / that** changed the world.	Er erfand Geräte, die die Welt veränderten.

Willst du Zugehörigkeit oder Besitz ausdrücken, verwendest du bei Personen und Dingen **whose**.

That's the **boy whose** parents are doctors.	Das ist der Junge, dessen Eltern Ärzte sind.
Edinburgh is a **city whose** centre is very old.	Edinburgh ist eine Stadt, deren Zentrum sehr alt ist.

(TEST YOURSELF) **Put in who, whose or which.**

1. Bell was a man —— had lots of fantastic ideas.
2. He even built a machine —— could fly.
3. One day he opened a school for people —— couldn't hear.
4. The phones —— people used fifty years ago are in museums now.
5. Many people —— are famous inventors come from Scotland.
6. This is the girl —— parents are from India.

(FÜR PROFIS)

Folgt <u>nach</u> who, which oder that ein Personalpronomen wie **I**, **you**, **he**, **she**, **it**, **we**, **they**, kannst du who, which oder that auch weglassen. Diesen Satz nennt man **contact clause**.

The lady (who) **we** saw on TV last night is my cousin.	Die Frau, die wir gestern im Fernsehen gesehen haben, ist meine Kusine.
Scotland is the country (which) **I** want to visit next year.	Schottland ist das Land, das ich nächstes Jahr besuchen möchte.

Language tip

G7 Das Gerundium

Gerund

*Spending a few days in Scotland is always
a great idea.*
I love looking at the sheep.

Ein paar Tage in Schottland zu
verbringen ist immer eine tolle Idee.
Ich liebe es, die Schafe anzuschauen.

Ein Gerundium bildet man, indem man **-ing** an ein Verb anhängt. Dadurch wird das Verb zu einem Nomen (Hauptwort). Mit dem Gerundium kann man über Tätigkeiten und Aktivitäten sprechen. Es steht am Satzanfang und ist **Subjekt / Satzgegenstand** des Satzes.

Watching TV can be interesting.	Fernsehen kann interessant sein.
Playing football is my favourite sport.	Fußballspielen ist mein Lieblingssport.

Das Gerundium kann aber auch nach dem Verb stehen und ist dann **Objekt / Satzergänzung** des Satzes. Das gilt besonders für Verben wie **love**, **(not) like** und **hate**.

I like **swimming**.	Ich schwimme gerne
I don't like **cleaning** my shoes.	Ich putze meine Schuhe nicht gerne.
Tim hates **tidying** his room.	Tim hasst es, sein Zimmer aufzuräumen.

 Das Gerundium darf man nicht mit dem **present progressive** verwechseln. Vergleiche:

I **am** walk**ing** on the beach.	Ich gehe gerade am Strand spazieren.
I **love** walk**ing** on the beach.	Ich mag es, am Strand spazieren zu gehen.

(TEST YOURSELF) Use the verbs to make the gerund.

1. —— (walk) with a dog can be fun.
2. —— (meet) friends is my favourite activity.
3. Rock —— (climb) can be very exciting.
4. Jane likes —— (stay) on a farm.
5. I hate —— (work) in the garden.
6. I don't like —— (write) tests.

(FÜR PROFIS)

Ein Gerundium kann auch nach Ausdrücken wie **be good at ...** oder **What about ...?** stehen.

I'm **good at playing** frisbee.	Ich bin gut im Frisbeespielen.
What about dancing?	Wie wär's mit Tanzen?

G8 R: Die Zukunft mit will

Revision: The will-future

Do you remember?

Mit dem **will-future** sprichst du über die Zukunft. Oft drückst du damit Hoffnungen, Wünsche und Vorhersagen aus. Dann beginnen diese Sätze mit **I hope**, **I think**, **I'm sure** oder **maybe**.
Du bildest das **will-future** mit **will** oder **won't** und der **Grundform des Verbs**. Häufig wird die Kurzform verwendet: I **will** go → I'll go

We'll **stay** at a campsite.	Wir werden auf einem Campingplatz übernachten.
Maybe we'll **see** Nessie.	Vielleicht sehen wir Nessie.
I hope it **won't rain** tomorrow.	Ich hoffe, es wird morgen nicht regnen.

Im Deutschen kann man über Zukünftiges mit der Zukunft oder der Gegenwart sprechen:

We'll **wait** for you.	Wir werden auf dich warten.
	Wir warten auf dich.

Auch wenn du dich in einer Situation ganz spontan für etwas Bestimmtes entscheidest, verwendest du das **will-future**.

I don't understand this exercise.	Ich verstehe diese Aufgabe nicht.
– Don't worry, I'll **help** you.	– Keine Sorge, ich helfe dir.
Look, it's sunny. I **won't take** a coat.	Schau, es ist sonnig. Ich nehme keine Jacke mit.

 Achtung! Verwechsle **will** (werden) nicht mit **want to** (wollen):

I **will** buy some souvenirs.	Ich **werde** ein paar Souvenirs kaufen.
I **want to** buy some souvenirs.	Ich **will** ein paar Souvenirs kaufen.

(TEST YOURSELF) Complete the sentences.

1. Maybe we —— (stay) in a cosy B&B in Inverness this summer.
2. I hope you —— (not be) ill on holiday.
3. Look, that's real Scottish food. – Great, I —— (have) that.
4. I don't have a map. – I —— (show) you the way.
5. Can you help us? – We —— (do) our best.
6. You can give her the money, she —— (not lose) it.

G9 Bedingungssätze Typ I

If-clauses type I

If it stops raining soon, I'll take a photo.

Wenn es bald aufhört zu regnen, mache ich ein Foto.

If-Sätze benutzt man, um Bedingungen und Folgen auszudrücken. Im if-Satz steht das **simple present**. Im Hauptsatz steht das **will-future**. Geht der **if**-Satz voran, steht am Ende des if-Satzes ein Komma.

Bedingung	Folge	
If it **rains**,	we'**ll stay** at home.	Wenn es regnet, bleiben wir zu Hause.
If it**'s** too dark,	I **won't take** any photos.	Wenn es zu dunkel ist, mache ich keine Fotos.

 Im **if**-Satz steht nie **will / won't**!

Bedingungssätze können auch mit dem Hauptsatz beginnen. Dann entfällt das Komma.

I'**ll be** unhappy if you **don't come** to my party.	Ich werde unglücklich sein, wenn du nicht zu meiner Party kommst.

(**TEST YOURSELF**) **Complete the sentences.**

1. If I —— (meet) Nancy, I —— (tell) her about the new swimming pool.
2. If Jake —— (go) to Scotland, he —— (not visit) a museum.
3. If Olivia —— (have) time on Saturday, she —— (go) shopping.
4. If Katie —— (not do) her homework, she —— (not be) good at Maths.
5. You —— (become) famous if you —— (take) a good photo of Nessie.
6. We —— (be) very unhappy if you —— (not visit) us at the weekend.

G10 Bedingungssätze Typ II

If-clauses type II

If I had a lot of money, I would buy a castle.

Wenn ich viel Geld hätte, würde ich ein Schloss kaufen.

Du kennst schon die Bedingungssätze Typ I. Bei Typ I steht die Bedingung im simple present und die Folge im will-future. (S. 158)

Bei Bedingungssätzen Typ II ist eine Bedingung unwahrscheinlich oder nicht erfüllbar. Du verwendest im if-Satz **simple past**. Im Hauptsatz steht **would / wouldn't + Grundform des Verbs**.

Bedingung	Folge	
If I **had** a dog,	I **would go** for a walk every day.	Wenn ich einen Hund hätte, würde ich jeden Tag spazieren gehen.
If it **rained**,	I **would take** my umbrella.	Wenn es regnen würde, würde ich meinen Regenschirm mitnehmen.

 Im if-Satz steht nie **would / wouldn't**.

Bedingungssätze können auch mit dem Hauptsatz beginnen. Dann entfällt das Komma.

I **would be** very sad if I **didn't find** my mobile again.	Ich wäre sehr traurig, wenn ich mein Handy nicht mehr finden würde.

 Achtung Besonderheit: Statt **If I was** … wird oft **If I were** … gebraucht.

If I **were** you, I **would call** her.	Wenn ich du wäre, würde ich sie anrufen.

Im Deutschen verwendet man in beiden Satzteilen **würde, wäre** oder **hätte (Konjunktiv)**.

If your mum **didn't work** so hard, she **wouldn't be** so tired.	Wenn deine Mutter nicht so schwer arbeiten **würde, wäre** sie nicht so müde.

(TEST YOURSELF) **Complete the sentences.**

1. If I ⸺ (have) more time, I ⸺ (go) camping with my friends.
2. If Sue ⸺ (be) older, she ⸺ (understand) the film.
3. If I ⸺ (be) in Northern Ireland, I ⸺ (visit) the Giant's Causeway.
4. I ⸺ (hear) you better if you ⸺ (speak) louder.
5. Your grandparents ⸺ (be) very sad, if you ⸺ (not visit) them.
6. Kate ⸺ (not stay) at home if she ⸺ (not be) ill.

G11 Steigerung und Vergleiche von Adjektiven

Clauses of comparison

My eyes are bigger than your eyes.

Meine Augen sind größer als deine Augen.

Adjektive mit **einer Silbe** steigerst du mit **-er / -est**:

cheap	cheap**er**	the cheap**est**	billig, billiger, am billigsten

Zweisilbige Adjektive, die auf **-y** enden, wie z. B. **happy**, **easy**, **crazy**, steigert man auch mit **-er / -est**.

happy	happ**ier**	the happ**iest**	glücklich, glücklicher, am glücklichsten

Alle anderen Adjektive **mit zwei und mehr Silben** steigerst du, indem du **more** und **the most** davor setzt.

expensive	**more** expensive **the most** expensive	teuer, teurer, am teuersten

Und so kannst du ausdrücken, dass etwas weniger oder am wenigsten ist:

interesting	**less** interesting **the least** interesting	interessant, weniger interessant, am wenigsten interessant

So kannst du Dinge miteinander vergleichen:

My big sister is **as** nice **as** my little brother.	Meine große Schwester ist genauso nett wie mein kleiner Bruder.
Mineral water is **not as** expensive **as** juice.	Mineralwasser ist nicht so teuer wie Saft.

 Achtung: Um ungleiche Dinge zu vergleichen, benutzt du **than**.

London is **bigger than** Berlin.	London ist größer als Berlin.

(TEST YOURSELF) **Compare these things.**

1. Northern Ireland is —— (small) than England.
2. Speaking English is —— (easy) than speaking French.
3. Watching a film can be —— (interesting) than surfing the internet.
4. Belfast is the —— (exciting) city in Northern Ireland.
5. A bike is —— (expensive) than a car.
6. Look, the black shoes are as —— (nice) as the white shoes.

G12 Some und any

Some and any

I need some milk but I don't need any cheese.

Ich brauche Milch, aber ich brauche keinen Käse.

Some oder **any** bedeuten im Deutschen **etwas**, **einige** oder **ein paar**.

 In positiven Aussagen benutzt du **some**. Es muss nicht immer übersetzt werden.

I'd like **some** fruit.	Ich möchte gerne (etwas) Obst.
I must buy **some** carrots.	Ich muss (ein paar) Karotten kaufen.

In verneinten Aussagen und in den meisten Fragen steht **any**. Es wird nicht immer übersetzt.

Do you have **any** milk at home?	Hast du Milch zu Hause?
Sorry, we don't have **any** bread.	Es tut mir leid, wir haben kein Brot.

Wie **some** und **any** werden auch ihre Zusammensetzungen verwendet:

something und **anything**	(irgend)etwas
somebody und **anybody**	(irgend)jemand
someone und **anyone**	(irgend)jemand
somewhere und **anywhere**	irgendwo

He told me **something**.	Er hat mir etwas gesagt.
Did he tell you **anything**?	Hat er dir etwas gesagt?
No, he didn't tell me **anything**.	Nein, er hat mir nichts gesagt.

 Achte auf folgende Übersetzungen:
not … anything → nichts; not … anybody / anyone → niemand; not … anywhere → nirgendwo

---

(TEST YOURSELF) **Put in <u>some</u> or <u>any</u>.**

1. Do you know —— facts about Northern Ireland?
2. Look, there are —— funny dancers in the street.
3. Let's buy —— food for the party.
4. Mr Taylor asked me —— questions about Belfast.
5. Do you have —— strawberries?
6. Sorry, we don't have —— strawberries today.

Unit 5

G13 Gegenüberstellung: Simple present und present progressive

Simple present and present progressive

I usually don't drink juice, but today I'm drinking green juice because it's St Patrick's Day.

Normalerweise trinke ich keinen Saft, aber heute trinke ich grünen Saft, weil St. Patrick's Day ist.

Present progressive

Wenn du sagen möchtest, was gerade passiert oder was jemand im Augenblick tut, verwendest du das **present progressive**.
So bildest du Aussagen im **present progressive: am / are / is + Verb + -ing**.
So verneinst du die Sätze: **am / are / is <u>not</u> + Verb + -ing**.
Bei Fragen stellst du **am / are / is** an den Satzanfang.

Signalwörter	
now	jetzt, nun
at the moment	im Moment

Listen, your mobile **is ring**ing.	Hör' mal, dein Handy klingelt gerade.
We **are not us**ing the computer at the moment.	Wir benutzen den Computer gerade nicht.
Are you prepar**ing** a snack?	Bereitest du gerade einen Imbiss vor?

Simple present

Wenn du einen Zustand beschreiben möchtest oder sagen willst, dass jemand etwas gewohnheitsmäßig tut oder dass etwas häufig oder regelmäßig geschieht, verwendest du das **simple present**.

 He, **she**, **it** – das **s** muss mit!

Signalwörter	
every ...	jede / r / s
always	immer
usually	normalerweise
often	oft
sometimes	manchmal
never	nie

Mit **don't** oder **doesn't** (bei he, she, it) kannst du sagen, was man **nicht** macht.
Bei Fragen mit Vollverben (z. B. sing, write, play etc.) musst du **do** oder **does** verwenden.

Every year Keith celebrate**s** St Patrick's Day.	Jedes Jahr feiert Keith den St. Patrick's Day.
Sue **doesn't** speak German.	Sue spricht kein Deutsch.
Do you often eat fish?	Isst du oft Fisch?

(TEST YOURSELF) Use simple present or present progressive.

1. Simon often —— (help) his grandma.
2. Listen, Maddy —— (practise) with her band.
3. —— you sometimes —— (eat) eggs?
4. Keith —— (not listen to) music now.
5. —— (you) —— (watch) TV at the moment?
6. Leo —— (not drink) tea every day.

G14 Possessivpronomen

Possessive pronouns

I found a mobile. Is it yours?

Ich habe ein Handy gefunden. Ist es deins?

Du kennst bereits die Possessiv**begleiter** (**my**, **your**, **his**, **her**, **our**, **their**). Sie stehen **vor** einem Nomen. Mit den Possessiv**pronomen** kannst du sagen, wem etwas gehört, wenn **kein** Nomen **folgt**.

Possessive determiner	Possessivbegleiter	Possessive pronoun	Possessivpronomen
That's **my** umbrella.	Das ist **mein** Schirm.	It's **mine**.	Das ist **meiner**.
Is that **your** coat?	Ist das **deine** Jacke?	Is it **yours**?	Ist das **deine**?
This is **his** toothbrush.	Das ist **seine** Zahnbürste.	It's **his**.	Das ist **seine**.
This is **her** shampoo.	Das ist **ihr** Shampoo.	It's **hers**.	Es ist **ihrs**.
Look at the cat and **its** ball.	Schau dir die Katze und **ihren** Ball an.	It's **its**.	Das ist **ihrer**.
They are **our** bags.	Es sind **unsere** Taschen.	They are **ours**.	Es sind **unsere**.
Are they **your** towels?	Sind das **eure** Handtücher?	Are they **yours**?	Sind das **eure**?
This is **their** new car.	Das ist **ihr** neues Auto.	It's **theirs**.	Das ist **ihrs**.

(TEST YOURSELF) Put in the correct word.

1. Your mobile just looks like —— (my / mine).
2. Have you put —— (your / yours) scarf in the bag, Leo?
3. Is that Maddy's bag? – Yes, it's —— (theirs / hers).
4. Their towels are white, —— (our / ours) are brown.
5. Is this the O'Brians' new car? – No, it isn't —— (their / theirs).
6. I think it's Conor's bike. – Well, I don't think it's —— (his / yours) bike.

G15 Modale Hilfsverben

Modal auxiliaries

You mustn't walk.

Du darfst nicht gehen.

Modale Hilfsverben verändern die Art und Weise eines Verbs. **Can**, **can't**, **must**, **needn't**, **mustn't**, **may**, **may not** kommen immer zusammen mit einem anderen Verb vor.

I **can** play tennis.	Ich kann Tennis spielen.
	(Ich habe es gelernt.)
I **can't** play tennis now.	Ich kann jetzt nicht Tennis spielen.
	(Ich muss meine Hausaufgaben machen.)
You **must** play tennis with Amy.	Du musst mit Amy Tennis spielen.
He **needn't** play tennis.	Er braucht nicht Tennis (zu) spielen.
	(Wir sind genug Spieler.)
She **mustn't** play tennis.	Sie darf nicht Tennis spielen.
	(Sie ist krank.)
We **may** play tennis later.	Wir spielen vielleicht später Tennis.
	(Jetzt ist der Platz besetzt.)
They **may not** play tennis then.	Sie spielen dann vielleicht nicht Tennis.
	(Also können wir spielen.)

 Aufgepasst bei **mustn't** (nicht dürfen) und **needn't** (nicht brauchen, nicht müssen):

You **mustn't** talk so loud.	Du darfst nicht so laut sprechen.
You **needn't** wait for me.	Du brauchst nicht auf mich (zu) warten.
	oder: Du musst nicht auf mich warten.

(TEST YOURSELF) **Choose the right word.**

1. —— (can / mustn't) I use your pen?
2. You —— (mustn't / needn't) eat ice cream in the classroom.
3. Sara —— (must / mustn't) do her homework.
4. You —— (may not / mustn't) have time to come to the party.
5. We —— (must / needn't) go now. It's already 7 o'clock.
6. You —— (can / needn't) worry. The children will be OK.

Lösungen

TEST YOURSELF

G1
1. buy
2. does
3. don't go
4. Do … go
5. are
6. Is

G2
1. had
2. didn't hear
3. Did … have
4. did … do
5. wasn't
6. Were

G3
1. myself
2. yourself
3. herself
4. ourselves
5. each other
6. itself

G4
1. carefully
2. good
3. well
4. clever
5. slowly
6. fast

G5
1. have … been
2. has … done
3. have / 've … had
4. have not / haven't asked
5. Have … forgotten
6. has … not / hasn't … called

G6
1. who
2. which
3. who
4. which
5. who
6. whose

G7
1. Walking
2. Meeting
3. climbing
4. staying
5. working
6. writing

G8
1. 'll / will stay
2. won't / will not be
3. 'll / will have
4. 'll / will show
5. 'll / will do
6. won't / will not lose

G9
1. meet, 'll / will tell
2. goes, won't / will not visit
3. has, 'll / will go
4. doesn't do, won't / will not be
5. 'll / will become, take
6. 'll / will be, don't visit

G10
1. had, would go
2. was, would understand
3. were, would visit
4. would hear, spoke
5. would be, didn't visit
6. wouldn't / would not stay, wasn't

G11
1. smaller
2. easier
3. more / less interesting
4. most exciting
5. less expensive
6. nice

G12
1. any
2. some
3. some
4. some
5. any
6. any

G13
1. helps
2. is practising
3. Do … eat
4. isn't listening to
5. Are … watching
6. doesn't drink

G14
1. mine
2. your
3. hers
4. ours
5. theirs
6. his

G15
1. Can
2. mustn't
3. must
4. may not
5. must
6. needn't

Methods

1-minute-presentation

Step 1
Nimm ein Blatt DIN A4-Papier quer und falte es so, dass das untere Drittel nach hinten wegknickt.

Step 2
Schreibe den Vortragstext auf die oberen zwei Drittel.
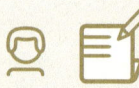

Step 3
Streiche nun die wichtigsten Stichpunkte im Text an. Notiere sie noch einmal auf dem unteren Drittel. Das ist dein Spickzettel.

Step 4
In deiner Präsentation verwendest du nur den Spickzettel. Wenn du steckenbleibst, darfst du ihn umknicken und kurz auf den Text oben schauen.

Bus stop
(Lerntempoduett)

Step 1
Bearbeite die Aufgabe zunächst allein. Schreibe deine Lösungen auf.

Step 2
Wenn du fertig bist, gehe zum „bus stop". Warte dort auf die nächste Person bzw. triff die Person, die dort schon wartet. Vergleicht und korrigiert eure Ergebnisse.

Step 3
Gehe danach wieder zu deinem Platz zurück. Bearbeite die nächste Aufgabe.

Double circle
(Kugellager)

Step 1
Teilt euch in zwei Gruppen A und B.
Gruppe A bildet den inneren Kreis. Gruppe B bildet den äußeren Kreis. Steht dabei so, dass ihr euch anseht.

Step 2
Wenn ein Signal ertönt, sprecht ihr mit der Person, die euch gegenübersteht.

Step 3
Beim nächsten Signal rückt der mittlere Kreis zwei Plätze weiter nach links. Wiederholt den Vorgang.

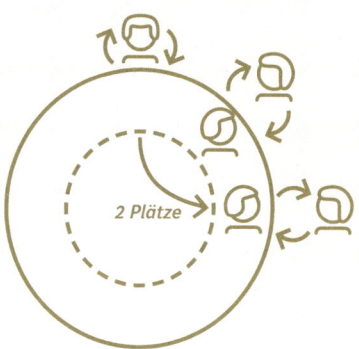

Dramatic reading
(Szenisches Lesen)

Step 1
Verteilt die Rollen innerhalb eurer Gruppe.

Step 2
Lies dir deinen Text lautlos oder ganz leise immer wieder vor, bis du ihn gut kennst.

Step 3
Übt euren Text in der Gruppe mit der Methode „Read and look up" (Seite 170).

Step 4
Überlegt euch, wie ihr euch in der Rolle fühlt und wie ihr euch bewegen würdet. Tragt euren Text so frei wie möglich vor.

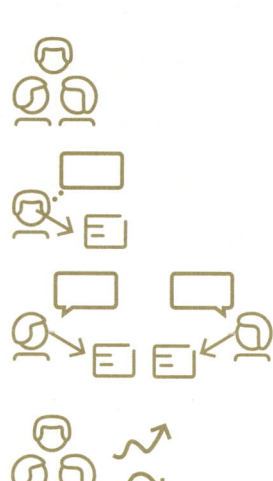

Gallery walk

Step 1
Hängt nach eurer Gruppenarbeit euer Produkt
gut sichtbar im Klassenzimmer auf.

Step 2
Einer von euch, der „Experte", bleibt bei eurem
Produkt stehen und erklärt es den anderen.
Die anderen gehen herum. Nach jedem Durchgang
wechselt der Experte.

Step 3
Seht euch die Produkte der anderen an und
bewertet sie.

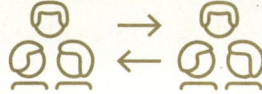

Step 4
Wertet im Anschluss eure Ergebnisse in der Klasse aus.

Milling around
(Marktplatz)

Step 1
Bearbeite die Aufgabe zunächst allein.
Auf ein Zeichen vom Lehrer oder der Lehrerin
steht ihr auf und geht durch den Raum.
Nimm die Aufgabe und einen Stift mit.

Step 2
Wenn ein Signal ertönt, bleibt ihr stehen.
Besprecht mit der Person die Aufgabe,
die euch am nächsten steht.

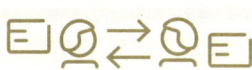

Step 3
Beim nächsten Signal trennt ihr euch und geht
weiter durch den Raum. Wiederholt den Vorgang.

Peer correction

(Partnerkontrolle)

Step 1
Bearbeite die Aufgabe zunächst selbstständig.

Step 2
Tausche deine Lösungen mit einem Partner/einer Partnerin.
Kontrolliere seine oder ihre Lösungen.

Step 3
Tauscht euch danach zu der Aufgabe aus und korrigiert den Text.

Placemat

(Platzdeckchen)

Step 1
Bildet Vierergruppen.

Step 2
Teilt ein großes Blatt Papier in fünf Bereiche ein.

Step 3
Setzt euch so hin, dass alle in eine Ecke des Blattes
schreiben können.

Step 4
Jedes Gruppenmitglied denkt allein über das Thema nach
und schreibt Ideen auf seinen Teil des Blattes.

Step 5
Tauscht euch über die Ideen aus. Einigt euch auf die besten
Ideen und schreibt diese in die Mitte des Blattes.

Read and look up
(Lesen und Aufschauen)

Step 1
Schaue auf deinen Text und präge dir die erste Zeile oder den ersten Satz ein. Schaue hoch und sprich deine Zeile/ deinen Satz lautlos oder leise vor dich hin. Nimm dir die nächste Zeile/den nächsten Satz vor.

Step 2
Übe nun mit einer Partnerin/einem Partner. Erzähle deinen Text, Zeile für Zeile oder Satz für Satz. Dazwischen schaust du immer wieder nach unten auf deinen Text.

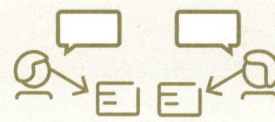

Step 3
Wiederhole alles, bis es gut klappt. Überlege dir, wo du stehen und wie du dich bewegen willst.

Round robin
(Blitzlicht)

Step 1
Bildet Gruppen und setzt euch in einen Kreis.

Step 2
Jedes Gruppenmitglied überlegt sich kurz einen Satz, der seine persönliche Meinung zum Thema ausdrückt.

Step 3
Wenn alle bereit sind, sagen die Gruppenmitglieder der Reihe nach ihre Meinung.

Step 4
Die anderen Gruppenmitglieder dürfen die Sätze nicht kommentieren.

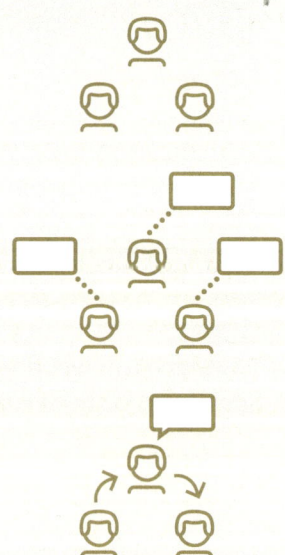

Think – pair – share

Step 1
Schreibe deine Ideen, Gedanken oder Lösungen zur Aufgabe auf.

Step 2
Tauscht eure Notizen zu zweit aus und besprecht sie.

Step 3
Präsentiert euer Ergebnis anderen Paaren oder der gesamten Klasse.

Tip top

Step 1
Sage zunächst, was dir gut gefallen hat – was „top" war.

Step 2
Sage nun, was noch nicht so gut war, und gib einen Tipp, was man noch verbessern könnte.

Writers' conference
(Schreibwerkstatt)

Step 1
Bildet Vierergruppen.

Step 2
Lest euch eure Sätze/Texte gegenseitig vor.

Step 3
Die anderen sagen, was ihnen gefallen hat.

Step 4
Die Zuhörer machen Verbesserungsvorschläge.

Step 5
Jede Gruppe wählt den besten Text aus und liest ihn der Klasse vor.

Vocabulary

Das Vocabulary enthält alle neuen Wörter und Wendungen. Sie stehen in der Reihenfolge, wie sie im Buch vorkommen.

Die Wortliste ist in drei Spalten aufgeteilt:

Links findest du das englische Wort mit der Lautschrift in Klammern. (Die Lautschrift wird ganz unten auf jeder Seite im *Dictionary* erklärt.)

In der mittleren Spalte steht die deutsche Übersetzung.

Rechts findest du Beispielsätze, Hinweise und Tipps, die dir beim Lernen helfen.

Die **fett** gedruckten Wörter musst du lernen.
Die blau gedruckten Wörter kannst du lernen, musst du aber nicht.
Die Wörter aus den Checkpoints musst du nicht lernen.

Symbole und Abkürzungen:

👄	Achte auf die Aussprache!	=	entspricht
🖊	Achte auf die Schreibung!	*(sg)*	Einzahl (Singular)
↔	ist das Gegenteil von	*(pl)*	Mehrzahl (Plural)
→	ist verwandt mit	Ⓡ	ähnlich wie im Russischen
sth	something	Ⓣ	ähnlich wie im Türkischen

Die *Word bank*-Seiten helfen dir, die *Your turn*-Aufgaben in den *Units* zu bearbeiten.
Du findest dort nützlichen individuellen Wortschatz zum Thema der *Unit*, der dir hilft, über deine eigene Situation zu sprechen oder zu schreiben. Diese Wörter findest du auch im *Dictionary*.

Wenn du ein Wort nicht weißt und im Wörterbuch nachschlagen willst, schau auf den *Dictionary*-Seiten ab S. 212 nach. Oder bei den *Instructions* auf S. 208.

Zoom in – The British Isles

p. 8	**The British Isles** [ðə ˌbrɪtɪʃ ˈaɪlz]	die Britischen Inseln	
	Northern Ireland [ˌnɔːðn̩ ˈaɪələnd]	Nordirland	
	The Republic of Ireland [ðə rɪˌpʌblɪk ˌəv ˈaɪələnd]	Irland	
	Wales [weɪlz]	Wales	
	The United Kingdom [ðə juːˌnaɪtɪd ˈkɪŋdəm]	Vereinigtes Königreich von Großbritannien und Nordirland	
	Great Britain [ˌɡreɪt ˈbrɪtn̩]	Großbritannien	
p. 9	**hobby** [ˈhɒbi]	Hobby	Ⓡ хобби Ⓣ hobi

Unit 1 England now and then

p. 10	**then** [ðen]	damals	We lived in Wales **then**.

Way in

	stone [stəʊn]	Stein	
	circle ['sɜ:kl]	Kreis; Ring	
	in the south of [ˌɪn ðə 'saʊθ ˌəv]	im Süden von	Stonehenge is **in the south of** England.
	the Romans [ðə 'rəʊmənz]	die Römer	**The Romans** built Hadrian's Wall.
	north [nɔ:θ]	Norden	**north** ↔ south
	to take [teɪk]	dauern	It **takes** two hours by train.
p. 11	**the Vikings** [ðə 'vaɪkɪŋz]	die Wikinger	**The Vikings** went to York.
	to invade [ɪn'veɪd]	einmarschieren (in); eindringen (in)	The Vikings **invaded** York.
	Denmark ['denmɑ:k]	Dänemark	**Denmark** is in the north of Europe.
	Norway ['nɔ:weɪ]	Norwegen	R Норвегия T Norveç
	the Normans [ðə 'nɔ:mənz]	die Normannen	In 1066 **the Normans** came from France.
	France [frɑ:ns]	Frankreich	T Fransa R Франция
	battle ['bætl]	Schlacht; Kampf	The Normans won a **battle**.
	against [ə'genst]	gegen	I fell **against** the tree.
	the English [ði 'ɪŋglɪʃ]	die Engländer	**The English** lost a battle near Hastings.
	Norman ['nɔ:mən]	Normanne; Normannin	A **Norman** became king of England.
	king [kɪŋ]	König	
	industry ['ɪndəstri]	Industrie	There is lots of **industry** in England.
	during ['djʊərɪŋ]	während	I ate my lunch **during** the break.
	Industrial Revolution [ɪnˌdʌstriəl revl'u:ʃn]	industrielle Revolution	The **Industrial Revolution** was from 1780 to 1840.
	sun [sʌn]	Sonne	
	sick [sɪk]	krank	She isn't at school because she is **sick**.
	grave [greɪv]	Grab	People found **graves** near Stonehenge.
	million ['mɪljən]	Million	**1 million** = 1,000,000

Station 1

Shops

souvenir shop ['suːvnɪə ˌʃɒp]	Souvenirladen	butcher's ['bʊtʃəz]	Metzgerei
baker's ['beɪkəz]	Bäckerei	jeweller's ['dʒuːələz]	Juwelierladen
newsagent's ['njuːzˌeɪdʒnts]	Zeitschriftenladen	greengrocer's ['griːnˌgrəʊsəz]	Obst- und Gemüseladen
		pet shop ['pet ˌʃɒp]	Tierhandlung

p. 12	way [weɪ]	Weg; Art und Weise	Do you know the way to the shops?
	to be interested in [bi: 'ɪntrəstɪd ˌɪn]	sich interessieren für; interessiert sein an	to be interested in = to like sth
	to learn about sth [ˌlɜːn ə'baʊt]	etwas erfahren über	I'd like to learn about the city.
	history ['hɪstri]	Geschichte	Ⓡ история
	what sth was like [ˌwɒt … 'wəz laɪk]	wie etwas war	It shows you what the city was like before.
	to cross [krɒs]	überqueren	We have to cross the road to get there.
	past [pɑːst]	vorbei (an)	Walk past the cinema, then cross the road.
	right [raɪt]	rechts	Turn right at the end of the road.
	left [left]	links	left ↔ right
	How do I get there? [ˌhaʊ du aɪ 'get ðeə]	Wie komme ich dahin?	Ganze Sätze am besten als Einheit lernen.
	down [daʊn]	entlang; herunter; hinunter	down ↔ up
	far [fɑː]	weit	far ↔ near
	a five minute walk [ə 'faɪv mɪnɪt ˌwɔːk]	fünf Minuten zu Fuß	It's just a five minute walk from here.
p. 13	to sell [sel], sold [səʊld], sold [səʊld]	verkaufen	to sell ↔ to buy
p. 15	near [nɪə]	nah	Excuse me, where's the nearest book shop?
	ticket ['tɪkɪt]	Fahrschein; Eintrittskarte	
	library ['laɪbri]	Bibliothek; Bücherei	
	street [striːt]	Straße	Walk down the second street on the left.

Station 2

<table>
<tr><td colspan="4">Talking about places</td></tr>
<tr><td>northwest [ˌnɔːˈθwest]</td><td>Nordwesten</td><td>tiny [ˈtaɪni]</td><td>klein; winzig</td></tr>
<tr><td>in the centre of [ˌɪn ðə ˈsentər_əv]</td><td>in der Mitte von</td><td>close [ˈkləʊs]</td><td>in der Nähe; nahe</td></tr>
<tr><td rowspan="2">quiet [ˈkwaɪət]</td><td rowspan="2">ruhig; leise; still</td><td>drive [draɪv]</td><td>Fahrt; Autofahrt</td></tr>
<tr><td>huge [hjuːdʒ]</td><td>riesig; riesengroß</td></tr>
<tr><td>noisy [ˈnɔɪzi]</td><td>laut</td><td rowspan="2">on the coast [ˌɒn ðə ˈkəʊst]</td><td rowspan="2">an der Küste</td></tr>
<tr><td>east [iːst]</td><td>Osten</td></tr>
<tr><td>west [west]</td><td>Westen</td><td></td><td></td></tr>
</table>

p. 16	**half a million** [ˌhɑːf_ə ˈmɪljən]	eine halbe Million	More than **half a million** people live there.
	inhabitant [ɪnˈhæbɪtnt]	Einwohner; Einwohnerin; Bewohner; Bewohnerin	**inhabitants** of a town = people who live in a town
	traffic [ˈtræfɪk]	Verkehr	It's a busy city with lots of **traffic**.
	past [pɑːst]	Vergangenheit	In the **past** Manchester had lots of industry.
	factory [ˈfæktri]	Fabrik; Werk	
	coal [kəʊl]	Kohle	**Coal** is black stones you use on a fire.
	mine [maɪn]	Bergwerk	You get coal from a coal **mine**.
	village [ˈvɪlɪdʒ]	Dorf	There are not many houses in a **village**.
	used to (live) [ˈjuːst tə]	(wohnte) früher	We **used to** live in Newcastle.
	goat [ɡəʊt]	Ziege	
	a lot of [ə ˈlɒt_əv]	viel; eine Menge	**a lot of** = lots of
	cow [kaʊ]	Kuh	
	only [ˈəʊnli]	nur; bloß; erst	**Only** about 400 people live there.
	worst [wɜːst]	schlimmste; schlechteste	That is the **worst** thing about our village.
	unfair [ʌnˈfeə]	unfair	I can't see my friends. It's so **unfair**!
p. 17	**mountain** [ˈmaʊntɪn]	Berg	
p. 18	**head first** [ˈhed fɜːst]	kopfüber	He fell into the mud, **head first**.
p. 19	**around** [əˈraʊnd]	herum; umher	I hang **around** with my friends.

Reading corner

p. 20	**deadly** ['dedli]	tod-; tödlich	It was **deadly** quiet in the house.
	silence ['saɪləns]	Stille; Schweigen; Ruhe	**silence** = no noise
	tunnel ['tʌnl]	Tunnel	R тоннель T tünel
	the dark [ðə 'dɑːk]	Dunkelheit	I sit in **the dark** every day.
	canary [kə'neəri]	Kanarienvogel	
	gas [gæs]	Gas	R газ T gaz
	to explode [ɪk'spləʊd]	explodieren	The gas in a mine can **explode**.
	explosion [ɪk'spləʊʒn]	Explosion	There was a big **explosion**.
	to kill [kɪl]	töten	An explosion **killed** 30 men.
	miner ['maɪnə]	Bergarbeiter; Bergarbeiterin	A **miner** works in a mine.
	to smell [smel], **smelt** [smelt], **smelt** [smelt]	riechen	A canary **smells** gas in the coal mine.
p. 21	**one day** [wʌn 'deɪ]	eines Tages	**One day** I stopped talking.
	to cough [kɒf]	husten	Bart **coughed** all the time.
	to die [daɪ]	sterben	He was really ill and **died**.
	could [kʊd]	konnte	I **couldn't** talk.
	to speak [spiːk], **spoke** [spəʊk], **spoken** ['spəʊkn]	sprechen	I opened my mouth, but couldn't **speak**.
	silent ['saɪlənt]	stumm; schweigsam	**silent** → silence
	truck [trʌk]	Wagen; Karre	
	nothing ['nʌθɪŋ]	nichts	**nothing** ↔ something
	time [taɪm]	Mal	This **time** I made a noise.
p. 22	**to breathe** [briːð]	atmen	I couldn't **breathe** in the mine.
	voice [vɔɪs]	Stimme	I could hear the miners' **voices**.
	to pick up [ˌpɪkˈʌp]	aufheben	One of the miners **picked** me **up**.
	dead [ded]	tot	I thought Billy was **dead**.
	to get out [ˌget 'aʊt]	herauskommen	We had to **get out** of the mine quickly.
	that [ðæt]	dass	I saw **that** everyone was OK.
	alive [ə'laɪv]	am Leben	**alive** ↔ dead

Film corner

p. 25	**Victorian era** [vɪkˌtɔːriən ˈɪərə]	viktorianisches Zeitalter	This was when Queen Victoria was the Queen.
	to **fall asleep** [ˌfɔːl̩ əˈsliːp]	einschlafen	I **fell asleep** at ten o'clock.
	to **dream** [driːm], **dreamt** [dremt], **dreamt** [dremt]	träumen	I **dreamt** that I was a teacher.
	century [ˈsenʃri]	Jahrhundert	a **century** = 100 years
	I'd rather [aɪd ˈrɑːðə]	ich würde lieber	**I'd rather** eat vegetables than meat.
	to **wish** [wɪʃ]	wünschen	I **wish** every day was Saturday.
	to **be asleep** [bi: əˈsliːp]	schlafen	You have **been asleep** all day.
	almost [ˈɔːlməʊst]	fast; beinahe	55 minutes is **almost** an hour.
	confused [kənˈfjuːzd]	verwirrt; wirr	I was **confused**, I didn't know where I was.

Checkpoint

project [ˈprɒdʒekt]	Projekt	informative [ɪnˈfɔːmətɪv]	informativ
presenter [prɪˈzentə]	Moderator; Moderatorin		

Reading skills

p. 31	**type** [taɪp]	Sorte; Typ; Art	What **type** of text is it?
	brochure [ˈbrəʊʃə]	Broschüre; Prospekt	R брошюра T broşür
	to **be about** [bi: əˈbaʊt]	gehen um; handeln von	The text **is about** a bike tour.
	queen [kwiːn]	Königin	
	inside [ˌɪnˈsaɪd]	in; innen in; im Innern	The Queen is **inside** the palace.

Word bank: Directions

on the left

on the right

beside / next to

opposite

on the corner

at the traffic lights

our house is on the right / left

turn right

turn left

go straight on

cross the road

walk down the road

go / walk past (a book shop)

Asking for help:
Excuse me, please.
Do you know where there is a … ?

Can I walk there?

Are there buses?

Does it take long?

Is it far away?

Getting help:
Can I help you?
Yes, I do.
No, I don't.
Yes, it's just a five minute walk.
Yes, it isn't far.
No, I'd take the bus / underground.
Yes, every five minutes.
No, there aren't.
Yes, about 30 minutes.
No, it doesn't take long.
Yes, it is.
No, it isn't.

Word bank: Where I live

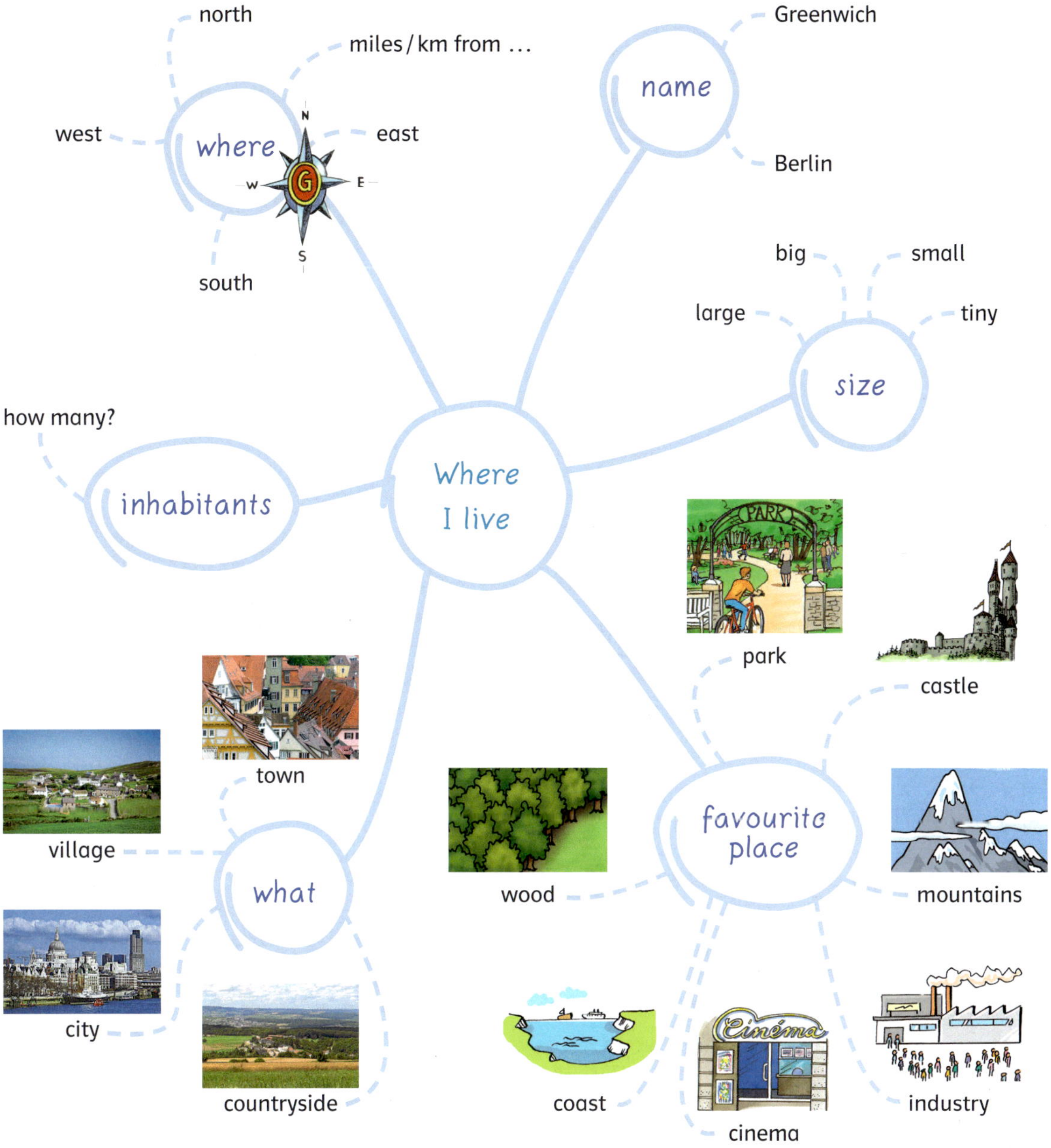

north

miles / km from …

Greenwich

west

where

east

name

N

W — G — E

S

Berlin

south

big   small

large   tiny

how many?

size

inhabitants

Where I live

park

castle

village

town

what

wood

favourite place

mountains

city

countryside

coast

cinema

industry

Unit 2 Adventures in Wales

p. 32	adventure [əd'ventʃə]	Abenteuer	We'll have lots of adventures in Wales.

Way in

Welsh [welʃ]	Walisisch; walisisch; Waliser; Waliserin	Welsh is a very old language.
sign [saɪn]	Schild; Zeichen	∅ Achtung Schreibweise! sign
zip line ['zɪp ˌlaɪn]	Seilrutsche	The longest zip line in Europe is in Wales.
skiing ['ski:ɪŋ]	Skifahren	

p. 33	capital (city) ['kæpɪtl (ˌsɪti)]	Hauptstadt	The capital of England is London.
	city centre [ˌsɪti 'sentə]	Stadtzentrum; Stadtmitte	There are lots of shops in the city centre.
	to try [traɪ]	ausprobieren	Have you ever been canoeing? Try it!
	water ['wɔ:tə]	Wasser	Penguins like water.
	sport [spɔ:t]	Sportart	Ⓡ спорт Ⓣ spor
	coast [kəʊst]	Küste	England has a lot of coast.
	rafting ['rɑ:ftɪŋ]	Rafting	You can do rafting in the sea or on a river.
	popular ['pɒpjələ]	beliebt	Canoeing and rafting are popular sports.
	volunteer [ˌvɒlən'tɪə]	Freiwilliger; Freiwillige; ehrenamtlicher Helfer; ehrenamtliche Helferin	Volunteers help people and don't get any money.
	lifeboat ['laɪfbəʊt]	Rettungsboot	Lifeboats are very important in Wales.
	important [ɪm'pɔ:tnt]	wichtig; einflussreich	Don't forget. It's very important!
	trouble ['trʌbl]	Schwierigkeiten; Problem; Ärger	They help people in trouble.
	teenager ['ti:nˌeɪdʒə]	Teenager; Teenagerin; Jugendliche; Jugendlicher	A teenager is between 13 and 19 years old.
	fluent ['flu:ənt]	fließend; flüssig	I'm German, but can speak fluent English.
	plant [plɑ:nt]	Pflanze	
	to mean [mi:n], meant [ment], meant [ment]	bedeuten; meinen	'Wurst' means 'sausage' in English.
	guest [gest]	Gast	We have guests for the weekend.

Station 1

Adjectives for sportspeople

slow [sləʊ]	langsam	**safe** [seɪf]	sicher; ungefährlich
tough [tʌf]	hart	**unfriendly** [ʌnˈfrendli]	unfreundlich
quick [kwɪk]	schnell	**small** [smɔ:l]	klein
strong [strɒŋ]	stark	**loud** [laʊd]	laut
fit [fɪt]	fit; in Form	**talented** [ˈtæləntɪd]	begabt; talentiert
friendly [ˈfrendli]	freundlich; nett	**exhausted** [ɪgˈzɔ:stɪd]	erschöpft
weak [wi:k]	schwach	**patient** [ˈpeɪʃnt]	geduldig
dry [draɪ]	trocken	**successful** [səkˈsesfl]	erfolgreich

p. 34	**outdoor** [ˌaʊtˈdɔ:]	Freiluft-; Outdoor-	Kayaking is an **outdoor** sport.
	activity centre [ækˈtɪvəti ˌsentə]	Jugendzentrum	The **activity centre** looks really good.
	to **take a trip** [ˌteɪk ə ˈtrɪp]	eine Fahrt machen	We **took** a canoeing **trip** down the river.
	rugby [ˈrʌgbi]	Rugby	Ⓡ регби Ⓣ rugbi
	rule [ru:l]	Regel	You can learn the **rules** quickly.
	indoor [ˌɪnˈdɔ:]	Hallen-; Innen-	**indoor** ↔ outdoor
	equipment [ɪˈkwɪpmənt]	Ausrüstung	**equipment**: helmet, special clothes, …
	myself [maɪˈself]	selbst; selber	It's nice. I often go there **myself**.
	enough [ɪˈnʌf]	genug; genügend	I'm strong **enough** for it.
	cheeky [ˈtʃi:ki]	frech	Mark was **cheeky** to Beth.
	to **climb** [klaɪm]	klettern; steigen; besteigen	𝄢 Achtung Schreibweise! clim**b**
	quite [kwaɪt]	ziemlich; ganz; völlig	I can climb **quite** well already.
	dangerous [ˈdeɪndʒrəs]	gefährlich	**dangerous** ↔ safe
	to **be scared** [bi: ˈskeəd]	Angst haben; erschrocken sein	I'm **scared** of dogs.
	each other [ˌi:tʃ ˈʌðə]	einander; sich; sich gegenseitig	We can tell **each other** about it later!
	self [self]	selbst; sich	**self**: myself, yourself, himself, herself, itself, ourselves, yourselves, themselves
p. 35	**instructor** [ɪnˈstrʌktə]	Lehrer; Lehrerin	All our **instructors** are friendly.
p. 36	**class** [klɑ:s]	Klasse	Our **class** went on a trip last week.
	camping [ˈkæmpɪŋ]	Camping; Zelten	We went on a **camping** trip to Wales.
p. 37	**because of** [bɪˈkɒz ˌəv]	wegen	I was late **because of** the weather.

What must you be like? [wɒt ˌmʌst ju ˈbiː laɪk]	Wie musst du sein?	Ganze Sätze am besten als Einheit lernen.

Station 2

Health and medicine

to **bleed** [bliːd], **bled** [bled], **bled** [bled]	bluten		cast [kɑːst]	Gips
to **cut** [kʌt], **cut** [kʌt], **cut** [kʌt]	(sich) schneiden		to **put on** [ˌpʊtˈɒn]	anlegen; anziehen
			bandage [ˈbændɪdʒ]	Verband
finger [ˈfɪŋgə]	Finger		to **cool** [kuːl]	kühlen
tooth (sg) [tuːθ], teeth (pl) [tiːθ]	Zahn		to **move** [muːv]	(sich) bewegen
			plaster [ˈplɑːstə]	Pflaster
knee [niː]	Knie		sleep [sliːp]	Schlaf
to **burn** [bɜːn], **burnt** [bɜːnt], **burnt** [bɜːnt]	verbrennen; brennen		medicine [ˈmedsn]	Medikamente; Medizin
to **sprain** [spreɪn]	verstauchen; verrenken		injection [ɪnˈdʒekʃn]	Spritze
			operation [ˌɒprˈeɪʃn]	Operation

p. 38	emergency [ɪˈmɜːdʒnsi]	Notfall	Help! It's an **emergency**.
	operator [ˈɒpreɪtə]	Vermittlung	You get the **operator** when you call 999.
	emergency service [ɪˈmɜːdʒnsi ˌsɜːvɪs]	Notdienst; Rettungsdienst	You call 999 for the **emergency services** in the UK.
	service [ˈsɜːvɪs]	Dienst	Which **service** do you need?
	ambulance [ˈæmbjələns]	Krankenwagen	
	to **hurry** [ˈhʌri]	sich beeilen	I need an ambulance. Please **hurry**!
	bad [bæd]	schlimm; böse; schlecht	His head doesn't look as **bad** as his leg.
	accident [ˈæksɪdnt]	Unfall	The man has had an **accident**.
	to **fall (over)** [ˌfɔːlˈəʊvə]	fallen; hinfallen; umfallen	I think he **fell** over on the beach.
	rock [rɒk]	Fels; Stein	
	awake [əˈweɪk]	bei Bewusstsein; wach	Is the man **awake**?
	phone number [ˈfəʊn ˌnʌmbə]	Telefonnummer	Give me your **phone number**, please!
	should [ʃʊd]	sollte	You **should** try something new this year.

to **do the right thing** [ˌduː ðə ˈraɪt θɪŋ]	das Richtige tun	It's OK. You've **done the right thing.**
police [pəˈliːs]	Polizei	R полиция T polis
caller [ˈkɔːlə]	Anrufer; Anruferin	**caller** → to call
emergency call [ɪˈmɜːdʒnsi ˌkɔːl]	Notruf	The phone number for **emergency calls** is 999.
p. 39 **cuddly toy** [ˈkʌdli ˌtɔɪ]	Kuscheltier	My little sister has lots of **cuddly toys.**
p. 40 **hand** [hænd]	Hand	
to hit [hɪt]	(sich) stoßen; anstoßen	He **hit** his head on the table.
p. 41 **training** [ˈtreɪnɪŋ]	Training	On Friday I have football **training.**
skateboard [ˈskeɪtbɔːd]	Skateboard	R скейтборд T skateboard
trick [trɪk]	Kunststück	I want to try some skateboard **tricks.**
back [bæk]	zurück	I have just sent it **back** to the shop.

Reading corner

p. 42 **reporter** [rɪˈpɔːtə]	Reporter; Reporterin	A **reporter** writes stories for magazines.
to **jump** [dʒʌmp]	zusammenzucken; erschrecken	The loud noise made us **jump.**
knight [naɪt]	Ritter	✎ Achtung Schreibweise! k̲night
cloud [klaʊd]	Wolke	
smoke [sməʊk]	Rauch	
corridor [ˈkɒrɪdɔː]	Gang; Flur; Korridor	There are lots of **corridors** at school.
p. 43 to **joust** [dʒaʊst]	einen Turnierzweikampf austragen; turnieren	We learned how to **joust.**
armour [ˈɑːmə]	Rüstung	
to hold [həʊld], **held** [held], **held** [held]	halten; festhalten	I **held** the door open for the film star.
sword [sɔːd]	Schwert	
still [stɪl]	dennoch	It wasn't real but it was **still** heavy.
to **make sb feel like sth** [ˌmeɪk … ˈfiːl laɪk]	jmdm. das Gefühl geben, etw. zu sein	It **made you feel like a real knight.**
jousting [ˈdʒaʊstɪŋ]	Turnierzweikampf	The **jousting** was super cool.

wheelchair [ˈwiːltʃeə]	Rollstuhl	
naughty [ˈnɔːti]	frech; böse	**naughty** ↔ good
stocks [stɒks]	Pranger	He put me in the **stocks**.
to **try out** [ˌtraɪˈaʊt]	ausprobieren	We **tried out** the stocks.
for fun [fə ˈfʌn]	zum Spaß	We did it just **for fun**.
lots [lɒts]	viel; jede Menge	We learned **lots** about Caldicot Castle.

Film corner

p. 45	**briefcase** [ˈbriːfkeɪs]	Aktenkoffer; Aktentasche	My dad puts things in his **briefcase**.
	to **answer the phone** [ˌɑːnsə ðə ˈfəʊn]	ans Telefon gehen	I **answered the phone** when you called.
	cannot [ˈkænɒt]	nicht können	The girls **cannot** open the briefcase.
	prop [prɒp]	Requisit	You need **props** for films and plays.
	ending [ˈendɪŋ]	Schluss; Ende	I didn't like the **ending**.
	to **expect** [ɪkˈspekt]	erwarten	I **expected** a happy ending.

Writing skills

p. 50	**review** [rɪˈvjuː]	Kritik	Read this **review** about the new book.
	to **enjoy** [ɪnˈdʒɔɪ]	*hier:* mögen	I really **enjoyed** the film.
	introduction [ˌɪntrəˈdʌkʃn]	Einleitung; Einführung	The **introduction** is very short.
	comedy [ˈkɒmədi]	Komödie	Ⓡ комедия Ⓣ komedi
	murderer [ˈmɜːdrə]	Mörder; Mörderin	You don't see the **murderer** until the end.
	to **run away** [ˌrʌn əˈweɪ]	weglaufen	She was scared and **ran away**.
	to **hide** [haɪd], **hid** [hɪd], **hidden** [ˈhɪdn]	(sich) verstecken	She ran away and **hid** behind the car.
	baker [ˈbeɪkə]	Bäcker; Bäckerin	
	enemy [ˈenəmi]	Feind; Feindin	**enemy** ↔ friend
	fight [faɪt]	Kampf; Streit	**fight** → to fight
	content [ˈkɒntent]	Inhalt	The **content** is about the film.
	writer [ˈraɪtə]	Verfasser; Verfasserin; Autor; Autorin	The **writer** of the review liked the book.
	location [ləʊˈkeɪʃn]	Drehort; Lage	The **location** of the film was beautiful.
	opinion [əˈpɪnjən]	Meinung	I gave my **opinion** and said what I thought.

star [stɑː]	Stern	In her review she gave the film four **stars**.
conclusion [kənˈkluːʒn]	Schlussfolgerung; Schluss	The **conclusion** is at the end.
to **get a job wrong** [ˌget ə dʒɒb ˈrɒŋ]	einen Auftrag vermasseln	The murderer **gets a job wrong**.
to **fall in love (with)** [ˌfɔːl ɪn ˈlʌv]	sich verlieben (in)	I **fell in love** with the actor in the film.
to **give sth a miss** [ˌgɪv sʌmθɪŋ ə ˈmɪs]	auf etw. verzichten; etw. bleiben lassen	**Give** the film **a miss**.
to **give reasons** [ˌgɪv ˈriːznz]	Gründe nennen; Gründe angeben	**Give** the **reasons** for your opinion.
to **rate** [reɪt]	bewerten; einstufen	The writer **rates** the film.
advice [ədˈvaɪs]	Rat; Ratschlag	Nichola gave me some good **advice**.
drama [ˈdrɑːmə]	Drama	R̲ драма T̲ dram
romance [ˈrəʊmæns]	Liebesgeschichte	**Romance** is also a type of film.
start [stɑːt]	Start; Anfang	**start** ↔ ending

p. 51 (to give reasons)

Word bank: Sports and activities

Water sports

swimming

surfing

windsurfing

canoeing

rafting

Activities

ride a bike

Ball sports

rugby

football

netball

handball

basketball

go rock climbing

Winter sports

skiing

snowboarding

ice skating

Equipment

boat

do skateboard tricks

Athletics

high jump

long jump

javelin

racket

paddle

go jogging

Racket sports

waterproofs

ball

tennis

badminton

squash

goggles

helmet

go hiking

Word bank: Emergency

Emergency services

police

ambulance

fire brigade

coastguard

cast

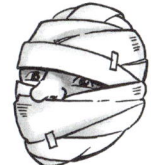

bandage

plaster

cut

Useful verbs the operator says

to cool

to move

to sit

bruise

Useful verbs the caller says

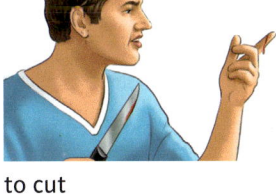

to cut

to break

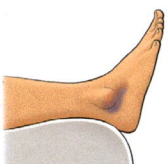

poison

wound

to hurt

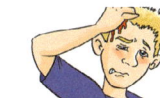

to bleed

to sprain

to breathe

to fall

Unit 3 Made in Scotland

Way in

p. 52	**inventor** [ɪnˈventə]	Erfinder; Erfinderin	Lots of **inventors** are from Scotland.
	to **be born** [bi: ˈbɔːn]	geboren werden	I **was born** in Germany.
	to **fight** [faɪt], **fought** [fɔːt], **fought** [fɔːt]	kämpfen; (sich) streiten	⬦ Achtung Schreibweise! fi**gh**t
	its [ɪts]	sein; ihr	The dog has **its** leg stuck in the mud.
p. 53	**clean** [kliːn]	sauber	**clean** ↔ dirty
	electricity [ˌelɪkˈtrɪsəti]	Strom; Elektrizität	Scotland has clean **electricity**.
	wind farm [ˈwɪnd fɑːm]	Windpark	A **wind farm** makes lots of electricity.
	lake [leɪk]	See	
	cottage [ˈkɒtɪdʒ]	Häuschen	
	to **enjoy** [ɪnˈdʒɔɪ]	genießen	I **enjoy** my garden in the summer.
	countryside [ˈkʌntrɪsaɪd]	Landschaft; Land	Tourists can enjoy the **countryside**.
	Scottish [ˈskɒtɪʃ]	schottisch	**Scottish** → Scotland
	tradition [trəˈdɪʃn]	Tradition	There are many **traditions** in Scotland.
	bagpipes (pl) [ˈbægpaɪps]	Dudelsack	In Scotland people play the **bagpipes**.
	kilt [kɪlt]	Schottenrock; Kilt	A **kilt** is a Scottish skirt, usually for men.
	Scot [skɒt]	Schotte; Schottin	**Scot** → Scotland
	porridge [ˈpɒrɪdʒ]	Haferbrei	Scots often eat **porridge** for breakfast.
	oat [əʊt]	Hafer	Porridge is made with **oats**.
	(wind) turbine [(wɪnd) ˈtɜːbaɪn]	Windrad	The **turbines** are very tall.
	to **protect** [prəˈtekt]	schützen	We must **protect** the animals.
	nature [ˈneɪtʃə]	Natur	Animals and plants are **nature**.

Station 1

Materials

plastic ['plæstɪk]	Plastik; Kunststoff		**cotton** ['kɒtn]	Baumwolle
metal ['metl]	Metall		**steel** [stiːl]	Stahl
wood [wʊd]	Holz		**cardboard** ['kɑːdbɔːd]	Pappe; Karton
rubber ['rʌbə]	Gummi		**silk** [sɪlk]	Seide
leather ['leðə]	Leder		**aluminium** [ˌæljə'mɪniəm]	Aluminium
paper ['peɪpə]	Papier			

p. 54	**who** [huː]	der; dem; den; die	There's the man **who** was in the film.
	to **change** [tʃeɪndʒ]	verändern; (sich) ändern	He was a Scot who **changed** the world.
	to **invent** [ɪn'vent]	erfinden	to **invent** → inventor
	telephone ['telɪfəʊn]	Telefon	R телефон T telefon
	to **grow up** [ˌgrəʊˈʌp], **grew up** [ˌgruːˈʌp], **grown up** [ˌgrəʊnˈʌp]	aufwachsen	She **grew up** in London.
	deaf [def]	gehörlos; schwerhörig; taub	She can't hear you. She's **deaf**.
	speech [spiːtʃ]	Sprache; Rede	Bell was very interested in **speech**.
	which [wɪtʃ]	die; der; dem; den; das	That's the dog **which** ate the food.
	sound [saʊnd]	Laut; Ton; Geräusch	Listen to the **sounds** of speech.
	Canada ['kænədə]	Kanada	**Canada** is north of America.
	USA (United States of America) [ˌjuːesˈeɪ (juːˌnaɪtɪd ˌsteɪts ˌəv əˈmerɪkə)]	USA (Vereinigte Staaten von Amerika)	Boston is in the **USA**.
	invention [ɪn'venʃn]	Erfindung	**invention** → to invent → inventor
	to **be made of** [bi 'meɪd ˌəv]	hergestellt sein aus	The house **is made of** stone.
	success [sək'ses]	Erfolg	Bell's telephone was a **success**.
	rich [rɪtʃ]	reich	He has a lot of money. He is **rich**.
	whose [huːz]	dessen; deren	He is a man **whose** invention saves time.
p. 55	to **start** [stɑːt]	gründen	He **started** a company in 2012.
	tube [tjuːb]	Schlauch; Rohr	There's a **tube** in the tyre.
	air [eə]	Luft	You have to put **air** in the tyres.

tyre [taɪə]	Reifen		
wheel [wiːl]	Rad		
solid ['sɒlɪd]	fest	They were made of **solid** rubber.
tyre [taɪə]	Reifen	**Tyres** are usually black.
p. 57	**steam engine** ['stiːm ˌendʒɪn]	Dampfmaschine	
	light bulb ['laɪt ˌbʌlb]	Glühbirne	

Station 2

Going on holiday

campsite ['kæmpsaɪt]	Campingplatz; Zeltplatz	to **check out** [ˌtʃek ˈaʊt]	auschecken
bed and breakfast (B&B) [ˌbed ˌən ˈbrekfəst]	Frühstückspension	to **pay the bill** [ˌpeɪ ðə ˈbɪl]	die Rechnung bezahlen
hostel ['hɒstl]	Herberge	to **make a reservation** [ˌmeɪk ˌə ˈrezəveɪʃn]	reservieren
caravan ['kærəvæn]	Wohnwagen	to **check in** [ˌtʃek ˈɪn]	einchecken
tent [tent]	Zelt		

p. 58	**trip** [trɪp]	Reise	It's time to plan our **trip**.
	to **decide** [dɪ'saɪd]	(sich) entscheiden	We have to **decide** where to go.
	cosy ['kəʊzi]	gemütlich	This hotel looks nice and **cosy**.
	could [kʊd]	könnten	You **could** show me the sights.
	hiking ['haɪkɪŋ]	Wandern	You know I love **hiking**.
	simple ['sɪmpl]	einfach	**simple** = easy
	outside [ˌaʊt'saɪd]	draußen; im Freien	We'll be **outside** every day.
	all day [ˌɔːl 'deɪ]	den ganzen Tag	They work **all day**.
	No way! [ˌnəʊ 'weɪ]	Auf keinen Fall!; Was?!; Echt?!	**No way!** I'm not going camping.
	to **freeze** [friːz], **froze** [frəʊz], **frozen** ['frəʊzn]	frieren; gefrieren	We'll **freeze** in a tent.
	insect ['ɪnsekt]	Insekt	
	Are you serious? [ˌɑː ju 'sɪəriəs]	Im Ernst?	Ganze Sätze am besten als Einheit lernen.
	buffet ['bʊfeɪ]	Büfett	R буфет T büfe

nice [naɪs]	*hier:* lecker; gut	The food is **nice** in a hotel.
not … either [nɒt … 'aɪðə]	auch nicht	I **don't** want to go camping **either**.
to **rent** [rent]	mieten	We could **rent** a holiday cottage.
a few [ə 'fjuː]	ein paar; wenige; einige	I looked again **a few** hours later.
tip [tɪp]	Tipp	We can get some **tips** about sights.
local ['ləʊkl]	hiesig; örtlich; lokal	I love the **local** food.
nobody ['nəʊbədi]	niemand	If **nobody** wants to go camping, fine.
monster ['mɒnstə]	Ungeheuer; Monster	Ⓡ монстр

p. 60	to **get cold** [ˌget 'kəʊld]	frieren	We will **get cold** if it rains.
	early ['ɜːli]	früh	I get up **early** at the weekend.
	haggis ['hægɪs]	Haggis *(schottisches Gericht aus Schafsinnereien)*	**Haggis** is a Scottish dish.

p. 61	**walking** ['wɔːkɪŋ]	Wandern	**Walking** in the mountains is fun.
	cycling ['saɪklɪŋ]	Radfahren	My favourite activity is **cycling**.
	bird watching ['bɜːd ˌwɒtʃɪŋ]	Vogelbeobachtung	**Bird watching** is an activity you can do.
	walk [wɔːk]	Spaziergang	A **walk** in the afternoon is nice.

Reading corner

p. 62	to **keep out** [ˌkiːp 'aʊt]	draußen halten	I will **keep** the English **out**.
	army ['ɑːmi]	Armee; Heer	Edward I has a strong **army**.
	to **beat** [biːt], **beat** [biːt], **beaten** ['biːtn]	besiegen; schlagen	We can't **beat** the English.
	soldier ['səʊldʒə]	Soldat; Soldatin	They have so many **soldiers**.
	like this [laɪk 'ðɪs]	so; auf diese Weise	I shouldn't hide **like this**.
	impossible [ɪm'pɒsəbl]	unmöglich	I think it's **impossible** to win.
p. 63	**spider** ['spaɪdə]	Spinne	
	amazing [ə'meɪzɪŋ]	erstaunlich; unglaublich; toll	This spider is **amazing**.
	web [web]	Spinnennetz; Netz	Look at its **web**.
	to **give up** [ˌgɪv 'ʌp]	aufgeben	The spider never **gives up**.
	must not/never [ˌmʌst 'nɒt/'nevə]	nicht/nie dürfen	I **must never** give up.
	brave [breɪv]	tapfer; mutig	We must be **brave**.

p. 64	**son** [sʌn]	Sohn	**son** ↔ daughter
	tactic ['tæktɪk]	Taktik; Vorgehensweise	We have good **tactics**. We can win.
	ground [graʊnd]	Boden; Erdboden	The **ground** is very wet.
p. 65	**proud (of)** [praʊd (əv)]	stolz (auf)	The Scots are **proud** of Robert the Bruce.
	peace [piːs]	Frieden	There was **peace** in Scotland.
	leader ['liːdə]	Führer; Führerin; Anführer; Anführerin	Robert the Bruce was a great **leader**.
	sad [sæd]	traurig	**sad** ↔ happy
p. 64	**hero** *(sg)* ['hɪərəʊ], **heroes** *(pl)* ['hɪərəʊz]	Held	He was the **hero** in the story.

Film corner

p. 67	**pay phone** ['peɪ fəʊn]	Münztelefon	I need some money for the **pay phone**.
	video chat ['vɪdɪəʊ ˌtʃæt]	Video-Chat	We can talk about it on the **video chat**.
	neighbour ['neɪbə]	Nachbar; Nachbarin	Our **neighbours** live next to us.
	to repair [rɪ'peə]	reparieren	Alicia **repairs** everything.
	radio ['reɪdɪəʊ]	Radio	R радио }radyo
	to be up to [biː 'ʌp tə]	vorhaben	I want to see what you**'re up** to.
	to attach [ə'tætʃ]	verbinden	You have to **attach** the two wires.
	pipe [paɪp]	Rohr	The machine has a water **pipe** in it.
	antenna [æn'tenə]	Antenne	The radio has an **antenna** on it.
	to connect [kə'nekt]	verbinden	**Connect** the wire to the radio.
	signal ['sɪgnl]	Empfang; Signal; Zeichen	Have you got a **signal**?

Checkpoint

advert (ad) ['ædvɜːt]	Anzeige	on duty [ɒn 'djuːti]	im Dienst
magical ['mædʒɪkl]	zauberhaft; magisch	garage ['gærɑːʒ]	Werkstatt; Tankstelle
wonderful ['wʌndəfl]	wunderbar	since [sɪns]	seit
offer ['ɒfə]	Angebot	petrol ['petrl]	Benzin
available [ə'veɪləbl]	erhältlich; verfügbar	free [friː]	kostenlos
full service [ˌfʊl 'sɜːvɪs]	Komplettservice	coffee ['kɒfi]	Kaffee
mechanic [mə'kænɪk]	Mechaniker; Mechanikerin	design [dɪ'zaɪn]	Design; Gestaltung
		message ['mesɪdʒ]	Botschaft

Word bank: Inventors and inventions

Talking about inventors

… was born in …	… invented …
… grew up in …	… also invented …
… moved to …	… was rich …
… died in … (place / year)	… was famous because …

Talking about inventions

is made of …

wood

plastic

metal

glass

is used for …

trolley suitcases

tyres

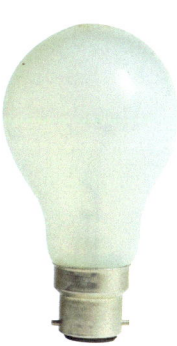

light bulbs

mirrors

tables

… is good because …

it is light	it is slow
it is heavy	it is recyclable
it is fast	it is washable

Word bank: **Places to stay**

B&B

hotel

guest house

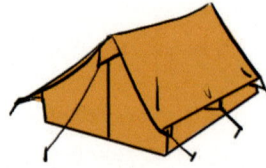
tent

campsite

hostel (youth hostel)

caravan

camper

static caravan

holiday flat

holiday cottage

farm

town

village

city

countryside

Words for describing places to stay

cheap	small
comfortable	clean
cosy	near …
big	good for …

Unit 4 In Northern Ireland

Way in

p. 74	**mural** ['mjʊərəl]	Wandgemälde	That **mural** on the building is great.
	Protestant ['prɒtɪstnt]	Protestant; Protestantin; protestantisch	There were problems between the **Protestants**
	Catholic ['kæθlɪk]	Katholik; Katholikin; katholisch	and the **Catholics**.
p. 75	**to run** [rʌn]	*hier:* betreiben; leiten; führen	My parents **run** a hotel.
	northwest of [ˌnɔːθ'west ˌəv]	nordwestlich	It is a town **northwest of** Belfast.
	free [friː]	kostenlos	The tickets are **free**.
	grandad ['grændæd]	Opa	
	every ['evri]	alle	Buses go **every** 30 minutes.
	adult ['ædʌlt]	Erwachsene; Erwachsener	**adult** ↔ child
	to cost [kɒst], **cost** [kɒst], **cost** [kɒst]	kosten	The tickets **cost** a lot of money.
	giant [dʒaɪənt]	Riese	
	probably ['prɒbəbli]	wahrscheinlich	We will **probably** go there in the summer.

Station 1

> **Adjectives for feelings**
>
> | | | | |
> |---|---|---|---|
> | **useful** ['juːsfl] | nützlich; hilfreich | **optimistic** [ˌɒptɪ'mɪstɪk] | optimistisch |
> | **lonely** ['ləʊnli] | einsam | **down** [daʊn] | deprimiert |
> | **positive** ['pɒzətɪv] | positiv | **dreadful** ['dredfl] | furchtbar |
> | **silly** ['sɪli] | dumm; doof | **hopeful** ['həʊpfl] | hoffnungsvoll |
> | **furious** ['fjʊəriəs] | wütend | **intelligent** [ɪn'telɪdʒnt] | intelligent; klug; vernünftig |
> | **smart** [smaːt] | schlau; klug; intelligent | | |
> | **confident** ['kɒnfɪdnt] | selbstsicher; selbstbewusst | **sure of oneself** ['ʃʊər ˌəv ˌwʌnself] | selbstsicher |
> | **horrible** ['hɒrəbl] | schrecklich; furchtbar | **annoyed** [ə'nɔɪd] | verärgert |

p. 76	**to be fed up (with)** [bi: fed ˌʌp (wɪð)]	die Nase voll haben (von); sauer sein	I'm **fed up** with school and homework.

not … any more [ˌnɒt … eni 'mɔː]	nicht mehr	They aren't friends **any more**.	
in the evenings [ɪn ði 'iːvnɪŋz]	abends	**In the evenings** they don't have time.	
to **nag** [næg]	nörgeln; meckern	They always **nag** me about my jobs.	
to **drive sb crazy** [draɪv … 'kreɪzi]	jmdn. verrückt machen	The guests sometimes **drive me crazy**.	
so much [ˌsəʊ 'mʌtʃ]	so sehr	I miss my friends **so much**.	
without [wɪ'ðaʊt]	ohne	I don't like it **without** you.	
to **hate** [heɪt]	hassen; nicht mögen	I **hate** snakes, but I love bears.	
milkshake ['mɪlkˌʃeɪk]	Milchmischgetränk; Milchshake		
p. 79 **coin** [kɔɪn]	Münze		
time travel ['taɪm ˌtrævl]	Zeitreise	He has invented a **time travel** machine.	
competition [ˌkɒmpə'tɪʃn]	Wettbewerb; Turnier	Dave won a prize in a **competition**!	

Station 2

Shopping

special offer [ˌspeʃl ˈɒfə]	Sonderangebot	**brand** [brænd]	Marke
customer ['kʌstəmə]	Kunde; Kundin	**exact** [ɪg'zækt]	exakt; genau
to **repeat** [rɪ'piːt]	wiederholen	to **change one's mind** [ˌtʃeɪndʒ wʌnz 'maɪnd]	seine Meinung ändern
to **run out of** [ˌrʌn ˈaʊt əv]	ausgehen (Ware)		

p. 80 **raspberry** ['rɑːzbri]	Himbeere		
jam [dʒæm]	Marmelade; Konfitüre	I like raspberry **jam** on my toast.	
one(s) [wʌn(z)]	*Platzhalter für ein Nomen*	This scarf is nice, but that **one** is nicer.	
tasty ['teɪsti]	lecker; schmackhaft	This jam is **tastier** than that jam.	
jar [dʒɑː]	Glas	**Jars** are made of glass.	
sliced bread [ˌslaɪst 'bred]	in Scheiben geschnittenes Brot	In England you buy **sliced bread**.	
loaf (sg) [ləʊf], **loaves** (pl) [ləʊvz]	Brotlaib	I'd like one **loaf** of farmer's bread, please.	
to **post** [pəʊst]	aufgeben (einen Brief); abschicken (einen Brief)	I have to **post** this to my aunt.	
letter ['letə]	Brief; Buchstabe	We don't write **letters**, we write e-mails.	

stamp [stæmp]	Briefmarke		
niece [ni:s]	Nichte	Sarah is her aunt's **niece**.	
less [les]	weniger	**less** ↔ more	
to **get** [get]	*hier:* verstehen	Sorry, I didn't **get** that.	
p. 81	to **check** [tʃek]	überprüfen; kontrollieren	Can you **check** my homework, please?
	peanut butter [ˌpiːnʌt ˈbʌtə]	Erdnussbutter	
	tissue [ˈtɪʃuː]	Taschentuch	**tissue** →
	mineral water [ˈmɪnrl ˌwɔːtə]	Mineralwasser	I drink juice with **mineral water**.
p. 82	**camel** [ˈkæml]	Kamel	
p. 83	**assistant** [əˈsɪstnt]	Verkäufer; Verkäuferin	The **assistant** helped me in the shop.

Reading corner

p. 84	**disaster** [dɪˈzɑːstə]	Katastrophe; Desaster; Unglück	My holiday was a **disaster**.
	to **hit** [hɪt]	gegen etw. fahren	The car **hit** the bike.
	iceberg [ˈaɪsbɜːg]	Eisberg	Ⓡ айсберг
	to **sink** [sɪŋk], **sank** [sæŋk], **sunk** [sʌŋk]	untergehen; sinken	The Titanic hit an iceberg and **sank**.
	after [ˈɑːftə]	danach; später	Two days **after** there were more facts.
	shipyard [ˈʃɪpjɑːd]	Werft	It was made in a Belfast **shipyard**.
	shortly [ˈʃɔːtli]	kurz	It happened **shortly** after the start.
	midnight [ˈmɪdnaɪt]	Mitternacht	**Midnight** is at twelve o'clock at night.
	voyage [ˈvɔɪɪdʒ]	Reise; Fahrt	The **voyage** started on April 15th.
	crew [kruː]	Crew; Besatzung; Mannschaft	The **crew** is the team who works on a ship.
	on board [ˈɒn bɔːd]	an Bord	Achtung Schreibweise! **on board**
	to **survive** [səˈvaɪv]	überleben	**to survive** ↔ to die
	gymnasium [dʒɪmˈneɪziəm]	*hier:* Fitnessraum	**gymnasium** ≠ Gymnasium
	ship builder [ˈʃɪp ˌbɪldə]	Schiffsbauer; Schiffsbauerin	The **ship's builders** said the ship was safe.
	half *(sg)* [hɑːf], halves *(pl)* [hɑːvz]	(die) Hälfte	**half** a lemon
p. 85	Dr [ˈdɒktə]	Dr. *(Anrede)*	My doctor is **Dr** Smith.

| however [haʊˈevə] | jedoch | **However**, we found out he was wrong. |
| to **save** [seɪv] | retten; bergen | The dog **saved** the people. |

Film corner

p. 87	**court** [kɔːt]	Spielfeld	You play tennis and basketball on a **court**.
	bench [benʃ]	Bank; Sitzbank	
	to **be sorry** [bi: ˈsɒri]	leid tun	I **was sorry** when I heard what happened.

Checkpoint

| author [ˈɔːθə] | Autor; Autorin | headteacher [ˌhedˈtiːtʃə] | Schulleiter; Schulleiterin |
| main [meɪn] | Haupt- | to **take place** [ˌteɪk ˈpleɪs] | stattfinden |

Speaking skills

p. 92	**upper** [ˈʌpə]	obere	In the **upper** left corner there is a bird.
	corner [ˈkɔːnə]	Ecke	
	in the background [ɪn ðə ˈbækgraʊnd]	im Hintergrund	The tree is **in the background**.
	in the middle [ɪn ðə ˈmɪdl]	in der Mitte	The car is **in the middle** of the road.
	lower [ˈləʊə]	untere	In the **lower** left corner there is a man.
	in the foreground [ɪn ðə ˈfɔːgraʊnd]	im Vordergrund	The dog is **in the foreground**.
p. 93	**van** [væn]	Lieferwagen; Transporter	

Word bank: **Giving advice**

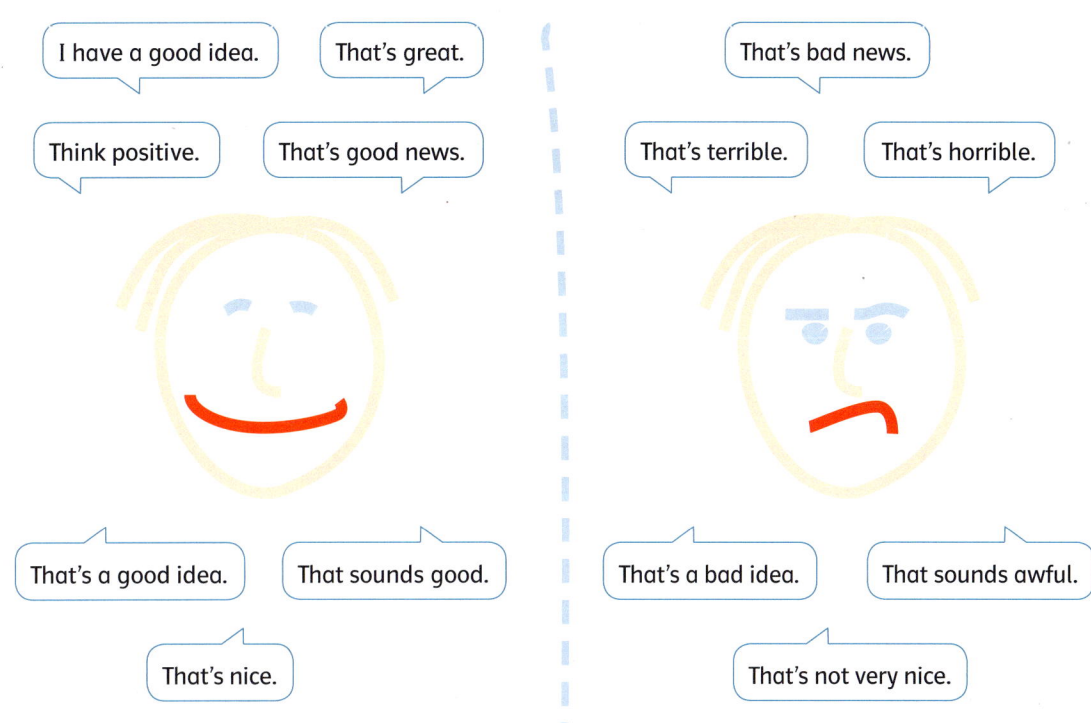

I have a good idea.

That's great.

That's bad news.

Think positive.

That's good news.

That's terrible.

That's horrible.

That's a good idea.

That sounds good.

That's a bad idea.

That sounds awful.

That's nice.

That's not very nice.

Suggestions:

Why don't you …
You can always …
Maybe you should …
How about you …
If I were you, I would …

If you told your mum / dad, …
If you talked to your mum's / dad's friend, …
If you …
Call me later.
Let's speak soon.

Word bank: Shopping

a bottle of

water   juice   ketchup   milk   lemonade

a bar of

chocolate

a can of

pet food   tomatoes   peaches

a jar of

jam   honey   peanut butter

a box of

tea bags   eggs

a bag of

flour   crisps   nuts   apples

a packet of

tissues   biscuits   tea   candles   sugar

a loaf of

bread

Where is …, please?
Where can I find …, please?
Have you got …, please?
Can you repeat that, please?
Sorry, I didn't understand / hear you.

How much is …, please?
Have you got this in a bigger size / box, please?
Have you got a different flavour, please?
Are these / Is this on special offer?
Could I have a …, please?

Unit 5 Welcome to Ireland

Way in

p. 94	**republic** [rɪˈpʌblɪk]	Republik	Ireland is called the green **republic**.
	euro [ˈjʊərəʊ]	Euro *(Währung)*	Ⓡ евро Ⓣ euro
	Irish [ˈaɪrɪʃ]	irisch; Irisch	There are many famous **Irish** bands.
	pub [pʌb]	Kneipe; Gasthaus	People often play music in **pubs**.
	youth *(no pl)* [juːθ]	Jugend-; Jugend	There are lots of **youth** groups in my town.
	orchestra [ˈɔːkɪstrə]	Orchester	Ⓡ оркестр Ⓣ orkestra
p. 95	**competition** [ˌkɒmpəˈtɪʃn]	Wettbewerb; Turnier	Dave won a prize in a **competition**!
	musical [ˈmjuːzɪkl]	Musik-; musikalisch	**musical** → music
	style [staɪl]	Stil	My favourite **style** is rock music.
	hip hop [ˈhɪphɒp]	Hip-Hop *(Musik)*	Keith's favourite style is **hip hop**.
	course [kɔːs]	Kurs	We have lots of different **courses**.
	acting [ˈæktɪŋ]	Schauspielen; Schauspielerei	There are courses in **acting** and dancing.
	to **care (for)** [ˈkeə (fɔː)]	sich kümmern (um)	He **cares** for old people.
	with special needs [wɪθ ˌspeʃl ˈniːdz]	mit Behinderung; mit besonderen Bedürfnissen	He helps children **with special needs**.
	guitar [gɪˈtɑː]	Gitarre	
	sign language [ˈsaɪn ˌlæŋgwɪdʒ]	Gebärdensprache; Zeichensprache	Keith knows **sign language**.

Station 1

In the bathroom

towel [ˈtaʊəl]	Handtuch		**shower gel** [ˈʃaʊə ˌdʒel]	Duschgel
shampoo [ʃæmˈpuː]	Shampoo		**body lotion** [ˈbɒdi ˌləʊʃn]	Körperlotion
toothbrush [ˈtuːθbrʌʃ]	Zahnbürste		**hair gel** [ˈheə ˌdʒel]	Haargel
nail scissors *(pl)* [ˈneɪl ˌsɪzəz]	Nagelschere		**soap** [səʊp]	Seife
comb [ˈkəʊm]	Kamm		**perfume** [ˈpɜːfjuːm]	Parfüm
toothpaste [ˈtuːθpeɪst]	Zahnpasta		**mirror** [ˈmɪrə]	Spiegel
hairdryer [ˈheəˌdraɪə]	Fön		**hairbrush** [ˈheəbrʌʃ]	Haarbürste

p. 96	to **take off** [ˌteɪkˈɒf]	ausziehen	You don't have to **take off** your shoes.
	fridge [frɪdʒ]	Kühlschrank	
	to **help oneself** [ˌhelp wʌnˈself]	sich bedienen	**Help yourself** to food and drinks.
	around [əˈraʊnd]	gegen; ungefähr um	We all meet for dinner **around** 6:30.
	on weekdays [ɒn ˈwiːkdeɪz]	unter der Woche; an Werktagen	**On weekdays** I have toast with jam.
	cereal [ˈsɪəriəl]	Müsli; Cornflakes	I eat **cereal** for breakfast.
	sweet [swiːt]	süß	Leo likes a **sweet** breakfast.
	except [ɪkˈsept]	außer	You can use all of them, **except** Maddy's.
	to **share** [ʃeə]	teilen	I'll **share** my room with you.
	to **practise** [ˈpræktɪs]	üben; trainieren	Today I have to **practise** with the band.
	adaptor [əˈdæptə]	Adapter	I can't find my **adaptor**.
	ours [aʊəz]	unsere	This room is for you and me. It's **ours**.
	to **prepare** [prɪˈpeə]	zubereiten; vorbereiten	Mum is **preparing** a snack for us.
	to **join** [dʒɔɪn]	sich anschließen	**Join** us when you're ready.
p. 97	**charger** [ˈtʃɑːdʒə]	Ladegerät	I need a **charger** for my phone.
	ID [ˌaɪˈdiː]	Ausweis; Personalausweis	You need your **ID** to visit another country.
	personal [ˈpɜːsnl]	persönlich	I have lots of **personal** things in my bag.
	raincoat [ˈreɪnkəʊt]	Regenmantel	I have a blue **raincoat**.
p. 98	**right now** [ˌraɪt ˈnaʊ]	gerade; jetzt gleich; sofort	I'm listening to music **right now**.
	German [ˈdʒɜːmən]	deutsch; aus Deutschland	I really like this **German** music.
	rapper [ˈræpə]	Rapper; Rapperin	Listen to this new German **rapper**.
	artist [ˈɑːtɪst]	Künstler; Künstlerin	Do you like the new hip hop **artist**?
	project [ˈprɒdʒekt]	Projekt	R проект T proje
	to **wash** [wɒʃ]	(sich) waschen; spülen	I **wash** my hair with shampoo.
	hair [heə]	Haar; Haare	
	cupboard [ˈkʌbəd]	Schrank	We always put the towels in the **cupboard**.
p. 99	**theirs** [ðeəz]	ihre	This is Dave's and Ann's room. It's **theirs**.
	partner [ˈpɑːtnə]	Partner; Partnerin	Ask what your **partner** is doing.

Station 2

Public transport

timetable ['taɪmˌteɪbl]	Fahrplan	**single ticket** ['sɪŋgl ˌtɪkɪt]	einfache Fahrkarte
to **change** [tʃeɪndʒ]	umsteigen	**station** ['steɪʃn]	Bahnhof; Haltestelle; Station
tram [træm]	Straßenbahn		
stop [stɒp]	Haltestelle; Halt	**daily** ['deɪli]	täglich
line [laɪn]	Linie	**weekly** ['wiːkli]	wöchentlich
on time [ɒn 'taɪm]	pünktlich	**monthly** ['mʌnθli]	monatlich
fare [feə]	Fahrpreis	**return ticket** [rɪ'tɜːn ˌtɪkɪt]	Hin- und Rückfahrkarte
valid ['vælɪd]	gültig		

p. 100	to **get around** [ˌget ə'raʊnd]	herumkommen	It's very easy to **get around** the city.
	striking ['straɪkɪŋ]	bemerkenswert; auffallend	He is a **striking** actor.
	move [muːv]	Bewegung	We will learn lots of new **moves**.
	dance [dɑːns]	Tanz	**dance** → to dance → dancer
	drumming ['drʌmɪŋ]	Trommel-	Let's try the **drumming** workshop.
	to **take part (in)** [ˌteɪk 'pɑːt]	teilnehmen (an)	We can **take part** in the workshop.
	I can't wait [aɪ ˌkɑːnt 'weɪt]	ich kann es kaum erwarten	**I can't wait** to go on holiday.
	journey ['dʒɜːni]	Fahrt; Reise	It's a long **journey** to London from here.
	public transport [ˌpʌblɪk 'trænspɔːt]	öffentliche Verkehrsmittel	**public transport**: buses, trams, trains
	by [baɪ]	bis (spätestens)	We must leave **by** 8:30 a.m.
	mustn't ['mʌsnt]	nicht dürfen	You **mustn't** forget to buy a ticket.
p. 102	**class** [klɑːs]	Unterricht	You can't eat during **class**.
	step [step]	Schritt	You must learn the new **steps**.
	to **follow** ['fɒləʊ]	befolgen; folgen	Please **follow** the rules.
	driver ['draɪvə]	Fahrer; Fahrerin	Don't talk to the **driver**!
	to **push** [pʊʃ]	schubsen; drängeln	Don't **push** other people!
p. 103	to **travel** ['trævl]	fahren	Dogs **travel** free.
	to **carry** ['kæri]	tragen	I can **carry** the heavy bag for you.

Reading corner

p. 104	**gold** [gəʊld]	Gold	My jewellery is made of **gold**.
	to **explain** [ɪkˈspleɪn]	erklären	I always have to **explain** my name.
	parade [pəˈreɪd]	Parade; Umzug	There are lots of **parades** and parties.
	shamrock [ˈʃæmrɒk]	Kleeblatt	
	rainbow [ˈreɪnbəʊ]	Regenbogen	
	gold [gəʊld]	golden; Gold-	The sweets are in **gold** paper.
	national [ˈnæʃnl]	National-; national	Look! There is the **national** team.
	flower [ˈflaʊə]	Blume	
	pot [pɒt]	Topf	The flower is in a **pot**.
	to **be homesick** [bi: ˈhəʊmsɪk]	Heimweh haben	It made me **be homesick**.
	call [kɔ:l]	Anruf; Ruf	They didn't answer my **calls**.
p. 105	to **cheer sb up** [ˌtʃɪərˈˌʌp]	jmdn. aufheitern; jmdn. aufmuntern	He tried to **cheer** me **up**.
	poem [ˈpəʊɪm]	Gedicht	I read a nice **poem** about summer.
	fable [ˈfeɪbl]	Fabel; Märchen	A **fable** is a kind of story.
	once [wʌns]	einst; einmal	at a time in the past
	to **foretell** [fɔ:ˈtel]	vorhersagen	She **foretold** my life.
	actually [ˈæktʃuəli]	tatsächlich; wirklich; eigentlich	**Actually**, I like your new dress.
	wealth [welθ]	Reichtum	My **wealth** is my family and friends.
	miserable [ˈmɪzrəbl]	elend; armselig; jämmerlich	I feel **miserable** today.
	to **feel sorry for** [ˌfi:l ˈsɒri fə]	Mitleid haben mit; bedauern	Niamh **felt sorry for** herself.
	I couldn't believe my eyes. [aɪ ˌkʊdnt bɪˌli:v maɪˈˌaɪz]	Ich traute meinen Augen nicht.	Ganze Sätze am besten als Einheit lernen.
	dressed [drest]	angezogen (wie); verkleidet (als)	They were all **dressed** in green clothes.
	I couldn't help but ... [ˌaɪ kʊdnt ˈhelp bʌt]	Ich konnte nicht anders als ...	**I couldn't help but** laugh.
	to **rush** [rʌʃ]	eilen; sich beeilen; stürzen	I **rushed** into my room.
	to **grab** [græb]	schnappen; greifen; ergreifen	Lucy was angry and **grabbed** her bag.
	outfit [ˈaʊtfɪt]	Outfit; Kleidung	I grabbed my Paddy's Day **outfit**.
	beginning [bɪˈgɪnɪŋ]	Anfang; Beginn	**beginning** ↔ end
	wonderful [ˈwʌndəfl]	wunderbar	**Wonderful!** = Great! = Fantastic!

Film corner

p. 107	to **impress** [ɪmˈpres]	beeindrucken	We **impressed** our English teacher.
	pineapple [ˈpaɪnæpl]	Ananas	
	wherever [weəˈrevə]	wo(hin) auch immer; egal wo(hin); überall wo(hin)	I go **wherever** the wind takes me.

Word bank: Things for a trip

toothbrush

hairbrush

scissors

money

towel

toiletries

toothpaste

extras

hairdryer

shower gel

soap

shampoo

key

umbrella

Things for a trip

visa

ticket

swimming things

coat

documents

skirt

clothes

T-shirt

sweater

identity card

passport

trousers / shorts

Word bank: Public transport

airport

plane

helicopter

station / stop

underground

train

bus

tram

other transport

skateboard

taxi

car

boat

motorbike / moped

bike / bicycle

ferry

You should take …
Use the … line.
Travel northbound / southbound / westbound / eastbound.
Then …
It's … stops.
It stops at …

You must / have to buy …
You needn't / don't have to …
It costs …
You can buy a single ticket / a return ticket.
Change buses / trains at …

Instructions

Act the dialogue • the role play.	**Spielt** den Dialog • das Rollenspiel.
Add more words.	**Ergänze** mehr Wörter.
Answer the questions.	**Beantworte** die Fragen.
Ask a partner.	**Frage** eine Partnerin/einen Partner.
Check the sentences.	**Überprüfe** die Sätze.
Choose one of the tasks • the right answer.	**Wähle** eine der Aufgaben • die richtige Antwort **aus**.
Collect ideas.	**Sammle** Ideen.
Compare with your partner.	**Vergleicht** zu zweit.
Complete the sentences • the dialogue.	**Vervollständige** die Sätze • den Dialog.
Copy the list.	**Schreibe** die Liste **ab**.
Correct the wrong sentences.	**Verbessere** die falschen Sätze.
Decide on the best order.	**Entscheide dich für** die beste Reihenfolge.
Describe the picture.	**Beschreibe** das Bild.
Discuss in groups.	**Besprecht euch** in Gruppen.
Draw a picture.	**Zeichne** ein Bild.
Exchange your lists.	**Tauscht** eure Listen **aus**.
Explain the rules.	**Erkläre** die Regeln.
Finish the sentences.	**Vervollständige** die Sätze.
Give feedback.	**Gib** Rückmeldung.
Give reasons.	**Gib** Gründe **an**.
Guess.	**Überlege.**
Interview your partner.	**Interviewe** deine Partnerin/deinen Partner.
Label the picture.	**Beschrifte** das Bild.
Listen to the dialogue.	**Höre** dir den Dialog **an**.
Look at the photos • pictures (again).	**Schau** dir die Fotos • Bilder (noch einmal) **an**.
Make a list • a chart • a mind map.	**Erstelle** eine Liste • eine Tabelle • ein Wörternetz.
Make notes.	**Mache** dir **Stichpunkte**.
Make up more verses.	**Denke dir** weitere Strophen **aus**.
Match the sentences with the pictures.	**Ordne** den Bildern die richtigen Sätze **zu**.
Name the place.	**Nenne** den Ort.
Plan your role play.	**Plant** euer Rollenspiel.
Practise with a partner.	**Übe** mit einer Partnerin/einem Partner.
Present your profile to the class.	**Stelle** dein Profil deiner Klasse **vor**.
Put in the right verbs.	**Setze** die richtigen Verben **ein**.
Put the words **in the right order**.	**Bringe** die Wörter **in die richtige Reihenfolge**.
Read the story **again**.	**Lies** die Geschichte **noch einmal**.
Record your dialogue.	**Nehmt** euren Dialog **auf**.
Rewrite the sentences.	**Schreibe** die Sätze **um**.

Say how you feel.	**Sage**, wie du dich fühlst.
Show your text to a partner.	**Zeige** deinen Text einer Partnerin/einem Partner.
Sort the words **into groups**.	**Sortiere** die Wörter **in Gruppen**.
Take notes.	**Mache** dir **Notizen**.
Talk about the photos.	**Rede** über die Fotos.
Tell the class.	**Erzähle** es der Klasse.
Think about the story.	**Denke über** die Geschichte **nach**.
Think of a number.	**Denke** dir eine Nummer **aus.**
Use your own ideas.	**Benutze** deine eigenen Ideen.
Watch the film.	**Schau** den Film **an**.
Write a poem • a heading • a draft.	**Schreibe** ein Gedicht • einen Titel • einen Entwurf.

Classroom phrases

You and your teacher

I'm sorry I'm late.	Tut mir leid, dass ich mich verspätet habe.
I'm sorry I don't have my exercise book.	Tut mir leid, ich habe mein Heft nicht dabei.
What's the homework?	Was haben wir als Hausaufgabe auf?
Can you help me, please?	Können Sie / Kannst du mir bitte helfen?
Can you say that again, please?	Können Sie / Kannst du das bitte wiederholen?
Can I go to the toilet, please?	Kann ich bitte auf Toilette gehen?
Mr / Mrs / Miss …, I don't feel well.	Herr / Frau …, mir geht es nicht gut.
What page is it, please?	Auf welcher Seite ist das?
What's the German / English word for …?	Was ist das deutsche / englische Wort für …?
How do you spell …?	Wie schreibt man …?
What does that mean?	Was heißt / bedeutet das?
Sorry, I don't understand/ I don't know.	Tut mir leid, ich verstehe das nicht/ ich weiß es nicht.

Working together

Can we work in pairs / groups?	Können wir zu zweit / in Gruppen arbeiten?
Do you want to work with me / us?	Willst du / Wollt ihr mit mir / uns arbeiten?
Let's make a / draw a …	Lass(t) uns ein … machen / zeichnen.
Whose turn is it? – It's my / your turn.	Wer ist dran? – Ich bin dran. / Du bist dran.

Your teacher can say …

Turn to page …	Schlagt Seite … auf.
Look at the board.	Schaut an die Tafel.
Put your hands up, please!	Meldet euch, bitte!
Try again!	Versuche es noch einmal.

List of irregular verbs

Hier findest du alle unregelmäßigen Verben, die im Buch vorkommen. Die Liste enthält jeweils alle drei Formen, auch wenn sie noch nicht alle in den Units vorgekommen sind.

infinitive	simple past	past participle	German
be [biː]	was, were [wɒz, wɜː]	been [biːn]	sein
beat [biːt]	beat [biːt]	beaten ['biːtn]	schlagen; besiegen
become [bɪ'kʌm]	became [bɪ'keɪm]	become [bɪ'kʌm]	werden
bleed [bliːd]	bled [bled]	bled [bled]	bluten
break [breɪk]	broke [brəʊk]	broken ['brəʊkn]	brechen
bring [brɪŋ]	brought [brɔːt]	brought [brɔːt]	bringen; mitbringen
build [bɪld]	built [bɪlt]	built [bɪlt]	bauen
burn [bɜːn]	burned/burnt [bɜːnt]	burned/burnt [bɜːnt]	brennen
buy [baɪ]	bought [bɔːt]	bought [bɔːt]	kaufen
choose [tʃuːz]	chose [tʃəʊz]	chosen ['tʃəʊzn]	auswählen; wählen
come [kʌm]	came [keɪm]	come [kʌm]	kommen
cost [kɒst]	cost [kɒst]	cost [kɒst]	kosten
cut [kʌt]	cut [kʌt]	cut [kʌt]	(sich) schneiden
do [duː]	did [dɪd]	done [dʌn]	machen; tun
draw [drɔː]	drew [druː]	drawn [drɔːn]	zeichnen
dream [driːm]	dreamed/dreamt [dremt]	dreamed/dreamt [dremt]	träumen
drink [drɪŋk]	drank [dræŋk]	drunk [drʌŋk]	trinken
eat [iːt]	ate [eɪt]	eaten ['iːtn]	essen
fall [fɔːl]	fell [fel]	fallen ['fɔːln]	fallen; hinfallen
feed [fiːd]	fed [fed]	fed [fed]	füttern; ernähren
feel [fiːl]	felt [felt]	felt [felt]	(sich) fühlen
fight [faɪt]	fought [fɔːt]	fought [fɔːt]	kämpfen; streiten
find [faɪnd]	found [faʊnd]	found [faʊnd]	finden
fly [flaɪ]	flew [fluː]	flown [fləʊn]	fliegen
forget [fə'get]	forgot [fə'gɒt]	forgotten [fə'gɒtn]	vergessen
freeze [friːz]	froze [frəʊz]	frozen ['frəʊzn]	frieren; gefrieren
get [get]	got [gɒt]	got [gɒt]	bekommen; werden
give [gɪv]	gave [geɪv]	given ['gɪvn]	geben
go [gəʊ]	went [went]	gone [gɒn]	gehen; fahren
grow up [ˌgrəʊ'ʌp]	grew up [ˌgruː'ʌp]	grown up [ˌgrəʊn'ʌp]	aufwachsen
hang [hæŋ]	hung [hʌŋ]	hung [hʌŋ]	hängen
have [hæv]	had [hæd]	had [hæd]	haben; besitzen
hear [hɪə]	heard [hɜːd]	heard [hɜːd]	hören
hide [haɪd]	hid [hɪd]	hidden ['hɪdn]	verstecken
hit [hɪt]	hit [hɪt]	hit [hɪt]	schlagen; treffen
hold [həʊld]	held [held]	held [held]	halten; festhalten
hurt [hɜːt]	hurt [hɜːt]	hurt [hɜːt]	verletzen; weh tun
keep [kiːp]	kept [kept]	kept [kept]	halten
know [nəʊ]	knew [njuː]	known [nəʊn]	wissen; kennen

infinitive	simple past	past participle	German
lay [leɪ]	laid [leɪd]	laid [leɪd]	legen; (den Tisch) decken
leave [li:v]	left [left]	left [left]	verlassen; lassen; abfahren
lend [lend]	lent [lent]	lent [lent]	leihen; verleihen
lose [lu:z]	lost [lɒst]	lost [lɒst]	verlieren
make [meɪk]	made [meɪd]	made [meɪd]	machen; tun; bilden
mean [mi:n]	meant [ment]	meant [ment]	bedeuten; meinen
meet [mi:t]	met [met]	met [met]	kennen lernen; (sich) treffen
pay [peɪ]	paid [peɪd]	paid [peɪd]	bezahlen
put [pʊt]	put [pʊt]	put [pʊt]	setzen; legen; stellen
read [ri:d]	read [red]	read [red]	lesen
ride [raɪd]	rode [rəʊd]	ridden ['rɪdn]	fahren; reiten
ring [rɪŋ]	rang [ræŋ]	rung [rʌŋ]	klingeln; läuten
run [rʌn]	ran [ræn]	run [rʌn]	laufen; rennen
say [seɪ]	said [sed]	said [sed]	sagen; sprechen
see [si:]	saw [sɔ:]	seen [si:n]	sehen
sell [sel]	sold [səʊld]	sold [səʊld]	verkaufen
send [send]	sent [sent]	sent [sent]	schicken; senden
show [ʃəʊ]	showed [ʃəʊd]	shown [ʃəʊn]	zeigen
sing [sɪŋ]	sang [sæŋ]	sung [sʌŋ]	singen
sink [sɪŋk]	sank [sæŋk]	sunk [sʌŋk]	untergehen; sinken
sit [sɪt]	sat [sæt]	sat [sæt]	sitzen
sleep [sli:p]	slept [slept]	slept [slept]	schlafen
smell [smel]	smelled/smelt [smelt]	smelled/smelt [smelt]	riechen
speak [spi:k]	spoke [spəʊk]	spoken ['spəʊkn]	sprechen
spell [spel]	spelled/spelt [spelt]	spelled/spelt [spelt]	buchstabieren
spend [spend]	spent [spent]	spent [spent]	ausgeben; verbringen
stand [stænd]	stood [stʊd]	stood [stʊd]	stehen
sweep [swi:p]	swept [swept]	swept [swept]	fegen
swim [swɪm]	swam [swæm]	swum [swʌm]	schwimmen
take [teɪk]	took [tʊk]	taken ['teɪkn]	nehmen; mitnehmen
tell [tel]	told [təʊld]	told [təʊld]	erzählen; sagen
think [θɪŋk]	thought [θɔ:t]	thought [θɔ:t]	denken; glauben
throw [θrəʊ]	threw [θru:]	thrown [θrəʊn]	werfen
understand [ˌʌndə'stænd]	understood [ˌʌndə'stʊd]	understood [ˌʌndə'stʊd]	verstehen
wake up [weɪk ˌʌp]	woke up [wəʊk ˌʌp]	woken up [ˌwəʊkn ˌʌp]	aufwachen
wear [weə]	wore [wɔ:]	worn [wɔ:n]	tragen
win [wɪn]	won [wʌn]	won [wʌn]	gewinnen; siegen
write [raɪt]	wrote [rəʊt]	written ['rɪtn]	schreiben

Dictionary

Im Dictionary kannst du Wörter nachschlagen!

Im *Dictionary* sind alle wichtigen Wörter aus deinem Buch enthalten. Die Wörter stehen in alphabetischer Reihenfolge. Englische Wörter schlägst du ab S. 212 nach, deutsche Wörter ab S. 247.

Die Abkürzungen geben an, wo das Wort zum ersten Mal im Buch erscheint.

across	[əˈkrɒs]	über	III	U1	11
englisches Wort	Aussprache	deutsche Übersetzung	Band 3	Unit 1	Seite

Die mit einem Sternchen (*) gekennzeichneten Verben sind unregelmäßige Verben (→ *List of irregular verbs*, S. 210 – 211).

Manche Wörter haben verschiedene Bedeutungen. Am besten liest du alle, bevor du dich für eine entscheidest.

practice [ˈpræktɪs] Training; Übung I[1]
to **accept** [əkˈsept] akzeptieren <III U4, 86>[3]

*to **spend** [spend] ausgeben; verbringen II[1]

actually [ˈæktʃuəli] tatsächlich; wirklich; eigentlich III U5, 105[2]
address [əˈdres] Adresse II[2]

1 Lernwortschatz für alle: schwarz; 2 Differenzierungswortschatz: blau; 3 kein Lernwortschatz: < >

A

a [ə] ein; eine I
  a bit [ə ˈbɪt] ein bisschen; ein wenig II
  a few [ə ˈfjuː] ein paar; wenige; einige III U3, 58
  a little [ə ˈlɪtl] ein bisschen II
  a lot [əˈlɒt] viel I; sehr II
  a lot of [ə ˈlɒt əv] eine Menge; viel I; viel; eine Menge III U1, 16
  a pair of [ə ˈpeər əv] ein Paar II
  a/one hundred [ˈhʌndrəd] einhundert; hundert I
  a/one thousand [ə/wʌn ˈθaʊznd] eintausend; tausend II
  a five minute walk [ə ˈfaɪv mɪnɪt ˌwɔːk] fünf Minuten zu Fuß III U1, 12
a.m. [ˌeɪˈem] vormittags II
about [əˈbaʊt] ungefähr; circa; etwa II
  to be about [bi: əˈbaʊt] gehen um; handeln von III U1, 31

about [əˈbaʊt] über II
  out and about [ˌaʊt ən əˈbaʊt] unterwegs I
to **accept** [əkˈsept] akzeptieren <III U4, 86>
accident [ˈæksɪdnt] Unfall III U2, 38
  stomach ache [ˈstʌmək ˌeɪk] Bauchweh; Bauchschmerzen II
across [əˈkrɒs] über II
to **act** [ækt] spielen II
  acting workshop [ˈæktɪŋ ˌwɜːkʃɒp] Schauspielworkshop II
acting [ˈæktɪŋ] Schauspielen; Schauspielerei III U5, 95
Action! [ˈækʃn] Achtung Aufnahme! <III U1, 27>
activity [ækˈtɪvəti] Aktivität I
  activity centre [ækˈtɪvəti ˌsentə] Jugendzentrum III U2, 34
actor [ˈæktə] Schauspieler; Schauspielerin II
actually [ˈæktʃuəli] tatsächlich; wirklich; eigentlich III U5, 105

adaptor [əˈdæptə] Adapter III U5, 96
to **add** [æd] hinzufügen II
address [əˈdres] Adresse II
adjective [ˈædʒɪktɪv] Adjektiv; Eigenschaftswort I
adult [ˈædʌlt] Erwachsene; Erwachsener III U4, 75
adventure [ədˈventʃə] Abenteuer III U2, 32
adverb [ˈædvɜːb] Adverb <III U2, 36>
advert (ad) [ˈædvɜːt] Anzeige <III U3, 68>
advice [ədˈvaɪs] Rat; Ratschlag III U2, 51
afraid [əˈfreɪd] ängstlich II
  to be afraid [bi: əˈfreɪd] sich fürchten; Angst haben II
after [ˈɑːftə] nach I; danach; später III U4, 84
  after that [ˌɑːftə ˈðæt] danach I
afternoon [ˌɑːftəˈnuːn] Nachmittag I
  in the afternoon [ɪn ðiˌɑːftəˈnuːn] am Nachmittag I

again [ə'gen] wieder; noch einmal II
Can you say that again, please?
[kæn ju: ˌseɪ ðæt ə'gen pli:s] Könntest du das bitte wiederholen? I
against [ə'genst] gegen III U1, 11
age [eɪdʒ] Alter I
ago [ə'gəʊ] vor II
to **agree** [ə'gri:] zustimmen II
to agree (on) [ə'gri: (ɒn)] sich
einigen (auf) <III U5, 108>
agreement [ə'gri:mənt] Vereinbarung
<III U5, 135>
air [eə] Luft III U3, 55
airport ['eəpɔ:t] Flughafen II
alarm clock [ə'lɑ:m ˌklɒk] Wecker I
alien ['eɪliən] Außerirdische; Außerirdischer I
alive [ə'laɪv] am Leben <III U1, 17>;
III U1, 22
all [ɔ:l] alle I
all day [ɔ:l 'deɪ] den ganzen Tag
III U3, 58
all right [ɔ:l 'raɪt] in Ordnung; alles
klar II
allergic to [ə'lɜ:dʒɪk tə] allergisch
gegen II
allergy ['ælədʒi] Allergie II
almost ['ɔ:lməʊst] fast; beinahe
III U1, 25
along [ə'lɒŋ] entlang I
alphabet ['ælfəbet] Alphabet I
already [ɔ:l'redi] schon; bereits II
aluminium [ˌæljə'mɪniəm] Aluminium
III U3, 55
always ['ɔ:lweɪz] immer I
am [æm] bin I
amazing [ə'meɪzɪŋ] erstaunlich;
unglaublich; toll III U3, 63
ambulance ['æmbjələns] Krankenwagen III U2, 38
an [ən] ein; eine I
and [ænd] und I
Anglo-Saxon [ˌæŋgləʊ'sæksn] angel-
sächsisch <III U1, 126>
the **Anglo-Saxons** [ði ˌæŋgləʊ'sæksnz]
die Angelsachsen <III U1, 127>
angry ['æŋgri] wütend; zornig; verärgert II

animal ['ænɪml] Tier I
animal rescue shelter [ˌænɪml
'reskju: ˌʃeltə] Tierheim I
ankle ['æŋkl] Fußgelenk; Fußknöchel
II
announcement [ə'naʊnsmənt] Durchsage; Ankündigung II
annoyed [ə'nɔɪd] verärgert III U4, 77
another [ə'nʌðə] ein andere; noch
ein II
answer ['ɑ:nsə] Antwort I
to **answer** ['ɑ:nsə] antworten; beantworten I
to answer the phone [ɑ:nsə ðə
'fəʊn] ans Telefon gehen III U2, 45
antenna [æn'tenə] Antenne III U3, 67
antique [æn'ti:k] Antiquität
<III U1, 30>
any ['eni] irgendwelche; irgendein II
Any idea? [ˌeni 'aɪdɪə] Irgendeine
Idee? I
not … any [ˌnɒt … eni] kein II
anything ['eniθɪŋ] irgendetwas II
Anything else? [eniθɪŋ 'els] Darf es
sonst noch etwas sein? I
anything to drink ['eniθɪŋ tə 'drɪŋk]
etwas zu trinken II
apple ['æpl] Apfel I
apple crumble [ˌæpl 'krʌmbl] Apfel-
auflauf (mit Streuseln bedeckt) II
April ['eɪprl] April I
archer ['ɑ:tʃə] Bogenschütze; Bogen-
schützin <III U1, 126>
archive ['ɑ:kaɪv] Archiv II
are [ɑ:] bist; sind I
Are you serious? [ˌɑ: ju 'sɪəriəs] Im
Ernst? III U3, 58
argument ['ɑ:gjəmənt] Auseinandersetzung; Streit II
armour ['ɑ:mə] Rüstung III U2, 43
army ['ɑ:mi] Armee; Heer III U3, 62
around [ə'raʊnd] herum; umher
III U1, 19
to get around [ˌget ə'raʊnd] herumkommen III U5, 100
around [ə'raʊnd] gegen; ungefähr
um III U5, 96

around the house [əˌraʊnd ðə
'haʊs] zu Hause I
to **arrive** [ə'raɪv] ankommen II
arrow ['ærəʊ] Pfeil <III U1, 127>
Art [ɑ:t] Kunst I
article ['ɑ:tɪkl] Artikel; Bericht
<III U5, 106>
artist ['ɑ:tɪst] Künstler; Künstlerin
III U5, 98
as … as [əz … əz] so … wie II
as [æz] als II; so <III U4, 133>
as [æz] wie II
to **ask** [ɑ:sk] fragen I
to ask about ['ɑ:sk əˌbaʊt] sich
erkundigen nach; fragen nach II
asking the way [ˌɑ:skɪŋ ðə 'weɪ]
nach dem Weg fragen I
*to be **asleep** [bi: ə'sli:p] schlafen
III U1, 25
to fall asleep [fɔ:l ə'sli:p] einschlafen III U1, 25
assistant [ə'sɪstnt] Verkäufer; Verkäuferin III U4, 83
shop assistant ['ʃɒp əˌsɪstnt] Verkäufer; Verkäuferin II
association football [əˌsəʊsieɪʃn
ˌfʊtbɔ:l] Assoziationsfußball (offizieller Name von Fußball) <III U1, 24>
at [æt] auf; an; in; um; bei; am I
at break [ət 'breɪk] in der Pause I
at home [ət 'həʊm] zu Hause I
at last [ət 'lɑ:st] endlich; zu guter
Letzt II
at school [ət 'sku:l] in der Schule I
at the seaside [ət ðə 'si:saɪd] am
Meer I
at the weekend [ət ðə ˌwi:k'end]
am Wochenende I
ate [eɪt] simple past von to eat II
athletics [æθ'letɪks] Leichtathletik
<III U2, 186>
to **attach** [ə'tætʃ] verbinden III U3, 67
attic ['ætɪk] Dachboden I
audition [ɔ:'dɪʃn] Vorspielen; Vorsprechen; Vorsingen; Vortanzen II
August ['ɔ:gəst] August I
in August [in 'ɔ:gəst] im August I
aunt [ɑ:nt] Tante II

author ['ɔ:θə] Autor; Autorin <III U4, 88>

available [ə'veɪləbl] erhältlich; verfügbar <III U3, 68>

avalanche ['ævla:nʃ] Lawine <III U3, 72>

awake [ə'weɪk] bei Bewusstsein; wach III U2, 38

away [ə'weɪ] weg; entfernt II

awful ['ɔ:fl] schrecklich; furchtbar I

B

back [bæk] Rückseite <III U5, 109>

back street ['bæk stri:t] Hinterhof <III U1, 17>

*to get **back** [ˌget ˌ'bæk] zurückkommen <III U2, 128>

back [bæk] zurück III U2, 41

back home [bæk 'həʊm] zu Hause II

background ['bækgraʊnd] Hintergrund III U4, 92

in the background [ɪn ðə 'bækgraʊnd] im Hintergrund III U4, 92

backseat ['bæksi:t] Rücksitz <III U1, 17>

bad [bæd] schlimm; böse; schlecht III U2, 38

badminton ['bædmɪntən] Badminton <III U2, 186>

bag [bæg] Tasche; Tüte; Sack I

tea bag ['ti: ˌbæg] Teebeutel <III U4, 200>

bagpipes *(pl)* ['bægpaɪps] Dudelsack III U3, 53

pasta **bake** [ˌpæstə 'beɪk] Nudelauflauf II

baker ['beɪkə] Bäcker; Bäckerin III U2, 50

baker's ['beɪkəz] Bäckerei III U1, 13

ball [bɔ:l] Ball II

cannon ball ['kænən ˌbɔ:l] Kanonenkugel II

balloon [bə'lu:n] Luftballon I

hot air balloon [ˌhɒt ˌ'eə bə'lu:n] Heißluftballon <III U2, 44>

banana [bə'nɑ:nə] Banane I

band [bænd] Band; Musikgruppe II

to start a band [ˌstɑ:t ə 'bænd] eine Band gründen II

bandage ['bændɪdʒ] Verband III U2, 39

a **bar** of chocolate [bɑ:r əv 'tʃɒklət] eine Tafel Schokolade I

barbecue ['bɑ:bɪkju:] Grill I

bargain ['bɑ:gɪn] Schnäppchen II

laundry **basket** ['lɔ:ndri ˌbɑ:skɪt] Wäschekorb <III U4, 86>

basketball ['bɑ:skɪtbɔ:l] Basketball II

bat [bæt] Fledermaus I

bathroom ['bɑ:θrʊm] Bad(ezimmer) I

batter ['bætə] Bierteig <III U3, 66>

battle ['bætl] Schlacht; Kampf III U1, 11

BC (= before Christ) [bi:'si:] vor Christus <III U5, 134>

*to **be** [bi:] sein I

to be about [bi: ə'baʊt] gehen um; handeln von III U1, 31

to be afraid [bi: ə'freɪd] sich fürchten; Angst haben II

to be asleep [bi: ə'sli:p] schlafen III U1, 25

to be born [bi: 'bɔ:n] geboren werden III U3, 52

to be called [bi: 'kɔ:ld] heißen; genannt werden II

to be careful [bi: 'keəfl] vorsichtig sein II

to be fed up (with) [bi: fed ˌ'ʌp (wɪð)] die Nase voll haben (von); sauer sein III U4, 76

to be good at [bi: 'gʊd ˌət] gut sein in; gut sein bei I

to be homesick [bi: 'həʊmsɪk] Heimweh haben III U5, 104

to be interested in [bi: 'ɪntrəstɪd ˌɪn] sich interessieren für; interessiert sein an III U1, 12

to be lucky [bi: 'lʌki] Glück haben <III U3, 72>

to be made of [bi: 'meɪd ˌəv] hergestellt sein aus III U3, 54

to be right [bi: 'raɪt] recht haben II

to be scared [bi: 'skeəd] Angst haben; erschrocken sein III U2, 34

to be sick [bi 'sɪk] sich übergeben I

to be sorry [bi: 'sɒri] leid tun III U4, 87

to be up to [bi: 'ʌp tə] vorhaben III U3, 67

beach [bi:tʃ] Strand I

to go beach combing [gəʊ 'bi:tʃ ˌkəʊmɪŋ] den Strand nach Strandgut absuchen II

*to **beat** [bi:t] besiegen; schlagen III U3, 62

beat [bi:t] simple past von *to beat* III U3, 62

beaten ['bi:tn] past participle von *to beat* III U3, 62

beautiful ['bju:tɪfl] schön; hübsch I

became [bɪ'keɪm] simple past von *to become* II

because [bɪ'kɒz] weil; da I

because of [bɪ'kɒz ˌəv] wegen III U2, 37

*to **become** [bɪ'kʌm] werden II

become [bɪ'kʌm] past participle von *to become* II

bed [bed] Bett I

bed and breakfast (B & B) [ˌbed ˌən 'brekfəst] Frühstückspension III U3, 58

to go to bed [gəʊ tə 'bed] ins Bett gehen I

bedroom ['bedrʊm] Schlafzimmer; Kinderzimmer I

beef [bi:f] Rindfleisch II

been [bi:n] past participle von *to be* II

before [bɪ'fɔ:] vorher; zuvor II

before [bɪ'fɔ:] bevor; bis zu II

*to **begin** [bɪ'gɪn] beginnen; anfangen <III U5, 135>

beginning [bɪ'gɪnɪŋ] Anfang; Beginn III U5, 105

behind [bɪ'haɪnd] hinter II

to **believe** [bɪ'li:v] glauben II

I couldn't believe my eyes [aɪ ˌkʊdnt bɪ'li:v maɪ ˌaɪz] Ich traute meinen Augen nicht. III U5, 105

bell [bel] Glocke II

bench [benʃ] Bank; Sitzbank III U4, 87

beside [bɪ'saɪd] neben <III U1, 178>

best [best] beste II
  the best [ðə ˈbest] die besten II
  Best wishes, [ˌbest ˈwɪʃɪz] Mit den besten Wünschen, I
between [bɪˈtwiːn] zwischen II
bicycle [ˈbaɪsɪkl] Fahrrad <III U5, 206>
big [bɪg] groß I
  big wheel [ˌbɪg ˈwiːl] Riesenrad II
bike [baɪk] Fahrrad I
bill [bɪl] Rechnung III U3, 59
  to pay the bill [ˌpeɪ ðə ˈbɪl] die Rechnung bezahlen III U3, 59
billion [ˈbɪliən] Milliarde II
biography [baɪˈɒgrəfi] Biografie <III U3, 54>
Biology [baɪˈɒlədʒi] Biologie I
bird [bɜːd] Vogel III U3, 61
  bird watching [ˈbɜːd ˌwɒtʃɪŋ] Vogelbeobachtung III U3, 61
birthday [ˈbɜːθdeɪ] Geburtstag I
  Happy birthday! [ˌhæpi ˈbɜːθdeɪ] Alles Gute zum Geburtstag! I
biscuit [ˈbɪskɪt] Keks II
  dog biscuit [ˈdɒg ˌbɪskɪt] Hundekeks II
a bit [ə ˈbɪt] ein bisschen; ein wenig II
black [blæk] schwarz I
to blaze [bleɪz] brennen; lodern <III U1, 17>
bled [bled] simple past, past participle von to bleed III U2, 38
*to bleed [bliːd] bluten III U2, 38
to blind [blaɪnd] blenden <III U1, 17>
blog [blɒg] Blog; Internettagebuch II
blouse [blaʊz] Bluse I
blue [bluː] blau I
  the blue one [ðə ˈbluː ˌwʌn] der blaue II
board [bɔːd] Tafel I
  on board [ˈɒn bɔːd] an Bord III U4, 84
boat [bəʊt] Boot II
  boat trip [ˈbəʊt ˌtrɪp] Bootsfahrt; Schiffsfahrt II
body [ˈbɒdi] Körper III U5, 97
  body lotion [ˈbɒdi ˌləʊʃn] Körperlotion III U5, 97

bodyguard [ˈbɒdigaːd] Leibwächter <III U3, 130>
book [bʊk] Buch; Heft I
  exercise book [ˈeksəsaɪz ˌbʊk] Übungsheft I
to book [bʊk] buchen; reservieren <III U2, 44>
to bookmark [ˈbʊkmaːk] zu … hinfügen II
boot [buːt] Stiefel II
boring [ˈbɔːrɪŋ] langweilig I
*to be born [biː ˈbɔːn] geboren werden III U3, 52
to borrow [ˈbɒrəʊ] ausleihen II
boss [bɒs] Boss; Chef II
both [bəʊθ] beide <III U2, 128>
  both … and … [ˈbəʊθ … ənd] sowohl … als auch … <III U1, 126>
a bottle of [ˈbɒtl] eine Flasche … I
  bottle bank [ˈbɒtl bæŋk] Altglascontainer II
bought [bɔːt] simple past von to buy I; past participle von to buy II
bowl [bəʊl] Schale; Schälchen; Schüssel II
box [bɒks] Box; Kiste I
  a box of [bɒks] eine Schachtel … I
  telephone box [ˈtelɪfəʊn ˌbɒks] Telefonzelle II
boy [bɔɪ] Junge I
brand [brænd] Marke III U4, 81
brave [breɪv] tapfer; mutig III U3, 63
sliced bread [ˌslaɪst ˈbred] in Scheiben geschnittenes Brot III U4, 80
bread [bred] Brot II
at break [ət ˈbreɪk] in der Pause I
  break of dawn [ˌbreɪk əv ˈdɔːn] Tagesanbruch <III U5, 101>
  to take a break [ˌteɪk ə ˈbreɪk] Pause machen II
*to break [breɪk] brechen; kaputt machen II
breakfast [ˈbrekfəst] Frühstück I
  bed and breakfast (B & B) [ˌbed ən ˈbrekfəst] Frühstückspension III U3, 58
  to have breakfast [ˌhæv ˈbrekfəst] frühstücken I

to breathe [briːð] atmen III U1, 22
bridge [brɪdʒ] Brücke II
briefcase [ˈbriːfkeɪs] Aktenkoffer; Aktentasche III U2, 45
brilliant [ˈbrɪliənt] toll I
*to bring [brɪŋ] bringen; mitbringen II
British [ˈbrɪtɪʃ] britisch II
brochure [ˈbrəʊʃə] Broschüre; Prospekt III U1, 31
broke [brəʊk] simple past von to break II
broken [ˈbrəʊkn] past participle von to break II
brother [ˈbrʌðə] Bruder I
brother-in-law [ˈbrʌðər ɪn lɔː] Schwager <III U1, 126>
brought [brɔːt] simple past von to bring II
brown [braʊn] braun I
bruise [bruːz] Bluterguss; blauer Fleck <III U2, 187>
speech bubble [ˈspiːtʃ ˌbʌbl] Sprechblase <III U2, 47>
buffet [ˈbʊfeɪ] Büfett III U3, 58
*to build [bɪld] bauen II
builder [ˈbɪldə] Bauarbeiter; Bauarbeiterin II
  ship builder [ˈʃɪp ˌbɪldə] Schiffsbauer; Schiffsbauerin III U4, 84
building [ˈbɪldɪŋ] Gebäude II
built [bɪlt] simple past, past participle von to build II
light bulb [ˈlaɪt ˌbʌlb] Glühbirne III U3, 57
burger [ˈbɜːgə] Hamburger II
*to burn [bɜːn] verbrennen; brennen III U2, 39
burnt [bɜːnt] simple past, past participle von to burn III U2, 39
bus [bʌs] Bus I
  bus stop [ˈbʌs ˌstɒp] Bushaltestelle II
  on the bus [ˌɒn ðə ˈbʌs] im Bus II
busy [ˈbɪzi] beschäftigt I; belebt <III U1, 30>
  a busy day [ə ˌbɪzi ˈdeɪ] ein ausgefüllter Tag I

busy

but [bʌt] aber I

butcher's [ˈbʊtʃəz] Metzgerei III U1, 13

butter [ˈbʌtə] Butter I
  peanut butter [ˌpiːnʌt ˈbʌtə] Erdnussbutter III U4, 81

to **buy [baɪ] kaufen I

by [baɪ] von II; vorbei <III U1, 17>; bis
  (spätestens) III U5, 100
  to go by (train) [ˌɡəʊ baɪ (ˈtreɪn)]
  mit (dem Zug) fahren I

Bye! [baɪ] Tschüss! I

C

cabbage [ˈkæbɪdʒ] Kohl; Kraut II

caber [ˈkeɪbə] Baumstamm
  <III U3, 130>
  caber toss [ˈkeɪbə ˌtɒs] Baumstammwerfen <III U3, 130>

cache [kæʃ] Cache *(Geheimschatz)* I
  cache box [ˈkæʃ ˌbɒks] *Schatzkiste*
  beim Geocaching I

café [ˈkæfeɪ] Café I

cafeteria [kæfəˈtɪəriə] Cafeteria;
  Mensa I

cage [keɪdʒ] Käfig I

cake [keɪk] Kuchen I

calculator [ˈkælkjəleɪtə] (Taschen-)
  Rechner I

calendar [ˈkæləndə] Kalender
  <III U2, 129>

call [kɔːl] Anruf; Ruf III U5, 104
  phone call [ˈfəʊn ˌkɔːl] Telefonanruf I

to **call** [kɔːl] rufen; anrufen II; nennen <III U1, 17>
  to be called [biː ˈkɔːld] heißen;
  genannt werden II
  call me [ˈkɔːl ˌmi] nenne mich I

caller [ˈkɔːlə] Anrufer; Anruferin
  III U2, 38

calm [kɑːm] ruhig; friedlich
  <III U4, 77>

came [keɪm] simple past von *to*
  come I

camel [ˈkæml] Kamel III U4, 82

camera [ˈkæmrə] Fotoapparat;
  Kamera <III U1, 27>

camp [kæmp] Camp; Lager II

camper [ˈkæmpə] Wohnmobil
  <III U3, 194>

camping [ˈkæmpɪŋ] Camping; Zelten
  III U2, 36
  to go camping [ˌɡəʊ ˈkæmpɪŋ]
  campen gehen; zelten II

campsite [ˈkæmpsaɪt] Campingplatz;
  Zeltplatz III U3, 58

a **can** of [kæn] eine Dose … I

can't [kɑːnt] nicht können I
  can [kæn; kən] können I
  Can I come back for it later? [kæn
  aɪ kʌm ˌbæk fərˌɪt ˈleɪtə] Kann ich
  später nochmal wiederkommen? I
  Can you say that again, please?
  [kæn juː ˌseɪ ðæt əˈgen pliːs] Könntest du das bitte wiederholen? I
  Can you tell me the way to …?
  [kæn juː ˌtel mi ðə ˈweɪ tə] Kannst
  du mir sagen, wie ich … komme? I
  I can't find … [aɪ kɑːnt ˈfaɪnd] ich
  kann … nicht finden I
  I can't wait [aɪ ˌkɑːnt ˈweɪt] ich
  kann es kaum erwarten III U5, 100

canary [kəˈneəri] Kanarienvogel
  III U1, 20

candle [ˈkændl] Kerze I

cannon [ˈkænən] Kanone II
  cannon ball [ˈkænən ˌbɔːl] Kanonenkugel II

cannot [ˈkænɒt] nicht können
  III U2, 45

canoeing [kəˈnuːɪŋ] Kanufahren I

cap [kæp] Kappe; Mütze I

capital (city) [ˈkæpɪtl (ˌsɪti)] Hauptstadt III U2, 33

captain [ˈkæptɪn] Kapitän; Kapitänin I

caption [ˈkæpʃn] Untertitel; Bildun-
  terschrift <II>

car [kɑː] Auto I
  car park [ˈkɑː ˌpɑːk] Parkplatz
  <III U4, 86>

caravan [ˈkærəvæn] Wohnwagen
  III U3, 59

static caravan [ˈstætɪk ˌkærəvæn]
  Mobilheim *(großer, fest stehender*
  Wohnwagen) <III U3, 194>

card [kɑːd] Karte; Spielkarte II
  prompt card [ˈprɒmt ˌkɑːd] Stichwortkarte <II>

cardboard [ˈkɑːdbɔːd] Pappe; Karton
  III U3, 55

to **care (for)** [ˈkeə (fɔː)] sich kümmern
  (um) III U5, 95

to be **careful [biː ˈkeəfl] vorsichtig
  sein II

caretaker [ˈkeəˌteɪkə] Hausmeister;
  Hausmeisterin I

carnival [ˈkɑːnɪvl] Karneval;
  Fasching I

carpenter [ˈkɑːpəntə] Zimmermann;
  Zimmerin; Tischler; Tischlerin II

carpet [ˈkɑːpɪt] Teppich I

carrot [ˈkærət] Karotte II
  carrot pudding [ˈkærət ˌpʊdɪŋ]
  indische Nachspeise I

to **carry** [ˈkæri] tragen III U5, 103

pencil **case** [ˈpensl ˌkeɪs] Federmäppchen I

cast [kɑːst] Gips III U2, 39

castle [ˈkɑːsl] Schloss; Burg II

cat [kæt] Katze I

catering college [ˈkeɪtərɪŋ ˌkɒlɪdʒ]
  Hotelfachschule II

Catholic [ˈkæθlɪk] Katholik; Katholikin; katholisch III U4, 74

to **cause** [kɔːz] verursachen
  <III U4, 132>

'**cause** (= because) [kɒz] weil
  <III U5, 101>

cave [keɪv] Höhle II

CD [ˌsiːˈdiː] CD I

ceiling [ˈsiːlɪŋ] Zimmerdecke I

to **celebrate** [ˈseləbreɪt] feiern I

Celt [kelt] Kelte; Keltin <III U5, 134>

Celtic [ˈkeltɪk] keltisch <III U5, 134>

centimetre (cm) [ˈsentɪˌmiːtə] Zentimeter (cm) I

centre [ˈsentə] Zentrum; Mitte; Center
  III U1, 16
  activity centre [ækˈtɪvəti ˌsentə]
  Jugendzentrum III U2, 34

p pen • b bed • t ten • d dad • k cat • ɡ grey • tʃ chair • dʒ joke • f fan • v very • θ three • ð the

city centre [ˌsɪti ˈsentə] Stadtzentrum; Stadtmitte III U2, 33

shopping centre [ˈʃɒpɪŋ ˌsentə] Einkaufszentrum I

in the centre of [ɪn ðə ˈsentər ˌəv] in der Mitte von III U1, 16

century [ˈsenʃri] Jahrhundert III U1, 25

cereal [ˈsɪərɪəl] Müsli; Cornflakes III U5, 96

chain [tʃeɪn] Kette <III U3, 131>

chair [tʃeə] Stuhl I

chamber of horrors [ˌtʃeɪmbər ˌəv ˈhɒrəz] Kammer des Schreckens <III U1, 30>

chance [tʃɑːns] Chance; Gelegenheit; Möglichkeit II

change [tʃeɪndʒ] Münzgeld; Wechselgeld II

to **change** [tʃeɪndʒ] wechseln II; ändern <III U1, 127>; (sich) ändern; verändern III U3, 54; umsteigen III U5, 100

to change one's mind [ˌtʃeɪndʒ wʌnz ˈmaɪnd] seine Meinung ändern <III U2, 44>; III U4, 81

charades [ʃəˈrɑːdz] Scharaden <II>

charger [ˈtʃɑːdʒə] Ladegerät III U5, 97

charity [ˈtʃærɪti] Wohltätigkeitsorganisation <III U2, 128>

chart [tʃɑːt] Tabelle; Diagramm <II>

video **chat** [ˈvɪdiəʊ ˌtʃæt] Video-Chat III U3, 67

to **chat** [tʃæt] chatten; plaudern II

cheap [tʃiːp] billig II

to **check** [tʃek] überprüfen; kontrollieren III U4, 81

to check in [ˌtʃek ˌɪn] einchecken III U3, 59

to check out [ˌtʃek ˌaʊt] auschecken III U3, 59

checklist [ˈtʃeklɪst] Checkliste <I>

checkpoint [ˈtʃekpɔɪnt] Kontrollpunkt <I>

cheeky [ˈtʃiːki] frech III U2, 34

to **cheer** sb up [ˌtʃɪər ˈʌp] jmdn. aufheitern; jmdn. aufmuntern III U5, 105

cheese [tʃiːz] Käse I

cheesecake [ˈtʃiːskeɪk] Käsekuchen II

chef [ʃef] Koch; Köchin II

head chef [ˈhed ˌʃef] Chefkoch II

chewing gum [ˈtʃuːɪŋ ˌɡʌm] Kaugummi I

chic [ʃɪk] schick; elegant I

chicken [ˈtʃɪkɪn] Huhn I; Hühnchen II

children *(pl)* [ˈtʃɪldrən] Kinder II

chilli [ˈtʃɪli] Chili II

chilli con carne [ˌtʃɪli kɒn ˈkɑːni] Chili con carne II

the **Chinese** [ðə ˌtʃaɪniːz] die Chinesen <III U1, 24>

chips *(pl)* [tʃɪps] Pommes I

fish and chips [ˌfɪʃ ən ˈtʃɪps] Pommes mit Fisch I

chocolate [ˈtʃɒklət] Schokolade I

*to **choose** [tʃuːz] wählen; auswählen II

chorus [ˈkɔːrəs] Refrain <I>

chose [tʃəʊz] simple past von *to choose* II

chosen [ˈtʃəʊzn] past participle von *to choose* II

Christianity [ˌkrɪstiˈænəti] Christentum <III U5, 134>

Christmas [ˈkrɪsməs] Weihnachten I

church [tʃɜːtʃ] Kirche II

cinema [ˈsɪnəmə] Kino I

circle [ˈsɜːkl] Kreis; Ring III U1, 10

city [ˈsɪti] Stadt; Großstadt II

city centre [ˌsɪti ˈsentə] Stadtzentrum; Stadtmitte III U2, 33

clan [klæn] Clan; Stamm <III U3, 130>

class [klɑːs] Klasse III U2, 36; Unterricht III U5, 102

classmate [ˈklɑːsmeɪt] Klassenkamerad; Klassenkameradin; Mitschüler; Mitschülerin <II>

classroom [ˈklɑːsrʊm] Klassenzimmer I

to **clean** [kliːn] sauber machen; putzen I

clean [kliːn] sauber III U3, 53

to **clear** the table [ˌklɪə ðə ˈteɪbl] den Tisch abräumen II

clever [ˈklevə] schlau; klug; intelligent II

to **click** [klɪk] klicken I

climb [klaɪm] Steigflug <III U3, 73>

to **climb** [klaɪm] besteigen; steigen; klettern III U2, 34

rock **climber** [ˈrɒk ˌklaɪmə] Kletterer; Kletterin <III U3, 72>

clock [klɒk] Uhr II

alarm clock [əˈlɑːm ˌklɒk] Wecker I

clock tower [ˈklɒk ˌtaʊə] Uhrenturm II

o'clock [əˈklɒk] Uhr *(Zeitangabe bei vollen Stunden)* I

to **close** [kləʊz] schließen; zumachen I

close [kləʊs] in der Nähe; nahe III U1, 17

clothes *(pl)* [kləʊðz] Kleider *(Pl.)*; Kleidung I

cloud [klaʊd] Wolke III U2, 42

cloudy [ˈklaʊdi] wolkig I

club [klʌb] Klub; Verein II

clue [kluː] Hinweis; Spur I

coach [kəʊtʃ] Trainer; Trainerin <III U2, 36>

coal [kəʊl] Kohle III U1, 16

coast [kəʊst] Küste III U2, 33

on the coast [ˌɒn ðə ˈkəʊst] an der Küste III U1, 17

coat [kəʊt] Jacke I

coffee [ˈkɒfi] Kaffee <III U3, 68>

coin [kɔɪn] Münze III U4, 79

coke [kəʊk] Cola I

cold [kəʊld] kalt I

to get cold [ˌget ˈkəʊld] frieren III U3, 60

collar [ˈkɒlə] Halsband I

to **collect** [kəˈlekt] sammeln I

catering **college** [ˈkeɪtərɪŋ ˌkɒlɪdʒ] Hotelfachschule II

colour [ˈkʌlə] Farbe I

colourful [ˈkʌləfl] bunt II

comb [ˈkəʊm] Kamm III U5, 97

combination [ˌkɒmbɪˈneɪʃn] Kombination II

*to **come** [kʌm] kommen I

to come out [ˌkʌm ˈaʊt] hervorkommen II

Come on! [ˌkʌm ˈɒn] Komm jetzt! I

come

comedy ['kɒmədi] Komödie III U2, 50

comfortable ['kʌmftəbl] bequem; angenehm II

comic ['kɒmɪk] Comic(heft) II

comment ['kɒment] Kommentar II

company ['kʌmpəni] Firma; Gesellschaft II

to compare [kəm'peə] vergleichen I

to compete (against) [kəm'pi:t] konkurrieren (gegen); sich messen (gegen) <III U3, 130>

competition [ˌkɒmpə'tɪʃn] Wettbewerb; Turnier III U5, 95

competitor [kəm'petɪtə] Mitbewerber; Mitbewerberin; Teilnehmer; Teilnehmerin <III U3, 131>

to complete [kəm'pli:t] vervollständigen I

complete [kəm'pli:t] vollständig <III U3, 131>

computer [ˌkəm'pju:tə] Computer I
computer game [ˌkəm'pju:tə geɪm] Computerspiel I

concert ['kɒnsət] Konzert II

conclusion [kən'klu:ʒn] Schlussfolgerung; Schluss III U2, 50

confident ['kɒnfɪdnt] selbstsicher; selbstbewusst III U4, 77

confused [kən'fju:zd] verwirrt; wirr III U1, 25

Congratulations! [kənˌgrætʃu'leɪʃnz] Glückwunsch! II

to connect [kə'nekt] verbinden III U3, 67

connecting [kə'nektɪŋ] verbindend <II>

conquest ['kɒŋkwest] Eroberung <III U1, 126>

content ['kɒntent] Inhalt III U2, 50

to control [kən'trəʊl] kontrollieren <III U1, 17>

to cook [kʊk] kochen II

to cool [ku:l] kühlen III U2, 39

cool [ku:l] cool; super; kühl I
to keep cool [ˌki:p 'ku:l] Ruhe bewahren <III U1, 27>

copy ['kɒpi] Kopie II; Abschrift <III U2, 51>

to copy ['kɒpi] kopieren II; abschreiben <III U2, 35>

corner ['kɔ:nə] Ecke III U4, 92
corner shop ['kɔ:nə ˌʃɒp] Tante-Emma-Laden I
film corner ['fi:lm ˌkɔ:nə] Filmecke <I>
reading corner ['ri:dɪŋ ˌkɔ:nə] Leseecke <I>

Cornish ['kɔ:nɪʃ] Cornish; aus Cornwall II

to correct [kə'rekt] verbessern I

correct [kə'rekt] richtig; korrekt <III U1, 25>

corridor ['kɒridɔ:] Gang; Flur; Korridor III U2, 42

cost [kɒst] Preis; Kosten <III U1, 30>

*to cost [kɒst] kosten III U4, 75

cost [kɒst] simple past, past participle von to cost III U4, 75

costume ['kɒstju:m] Kostüm I

cosy ['kəʊzi] gemütlich III U3, 58

cottage ['kɒtɪdʒ] Häuschen III U3, 53
holiday cottage ['hɒlədeɪ ˌkɒtɪdʒ] Ferienhäuschen <III U3, 194>

cotton ['kɒtn] Baumwolle III U3, 55

to cough [kɒf] husten III U1, 21

could [kʊd] konnte III U1, 21; könnten III U3, 58

country ['kʌntri] ländliche Gegend; Land I

countryside ['kʌntrɪsaɪd] Landschaft; Land III U3, 53

course [kɔ:s] Kurs III U5, 95
main course [ˌmeɪn 'kɔ:s] Hauptgericht II
of course [əv 'kɔ:s] natürlich; selbstverständlich II

court [kɔ:t] Spielfeld III U4, 87

cousin ['kʌzn] Cousin; Cousine II

to cover ['kʌvə] überziehen <III U3, 66>

cow [kaʊ] Kuh III U1, 16

crazy ['kreɪzi] verrückt I
to drive sb crazy [draɪv … 'kreɪzi] jmdn. verrückt machen III U4, 76

credit card ['kredɪt ˌka:d] Kreditkarte <III U4, 86>

crew [kru:] Crew; Besatzung; Mannschaft III U4, 84

cricket ['krɪkɪt] Kricket II

crime [kraɪm] Verbrechen <III U4, 77>

financial crisis [faɪˌnænʃl 'kraɪsɪs] Wirtschaftskrise <III U5, 135>

crisp [krɪsp] Kartoffelchip I

crisp [krɪsp] knusprig; kross <III U3, 66>

crocodile ['krɒkədaɪl] Krokodil I

to cross [krɒs] überqueren III U1, 12

crowd [kraʊd] Menschenmenge II

to cry [kraɪ] weinen; rufen; schreien <III U4, 77>

CU (See you!) ['si: ˌju] Bis später! II

cuddly ['kʌdli] knuddelig III U2, 39
cuddly toy ['kʌdli ˌtɔɪ] Kuscheltier III U2, 39

cuju ['tsuju] Cuju (asiatischer Vorgänger des Fußballs) <III U1, 24>

culture ['kʌltʃə] Kultur <I>

cup [kʌp] Tasse II

cupboard ['kʌbəd] Schrank III U5, 98

curry ['kʌri] Curry II

custard ['kʌstəd] Vanillesauce II

customer ['kʌstəmə] Kunde; Kundin III U4, 80

cut [kʌt] Schnittverletzung <III U2, 187>

*to cut [kʌt] schneiden III U2, 39

cut [kʌt] simple past, past participle von to cut III U2, 39

cute [kju:t] niedlich; süß II

cycling ['saɪklɪŋ] Radfahren III U3, 61

D

dad [dæd] Papa; Vati I

daily ['deɪli] täglich III U5, 101

dance [da:ns] Tanz III U5, 100

to dance [da:ns] tanzen I

dancer ['da:nsə] Tänzer; Tänzerin I

dancing ['da:nsɪŋ] Tanzen; Tanz- <III U3, 131>

danger ['deɪndʒə] Gefahr <III U2, 128>

dangerous ['deɪndʒrəs] gefährlich III U2, 34

the **dark** [ðə 'dɑːk] Dunkelheit III U1, 20

dark [dɑːk] dunkel I

darkness ['dɑːknəs] Dunkelheit <III U5, 101>

date [deɪt] Zeitpunkt; Datum I

daughter ['dɔːtə] Tochter I

break of **dawn** [ˌbreɪk əv 'dɔːn] Tagesanbruch <III U5, 101>

day [deɪ] Tag I

a busy day [ə ˌbɪzi 'deɪ] ein ausgefüllter Tag I

all day [ˌɔːl 'deɪ] den ganzen Tag III U3, 58

lucky day [ˌlʌki 'deɪ] Glückstag II

one day [wʌn 'deɪ] eines Tages III U1, 21

four hours a day [ˌfɔːr aʊəz ə 'deɪ] vier Stunden täglich I

dead [ded] tot III U1, 22

deadly ['dedli] tod-; tödlich III U1, 20

deaf [def] gehörlos; schwerhörig; taub III U3, 54

Dear …, [dɪə] Liebe(r) …, (Anrede in Briefen) I

oh dear [əʊ 'dɪə] oje III U4, 80

debit card ['debɪt ˌkɑːd] EC-Karte <III U4, 86>

December [dɪ'sembə] Dezember I

to **decide** [dɪ'saɪd] (sich) entscheiden III U3, 58

deep fried [ˌdiːp'fraɪd] frittiert; in Fett ausgebacken <III U3, 66>

definition [ˌdefɪ'nɪʃn] Definition <III U3, 59>

delicious [dɪ'lɪʃəs] köstlich II

department [dɪ'pɑːtmənt] Abteilung II

department store [dɪ'pɑːtmənt ˌstɔː] Kaufhaus II

to **describe** [dɪ'skraɪb] beschreiben <I>

design [dɪ'zaɪn] Design; Gestaltung <III U3, 69>

Design Technology (DT) [dɪˌzaɪn tek'nɒlədʒi ˌdiː'tiː] Technik I

to **design** [dɪ'zaɪn] entwerfen; gestalten <III U3, 69>

information **desk** [ɪnfə'meɪʃn ˌdesk] Information II

dessert [dɪ'zɜːt] Nachspeise II

detail ['diːteɪl] Detail; Einzelheit <II>

detective [dɪ'tektɪv] Detektiv; Detektivin <I>

dialogue ['daɪəlɒg] Dialog; Gespräch <I>

diamond ['daɪəmənd] Diamant <II>

diary ['daɪəri] Tagebuch I

dictionary ['dɪkʃnri] Wörterbuch <III U3, 73>

did [dɪd] simple past von to do I

to **die** [daɪ] sterben III U1, 21

difficult ['dɪfɪklt] schwierig II

dining room ['daɪnɪŋ ˌrʊm] Esszimmer I

dinner ['dɪnə] Mittagessen; Abendessen II

directions [dɪ'rekʃnz] Anweisungen; Wegbeschreibung <III U1, 15>

director [dɪ'rektə] Regisseur; Regisseurin II

dirty ['dɜːti] dreckig; schmutzig I

to **disagree** [ˌdɪsə'griː] anderer Meinung sein; nicht einverstanden sein II

disagreement [ˌdɪsə'griːmnt] Meinungsverschiedenheit; Streit <III U4, 132>

disaster [dɪ'zɑːstə] Katastrophe; Desaster; Unglück III U4, 84

to **discover** [dɪ'skʌvə] entdecken <III U1, 30>

dish [dɪʃ] Gericht; Speise II

*to **do** [duː] machen; tun I

to do homework [ˌduː 'həʊmwɜːk] Hausaufgabe(n) machen I

to do the right thing [ˌduː ðə 'raɪt θɪŋ] das Richtige tun III U2, 38

to do the shopping [ˌduː ðə 'ʃɒpɪŋ] Einkäufe machen; Besorgungen machen II

to do the washing up [ˌduː ðə 'wɒʃɪŋ ˌʌp] abspülen II

dos and don'ts [ˌduːz ən 'dəʊnts] Verhaltensregel <III U2, 44>

doctor ['dɒktə] Arzt; Ärztin II

document ['dɒkjəmənt] Dokument <III U5, 206>

dog [dɒg] Hund I

dog biscuit ['dɒg ˌbɪskɪt] Hundekeks II

to take the dog for a walk [ˌteɪk ðə dɒg fɔːr ə 'wɔːk] den Hund ausführen I

dome [dəʊm] Kuppel II

dos and **don'ts** [ˌduːz ən 'dəʊnts] Verhaltensregeln <III U2, 44>

done [dʌn] past participle von to do II

door [dɔː] Tür II

doorbell ['dɔːbel] Türklingel I

down [daʊn] entlang; herunter; hinunter III U1, 12

down [daʊn] traurig III U4, 77

to **download** [ˌdaʊn'ləʊd] herunterladen II

Dr ['dɒktə] Dr. (Anrede) III U4, 85

draft [drɑːft] Entwurf <II>

drama ['drɑːmə] Theater II; Drama III U2, 51

drank [dræŋk] simple past von to drink II

*to **draw** [drɔː] zeichnen II

drawn [drɔːn] past participle von to draw II

dreadful ['dredfl] furchtbar III U4, 77

dream [driːm] Traum II

*to **dream** [driːm] träumen III U1, 25

dreamt [dremt] simple past, past participle von to dream III U1, 25

dress [dres] Kleid II

fancy dress [ˌfænsi 'dres] Verkleidung; Kostüm I

dressed [drest] angezogen (wie); verkleidet (als) III U5, 105

*to get **dressed** [ˌget 'drest] sich anziehen II

drew [druː] simple past von to draw II

drink [drɪŋk] Getränk II

*to **drink** [drɪŋk] trinken II

anything to drink ['eniθɪŋ tə 'drɪŋk] etwas zu trinken II

drive [draɪv] Fahrt; Autofahrt III U1, 17

drive

*to **drive** [draɪv] treiben <III U5, 134>
  to drive sb crazy [draɪv … ˈkreɪzi] jmdn. verrückt machen III U4, 76
driver [ˈdraɪvə] Fahrer; Fahrerin III U5, 102
  lorry driver [ˈlɒri ˌdraɪvə] LKW-Fahrer; LKW-Fahrerin II
to **drown** [draʊn] ertrinken <III U5, 134>
drumming [ˈdrʌmɪŋ] Trommeln- III U5, 100
drunk [drʌŋk] past participle von *to drink* II
dry [draɪ] trocken III U2, 35
duke [djuːk] Herzog <III U1, 126>
dumpling [ˈdʌmplɪŋ] Kloß II
duration [djʊˈreɪʃn] Dauer <III U1, 30>
during [ˈdjʊərɪŋ] während III U1, 11
on **duty** [ɒn ˈdjuːti] im Dienst <III U3, 68>
DVD [ˌdiːviːˈdiː] DVD I

E

each [iːtʃ] jede <III U4, 79>
  each other [iːtʃ ˈʌðə] einander; sich; sich gegenseitig III U2, 34
each [iːtʃ] pro Stück II
ear [ɪə] Ohr II
early [ˈɜːli] früh III U3, 60
  early settler [ˈɜːli ˈsetlə] früher Siedler; frühe Siedlerin <III U5, 134>
east [iːst] Osten III U1, 17
eastbound [ˈiːstbaʊnd] in Richtung Osten <III U5, 207>
easy [ˈiːzi] einfach; leicht I
*to **eat** [iːt] essen I
eaten [ˈiːtn] past participle von *to eat* II
economy [ɪˈkɒnəmi] Wirtschaft <III U5, 135>
egg [eg] Ei II
  scrambled egg [ˌskræmbldˈeg] Rührei II
Eid [iːd] Eid *(muslimisches Fest)* I
eight [eɪt] acht I
eighteen [ˌeɪˈtiːn] achtzehn I
eighty [ˈeɪti] achtzig I

not … **either** [nɒt … ˈaɪðə] auch nicht III U3, 58
electricity [ˌelɪkˈtrɪsəti] Strom, Elektrizität III U3, 53
elephant [ˈelɪfənt] Elefant I
eleven [ɪˈlevn] elf I
e-mail [ˈiːmeɪl] E-Mail II
embarrassed [ɪmˈbærəst] verlegen II
emergency [ɪˈmɜːdʒnsi] Notfall III U2, 38
  emergency call [ɪˈmɜːdʒnsi ˌkɔːl] Notruf III U2, 38
  emergency service [ɪˈmɜːdʒnsi ˌsɜːvɪs] Notdienst; Rettungsdienst III U2, 38
to **emigrate** [ˈemɪgreɪt] auswandern <III U5, 135>
end [end] Ende; Schluss II
  in the end [ɪn ði ˈend] schließlich; zum Schluss II
to **end** [end] enden <II>
ending [ˈendɪŋ] Schluss; Ende III U2, 45
enemy [ˈenəmi] Feind; Feindin III U2, 50
steam **engine** [ˈstiːm ˌendʒɪn] Dampfmaschine III U3, 57
engineer [ˌendʒɪˈnɪə] Ingenieur; Ingenieurin; Techniker; Technikerin II
English [ˈɪŋglɪʃ] Englisch I
the **English** [ði ˈɪŋglɪʃ] die Engländer III U1, 11
to **enjoy** [ɪnˈdʒɔɪ] mögen III U2, 50; genießen III U3, 53
enough [ɪˈnʌf] genug; genügend III U2, 34
enough [ɪˈnʌf] genug; genügend <III U1, 127>
entry [ˈentri] Eintrag <III U3, 73>
  entry form [ˈentri ˌfɔːm] Anmeldeformular II
equipment [ɪˈkwɪpmənt] Ausrüstung III U2, 34
Victorian **era** [vɪkˌtɔːriən ˈɪərə] viktorianisches Zeitalter III U1, 25
eraser [ɪˈreɪzə] Radiergummi I
escalator [ˈeskəleɪtə] Rolltreppe II

to **escape** [ɪˈskeɪp] entkommen; fliehen; entfliehen; flüchten <III U3, 72>
euro [ˈjʊərəʊ] Euro *(Währung)* III U5, 94
European [ˌjʊərəˈpiːən] europäisch <III U5, 135>
even [ˈiːvn] noch; sogar II
evening [ˈiːvnɪŋ] Abend I
  in the evenings [ɪn ði ˈiːvnɪŋz] abends III U4, 76
event [ɪˈvent] Ereignis; Veranstaltung <III U2, 129>; <III U4, 88>
ever [ˈevə] jemals II
every [ˈevri] jede I
every [ˈevri] alle III U4, 75
everyone [ˈevriwʌn] jeder I; zusammen; alle II
everything [ˈevriθɪŋ] alles II
exact [ɪgˈzækt] exakt; genau III U4, 81
example [ɪgˈzɑːmpl] Beispiel <III U3, 69>
except [ɪkˈsept] außer III U5, 96
exchange [ɪksˈtʃeɪndʒ] Austausch <III U5, 106>
to **exchange** [ɪksˈtʃeɪndʒ] tauschen; austauschen <III U2, 41>
excited [ɪkˈsaɪtɪd] aufgeregt; begeistert II
exciting [ɪkˈsaɪtɪŋ] spannend; aufregend I
Excuse me. [ɪkˈskjuːz mi] Entschuldigung. I
exercise book [ˈeksəsaɪz ˌbʊk] Übungsheft I
exhausted [ɪgˈzɔːstɪd] erschöpft III U2, 35
to **expect** [ɪkˈspekt] erwarten III U2, 45
expensive [ɪkˈspensɪv] teuer II
experiment [ɪkˈsperɪmənt] Versuch II
to **explain** [ɪkˈspleɪn] erklären III U5, 104
to **explode** [ɪkˈspləʊd] explodieren III U1, 20
to **explore** [ɪkˈsplɔː] erkunden; erforschen II
explosion [ɪkˈspləʊʒn] Explosion III U1, 20

extra ['ekstrə] Extra; Zusatz
<III U5, 206>

extra ['ekstrə] zusätzlich; Zusatz- II
extra practice [ˌekstrə 'præktɪs]
Zusatzübungen <I>

eye [aɪ] Auge II
I couldn't believe my eyes. [aɪ
ˌkʊdnt bɪˌliːv maɪ ˈaɪz] Ich traute
meinen Augen nicht. III U5, 105

F

fable ['feɪbl] Fabel; Märchen
III U5, 105

face [feɪs] Gesicht I

fact [fækt] Fakt; Tatsache II

factory ['fæktri] Fabrik; Werk III U1, 16

fair [feə] gerecht; fair <III U1, 24>

*** to fall** [fɔːl] fallen; hinfallen I
to fall (over) [fɔːlˈəʊvə] fallen;
hinfallen; umfallen III U2, 38
to fall apart [ˌfɔːlˌəˈpaːt] zusam-
menbrechen <III U4, 77>
to fall asleep [ˌfɔːlˌəˈsliːp] einschlafen III U1, 25
to fall in love (with) [ˌfɔːlˌɪn ˈlʌv]
sich verlieben (in) III U2, 50

family ['fæmli] Familie I
host family ['həʊst ˌfæmli] Gastfamilie <III U5, 99>

famine ['fæmɪn] Hungersnot
<III U5, 135>

famous ['feɪməs] berühmt I

fan [fæn] Fan I

fancy dress [ˌfænsi 'dres] Verkleidung;
Kostüm I

fantastic [fæn'tæstɪk] fantastisch;
großartig II

fantasy ['fæntəsi] Fantasie; Fantasy II
fantasy trip ['fæntəsi ˌtrɪp] Fantasieausflug I

far [faː] weit III U1, 12

fare [feə] Fahrpreis III U5, 100

farewell speech [feəˈwel spiːtʃ]
Abschiedsrede II

farm ['faːm] Bauernhof I
wind farm ['wɪndfaːm] Windpark
III U3, 53

farmer ['faːmə] Bauer; Bäuerin;
Landwirt; Landwirtin I

fashionable ['fæʃnəbl] modisch II

fast [faːst] schnell II
fast food restaurant [ˌfaːst fuːd
'restrɒnt] Fastfood-Restaurant I
the fastest [ðə 'faːstɪst] der/die/
das schnellste I

father ['faːðə] Vater I
It was my **fault**. [ɪt wəz ˌmaɪ 'fɔːlt] Es
war meine Schuld. II

favourite ['feɪvrɪt] Lieblings- I

fear [fɪə] Angst; Furcht <III U4, 77>

feature ['fiːtʃə] Merkmal <III U4, 88>

February ['februri] Februar I

fed [fed] simple past von *to feed* I;
past participle von *to feed* II

*** to be fed up (with)** [biː fed ʌp (wɪð)]
die Nase voll haben (von); sauer
sein III U4, 76

*** to feed** [fiːd] füttern I

feedback ['fiːdbæk] Feedback; Rück-
meldung <II>

*** to feel** [fiːl] (sich) fühlen II
to feel sorry [ˌfiːl 'sɒri] Mitleid
haben mit; bedauern III U5, 105
to make sb feel like sth [ˌmeɪk …
'fiːl laɪk] jmdm. das Gefühl geben,
etw. zu sein III U2, 43

feeling ['fiːlɪŋ] Gefühl <III U4, 87>

foot *(sg)* [fʊt], **feet** *(pl)* [fiːt] Fuß I

fell [fel] simple past von *to fall* I

felt-tip [ˌfelt'tɪp] Filzstift I

felt [felt] simple past von *to feel* II

female ['fiːmeɪl] weiblich <III U1, 24>

ferry ['feri] Fähre <III U5, 207>

a **few** [ə 'fjuː] ein paar; wenige;
einige III U3, 58

science **fiction** [ˌsaɪəns 'fɪkʃn] Science-
Fiction I

fifteen [ˌfɪf'tiːn] fünfzehn I

fifty ['fɪfti] fünfzig I

fight [faɪt] Kampf; Streit III U2, 50

*** to fight** [faɪt] kämpfen; (sich) streiten III U3, 52

fighting ['faɪtɪŋ] Kämpfen; Kämpfe
<III U4, 132>

file [faɪl] Datei II

to fill [fɪl] (sich) füllen <III U1, 17>

film [fɪlm] Film I
film corner ['fiːlm ˌkɔːnə] Filmecke
<I>
film maker ['fɪlm ˌmeɪkə] Filmemacher; Filmemacherin <III U5, 107>

to film [fɪlm] filmen; drehen
<III U1, 26>

finally ['faɪnli] schließlich; zum
Schluss II

financial crisis [faɪˌnænʃl 'kraɪsɪs]
Wirtschaftskrise <III U5, 135>

*** to find** [faɪnd] finden; herausfinden I
to find out [ˌfaɪnd 'aʊt] herausfinden I
I can't find … [aɪ kaːnt 'faɪnd] ich
kann … nicht finden I

fine [faɪn] gut; in Ordnung; schön II
I'm fine. [aɪm 'faɪn] Mir geht es
gut. II

finger ['fɪŋɡə] Finger III U2, 39

fingerprint ['fɪŋɡəprɪnt] Fingerabdruck II

to finish ['fɪnɪʃ] beenden; enden;
aufhören; fertigstellen; vervollständigen II

fire [faɪə] Feuer II
fire engine ['faɪərˌendʒɪn] Feuerwehrauto II

first [fɜːst] zuerst; als Erstes; erste I
first name [ˌfɜːst 'neɪm] Vorname
<III U1, 127>
the first time [ðə ˌfɜːst 'taɪm] das
erste Mal I

fish *(sg)* [fɪʃ], **fish** *(pl)* [fɪʃ] Fisch I
fish and chips [ˌfɪʃ ən 'tʃɪps] Pom-
mes mit Fisch I

to fit [fɪt] passen II

fit [fɪt] fit; in Form III U2, 34

five [faɪv] fünf I

flag [flæɡ] Flagge; Fahne II

flamingo [fləˈmɪŋɡəʊ] Flamingo I

flare [fleə] Leuchtsignal; Leuchtfa-
ckel <III U5, 101>

flat [flæt] Wohnung I
holiday flat ['hɒlədeɪ ˌflæt] Ferienwohnung <III U3, 194>

flat

flavour ['fleɪvə] Geschmack; Geschmacksrichtung; Sorte <III U4, 200>

flew [flu:] simple past von *to fly* II

flip flop ['flɪp flɒp] Flipflop <III U2, 44>

floor [flɔ:] Stockwerk II; <III U1, 30>

flour [flaʊə] Mehl I

flower ['flaʊə] Blume III U5, 104

flown [fləʊn] past participle von *to fly* II

fluent ['flu:ənt] fließend; flüssig III U2, 33

***to fly** [flaɪ] fliegen II; wehen <III U1, 30>

flyer ['flaɪə] Flyer; Faltblatt II

flying ['flaɪɪŋ] Fliegen <III U1, 30>

foggy ['fɒgi] neblig I

to follow ['fɒləʊ] befolgen; folgen III U5, 102

food [fu:d] Essen; Lebensmittel I
food stall ['fu:d ˌstɔ:l] Essensstand II

foot *(sg)* [fʊt], **feet** *(pl)* [fi:t] Fuß I
to go on foot [ˌgəʊ ɒn 'fʊt] zu Fuß gehen I

football ['fʊtbɔ:l] Fußball I
association football [əˈsəʊsieɪʃn ˌfʊtbɔ:l] Assoziationsfußball *(offizieller Name von Fußball)* <III U1, 24>
football association ['fʊtbɔ:l ˌəsəʊsieɪʃn] Fußballverband ‹III U1, 24›

for [fɔ:; fə] lang <III U5, 134>
for example [fərˌɪgˈza:mpl] zum Beispiel <III U1, 24>
for five months [fə ˌfaɪv 'mʌnθs] fünf Monate lang I
for fun [fə 'fʌn] zum Spaß III U2, 43
for service [fə 'sɜ:vɪs] um bedient zu werden <III U4, 86>

for [fɔ:] für I; seit <III U2, 129>

foreground ['fɔ:graʊnd] Vordergrund III U4, 92
in the foreground [ɪn ðə 'fɔ:graʊnd] im Vordergrund III U4, 92

to foretell [fɔ:ˈtel] vorhersagen III U5, 105

forever [fəˈrevə] für immer; ewig II

***to forget** [fəˈget] vergessen I

forgot [fəˈgɒt] simple past von *to forget* II

forgotten [fəˈgɒtn] past participle von *to forget* II

fork [fɔ:k] Gabel II

form [fɔ:m] Form <III U5, 98>
entry form ['entri ˌfɔ:m] Anmeldeformular II

forty ['fɔ:ti] vierzig I

fought [fɔ:t] simple past, past participle von *to fight* III U3, 52

found [faʊnd] simple past von *to find* II

four [fɔ:] vier I

fourteen [ˌfɔ:ˈti:n] vierzehn I

fourth [fɔ:θ] vierte I

free [fri:] kostenlos III U4, 75
free range [ˌfri: 'reɪndʒ] Freiland- II
free time [ˌfri: 'taɪm] Freizeit I

***to freeze** [fri:z] frieren; gefrieren III U3, 58
freeze frame ['fri:z ˌfreɪm] Standbild <II>

French [frentʃ] Französisch I

French [frenʃ] französisch <III U1, 130>

fresh [freʃ] frisch II

Friday ['fraɪdeɪ] Freitag I

fridge [frɪdʒ] Kühlschrank III U5, 96
deep fried [ˌdi:pˈfraɪd] frittiert; in Fett ausgebacken ‹III U3, 66›

fried [fraɪd] (in der Pfanne) gebraten II

friend [frend] Freund; Freundin I
to make friends [ˌmeɪk 'frendz] Freundschaften schließen I

friendly ['frendli] freundlich; nett III U2, 35

frisbee ['frɪzbi] Frisbeescheibe I

from [frɒm] aus; von I
I'm from … ['aɪm ˌfrɒm] ich komme aus … I
Where are you from? [ˌweər ə ju 'frɒm] Woher kommst du? I

in front of [ɪn 'frʌnt ˌəv] vor; davor <III U4, 93>

froze [frəʊz] simple past von *to freeze* III U3, 58

frozen ['frəʊzn] past participle von *to freeze* III U3, 58

fruit [fru:t] Frucht; Obst I

to fry [fraɪ] frittieren <III U3, 66>

full service [ˌfʊl 'sɜ:vɪs] Komplettservice <III U3, 68>

fun [fʌn] Freude; Spaß I
for fun [fə 'fʌn] zum Spaß III U2, 43

fundraising ['fʌndˌreɪzɪŋ] Spendenaktionen <III U2, 128>

funny ['fʌni] merkwürdig; komisch; lustig; witzig I

furious ['fjʊəriəs] wütend III U4, 77

future ['fju:tʃə] Zukunft <II>

G

game [geɪm] Spiel I
computer game [kəmˈpju:tə geɪm] Computerspiel I

gamer ['geɪmə] Spieler *(Computer)*; Spielerin *(Computer)* II

garage ['gæra:ʒ] Werkstatt; Tankstelle <III U3, 68>

garden ['ga:dn] Garten I

garlic ['ga:lɪk] Knoblauch II

gas [gæs] Gas III U1, 20

gave [geɪv] simple past von *to give* II

gel [dʒel] Gel III U5, 97
hair gel ['heə ˌdʒel] Haargel III U5, 97
shower gel ['ʃaʊə ˌdʒel] Duschgel III U5, 97

gently ['dʒentli] sanft <III U4, 86>

geocaching ['dʒiəʊkæʃɪŋ] Geocaching *(eine Art elektronische Schatzsuche)* I

Geography [dʒiˈɒgrəfi] Geografie; Erdkunde I

German ['dʒɜ:mən] Deutsch I

German ['dʒɜ:mən] deutsch; aus Deutschland III U5, 98

***to get** [get] bekommen I; verstehen III U4, 80

to get a job wrong [ˌget ə dʒɒb 'rɒŋ] einen Auftrag vermasseln III U2, 50

to get around [ˌget ə'raʊnd] herumkommen III U5, 100

to get back [ˌget 'bæk] zurückkommen <III U2, 128>

to get cold [ˌget 'kəʊld] frieren III U3, 60

to get dressed [ˌget 'drest] sich anziehen II

to get in [ˌget ɪn] hereinkommen I

to get into trouble [ˌget ɪntə 'trʌbl] in Schwierigkeiten geraten <III U2, 128>

to get married [ˌget 'mærɪd] heiraten II

to get off [ˌget 'ɒf] aussteigen II

to get out [ˌget 'aʊt] herauskommen III U1, 22

to get ready [ˌget 'redi] sich vorbereiten; sich fertig machen <III U1, 27>; <III U2, 44>

to get to [ˈget tə] hinkommen zu; gelangen <III U2, 128>

to get to know [ˌget tə 'nəʊ] kennen lernen II

to get up [ˌget ˈʌp] aufstehen I

ghost [gəʊst] Geist II

giant [dʒaɪənt] Riese III U4, 75

giraffe [dʒɪ'rɑːf] Giraffe I

girl [gɜːl] Mädchen I

***to give** [gɪv] geben I

to give a talk [ˌgɪv ə 'tɔːk] einen Vortrag halten <III U1, 19>

to give reasons [ˌgɪv 'riːznz] Gründe nennen; Gründe angeben III U2, 51

to give sth a miss [ˌgɪv sʌmθɪŋ ə 'mɪs] auf etw. verzichten; etw. bleiben lassen III U2, 50

to give up [ˌgɪv ˈʌp] aufgeben III U3, 63

glad [glæd] froh II

glass [glɑːs] Glas II

glove [glʌv] Handschuh <III U2, 44>

to glow [gləʊ] leuchten <III U5, 101>

glue [gluː] Klebstoff I

***to go** [gəʊ] gehen; fahren I

to go beach combing [gəʊ 'biːtʃ ˌkəʊmɪŋ] den Strand nach Strandgut absuchen II

to go by (train) [ˌgəʊ baɪ ('treɪn)] mit (dem Zug) fahren I

to go camping [gəʊ 'kæmpɪŋ] campen gehen; zelten II

to go for a walk [gəʊ fər ə 'wɔːk] spazieren gehen I

to go on foot [gəʊ ɒn 'fʊt] zu Fuß gehen I

to go shopping [gəʊ 'ʃɒpɪŋ] einkaufen gehen II

to go sightseeing [gəʊ 'saɪtsiːɪŋ] eine Besichtigungstour machen II

to go swimming [gəʊ 'swɪmɪŋ] schwimmen gehen I

to go to bed [gəʊ tə 'bed] ins Bett gehen I

goat [gəʊt] Ziege III U1, 16

goggles (pl) ['gɒglz] Schutzbrille <III U2, 44>

gold [gəʊld] Gold III U5, 104

gold [gəʊld] golden; Gold- III U5, 104

gone [gɒn] past participle von to go II

gonna (= going to) ['gɒnə] werden III U4, 77

good [gʊd] gut I

to be good at [bi 'gʊd ət] gut sein in; gut sein bei I

Good morning. [gʊd 'mɔːnɪŋ] Guten Morgen. II

good luck [gʊd 'lʌk] viel Glück II

Goodbye. [gʊd'baɪ] Auf Wiedersehen. I

gooey ['guːi] zähflüssig <III U3, 66>

got [gɒt] simple past von to get I

GPS (Global Positioning System) [ˌdʒiːpiːˈes] GPS (ein satellitengestütztes System zur weltweiten Positionsbestimmung) I

gr8 (great) [greɪt] großartig; toll II

to **grub** [grʌb] schnuppen; greifen; ergreifen III U5, 105

grammar ['græmə] Grammatik <I>

grandad ['grændæd] Opa III U4, 75

great-great-grandad [ˌgreɪt greɪt 'grændæd] Ururopa I

grandfather ['grænˌfɑːðə] Großvater II

grandma ['grænmɑː] Oma II

grandmother ['grænˌmʌðə] Großmutter II

grandparents (pl) ['grænˌpeərənts] Großeltern II

grave [greɪv] Grab III U1, 11

great [greɪt] großartig; toll I; groß; riesig <III U5, 135>

green [griːn] grün I

greengrocer's ['griːnˌgrəʊsəz] Obst- und Gemüseladen III U1, 13

grew [gruː] simple past von to grow <III U5, 135>

grew up [gruː ˈʌp] simple past von to grow up III U3, 54

grey [greɪ] grau I

ground [graʊnd] Boden; Erdboden III U3, 64

group [gruːp] Gruppe I

group skills ['gruːp ˌskɪlz] Fertigkeit Kooperatives Lernen <I>

tutor group ['tjuːtə ˌgruːp] Klasse I

***to grow** [grəʊ] wachsen <III U5, 135>

to grow up [ˌgrəʊ ˈʌp] aufwachsen III U3, 54

grown up [ˌgrəʊn ˈʌp] past participle von to grow up III U3, 54

to **guess** [ges] erraten; raten; überlegen II

Guess what? [ges 'wɒt] Weißt du was? I

guest [gest] Gast III U2, 33

guinea pig ['gɪni pɪg] Meerschweinchen II

guitar [gɪ'tɑː] Gitarre III U5, 95

guys [gaɪz] Leute II

gymnasium [dʒɪm'neɪziəm] Fitnessraum III U4, 84

gymnasium

H

had [hæd] simple past von *to have* I; past participle von *to have* II
had to ['hæd tə] simple past von *to have to* II
haggis ['hægɪs] Haggis *(schottisches Gericht aus Schafsinnereien)* III U3, 60
hair gel ['heə ˌdʒel] Haargel III U5, 97
hair [heə] Haar; Haare III U5, 98
   hair straightener ['heə ˌstreɪtnə] Haarglätter I
hairbrush ['heəbrʌʃ] Haarbürste III U5, 97
haircut ['heəkʌt] Haarschnitt II
   to have a haircut ['heəkʌt] sich die Haare schneiden lassen II
hairdresser ['heəˌdresə] Friseur; Friseurin II
hairdryer ['heəˌdraɪə] Fön III U5, 97
half *(sg)* [hɑːf], halves *(pl)* [hɑːvz] (die) Hälfte III U4, 84
half past (two) [ˌhɑːf 'pɑːst] halb (drei) I
half [hɑːf] halb III U1, 16
   half a million [ˌhɑːf ə 'mɪljən] eine halbe Million III U1, 16
Halloween [ˌhæləʊ'iːn] Halloween I
ham [hæm] Schinken II
hammer throw ['hæmə ˌθrəʊ] Hammerwurf <III U3, 131>
hand [hænd] Hand III U2, 40
handball ['hændbɔːl] Handball <III U2, 186>
***to hang** [hæŋ] hängen II
to happen ['hæpn] geschehen; passieren II
happy ['hæpi] glücklich; froh I
   Happy birthday! [ˌhæpi 'bɜːθdeɪ] Alles Gute zum Geburtstag! I
harbour ['hɑːbə] Hafen II
hard [hɑːd] hart; schwer; schwierig II
hat [hæt] Hut II
to hate [heɪt] hassen; nicht mögen III U4, 76
***to have** [hæv] haben; besitzen I

to have a haircut ['heəkʌt] sich die Haare schneiden lassen II
to have a look [ˌhæv ə 'lʊk] anschauen II
to have breakfast [ˌhæv 'brekfəst] frühstücken I
to have to ['hæv tə] müssen II
have you got [ˌhæv ju: 'gɒt] hast du II
Have you ever been to …? [ˌhæv ju ˌevə 'biːn tə] Warst du schon in …? II
Have you finished yet? [ˌhæv ju: 'fɪnɪʃt jet] Seid ihr schon fertig? II
he [hiː] er I
head [hed] Kopf II
   head chef ['hed ˌʃef] Chefkoch II
   head first ['hed fɜːst] kopfüber III U1, 18
headache ['hedeɪk] Kopfschmerzen; Kopfweh II
heading ['hedɪŋ] Überschrift; Titel <III U1, 22>
headline ['hedlaɪn] Schlagzeile <III U4, 79>
headteacher [ˌhed'tiːtʃə] Schulleiter; Schulleiterin <III U4, 88>
***to hear** [hɪə] hören I
heard [hɜːd] simple past von *to hear* I; past participle von *to hear* II
heart [hɑːt] Herz <III U3, 66>
heavy ['hevi] schwer; stark II
height [haɪt] Höhe II
held [held] simple past, past participle von *to hold* III U2, 43
helicopter ['helɪkɒptə] Helikopter; Hubschrauber I
Hello. [hə'ləʊ] Hallo. I
helm [helm] Steuermann <III U2, 129>
helmet ['helmət] Helm I
help [help] Hilfe II
to help [help] helfen I
   to help oneself [ˌhelp wʌn'self] sich bedienen III U5, 96
   Help yourselves! [ˌhelp jɔː'selvz] Bedient euch!; Bedienen Sie sich! II

How can I help you? [ˌhaʊ kæn aɪ 'help ju:] Was kann ich für dich tun? I
I couldn't help but … [aɪ ˌkʊdnt 'help bʌt] Ich konnte nicht anders als … III U5, 105
her [hɜː] ihr I
here [hɪə] hier I
   Here you are. [ˌhɪə ju ˌ'ɑː] Bitte schön. I
   Here's your change. [ˌhɪəz jɔː 'tʃeɪndʒ] Hier ist dein Wechselgeld. I
hero *(sg)* ['hɪərəʊ], **heroes** *(pl)* ['hɪərəʊz] Held III U3, 64
hers [hɜːz] ihre II
herself [hɜː'self] sie selbst; sich selbst III U2, 152
Hi. [haɪ] Hi.; Hallo. I
   Say hi to … [seɪ 'haɪ tə] Grüße … von mir. I
hid [hɪd] simple past von *to hide* III U2, 50
hidden ['hɪdn] past participle von *to hide* III U2, 50
***to hide** [haɪd] (sich) verstecken III U2, 50
high [haɪ] hoch; groß I
   high jump ['haɪ ˌdʒʌmp] Hochsprung <III U2, 186>
   high school ['haɪ ˌskuːl] High School *(weiterführende Schule, Oberstufe)* <III U2, 129>
highlight ['haɪlaɪt] Highlight; Höhepunkt <III U5, 134>
highlighted ['haɪlaɪtɪd] markiert <III U1, 31>
to hike [haɪk] wandern II
hiking ['haɪkɪŋ] Wandern III U3, 58
him [hɪm] ihn; ihm I
himself [hɪm'self] er selbst; sich (selbst) III U2, 34
hip hop ['hɪphɒp] Hip-Hop *(Musik)* III U5, 95
his [hɪz] sein I; seins; seiner II
History ['hɪstri] Geschichte I
history ['hɪstri] Geschichte III U1, 12
hit [hɪt] Hit; Treffer <III U3, 73>

*to **hit** [hɪt] treffen; schlagen II; (sich) stoßen; anstoßen III U2, 40; gegen etw. fahren III U4, 84

hit [hɪt] simple past, past participle von *to hit* II

hobby ['hɒbi] Hobby III ZI 9

*to **hold** [həʊld] halten; festhalten III U2, 43

hole [həʊl] Loch I

holiday ['hɒlədeɪ] Ferien; Urlaub II
holiday cottage ['hɒlədeɪ ˌkɒtɪdʒ] Ferienhäuschen <III U3, 194>
holiday flat ['hɒlədeɪ ˌflæt] Ferienwohnung <III U3, 194>

home [həʊm] Zuhause; Heim I
at home [ət 'həʊm] zu Hause I
back home [bæk 'həʊm] zu Hause II

*to be **homesick** [bi: 'həʊmsɪk] Heimweh haben III U5, 104

*to do **homework** [ˌdu: 'həʊmwɜːk] Hausaufgabe(n) machen I

honey ['hʌni] Honig <III U4, 200>

hood [hʊd] Kapuze <III U1, 17>

Hooray! [hʊ'reɪ] Hurra! III U3, 65

to **hoover** ['huːvə] staubsaugen II

to **hope** [həʊp] hoffen II

hopeful ['həʊpfl] hoffnungsvoll III U4, 77

horrible ['hɒrəbl] schrecklich; furchtbar III U4, 77

chamber of **horrors** [ˌtʃeɪmbər əv 'hɒrəz] Kammer des Schreckens <III U1, 30>

horse [hɔːs] Pferd I
horse riding ['hɔːs ˌraɪdɪŋ] Reiten I

hospital ['hɒspɪtl] Krankenhaus I

host family ['həʊst ˌfæmli] Gastfamilie <III U5, 99>

hostel ['hɒstl] Herberge III U3, 59

hot [hɒt] heiß I
hot air balloon [ˌhɒt 'eə bəˌluːn] Heißluftballon <III U2, 44>

hotel [həʊ'tel] Hotel II

40 kilometres an **hour** [kɪ'lɒmiːtəz ən ˌaʊə] 40 Kilometer pro Stunde I

house [haʊs] Haus I

around the house [əˌraʊnd ðə 'haʊs] zu Hause I

tree house ['triː ˌhaʊs] Baumhaus I

how [haʊ] wie I
How are you? [ˌhaʊ 'jɑː jə] Wie geht es dir? I
How can I help you? [ˌhaʊ kæn aɪ 'help ju:] Was kann ich für dich tun? I
How do I get there? [ˌhaʊ du aɪ 'get ðeə] Wie komme ich dahin? III U1, 12
how many [ˌhaʊ 'meni] wie viele II
How much (is/are) …? [ˌhaʊ 'mʌtʃ ɪz/ɑː] Wie viel (kostet/kosten) …? I
How old are you? [haʊ ˌəʊld ə ˌju:] Wie alt bist du? I
How to … ['haʊ tə] Wie man … II

however [haʊ'evə] jedoch III U4, 85

huge [hjuːdʒ] riesig; riesengroß III U1, 17; gewaltig <III U3, 72>

a/one **hundred** ['hʌndrəd] einhundert; hundert I

hung [hʌŋ] simple past von *to hang* II

hungry ['hʌŋgri] hungrig I

to **hurry** ['hʌri] sich beeilen III U2, 38

*to **hurt** [hɜːt] weh tun; verletzen II

hurt [hɜːt] simple past, past participle von *to hurt* II

I

I [aɪ] ich I
I can't wait [aɪ ˌkɑːnt 'weɪt] ich kann es kaum erwarten III U5, 100
I don't know! [ˌaɪ dəʊnt 'nəʊ] Ich weiß (es) nicht! I
I don't like [aɪ ˌdəʊnt 'laɪk] ich mag nicht; gefällt mir nicht I
I like [aɪ 'laɪk] ich mag; gefällt mir I
I spy with my little eye … [aɪ spaɪ wɪð ˌmaɪ lɪtl 'aɪ] Ich sehe was, was du nicht siehst … I
I wouldn't like (to) … [aɪ 'wʊdnt laɪk (tə)] ich möchte nicht …; ich würde nicht gerne … I

I'd like (to) … (= I would like to) [aɪd 'laɪk (tə)] ich möchte …; ich würde gerne … I

I'd rather [aɪd 'rɑːðə] ich würde lieber III U1, 25

I'm fine. [aɪm 'faɪn] Mir geht es gut. II

I'm from … ['aɪm ˌfrɒm] ich komme aus … I

I've (I have) got [ˌaɪv 'gɒt] ich habe II

ice skating ['aɪs ˌskeɪtɪŋ] Schlittschuhlaufen <III U2, 186>
ice cream [ˌaɪs 'kriːm] Eiscreme; Eis II

iceberg ['aɪsbɜːg] Eisberg III U4, 84

ID [ˌaɪ'diː] Ausweis; Personalausweis III U5, 97

idea [aɪ'dɪə] Idee I
Any idea? [ˌeni 'aɪdɪə] Irgendeine Idee? I

identity card [aɪ'dentəti ˌkɑːd] Ausweis; Personalausweis <III U5, 206>

if [ɪf] wenn II

ill [ɪl] krank; schlecht II

important [ɪm'pɔːtnt] wichtig; einflussreich III U2, 33

impossible [ɪm'pɒsəbl] unmöglich III U3, 62

to **impress** [ɪm'pres] beeindrucken III U5, 107

in [ɪn] in; im I
in August [ɪn 'ɔːgəst] im August I
in front of [ɪn 'frʌnt əv] vor; davor <III U4, 93>
in need [ɪn 'niːd] bedürftig; in Not <III U4, 77>
in the background [ɪn ðə 'bækgraʊnd] im Hintergrund III U4, 92
in the foreground [ɪn ðə 'fɔːgraʊnd] im Vordergrund III U4, 92
in the middle [ɪn ðə 'mɪdl] in der Mitte III U4, 92
in vain [ɪn 'veɪn] umsonst; vergeblich <III U5, 101>

in

include

in the centre of [ɪn ðə 'sentər‿əv] in der Mitte von III U1, 16

in the end [ɪn ði 'end] schließlich; zum Schluss II

in the evenings [ɪn ði 'i:vnɪŋz] abends III U4, 76

in the south of [ɪn ðə 'saʊθ‿əv] im Süden von III U1, 10

in the world [ɪn ðə 'wɜ:ld] auf der Welt II

to include [ɪn'klu:d] enthalten <III U3, 66>

Indian ['ɪndiən] indisch II

indoor [ˌɪn'dɔ:] Hallen-; Innen- III U2, 34

Industrial Revolution [ɪnˌdʌstriəl revl'u:ʃn] industrielle Revolution III U1, 11

industry ['ɪndəstri] Industrie III U1, 11

information desk [ɪnfə'meɪʃn ˌdesk] Information II

informative [ɪn'fɔ:mətɪv] informativ <III U1, 27>

ingredient [ɪn'gri:diənt] Zutat II

inhabitant [ɪn'hæbɪtnt] Einwohner; Einwohnerin; Bewohner; Bewohnerin III U1, 16

injection [ɪn'dʒekʃn] Spritze III U2, 39

insect ['ɪnsekt] Insekt III U3, 58

inside [ˌɪn'saɪd] in … hinein II

inside [ˌɪn'saɪd] in; innen in; im Innern III U1, 31

institution [ˌɪnstɪ'tju:ʃn] Einrichtung; Organisation; Institution <III U2, 128>

instructor [ɪn'strʌktə] Lehrer; Lehrerin III U2, 35

intelligent [ɪn'telɪdʒnt] intelligent; klug; vernünftig III U4, 77

*to be interested in [bi: 'ɪntrəstɪd‿ɪn] sich interessieren für; interessiert sein an III U1, 12

interesting ['ɪntrəstɪŋ] interessant I

internet ['ɪntənet] Internet II
    to surf the internet [ˌsɜ:f ði 'ɪntənet] im Internet surfen II

interview ['ɪntəvju:] Interview; Befragung II

to interview ['ɪntəvju:] interviewen; befragen I

into ['ɪntə] in; drin <III U1, 17>

introduction [ˌɪntrə'dʌkʃn] Einleitung; Einführung III U2, 50

to invade [ɪn'veɪd] einmarschieren (in); eindringen (in) III U1, 11

to invent [ɪn'veñt] erfinden III U3, 54

invention [ɪn'venʃn] Erfindung III U3, 54

inventor [ɪn'ventə] Erfinder; Erfinderin III U3, 52

invitation [ˌɪnvɪ'teɪʃn] Einladung I

to invite [ɪn'vaɪt] einladen I

Irish ['aɪrɪʃ] irisch; Irisch III U5, 94

is [ɪz] ist I
    … is 99p [ɪz ˌnaɪntiˌnaɪn 'pens] … kostet 99 Pence I
    is something wrong [ɪz 'sʌmθɪŋ rɒŋ] stimmt etwas nicht II

island ['aɪlənd] Insel II

isn't it? ['ɪznt‿ɪt] nicht wahr?; stimmt's? II

it [ɪt] es I
    it isn't up to you [ɪt‿ɪznt‿ʌp tə 'ju:] es ist nicht deine Sache <III U1, 17>
    It was my fault. [ɪt wəz ˌmaɪ 'fɔ:lt] Es war meine Schuld. II
    It's me! [ɪts 'mi:] Ich bin es! I
    It's time to go. [ɪts ˌtaɪm tə 'gəʊ] Es ist Zeit zu gehen. I

IT (Information Technology) [ˌaɪ'ti:] Informatik; Informationstechnik I

its [ɪts] sein; ihr III U3, 52

itself [ɪt'self] (sich) selbst III U2, 152

J

jacket ['dʒækɪt] Jacke II
    jacket potato [ˌdʒækɪt pə'teɪtəʊ] Ofenkartoffel II

jam [dʒæm] Marmelade; Konfitüre III U4, 80

Jamaican [dʒə'meɪkən] jamaikanisch II

January ['dʒænjuri] Januar I

jar [dʒɑ:] Glas III U4, 80

javelin ['dʒævlɪn] Speerwerfen <III U2, 186>

jealous ['dʒeləs] eifersüchtig; neidisch II

jeans (pl) [dʒi:nz] Jeans I

jerk [dʒɜ:k] in Gewürzen mariniertes und über Holzfeuer gegrilltes Essen II

jeweller's ['dʒu:ələz] Juwelierladen III U1, 13

jewellery ['dʒu:əlri] Schmuck II

job [dʒɒb] Job; Aufgabe; Tätigkeit; Arbeit; Beruf II

jogging ['dʒɒgɪŋ] Joggen <III U2, 186>

to join [dʒɔɪn] Mitglied werden in <III U2, 129>; sich anschließen III U5, 96

joke [dʒəʊk] Witz I

journey ['dʒɜ:ni] Fahrt; Reise III U5, 100

to joust [dʒaʊst] einen Turnierzweikampf austragen; turnieren III U2, 43

jousting ['dʒaʊstɪŋ] Turnierzweikampf III U2, 43

judge [dʒʌdʒ] Juror; Jurorin II

to judge [dʒʌdʒ] beurteilen; bewerten <III U4, 77>

juice [dʒu:s] Saft II

July [dʒʊ'laɪ] Juli I
    on 7th July [ɒn ðə ˌsevnθ əv 'dʒʊlaɪ] am 7. Juli I

jumble sale ['dʒʌmbl ˌseɪl] Flohmarkt II

high jump ['haɪ ˌdʒʌmp] Hochsprung <III U2, 186>
    long jump ['lɒŋ ˌdʒʌmp] Weitsprung <III U2, 186>

to jump [dʒʌmp] zusammenzucken; erschrecken III U2, 42

June [dʒu:n] Juni I

just [dʒʌst] gerade (eben); soeben; nur II

K

kayak [ˈkaɪæk] Kajak <III U2, 128>

kayaking [ˈkaɪækɪŋ] Kajakfahren <III U2, 128>

*to **keep** [kiːp] halten II
  to keep cool [ˌkiːp ˈkuːl] Ruhe bewahren <III U1, 27>
  to keep in touch [ˌkiːp ɪn ˈtʌtʃ] in Verbindung bleiben II
  to keep out [ˌkiːpˈaʊt] draußen halten III U3, 62

kept [kept] simple past, past participle von *to keep* II

ketchup [ˈketʃʌp] Ketchup II

kid [kɪd] Kind II

to kill [kɪl] töten III U1, 20

7 kilograms a day [ˌkɪləgræmz ə ˈdeɪ] sieben Kilogramm täglich I

40 kilometres an hour [kɪˈlɒmiːtəz ən ˈaʊə] 40 Kilometer pro Stunde I

kilt [kɪlt] Schottenrock; Kilt III U3, 53

king [kɪŋ] König III U1, 11

kiss [kɪs] Kuss II

kitchen [ˈkɪtʃɪn] Küche I

knee [niː] Knie III U2, 39

knife *(sg)* [naɪf], **knives** *(pl)* [naɪvz] Messer II

knight [naɪt] Ritter III U2, 42

*to **know** [nəʊ] kennen; wissen I
  to get to know [ˌget tə ˈnəʊ] kennen lernen II
  I don't know! [ˌaɪ dəʊnt ˈnəʊ] Ich weiß (es) nicht! I

L

to label [ˈleɪbl] beschriften <III U2, 43>

lace [leɪs] Schnürsenkel <III U1, 17>

ladder [ˈlædə] Leiter I

laid [leɪd] simple past, past participle von *to lay* II

lake [leɪk] See III U3, 53

lamb [læm] Lamm II

lamp [læmp] Lampe I

land [lænd] Land II

landlord [ˈlændlɔːd] Eigentümer II

language [ˈlæŋgwɪdʒ] Sprache II

language tip [ˌlæŋgwɪdʒ ˈtɪp] Grammatikhinweis <I>

sign language [ˈsaɪn ˌlæŋgwɪdʒ] Gebärdensprache; Zeichensprache III U5, 95

large [lɑːdʒ] groß II

lasagne [ləˈzænjə] Lasagne II

last [lɑːst] letzte I
  at last [ət ˈlɑːst] endlich; zu guter Letzt II

late [leɪt] (zu) spät II

later [ˈleɪtə] später I

to laugh [lɑːf] lachen II
  LOL (Laugh out loud!) [ˈlɑːf aʊt ˌlaʊd] Laut lachen! II

laundry basket [ˈlɔːndri ˌbɑːskɪt] Wäschekorb <III U4, 86>

*to **lay** [leɪ] decken; legen II
  to lay the table [ˌleɪ ðə ˈteɪbl] den Tisch decken II

*to **lead** [liːd] anführen; leiten <III U2, 129>

leader [ˈliːdə] Führer; Führerin; Anführer; Anführerin III U3, 65

to learn [lɜːn] lernen II
  to learn about sth [ˌlɜːn əˈbaʊt] etwas erfahren über III U1, 12

leather [ˈleðə] Leder III U3, 55

leave [liːv] abfahren; verlassen; lassen II

leaving [ˈliːvɪŋ] Abschieds- II

left [left] simple past, past participle von *to leave* II

left [left] links III U1, 12
  to turn left (into …) [ˌtɜːn ˈleft] (nach) links abbiegen I
  on the left [ɒn ðə ˈleft] auf der linken Seite; links I

leg [leg] Bein II

legend [ˈledʒənd] Legende; Sage <III U3, 130>

lemon [ˈlemən] Zitrone II

lemonade [ˌleməˈneɪd] Limonade II

*to **lend** [lend] leihen; verleihen II

lent [lent] simple past von *to lend* II

less [les] weniger III U4, 80

lesson [ˈlesn] Schulstunde; Unterricht I

*to **let** go [ˌlet ˈgəʊ] loslassen <III U3, 131>
  let us [ˈlet ʌs] lass(t) uns <III U2, 44>
  let's (= let us) [lets] lass(t) uns I

letter [ˈletə] Buchstabe; Brief III U4, 80

lettuce [ˈletɪs] Kopfsalat II

library [ˈlaɪbri] Bibliothek; Bücherei III U1, 15

life *(sg)* [laɪf], **lives** *(pl)* [laɪvz] Leben I

school life [ˈskuːˌlaɪf] Schulalltag <I>

lifeboat [ˈlaɪfbəʊt] Rettungsboot III U2, 33

light [laɪt] Licht <III U1, 17>
  light bulb [ˈlaɪt ˌbʌlb] Glühbirne III U3, 57
  traffic light [ˈtræfɪk ˌlaɪt] (Verkehrs-)Ampel <III U1, 178>

*to **light** up [ˌlaɪt ˈʌp] (sich) erhellen; anzünden <III U5, 101>

light [laɪt] leicht; hell <III U3, 193>

to like [laɪk] mögen; gern haben I
  would like [wəd ˈlaɪk] würde(n) gern; hätte(n) gern II
  I don't like [aɪ ˌdəʊnt ˈlaɪk] ich mag nicht; gefällt mir nicht I
  I like [aɪ ˈlaɪk] ich mag; gefällt mir I
  I wouldn't like (to) … [aɪ ˈwʊdnt laɪk (tə)] ich möchte nicht …; ich würde nicht gerne … I
  I'd like (to) … (= I would like to) [aɪd ˈlaɪk (tə)] ich möchte …; ich würde gerne … I
  Would you like (to)…? [wʊd jə ˈlaɪk (tə)] Möchtest du? I

like [laɪk] wie II
  like that [laɪk ˈðæt] so I
  like this [laɪk ˈðɪs] so; auf diese Weise III U3, 62
  What must you be like? [wɒt ˌmʌst ju ˈbiː laɪk] Wie musst du sein? III U2, 37

line [laɪn] Zeile <I>; Linie III U5, 100

lines [laɪnz] Text II

lion [ˈlaɪən] Löwe I

list [lɪst] Liste II
  shopping list [ˈʃɒpɪŋ ˌlɪst] Einkaufszettel I

list

to **listen** (to) ['lɪsn (tə)] hören; anhören; zuhören I

listening ['lɪsnɪŋ] Hörverstehen <I>
listening skills ['lɪsnɪŋ ˌskɪlz] Fertigkeit Hören <I>

little ['lɪtl] klein II
a little [ə 'lɪtl] ein bisschen II

to **live** [lɪv] wohnen; leben I

liver ['lɪvə] Leber <III U3, 66>

living room ['lɪvɪŋ ˌrʊm] Wohnzimmer I

loaf (sg) [ləʊf], **loaves** (pl) [ləʊvz] Brotlaib III U4, 80

local ['ləʊkl] hiesig; örtlich; lokal III U3, 58

location [ləʊ'keɪʃn] Drehort; Lage III U2, 50

LOL (Laugh out loud!) ['laf aʊt ˌlaʊd] Laut lachen! II

lonely ['ləʊnli] einsam III U4, 76

long [lɒŋ] lang I
long jump ['lɒŋ ˌdʒʌmp] Weitsprung <III U2, 186>

*to have a **look** [ˌhæv ə 'lʊk] anschauen II

to **look** [lʊk] (nach)schauen I; aussehen; sehen II
to look after [ˌlʊk 'ɑːftə] aufpassen; hüten II
to look at ['lʊk ˌət] anschauen I
to look for ['lʊk ˌfə] suchen I
Well, look … [wel 'lʊk] Na ja, schau mal … nach. I

lookout point ['lʊkaʊt ˌpɔɪnt] Aussichtspunkt II

loose [luːs] locker; lose II

lorry driver ['lɒri ˌdraɪvə] LKW-Fahrer; LKW-Fahrerin II

*to **lose** [luːz] verlieren II

lost [lɒst] simple past von to lose II; past participle von to lose III U3, 62

a **lot** [ə'lɒt] viel I; sehr II
a lot of [ə 'lɒt ˌəv] eine Menge; viel I; viel; eine Menge III U1, 16

body **lotion** ['bɒdi ˌləʊʃn] Körperlotion III U5, 97

lots [lɒts] viel; jede Menge III U2, 43
lots of ['lɒts ˌəv] viel; jede Menge I

loud [laʊd] laut III U2, 35

*to fall in **love** (with) [ˌfɔːl ɪn 'lʌv] sich verlieben (in) III U2, 50

to **love** [lʌv] lieben; gern mögen I

lovely ['lʌvli] schön; herrlich; hübsch II

low [ləʊ] niedrig II

lower ['ləʊə] untere III U4, 92

*to be **lucky** [bi: 'lʌki] Glück haben <III U3, 72>
lucky day [ˌlʌki 'deɪ] Glückstag II

luminous ['luːmɪnəs] leuchtend <III U5, 101>

lunch [lʌnʃ] Mittagessen I
packed lunch [ˌpækt 'lʌnʃ] Lunchpaket; Vesper II

lunchtime ['lʌnʃtaɪm] Mittagszeit; Mittagspause I

lung [lʌŋ] Lunge <III U3, 66>

lyrics ['lɪrɪks] Liedtext <II>

M

machine [mə'ʃiːn] Automat; Maschine II
payment machine ['peɪmənt ˌməʃiːn] Bezahlautomat II

made [meɪd] past participle von to make II
to be made of [bi: 'meɪd əv] hergestellt sein aus III U3, 54

magazine [ˌmægə'ziːn] Zeitschrift I

magic ['mædʒɪk] Magie; Zauberei II

magical ['mædʒɪkl] zauberhaft; magisch <III U3, 68>

main [meɪn] Haupt- <III U4, 88>
main course [ˌmeɪn 'kɔːs] Hauptgericht II

*to **make** [meɪk] erstellen; machen; tun I
to make a reservation [ˌmeɪk ə ˌrezə'veɪʃn] reservieren III U3, 59
to make friends [ˌmeɪk 'frendz] Freundschaften schließen I
to make sb feel like sth [ˌmeɪk … 'fiːl laɪk] jmdm. das Gefühl geben, etw. zu sein III U2, 43

it's made with [ˌɪts 'meɪd wɪð] es wird aus gemacht II

film **maker** ['fɪlm ˌmeɪkə] Filmemacher; Filmemacherin <III U5, 107>

mama ['mæmə] Mama II

man (sg) [mæn], **men** (pl) [men] Mann I

many ['meni] viele II
how many [haʊ 'meni] wie viele II

map [mæp] Stadtplan; Landkarte I

March [mɑːtʃ] März I

market ['mɑːkɪt] Markt II

*to get **married** [ˌget 'mærɪd] heiraten II

mashed potatoes [ˌmæʃt pə'teɪtəʊz] Kartoffelbrei II

to **match** [mætʃ] zuordnen I

material [mə'tɪəriəl] Material; Stoff <III U3, 55>

Maths [mæθs] Mathe I

It doesn't **matter**. [ɪt ˌdʌznt 'mætə] Es ist egal. II

won't **matter** [ˌwəʊnt 'mætə] wird nicht von Bedeutung sein; wird nichts ausmachen <III U5, 101>

May [meɪ] Mai I

may [meɪ] vielleicht; dürfen; können II

maybe ['meɪbi] vielleicht II

mayonnaise [ˌmeɪə'neɪz] Mayonnaise II

me [miː] ich; mich; mir I
Excuse me. [ɪk'skjuːz mi] Entschuldigung. I
call me ['kɔːl ˌmi] nenne mich I
It's me! [ɪts 'miː] Ich bin es! I

meal [miːl] Essen; Mahlzeit II

*to **mean** [miːn] bedeuten; meinen III U2, 33

meaning ['miːnɪŋ] Bedeutung; Sinn <III U3, 73>

meant [ment] simple past, past participle von to mean III U2, 33

meat [miːt] Fleisch I

mechanic [mə'kænɪk] Mechaniker; Mechanikerin <III U3, 68>

mediation [ˌmiːdi'eɪʃn] Sprachmittlung <I>

mediation skills [ˌmiːdiˈeɪʃn ˌskɪlz] Fertigkeit Sprachmitteln <I>

medicine [ˈmedsn] Medikamente; Medizin III U2, 39

*to **meet** [miːt] kennen lernen I; (sich) treffen II

meeting [ˈmiːtɪŋ] Treffen; Treff- <III U1, 30>

meeting point [ˈmiːtɪŋ ˌpɔɪnt] Treffpunkt <III U1, 30>

member [ˈmembə] Mitglied <III U1, 30>; <III U2, 128>

menu [ˈmenjuː] Speisekarte II

mess [mes] Unordnung; Durcheinander I

message [ˈmesɪdʒ] Nachricht; SMS II; Botschaft <III U3, 69>

text message [ˈtekst ˌmesɪdʒ] Textnachricht (SMS) I

met [met] simple past von *to meet* I

metal [ˈmetl] Metall III U3, 54

metre [ˈmiːtə] Meter I

microwave [ˈmaɪkrəweɪv] Mikrowelle II

middle [ˈmɪdl] Mitte III U4, 92

in the middle [ɪn ðə ˈmɪdl] in der Mitte III U4, 92

midnight [ˈmɪdnaɪt] Mitternacht III U4, 84

mild [maɪld] mild I

mile [maɪl] Meile II

milk [mɪlk] Milch II

milkshake [ˈmɪlkˌʃeɪk] Milchmischgetränk; Milchshake III U4, 76

million [ˈmɪljən] Million III U1, 11

half a million [ˌhaːf ə ˈmɪljən] eine halbe Million III U1, 16

mind [maɪnd] Geist; Verstand <III U1, 17>

mind map [ˈmaɪnd ˌmæp] Wörternetz <III U4, 88>

Never mind. [ˌnevə ˈmaɪnd] Macht nichts.; Schon gut.; Mach dir nichts draus. II

mine [maɪn] Bergwerk III U1, 16

mine [maɪn] meins; meine II

of mine [əv ˈmaɪn] von mir II

miner [ˈmaɪnə] Bergarbeiter; Bergarbeiterin III U1, 20

mineral water [ˈmɪnrl ˌwɔːtə] Mineralwasser III U4, 81

prime minister [ˌpraɪm ˈmɪnɪstə] Premierminister; Ministerpräsident; Ministerpräsidentin; Premierministerin <III U5, 135>

minute [ˈmɪnɪt] Minute II

mirror [ˈmɪrə] Spiegel <III U3, 193>; III U5, 97

miserable [ˈmɪzrəbl] elend; armselig; jämmerlich III U5, 105

*to give sth a **miss** [ˌgɪv sʌmθɪŋ ə ˈmɪs] auf etw. verzichten; etw. bleiben lassen III U2, 50

to miss [mɪs] vermissen II

to mix [mɪks] mischen <III U2, 46>

mixed [mɪkst] gemischt <III U4, 133>

mobile (phone) [ˈməʊbaɪl (ˌfəʊn)] Handy I

modern [ˈmɒdn] modern I

moment [ˈməʊmənt] Moment; Augenblick II

Monday [ˈmʌndeɪ] Montag I

money [ˈmʌni] Geld I

monkey [ˈmʌŋki] Affe I

monster [ˈmɒnstə] Ungeheuer; Monster III U3, 58

month [mʌnθ] Monat I

monthly [ˈmʌnθli] monatlich III U5, 101

monument [ˈmɒnjəmənt] Denkmal II

moon [muːn] Mond <III U5, 101>

moped [ˈməʊped] Moped <III U5, 207>

more [mɔː] mehr <I>; mehr II

once more [ˈwʌns ˌmɔː] noch einmal II

morning [ˈmɔːnɪŋ] Morgen; Vormittag I

Good morning. [ˌgʊd ˈmɔːnɪŋ] Guten Morgen. II

mosque [mɒsk] Moschee II

most [məʊst] die meisten; die Mehrheit <III U1, 127>

the most famous [ðə ˈməʊst ˌfeɪməs] der berühmteste II

mother [ˈmʌðə] Mutter I

motorbike [ˈməʊtəbaɪk] Motorrad I

mountain [ˈmaʊntɪn] Berg III U1, 17

mouse *(sg)* [maʊs], **mice** *(pl)* [maɪs] Maus I

moussaka [muˈsaːkə] Moussaka II

mouth [maʊθ] Mund II

move [muːv] Bewegung III U5, 100

to move [muːv] (sich) bewegen III U2, 39

to move (house) [muːv] umziehen II

movie [ˈmuːvi] Film I

Mr [ˈmɪstə] Herr *(Anrede)* I

Mrs [ˈmɪsɪz] Frau *(Anrede)* I

Ms [mɪz] Frau *(Anrede)* I

much [mʌtʃ] viel I

so much [ˌsəʊ ˈmʌtʃ] so sehr III U4, 76

too much [tu: ˈmʌtʃ] zu sehr II

How much (is/are) …? [ˌhaʊ ˈmʌtʃ ɪz/aː] Wie viel (kostet/kosten) …? I

mud [mʌd] Schlamm; Matsch I

stuck in the mud [ˌstʌk ɪn ðə ˈmʌd] im Schlamm festgesteckt I

mum [mʌm] Mama; Mutti I

mural [ˈmjʊərəl] Wandgemälde III U4, 74

murderer [ˈmɜːdrə] Mörder; Mörderin III U2, 50

museum [mjuːˈziːəm] Museum II

music [ˈmjuːzɪk] Musik I

musical [ˈmjuːzɪkl] Musical <III U3, 73>

musical [ˈmjuːzɪkl] Musik-; musikalisch III U5, 95

Muslim [ˈmʊzlɪm] Muslim; Muslimin I

must not/never [ˌmʌst ˈnɒt/ˈnevə] nicht/nie dürfen III U3, 63

must [mʌst] müssen I

mustard [ˈmʌstəd] Senf II

mustn't [ˈmʌsnt] nicht dürfen III U5, 100

my [maɪ] mein I

My name is … [maɪ ˈneɪm ɪz] Ich heiße … I

myself [maɪˈself] selbst; selber III U2, 34

mystery [ˈmɪstri] Rätsel; Geheimnis I

N

to **nag** [næg] nörgeln; meckern
III U4, 76

nail [neɪl] Nagel III U5, 97

nail scissors [ˈneɪl ˌsɪzəz] Nagelschere III U5, 97

name [neɪm] Name I

first name [ˌfɜːst ˈneɪm] Vorname
<III U1, 127>

My name is … [maɪ ˈneɪm ˌɪz] Ich
heiße … I

napkin [ˈnæpkɪn] Serviette II

narrator [nəˈreɪtə] Erzähler; Erzählerin I

national [ˈnæʃnl] National-; national
III U5, 104

nature [ˈneɪtʃə] Natur III U3, 53

naughty [ˈnɔːti] frech; böse III U2, 43

near [nɪə] nah III U1, 15

near [nɪə] in der Nähe von I

to **need** [niːd] brauchen II

needn't [ˈniːdnt] nicht brauchen;
nicht müssen I

with special **needs** [wɪθ ˌspeʃl ˈniːdz]
mit Behinderung; mit besonderen
Bedürfnissen III U5, 95

neighbour [ˈneɪbə] Nachbar; Nachbarin III U3, 67

nervous [ˈnɜːvəs] nervös; aufgeregt II

netball [ˈnetbɔːl] Korbball I

never [ˈnevə] nie; niemals I

Never mind. [ˌnevə ˈmaɪnd] Macht
nichts.; Schon gut.; Mach dir nichts
draus. II

new [njuː] neu I

news [njuːz] Neuigkeit(en);
Nachricht(en) II

newsagent's [ˈnjuːzˌeɪdʒnts] Zeitschriftenladen III U1, 13

newspaper [ˈnjuːsˌpeɪpə] Zeitung <I>

next [nekst] nächste I

next to [ˈnekst tə] neben I

next [nekst] als Nächstes II

nice [naɪs] nett; schön I; lecker; gut
III U3, 58

Nice to meet you. [ˌnaɪs tə ˈmiːt juː]
Nett, dich kennen zu lernen. I

nickname [ˈnɪkneɪm] Spitzname
<III U1, 127>

niece [niːs] Nichte III U4, 80

night [naɪt] Nacht I

night walk [ˈnaɪt wɔːk] Nachtwanderung I

nine [naɪn] neun I

nineteen [ˌnaɪnˈtiːn] neunzehn I

ninety [ˈnaɪnti] neunzig I

no [nəʊ] kein; keine; nein I

no one [ˈnəʊ wʌn] niemand I

No way! [ˌnəʊ ˈweɪ] Auf keinen
Fall!; Was?!; Echt?! III U3, 58

no vacancies [ˌnəʊ ˈveɪknsɪz] kein
Zimmer frei <III U4, 86>

nobody [ˈnəʊbədi] niemand III U3, 58

noise [nɔɪz] Geräusch I

noisy [ˈnɔɪzi] laut III U1, 16

non [nɒn] nicht <III U4, 86>

Norman [ˈnɔːmən] Normanne; Normannin III U1, 11

the **Normans** [ðə ˈnɔːmənz] die Normannen III U1, 11

Norman [ˈnɔːmən] normannisch
<III U1, 126>

north [nɔːθ] Norden III U1, 10

northbound [ˈnɔːθbaʊnd] in Richtung
Norden <III U5, 207>

northwest [ˌnɔːθˈwest] Nordwesten
III U1, 16

northwest of [ˌnɔːθˈwest əv] nordwestlich III U4, 75

nose [nəʊz] Nase I

not [nɒt] nicht I

not … any [ˌnɒt … eni] kein II

not … any more [ˌnɒt … eni ˈmɔː]
nicht mehr III U4, 76

not … either [ˌnɒt … ˈaɪðə] auch
nicht III U3, 58

not … yet [ˌnɒt … ˈjet] noch nicht II

note [nəʊt] Geldschein II

***to take notes** [ˌteɪk ˈnəʊts] sich Noti-
zen machen I

nothing [ˈnʌθɪŋ] nichts III U1, 21

noun [naʊn] Nomen; Hauptwort <I>

November [nəˈvembə] November I

now [naʊ] jetzt; nun I; heutzutage II

right now [ˌraɪt ˈnaʊ] gerade; jetzt
gleich; sofort III U5, 98

nowadays [ˈnaʊədeɪz] heutzutage
<III U1, 24>

number [ˈnʌmbə] Nummer; Zahl I

phone number [ˈfəʊn ˌnʌmbə]
Telefonnummer III U2, 38

nurse [nɜːs] Krankenschwester; Krankenpfleger II

nut [nʌt] Nuss I

O

o'clock [əˈklɒk] Uhr *(Zeitangabe bei
vollen Stunden)* I

oat [əʊt] Hafer III U3, 53

oatmeal [ˈəʊtmiːl] Haferflocken
<III U3, 66>

object [ˈɒbdʒɪkt] Objekt; Gegenstand
<III U5, 105>

October [ɒkˈtəʊbə] Oktober I

the **odd** one out [ˌɒd wʌn ˈaʊt] das
Wort, das nicht in die Gruppe
passt <III U5, 101>

a photo **of** [ə ˈfəʊtəʊ əv] ein Foto
von I

to be made of [biː ˈmeɪd əv] hergestellt sein aus III U3, 54

of course [əv ˈkɔːs] natürlich;
selbstverständlich II

of mine [əv ˈmaɪn] von mir II

offer [ˈɒfə] Angebot <III U3, 68>

special offer [ˌspeʃl ˈɒfə] Sonderangebot III U4, 80

office [ˈɒfɪs] Büro II

post office [ˈpəʊst ˌɒfɪs] Postamt I

police **officer** [pəˈliːs ˌɒfɪsə] Polizeibeamter; Polizeibeamtin I

often [ˈɒfn] oft; häufig I

oh [əʊ] null *(bei Uhrzeiten und Tele-
fonnummern)* I

oh dear [ˌəʊ ˈdɪə] oje III U4, 80

oil [ɔɪl] Öl <III U3, 66>

OK [əʊˈkeɪ] okay I

old [əʊld] alt I

How old are you? [haʊ ˈəʊld ə juː]
Wie alt bist du? I

on [ɒn] auf; an; am I

on board ['ɒn bɔ:d] an Bord
III U4, 84

on duty [ɒn 'dju:ti] im Dienst
<III U3, 68>

on time [ɒn 'taɪm] pünktlich
III U5, 100

on weekdays [ɒn 'wi:kdeɪz] unter
der Woche; an Werktagen III U5, 96

to try on [ˌtraɪ 'ɒn] anprobieren II

on purpose [ɒn 'pɜ:pəs] absichtlich
II

on Saturdays [ɒn 'sætədeɪz] samstags I

on 7th July [ɒn ðə ˌsevnθ əv 'dʒʊlaɪ]
am 7. Juli I

on the bus [ɒn ðə 'bʌs] im Bus II

on the left [ɒn ðə 'left] auf der
linken Seite; links I

on the right [ɒn ðə 'raɪt] auf der
rechten Seite; rechts I

on Tuesday [ˌɒn 'tju:zdeɪ] am
Dienstag I

once [wʌns] einst; einmal III U5, 105
once more ['wʌns ˌmɔ:] noch
einmal II

one [wʌn] eins I
a/one hundred ['hʌndrəd] einhundert; hundert I
no one ['nəʊ wʌn] niemand I
one day [wʌn 'deɪ] eines Tages
III U1, 21

one(s) [wʌn(z)] Platzhalter für ein
Nomen III U4, 80
the blue one [ðə 'blu: ˌwʌn] der
blaue II

to help oneself [ˌhelp wʌn'self] sich
bedienen III U5, 96

onion ['ʌnjən] Zwiebel II

online [ɒn'laɪn] online II

only ['əʊnli] einzige II; nur; bloß; erst
III U1, 16

to open ['əʊpn] öffnen; aufmachen I

operation [ˌɒpr'eɪʃn] Operation
III U2, 39

operator ['ɒpreɪtə] Vermittlung
III U2, 38

opinion [ə'pɪnjən] Meinung III U2, 50

opposite ['ɒpəzɪt] gegenüber I;
Gegenteil <II>

optimistic [ˌɒptɪ'mɪstɪk] optimistisch
III U4, 77

or [ɔ:] oder I

orange ['ɒrɪndʒ] orange; Orange I

orchestra ['ɔ:kɪstrə] Orchester
III U5, 94

order ['ɔ:də] Reihenfolge <III U2, 47>

to order ['ɔ:də] bestellen II

ordinal number [ˌɔ:dɪnəl 'nʌmbə]
Ordinalzahl I

to organize ['ɔ:gənaɪz] organisieren II

other ['ʌðə] andere I
each other [i:tʃ'ʌðə] einander;
sich; sich gegenseitig III U2, 34

others ['ʌðəz] anderen II

our [aʊə] unser I

ours [aʊəz] unsere III U5, 96

ourselves [ˌaʊə'selvz] selber; selbst
III U2, 152

out [aʊt] heraus II
to keep out [ki:p 'aʊt] draußen
halten III U3, 62

out and about [ˌaʊt ən ə'baʊt] unterwegs I
out of ['aʊt əv] aus … heraus I

outdoor [aʊt'dɔ:] Freiluft-; Outdoor-
III U2, 34

outfit ['aʊtfɪt] Outfit; Kleidung
III U5, 105

outline Skizze; Kontur; Überblick
<III U5, 105>

outside [aʊt'saɪd] draußen; im Freien
III U3, 58

over ['əʊvə] über <III U4, 93>
over there [ˌəʊvə 'ðeə] da drüben;
dort drüben II

to own [əʊn] besitzen II

own [əʊn] eigene <I>; eigene II

P

p.m. [ˌpi:'em] nachmittags II

to pack [pæk] packen; einpacken II
to pack up [ˌpæk 'ʌp] packen;
einpacken II

packed lunch [ˌpækt 'lʌnʃ] Lunchpaket; Vesper II

a packet of ['pækɪt] eine Packung …;
eine Tüte … I

paddle ['pædl] Paddel <III U2, 186>

paid [peɪd] simple past, past participle von to pay II

to paint [peɪnt] streichen; anmalen;
malen II

pair [peə] Paar <III U2, 41>
a pair of [ə 'peər əv] ein Paar II

palace ['pælɪs] Palast <III U1, 30>

pancake ['pænkeɪk] Pfannkuchen II

to panic ['pænɪk] panisch werden II

pantomime ['pæntəmaɪm] Weihnachtstheaterstück II

paper ['peɪpə] Papier III U3, 55

parade [pə'reɪd] Parade; Umzug
III U5, 104

paragraph ['pærəgra:f] Paragraph;
Absatz <III U5, 104>

Pardon? ['pa:dn] Wie bitte? I

parents (pl) ['peərnts] Eltern II

park [pa:k] Park I
theme park ['θi:m ˌpa:k] Freizeitpark I

part [pa:t] Rolle; Teil II
to take part (in) [teɪk 'pa:t] teilnehmen (an) III U5, 100

partner ['pa:tnə] Partner; Partnerin
III U5, 99

party ['pa:ti] Party; Feier I

to pass [pa:s] reichen II

passenger ['pæsndʒə] Passagier;
Passagierin II

passport ['pa:spɔ:t] (Reise-)Pass
<III U5, 206>

simple past [ˌsɪmpl 'pa:st] einfache
Vergangenheit <III U2, 41>

past [pa:st] Vergangenheit III U1, 16

past [pa:st] nach (bei Uhrzeitangaben) I; vorbei (an) III U1, 12
half past (two) [ha:f 'pa:st] halb
(drei) I

pasta ['pæstə] Pasta; Nudeln II
pasta bake ['pæstə 'beɪk] Nudelauflauf II

to paste [peɪst] einfügen II

paste

pasty ['pæsti] Pastete II

patient ['peɪʃnt] Patient; Patientin II

patient ['peɪʃnt] geduldig III U2, 35

patron saint [ˌpeɪtrn 'seɪnt] Schutzheiliger; Schutzheilige <III U5, 134>

patterned ['pætənd] gemustert II

***to pay** [peɪ] bezahlen II

to **pay back** [ˌpeɪ 'bæk] zurückzahlen II

to **pay the bill** [ˌpeɪ ðə 'bɪl] die Rechnung bezahlen III U3, 59

pay phone ['peɪ fəʊn] Münztelefon III U3, 67

payment machine ['peɪmənt ˌməʃiːn] Bezahlautomat II

PE (Physical Education) [ˌpiːˈiː, ˌfɪzɪkl edʒʊˈkeɪʃn] Sportunterricht I

peace [piːs] Frieden III U3, 65

peach [piːtʃ] Pfirsich I

peanut butter [ˌpiːnʌt 'bʌtə] Erdnussbutter III U4, 81

pen [pen] Füller; Stift I

pence *(pl)* [pens], **penny** *(sg)* ['peni] Pence *(brit. Währungseinheit)* I

… is 99p [ɪz ˌnaɪntinaɪn 'pens] … kostet 99 Pence I

pencil ['pensl] Bleistift I

pencil case ['pensl ˌkeɪs] Federmäppchen I

pencil sharpener ['pensl ˌʃɑːpnə] Anspitzer I

penguin ['peŋgwɪn] Pinguin I

people ['piːpl] Leute; Menschen I; Volk <III U5, 134>

pepper ['pepə] Pfeffer II

per [pɜː] pro <III U2, 128>

percent (%) [pəˈsent] Prozent <III U4, 86>

present **perfect** [ˌpreznt 'pɜːfɪkt] das Perfekt <III U2, 41>

perfume ['pɜːfjuːm] Parfüm III U5, 97

person ['pɜːsn] Person; Mensch II

personal ['pɜːsnl] persönlich III U5, 97

pet [pet] Haustier I

pet shop ['pet ʃɒp] Tierhandlung III U1, 13

petrol ['petrl] Benzin <III U3, 68>

Phew! [fjuː] Puh! III U4, 75

mobile (phone) ['məʊbaɪl (ˌfəʊn)] Handy I

phone [fəʊn] Telefon II

to answer the phone [ˌɑːnsə ðə 'fəʊn] ans Telefon gehen III U2, 45

pay phone ['peɪ fəʊn] Münztelefon III U3, 67

phone call ['fəʊn ˌkɔːl] Telefonanruf I

phone number ['fəʊn ˌnʌmbə] Telefonnummer III U2, 38

to **phone** [fəʊn] anrufen; telefonieren I

photo ['fəʊtəʊ] Foto I

to take a photo [ˌteɪk ə 'fəʊtəʊ] ein Foto machen I

phrase [freɪz] Ausdruck <III U1, 17>; Redewendung; Satz <III U4, 79>

to **pick up** [pɪk ˈʌp] aufheben III U1, 22

picnic ['pɪknɪk] Picknick I

picture ['pɪktʃə] Bild I

pie [paɪ] Kuchen; Pastete II

piece [piːs] Stück II

pierogi [pjɜːˈrɒgi] Pirogge II

pig [pɪg] Schwein <III U1, 127>

pinch [pɪntʃ] Prise II

pineapple ['paɪnæpl] Ananas III U5, 107

pink [pɪŋk] pink; rosa I

pipe [paɪp] Rohr III U3, 67

pirate ['paɪrət] Pirat; Piratin I

pizza ['piːtsə] Pizza I

place [pleɪs] Platz; Stelle; Ort I

to take place [ˌteɪk 'pleɪs] stattfinden <III U3, 130>; <III U4, 89>

plain [pleɪn] schlicht; einfach II

plan [plæn] Plan II

to **plan** [plæn] planen II

plane [pleɪn] Flugzeug II

plant [plɑːnt] Pflanze III U2, 33

plantain ['plæntɪn] Kochbanane II

plaster ['plɑːstə] Pflaster III U2, 39

plastic ['plæstɪk] Plastik; Kunststoff III U3, 54

plate [pleɪt] Teller II

play [pleɪ] Theaterstück II

to **play** [pleɪ] spielen I

player ['pleɪə] Spieler; Spielerin II

playground ['pleɪgraʊnd] Schulhof; Pausenhof; Spielplatz I

please [pliːz] bitte I

poem ['pəʊɪm] Gedicht III U5, 105

lookout **point** ['lʊkaʊt ˌpɔɪnt] Aussichtspunkt II

meeting point ['miːtɪŋ ˌpɔɪnt] Treffpunkt <III U1, 30>

starting point ['stɑːtɪŋ ˌpɔɪnt] Ausgangspunkt <III U5, 101>

poison ['pɔɪzn] Gift <III U2, 187>

pole [pəʊl] Pfahl; Stange <III U3, 130>

police [pəˈliːs] Polizei III U2, 38

police officer [pəˈliːs ˌɒfɪsə] Polizeibeamter; Polizeibeamtin I

polite [pəˈlaɪt] höflich II

swimming **pool** ['swɪmɪŋ ˌpuːl] Schwimmbad I

poor [pɔː] arm <III U5, 135>

popcorn ['pɒpkɔːn] Popcorn I

popular ['pɒpjələ] beliebt III U2, 33

pork [pɔːk] Schweinefleisch II

porridge ['pɒrɪdʒ] Haferbrei III U3, 53

positive ['pɒzətɪv] positiv III U4, 76

possessive pronoun [pəˈsesɪv ˌprəʊnaʊn] Possessivpronomen <III U5, 99>

post office ['pəʊst ˌɒfɪs] Postamt I

to **post** [pəʊst] aufgeben *(einen Brief)*; abschicken *(einen Brief)* III U4, 80

postcard ['pəʊstkɑːd] Postkarte I

poster ['pəʊstə] Poster I

postman ['pəʊsmən] Postbote <III U2, 129>

pot [pɒt] Topf III U5, 104

potato *(sg)* [pəˈteɪtəʊ], **potatoes** *(pl)* [pəˈteɪtəʊz] Kartoffel II

jacket potato [ˌdʒækɪt pəˈteɪtəʊ] Ofenkartoffel II

mashed potatoes [ˌmæʃt pəˈteɪtəʊz] Kartoffelbrei II

pound [paʊnd] Pfund *(brit. Währungseinheit)* I

practice ['præktɪs] Training; Übung I

to **practise** ['præktɪs] üben; trainieren III U5, 96

to **prefer** [prɪˈfɜ:] vorziehen II
  I prefer working [aɪ prɪˈfɜ: ˌwɜ:kɪŋ] ich arbeite lieber II
to **prepare** [prɪˈpeə] zubereiten; vorbereiten III U5, 96
present [ˈpreznt] Geschenk I
  present perfect [ˌpreznt ˈpɜ:fɪkt] das Perfekt <III U2, 41>
  present progressive [ˌpreznt prəˈgresɪv] Verlaufsform der Gegenwart <III U4, 93>
  simple present [ˌsɪmpl ˈpreznt] Gegenwart; Präsens <III U5, 98>
to **present** [prɪˈzent] präsentieren I
presentation [ˌpreznˈteɪʃn] Präsentation; Vortrag <III U5, 104>
presenter [prɪˈzentə] Moderator; Moderatorin <III U1, 26>
pretty [ˈprɪti] hübsch II
price [praɪs] Preis II
prime minister [ˌpraɪm ˈmɪnɪstə] Premierminister; Ministerpräsident; Ministerpräsidentin; Premierministerin <III U5, 135>
prison [ˈprɪzn] Gefängnis II
private [ˈpraɪvɪt] Privat-; privat <III U4, 86>
prize [praɪz] Preis II
probably [ˈprɒbəbli] wahrscheinlich III U4, 75
problem [ˈprɒbləm] Problem I
process [ˈprəʊses] Prozess <III U5, 135>
product [ˈprɒdʌkt] Produkt <III U3, 68>
profile [ˈprəʊfaɪl] Profil; Steckbrief <I>
present **progressive** [ˌpreznt prəˈgresɪv] Verlaufsform der Gegenwart <III U4, 93>
project [ˈprɒdʒekt] Projekt III U5, 98
prompt card [ˈprɒmt ˌka:d] Stichwortkarte <II>
possessive **pronoun** [pəˈsesɪv ˌprəʊnaʊn] Possessivpronomen <III U5, 99>
prop [prɒp] Requisit III U2, 45
to **protect** [prəˈtekt] schützen III U3, 53
Protestant [ˈprɒtɪstnt] Protestant; Protestantin; protestantisch III U4, 74

proud (of) [praʊd (əv)] stolz (auf) III U3, 65
pub [pʌb] Kneipe; Gasthaus III U5, 94
public transport [ˌpʌblɪk ˈtrænspɔ:t] öffentliche Verkehrsmittel III U5, 100
pudding [ˈpʊdɪŋ] Nachspeise; Pudding II
to **pull** [pʊl] ziehen I
purple [ˈpɜ:pl] lila; violett I
on **purpose** [ɒn ˈpɜ:pəs] absichtlich II
to **push** [pʊʃ] schieben I; schubsen; drängeln III U5, 102
*to **put** [pʊt] setzen; legen; stellen II
  to put in [ˌpʊtˈɪn] einsetzen I
  to put in the right order [ˌpʊtˌɪn ðə ˈraɪt ɔ:də] in die richtige Reihenfolge bringen I
  to put on [ˌpʊtˈɒn] anlegen; anziehen III U2, 39
  to put up [ˌpʊtˈʌp] hochhalten <III U2, 128>
  Put your hands up. [pʊt jɔ: ˌhændzˌˈʌp] Meldet euch. I
put [pʊt] simple past von to put II

Q

quarter past [ˈkwɔ:tə pa:st] Viertel nach I
  quarter to [ˈkwɔ:tə tə] Viertel vor I
queen [kwi:n] Königin III U1, 31
question [ˈkwestʃən] Frage I
queue [kju:] Warteschlange II
quick [kwɪk] schnell III U2, 34
quickly [ˈkwɪkli] schnell II
quiet [ˈkwaɪət] ruhig; leise; still III U1, 16
quite [kwaɪt] ziemlich; ganz; völlig III U2, 34

R

raccoon [rəˈku:n] Waschbär I
race [reɪs] Wettrennen; Rennen I
racket [ˈrækɪt] Schläger <III U2, 186>
radio [ˈreɪdiəʊ] Radio III U3, 67
rafting [ˈra:ftɪŋ] Rafting III U2, 33

to **rain** [reɪn] regnen I
rainbow [ˈreɪnbəʊ] Regenbogen III U5, 104
raincoat [ˈreɪnkəʊt] Regenmantel III U5, 97
ran [ræn] simple past von to run III U4, 75
rang [ræŋ] simple past von to ring II
rap [ræp] Rap <I>
to **rap** [ræp] rappen II
rapper [ˈræpə] Rapper; Rapperin III U5, 98
raspberry [ˈra:zbri] Himbeere III U4, 80
to **rate** [reɪt] bewerten; einstufen III U2, 51
I'd **rather** [aɪd ˈra:ðə] ich würde lieber III U1, 25
rating [ˈreɪtɪŋ] Bewertung <III U2, 51>
*to **read** [ri:d] lesen I
reading [ˈri:dɪŋ] Lesen <I>
  reading corner [ˈri:dɪŋ ˌkɔ:nə] Leseecke <I>
  reading skills [ˈri:dɪŋ ˌskɪlz] Fertigkeit Lesen <I>
ready [ˈredi] fertig; bereit I
  to get ready [get ˈredi] sich vorbereiten; sich fertig machen <III U1, 27>; <III U2, 44>
real [rɪəl] echt; richtig; wirklich II
really [ˈrɪəli] echt II
Really? [ˈrɪəli] Wirklich? I
reason [ˈri:zn] Grund III U2, 51
  to give reasons [gɪv ˈri:znz] Gründe nennen; Gründe angeben III U2, 51
receipt [riˈsi:t] Quittung II
recipe [ˈresɪpi] Rezept II
to **record** [rɪˈkɔ:d] aufnehmen <III U2, 43>
recording [rɪˈkɔ:dɪŋ] Aufnahme <III U2, 43>
recyclable [ˌri:ˈsaɪkləbl] wiederverwertbar; recycelbar <III U3, 193>
red [red] rot I
registration [ˌredʒɪˈstreɪʃn] Überprüfung der Anwesenheit I; Anmeldung II

registration

relaxed [rɪˈlækst] entspannt; locker; gelassen II

religion [rɪˈlɪdʒn] Religion <III U4, 132>

RE (Religious Education) [ˌɑːˈriː, rɪˌlɪdʒəsˌedʒʊˈkeɪʃn] Religionsunterricht I

to **remember** [rɪˈmembə] sich merken; sich erinnern (an) II

rent [rent] Miete II

to **rent** [rent] mieten III U3, 58

to **repair** [rɪˈpeə] reparieren III U3, 67

to **repeat** [rɪˈpiːt] wiederholen III U4, 80

report [rɪˈpɔːt] Bericht <I>

reporter [rɪˈpɔːtə] Reporter; Reporterin III U2, 42

republic [rɪˈpʌblɪk] Republik III U5, 94

are **required** [ˌɑː rɪˈkwaɪəd] werden gebeten <III U4, 86>

animal **rescue** shelter [ˈænɪml ˈreskjuːˌʃeltə] Tierheim I

rescue [ˈreskjuː] Rettung <III U2, 128>

to **rescue** [ˈreskjuː] retten <III U2, 128>

rescued [ˈreskjuːd] gerettet <III U2, 129>

reservation [ˌrezəˈveɪʃn] Reservierung III U3, 59

to make a reservation [ˌmeɪk ə ˈrezəveɪʃn] reservieren III U3, 59

to **rest** [rest] rasten; ausruhen; liegen II

restaurant [ˈrestrɒnt] Restaurant II

fast food restaurant [ˌfɑːst fuːd ˈrestrɒnt] Fastfood-Restaurant I

result [rɪˈzʌlt] Ergebnis II

return ticket [rɪˈtɜːn ˌtɪkɪt] Hin- und Rückfahrkarte III U5, 101

review [rɪˈvjuː] Kritik III U2, 50

Industrial **Revolution** [ɪnˌdʌstriəl revlˈuːʃn] industrielle Revolution III U1, 11

rice [raɪs] Reis II

rich [rɪtʃ] reich III U3, 54

ridden [ˈrɪdn] past participle von to ride II

ride [raɪd] Fahrt; Ritt II

*to **ride** [raɪd] fahren; reiten II

horse **riding** [ˈhɔːs ˌraɪdɪŋ] Reiten I

right [raɪt] richtig; korrekt I; rechts III U1, 12

all right [ɔːl ˈraɪt] in Ordnung; alles klar II

to be right [biː ˈraɪt] recht haben II

to do the right thing [duː ðə ˈraɪt θɪŋ] das Richtige tun III U2, 38

to turn right (into …) [ˌtɜːn ˈraɪt] rechts abbiegen I

on the right [ɒn ðə ˈraɪt] auf der rechten Seite; rechts I

You're right. [jɔː ˈraɪt] Du hast recht. I

right now [raɪt ˈnaʊ] gerade; jetzt gleich; sofort III U5, 98

*to **ring** [rɪŋ] läuten; klingeln II

river [ˈrɪvə] Fluss I

road [rəʊd] Straße I

rock [rɒk] Fels; Stein III U2, 38

rock climber [ˈrɒk ˌklaɪmə] Kletterer; Kletterin <III U3, 72>

rock climbing [ˈrɒk ˌklaɪmɪŋ] Klettern I

space **rocket** [ˈspeɪs ˌrɒkɪt] Raumschiff <III U1, 30>

rode [rəʊd] simple past von to ride II

role play [ˈrəʊl ˌpleɪ] Rollenspiel <II>

roller coaster [ˈrəʊlə ˌkəʊstə] Achterbahn II

the **Romans** [ðə ˈrəʊmənz] die Römer III U1, 10

romance [ˈrəʊmæns] Liebesgeschichte III U2, 51

roof [ruːf] Dach II

room [ruːm] Zimmer; Raum I

dining room [ˈdaɪnɪŋ ˌruːm] Esszimmer I

rope [rəʊp] Seil I

royal [ˈrɔɪəl] königlich II

rubber [ˈrʌbə] Gummi III U3, 55

rubbish [ˈrʌbɪʃ] Müll; Abfall II

rugby [ˈrʌɡbi] Rugby III U2, 34

to **ruin** [ˈruːɪn] ruinieren; zerstören II

rule [ruːl] Regel III U2, 34

ruler [ˈruːlə] Lineal I

run [rʌn] Lauf <III U2, 129>

*to **run** [rʌn] rennen; laufen I; betreiben; leiten; führen III U4, 75

to run away [ˌrʌn əˈweɪ] weglaufen III U2, 50

to run out of [ˌrʌn ˈaʊt əv] ausgehen *(Ware)* III U4, 81

run [rʌn] past participle von to run III U4, 75

rung [rʌŋ] past participle von to ring III U5, 96

to **rush** [rʌʃ] eilen; sich beeilen; stürzen III U5, 105

S

sad [sæd] traurig III U3, 65

safe [seɪf] sicher; ungefährlich III U2, 35

safety [ˈseɪfti] Sicherheit <III U2, 128>

said [sed] simple past von to say I

to **sail** [seɪl] segeln <III U1, 126>

patron **saint** [ˌpeɪtrn ˈseɪnt] Schutzheiliger; Schutzheilige <III U5, 134>

salad [ˈsæləd] Salat II

sale [seɪl] Schlussverkauf; Ausverkauf II; Verkauf <III U2, 129>

jumble sale [ˈdʒʌmbl ˌseɪl] Flohmarkt II

salt [sɔːlt] Salz II

the **same** [ðə ˈseɪm] derselbe; gleich II

sand [sænd] Sand II

sandal [ˈsændl] Sandale <III U2, 44>

sandwich [ˈsænwɪdʒ] Sandwich; belegtes Brot I

sang [sæŋ] simple past von to sing II

sank [sæŋk] simple past von to sink III U4, 84

on **Saturdays** [ɒn ˈsætədeɪz] samstags I

Saturday [ˈsætədeɪ] Samstag I

sauce [sɔːs] Soße II

sausage [ˈsɒsɪdʒ] Wurst; Bratwurst II

sausage roll [ˈsɒsɪdʒ ˌrəʊl] *Blätterteig mit Wurstfüllung* II

to **save** [seɪv] speichern II; retten; bergen III U4, 85

saw [sɔː] simple past von to see I

saxophone [ˈsæksəfəʊn] Saxofon I

*to **say** [seɪ] nachsprechen; nennen; sagen; sprechen I
  to say sorry [ˌseɪ ˈsɒri] sich entschuldigen II
  Can you say that again, please? [kæn ju: ˌseɪ ðæt əˈgen pli:s] Könntest du das bitte wiederholen? I
  Say hi to … [seɪ ˈhaɪ tə] Grüße … von mir. I
to **scan** [skæn] scannen; nach Details durchsuchen <III U1, 31>
to **scare** [skeə] erschrecken II
*to be **scared** [bi: ˈskeəd] Angst haben; erschrocken sein III U2, 34
scared [skeəd] verängstigt I
scarf (sg) [skɑ:f], **scarves** (pl) [skɑ:vz] Schal; Tuch II
scary [ˈskeəri] gruselig; beängstigend I
scene [si:n] Szene II
school [sku:l] Schule I
  at school [ət ˈsku:l] in der Schule I
  high school [ˈhaɪ ˌsku:l] High School (weiterführende Schule, Oberstufe) <III U2, 129>
  school life [ˈsku: ˌlaɪf] Schulalltag <I>
Science [saɪəns] Wissenschaft; Naturwissenschaft I
  science fiction [saɪəns ˈfɪkʃn] Science-Fiction I
scissors (pl) [ˈsɪzəz] Schere III U5, 97
  nail scissors [ˈneɪl ˌsɪzəz] Nagelschere III U5, 97
scone [skɒn] Scone (eine Art süßes Brötchen) II
Scot [skɒt] Schotte; Schottin III U3, 53
Scottish [ˈskɒtɪʃ] schottisch III U3, 53
scrambled egg [ˌskræmbld ˈeg] Rührei II
script [skrɪpt] Drehbuch; Skript <III U1, 27>
sea [si:] Meer I
search [sɜ:tʃ] Suche <III U3, 73>
to **search** [sɜ:tʃ] durchsuchen <III U3, 65>
seasick [ˈsi:sɪk] seekrank <III U2, 128>

at the **seaside** [ət ðə ˈsi:saɪd] am Meer I
second [ˈseknd] Sekunde II
second [ˈseknd] zweite I
secret [ˈsi:krət] Geheimnis II
secret [ˈsi:krət] geheim II
section [ˈsekʃn] Abschnitt <III U1, 22>
*to **see** [si:] sehen I
  CU (See you!) [ˈsi: ju] Bis später! II
  See you! [ˈsi: ju:] Tschüss!; Bis bald! I
  See you soon! [ˌsi: ju: ˈsu:n] Bis bald! I
seen [si:n] past participle von to see II
self [self] selbst; sich III U2, 34
*to **sell** [sel] verkaufen III U1, 13
*to **send** [send] schicken; senden I
sent [sent] simple past von to send I; past participle von to send II
sentence [ˈsentəns] Satz <I>
to **separate** [ˈsepreɪt] trennen <III U4, 133>
separate [ˈseprət] getrennt; separat; verschieden <III U4, 132>
September [sepˈtembə] September I
series (no pl) [ˈsɪəri:z] Serie <III U4, 133>
serious [ˈsɪəriəs] ernst III U3, 58
Are you **serious**? [ɑ: ju ˈsɪəriəs] Im Ernst? III U3, 58
to **serve** [sɜ:v] servieren <III U3, 66>
service [ˈsɜ:vɪs] Dienst III U2, 38
  emergency service [ɪˈmɜ:dʒnsi ˌsɜ:vɪs] Notdienst; Rettungsdienst III U2, 38
  full service [ˌfʊl ˈsɜ:vɪs] Komplettservice <III U3, 68>
  for service [fə ˈsɜ:vɪs] um bedient zu werden <III U4, 86>
*to **set** free [set ˈfri:] freilassen <III U4, 77>
  to set off [set ˈɒf] auslösen <III U3, 72>
to **settle** (in) [ˈsetl] besiedeln; sich niederlassen (in) <III U4, 132>
early **settler** [ˌɜ:li ˈsetlə] früher Siedler; frühe Siedlerin <III U5, 134>

seven [ˈsevn] sieben I
seventeen [ˌsevnˈti:n] siebzehn I
seventy [ˈsevnti] siebzig I
shampoo [ʃæmˈpu:] Shampoo III U5, 96
shamrock [ˈʃæmrɒk] Kleeblatt III U5, 104
shape [ʃeɪp] Form <III U5, 105>
to **share** [ʃeə] teilen III U5, 96
shark [ʃɑ:k] Hai I
pencil **sharpener** [ˈpensl ˌʃɑ:pnə] Anspitzer I
she [ʃi:] sie I
sheep (sg) [ʃi:p], **sheep** (pl) [ʃi:p] Schaf I
shelf (sg) [ʃelf], **shelves** (pl) [ʃelvz] Regal; Regalbrett I
animal rescue **shelter** [ænɪml ˈreskju: ˌʃeltə] Tierheim I
*to **shine** [ʃaɪn] scheinen <III U5, 101>
ship [ʃɪp] Schiff I
  ship builder [ˈʃɪp ˌbɪldə] Schiffsbauer; Schiffsbauerin III U4, 84
shipyard [ˈʃɪpjɑ:d] Werft III U4, 84
shirt [ʃɜ:t] Hemd; Shirt II
shoe [ʃu:] Schuh II
*to **shoot** (a film) [ˌʃu:t (ə ˈfɪlm)] (einen Film) drehen <III U5, 107>
shop [ʃɒp] Geschäft; Laden I
  corner shop [ˈkɔ:nə ˌʃɒp] Tante-Emma-Laden I
  shop assistant [ˈʃɒpˌəˌsɪstnt] Verkäufer; Verkäuferin II
  sports shop [ˈspɔ:ts ˌʃɒp] Sportgeschäft I
shopping [ˈʃɒpɪŋ] Einkaufen I
  to do the shopping [ˌdu: ðə ˈʃɒpɪŋ] Einkäufe machen; Besorgungen machen II
  to go shopping [ˌgəʊ ˈʃɒpɪŋ] einkaufen gehen II
  shopping centre [ˈʃɒpɪŋ ˌsentə] Einkaufszentrum I
  shopping list [ˈʃɒpɪŋ ˌlɪst] Einkaufszettel I
short [ʃɔ:t] kurz II
shortly [ˈʃɔ:tli] kurz III U4, 84
shorts (pl) [ʃɔ:ts] Shorts; kurze Hose I

should [ʃʊd] sollte III U2, 38

shout [ʃaʊt] Schrei I

to shout [ʃaʊt] schreien; rufen II

talent show ['tælənt ˌʃəʊ] Talentwettbewerb I

TV show [ˌtiː'viː ˌʃəʊ] Fernsehsendung II

*to show [ʃəʊ] zeigen II

shower ['ʃaʊə] Dusche III U5, 97

shower gel ['ʃaʊə ˌdʒel] Duschgel III U5, 97

sick [sɪk] krank III U1, 11

to be sick [bi 'sɪk] sich übergeben I

side [saɪd] Seite II

sight [saɪt] Sehenswürdigkeit II

*to go sightseeing [gəʊ 'saɪtsiːɪŋ] eine Besichtigungstour machen II

sign [saɪn] Schild; Zeichen III U2, 32

sign language ['saɪn ˌlæŋgwɪdʒ] Gebärdensprache; Zeichensprache III U5, 95

to sign [saɪn] unterschreiben; unterzeichnen <III U5, 135>

signal ['sɪgnl] Empfang; Signal; Zeichen III U3, 67

silence ['saɪləns] Stille; Schweigen; Ruhe III U1, 20

silent ['saɪlənt] stumm; schweigsam III U1, 21

silk [sɪlk] Seide III U3, 55

silly ['sɪli] albern II; dumm; doof III U4, 76

similarity [ˌsɪmɪ'lærəti] Ähnlichkeit <III U1, 24>

simple ['sɪmpl] einfach III U3, 58

simple past [ˌsɪmpl 'paːst] einfache Vergangenheit <III U2, 41>

simple present [ˌsɪmpl 'preznt] Gegenwart; Präsens <III U5, 98>

since [sɪns] seit <III U2, 128>; <III U3, 68>; seitdem <III U4, 132>

*to sing [sɪŋ] singen I

singer ['sɪŋə] Sänger; Sängerin I

single ticket ['sɪŋgl ˌtɪkɪt] einfache Fahrkarte III U5, 101

*to sink [sɪŋk] untergehen; sinken III U4, 84

siren ['saɪrən] Sirene; Martinshorn <III U1, 17>

sister ['sɪstə] Schwester I

*to sit (down) [sɪt 'daʊn] sich (hin)setzen I

situation [ˌsɪtjuˈeɪʃn] Situation II

six [sɪks] sechs I

sixteen [ˌsɪk'stiːn] sechzehn I

sixty ['sɪksti] sechzig I

size [saɪz] Größe II

skateboard ['skeɪtbɔːd] Skateboard III U2, 41

ice skating ['aɪs ˌskeɪtɪŋ] Schlittschuhlaufen <III U2, 186>

to ski [skiː] Ski fahren II

skiing ['skiːɪŋ] Skifahren III U2, 32

to skim [skɪm] überfliegen <III U1, 31>

skin [skɪn] Haut <III U2, 44>

skirt [skɜːt] Rock I

sleep [sliːp] Schlaf <III U1, 17>; III U2, 39

*to sleep [sliːp] schlafen I

sleepover ['sliːpˌəʊvə] Übernachtung I

slept [slept] simple past, past participle von to sleep II

sliced bread [ˌslaɪst 'bred] in Scheiben geschnittenes Brot III U4, 80

slow [sləʊ] langsam III U2, 34

small [smɔːl] klein III U2, 35

smart [smaːt] schlau; klug; intelligent III U4, 77

*to smell [smel] riechen III U1, 20

smelt [smelt] simple past, past participle von to smell III U1, 20

smoke [sməʊk] Rauch III U2, 42

smuggler ['smʌglə] Schmuggler; Schmugglerin II

smurf [smɜːf] Schlumpf I

snack [snæk] Snack; Imbiss I

snake [sneɪk] Schlange I

snow [snəʊ] Schnee <III U3, 72>

snowboarding ['snəʊbɔːdɪŋ] Snowboarden <III U2, 186>

so [səʊ] so II

so much [ˌsəʊ 'mʌtʃ] so sehr III U4, 76

so [səʊ] deshalb; also I

soap [səʊp] Seife III U5, 97

soccer (AE) ['sɒkə] Fußball <III U1, 24>

sock [sɒk] Socke I

sofa ['səʊfə] Sofa II

software ['sɒftweə] Software II

sold [səʊld] simple past, past participle von to sell III U1, 13

soldier ['səʊldʒə] Soldat; Soldatin III U3, 62

solid ['sɒlɪd] fest III U3, 55

to solve [sɒlv] lösen I

some [sʌm] einige; etwas I

something ['sʌmθɪŋ] etwas I

sometimes ['sʌmtaɪmz] manchmal II

son [sʌn] Sohn III U3, 64

song [sɒŋ] Lied <I>

soon [suːn] bald II

See you soon! [ˌsi ju 'suːn] Bis bald! I

sore [sɔː] schmerzhaft; wund II

sore throat [ˌsɔː 'θrəʊt] Halsschmerzen II

*to be sorry [bi 'sɒri] leid tun III U4, 87

*to feel sorry [ˌfiːl 'sɒri fə] Mitleid haben mit; bedauern III U5, 105

Sorry. ['sɒri] Tut mir leid.; Entschuldigung. I

to say sorry [ˌseɪ 'sɒri] sich entschuldigen II

sort [sɔːt] Sorte; Art II

to sort [sɔːt] sortieren <III U1, 17>

sound [saʊnd] Laut; Ton Geräusch III U3, 54

to sound [saʊnd] klingen II

sounds [saʊndz] Laute <I>

soup [suːp] Suppe II

south [saʊθ] Süden III U1, 10

in the south of [ˌɪn ðə 'saʊθ ˌəv] im Süden von III U1, 10

southbound ['saʊθbaʊnd] in Richtung Süden <III U5, 207>

souvenir [ˌsuːvn'ɪə] Souvenir; Andenken III U1, 12

souvenir shop ['suːvnɪə ˌʃɒp] Souvenirladen III U1, 12

space rocket ['speɪs ˌrɒkɪt] Raumschiff <III U1, 30>

spaghetti [spə'geti] Spaghetti II

*to **speak** [spiːk] sprechen III U1, 21

speaking [ˈspiːkɪŋ] Sprechen <I>
speaking skills [ˈspiːkɪŋ ˌskɪlz] Fertigkeit Sprechen <I>

special [ˈspeʃl] besonders; speziell I
special offer [ˌspeʃl ˈɒfə] Sonderangebot III U4, 80

with **special** needs [wɪθ ˌspeʃl ˈniːdz] mit Behinderung; mit besonderen Bedürfnissen III U5, 95

speech [spiːtʃ] Sprache; Rede III U3, 54
farewell speech [feəˈwel spiːtʃ] Abschiedsrede II
speech bubble [ˈspiːtʃ ˌbʌbl] Sprechblase <III U2, 47>

*to **spell** [spel] buchstabieren I

spelling [ˈspelɪŋ] Rechtschreibung I

*to **spend** [spend] ausgeben (Geld); verbringen (Zeit) II

spent [spent] simple past, past participle von to spend II

spice [spaɪs] Gewürz II

spider [ˈspaɪdə] Spinne III U3, 63

*to **split** [splɪt] teilen; spalten <III U5, 135>

spoke [spəʊk] simple past von to speak III U1, 21

spoken [ˈspəʊkn] past participle von to speak III U1, 21

spoon [spuːn] Löffel II

sport [spɔːt] Sport I; Sportart III U2, 33
sports shop [ˈspɔːts ˌʃɒp] Sportgeschäft I

to **spot** [spɒt] sehen; erkennen <III U2, 128>

to **sprain** [spreɪn] verstauchen; verrenken III U2, 39

spring roll [ˌsprɪŋ ˈrəʊl] Frühlingsrolle II

I **spy** with my little eye … [aɪ spaɪ wɪð ˌmaɪ lɪtl ˈaɪ] Ich sehe was, was du nicht siehst … I

square [skweə] Platz II

squash [skwɒʃ] Squash <III U2, 186>

stadium [ˈsteɪdiəm] Stadion II

stage [steɪdʒ] Bühne II

food **stall** [ˈfuːd ˌstɔːl] Essensstand II

stallholder [ˈstɔːlˌhəʊldə] Standinhaber; Standinhaberin II

stamp [stæmp] Briefmarke III U4, 80

*to **stand** [stænd] stehen II

star [stɑː] Star I; Stern III U2, 50
You're a star. [jɔːr ə ˈstɑː] Du bist fantastisch. II

start [stɑːt] Start; Anfang III U2, 51

to **start** [stɑːt] anfangen; beginnen; starten II; gründen III U3, 55
to start a band [stɑːt ə ˈbænd] eine Band gründen II
starting point [ˈstɑːtɪŋ ˌpɔɪnt] Ausgangspunkt <III U5, 101>

static caravan [ˈstætɪk ˌkærəvæn] Mobilheim (großer, fest stehender Wohnwagen) <III U3, 194>

station [ˈsteɪʃn] Haltestelle; Station; Bahnhof III U5, 101

to **stay** [steɪ] übernachten; bleiben II

steam engine [ˈstiːm ˌendʒɪn] Dampfmaschine III U3, 57

steel [stiːl] Stahl III U3, 55

steep [stiːp] steil <III U3, 73>

step [step] Schritt III U5, 102; Stufe II

sticker [ˈstɪkə] Aufkleber II

sticky [ˈstɪki] klebrig <III U3, 66>

still [stɪl] dennoch III U2, 43

to **stir** [stɜː] rühren; umrühren II

stocks [stɒks] Pranger III U2, 43

stomach [ˈstʌmək] Magen; Bauch II
stomach ache [ˈstʌmək ˌeɪk] Bauchweh; Bauchschmerzen II

stone [stəʊn] Stein III U1, 10
stone put [ˈstəʊn ˌpʊt] Steinwurf <III U3, 131>

stood [stʊd] simple past, past participle von to stand II

stop [stɒp] Haltestelle; Halt III U5, 100
bus stop [ˈbʌs ˌstɒp] Bushaltestelle II
Stop it! [ˈstɒp ˌɪt] Hör(t) auf! II

department **store** [dɪˈpɑːtmənt ˌstɔː] Kaufhaus II

storm [stɔːm] Sturm I

story [ˈstɔːri] Geschichte I

straight on [streɪt ˈɒn] geradeaus I

hair **straightener** [ˈheə ˌstreɪtnə] Haarglätter I

strange [streɪndʒ] merkwürdig; seltsam II

stranger [ˈstreɪndʒə] Fremder; Fremde <III U1, 17>

straw [strɔː] Trinkhalm II

strawberry [ˈstrɔːbri] Erdbeere II

stream [striːm] Bach II

street [striːt] Straße III U1, 15
back street [ˈbæk striːt] Hinterhof <III U1, 17>

striking [ˈstraɪkɪŋ] bemerkenswert; auffallend III U5, 100

strong [strɒŋ] stark III U2, 34

structure [ˈstrʌktʃə] Struktur; Aufbau <III U2, 51>

*to be **stuck** [bi ˈstʌk] feststecken; nicht weg können I
stuck in the mud [stʌk ˌɪn ðə ˈmʌd] im Schlamm festgesteckt I

student [ˈstjuːdnt] Schüler; Schülerin I

TV **studio** [ˌtiːˈviː ˌstjuːdiəʊ] Fernsehstudio II

study skills [ˌstʌdi ˈskɪlz] Fertigkeit Lern- und Arbeitstechniken <I>

style [staɪl] Stil III U5, 95

subject [ˈsʌbdʒɪkt] Schulfach I

submarine [ˌsʌbmrˈiːn] U-Boot I

success [səkˈses] Erfolg III U3, 54

successful [səkˈsesfl] erfolgreich III U2, 35

such as [ˈsʌtʃ əz] wie <III U1, 24>

suddenly [ˈsʌdnli] plötzlich; auf einmal II

suit [suːt] Anzug <III U2, 44>

to **suit** [suːt] stehen; passen II

suitcase [ˈsuːtkeɪs] Koffer II

summary [ˈsʌmri] Zusammenfassung <III U1, 25>

summer [ˈsʌmə] Sommer II

sun [sʌn] Sonne III U1, 11

to **sunbathe** [ˈsʌnbeɪð] sonnenbaden II

Sunday [ˈsʌndeɪ] Sonntag I

sunglasses (pl) [ˈsʌnˌglɑːsɪz] Sonnenbrille II

sunk [sʌŋk] past participle von *to sink* III U4, 84

sunny ['sʌni] sonnig I

superman ['su:pəmæn] Superman I

supermarket ['su:pə,ma:kɪt] Supermarkt II

sure [ʃʊə] sicher II
sure of oneself ['ʃʊər‿əv ,wʌnself] selbstsicher III U4, 77

to surf [sɜ:f] surfen; wellenreiten II
to surf the internet [,sɜ:f ði 'ɪntənet] im Internet surfen II

surfing ['sɜ:fɪŋ] Wellenreiten; Surfen <III U2, 186>

surname ['sɜ:neɪm] Nachname; Familienname <III U1, 127>

surprise [sə'praɪz] Überraschung I

surprised [sə'praɪzd] überrascht II

surprising [sə'praɪzɪŋ] überraschend <III U4, 133>

survey ['sɜ:veɪ] Umfrage II

to survive [sə'vaɪv] überleben III U4, 84

swam [swæm] simple past von *to swim* II

sweater ['swetə] Pullover <III U5, 206>

sweatshirt ['swetʃɜ:t] Sweatshirt I

*__to sweep__ [swi:p] fegen II; mitreißen <III U3, 72>
to sweep through [,swi:p 'θru:] durchziehen <III U3, 73>

sweet [swi:t] Süßigkeit; Bonbon I

sweet [swi:t] süß III U5, 96

swept [swept] simple past, past participle von *to sweep* II

*__to swim__ [swɪm] schwimmen II

*__to go swimming__ [,gəʊ 'swɪmɪŋ] schwimmen gehen I
swimming pool ['swɪmɪŋ ,pu:l] Schwimmbad I
swimming things ['swɪmɪŋ ,θɪŋz] Schwimmsachen <III U5, 206>

*__to swing__ [swɪŋ] schwingen; schwenken <III U3, 131>

sword [sɔ:d] Schwert III U2, 43

swum [swʌm] past participle von *to swim* II

T

table ['teɪbl] Tisch I; Tabelle <III ZI, 9>
table tennis ['teɪbl ,tenɪs] Tischtennis II

tablespoon ['teɪblspu:n] Esslöffel II

tablet ['tæblət] Tablette II

tactic ['tæktɪk] Taktik; Vorgehensweise III U3, 64

take [teɪk] Aufnahme <III U1, 27>

*__to take__ [teɪk] nehmen; mitnehmen; bringen; mitbringen; hinbringen II; dauern III U1, 10
to take a break [,teɪk ə 'breɪk] Pause machen II
to take a photo [,teɪk ə 'fəʊtəʊ] ein Foto machen I
to take a trip [,teɪk ə 'trɪp] eine Fahrt machen III U2, 34
to take notes [teɪk 'nəʊts] sich Notizen machen I
to take off [teɪk ‿'ɒf] ausziehen III U5, 96
to take out [,teɪk ‿'aʊt] herausnehmen I
to take part (in) [teɪk 'pa:t] teilnehmen (an) III U5, 100
to take place [teɪk 'pleɪs] stattfinden <III U3, 130>; <III U4, 89>
to take turns [,teɪk 'tɜ:nz] sich abwechseln <II>
to take the dog for a walk [,teɪk ðə dɒg fɔ:r‿ə 'wɔ:k] den Hund ausführen I

takeaway ['teɪkəweɪ] Essen zum Mitnehmen II

taken ['teɪkn] past participle von *to take* II

talent show ['tælənt ,ʃəʊ] Talentwettbewerb I
What's your talent? [wɒts jɔ: 'tælənt] Was ist dein Talent? I

talented ['tæləntɪd] talentiert III U2, 35

talk [tɔ:k] Vortrag; Rede <III U1, 19>
to give a talk [gɪv ə 'tɔ:k] einen Vortrag halten <III U1, 19>

to talk (to) [tɔ:k] sprechen (mit); reden (mit) I
to talk about ['tɔ:k ‿ə,baʊt] sprechen über II
TTYL (Talk to you later!) ['tɔ:k tə ju ,leɪtə] Wir reden später! II
don't talk [dəʊnt 'tɔ:k] sei still; rede nicht I

tall [tɔ:l] groß; hoch II

tapestry ['tæpɪstri] Wandteppich <III U1, 127>

task [ta:sk] Aufgabe; Auftrag <I>

tasty ['teɪsti] lecker; schmackhaft III U4, 80

taxi ['tæksi] Taxi II

tea bag ['ti: ,bæg] Teebeutel <III U4, 200>

tea [ti:] Tee; (frühes) Abendessen I

teacher ['ti:tʃə] Lehrer; Lehrerin I

team [ti:m] Team; Gruppe I

teamwork ['ti:mwɜ:k] Teamwork II

tear [tɪə] Träne <III U4, 77>

teaspoon ['ti:spu:n] Teelöffel II

Design Technology (DT) [dɪ,zaɪn tek'nɒlədʒi ,di:'ti:] Technik I

technology [tek'nɒlədʒi] Technologie <III U1, 30>

teen [ti:n] Jugend-; Teenager; Jugendliche; Jugendlicher II

teenage ['ti:neɪdʒ] jugendlich <III U2, 128>

teenager ['ti:n,eɪdʒə] Teenager; Teenagerin; Jugendliche; Jugendlicher III U2, 33

telephone ['telɪfəʊn] Telefon III U3, 54
telephone box ['telɪfəʊn ,bɒks] Telefonzelle II

*__to tell__ [tel] erzählen; sagen I
Can you tell me the way to …? [kæn ju: ,tel mi ðə 'weɪ tə] Kannst du mir sagen, wie ich … komme? I

ten [ten] zehn I

tennis ['tenɪs] Tennis I

tent [tent] Zelt III U3, 61

to test [test] testen; prüfen II

text [tekst] Text II
text message ['tekst ,mesɪdʒ] Textnachricht (SMS) I

to **text** [tekst] texten; eine SMS schreiben II

texter ['tekstə] SMS-Schreiber; SMS-Schreiberin II

than [ðæn] als II

Thank you. ['θæŋk ju] Danke. I

Thanks. [θæŋks] Danke. I

that [ðæt] dass III U1, 22

that [ðæt] das I
after that [ˌɑːftə 'ðæt] danach I
that's £2.24 [ðæts ˌtuː paʊndz twentiˈfɔː] das macht 2 Pfund und 24 Pence I

the [ðə] der; die; das I
the same [ðə 'seɪm] derselbe; gleich II

theatre ['θɪətə] Theater II

their [ðeə] ihr I

theirs [ðeəz] ihre III U5, 99

them [ðem] sie II

theme park ['θiːm ˌpɑːk] Freizeitpark I

themselves [ðəm'selvz] selber; sie selbst; sich selbst; selbst III U2, 152

then [ðen] dann; danach I; damals III U1, 10

there [ðeə] da; dort I
over there [ˌəʊvə 'ðeə] da drüben; dort drüben II
there are [ðeər_'ɑː] da sind; es gibt I
there is (= there's) [ðeə_'ɪz] da ist; es gibt I

these [ðiːz] diese II

they [ðeɪ] sie (Pl.) I

thing [θɪŋ] Sache; Ding II

*to **think** [θɪŋk] denken I
to think of ['θɪŋk_əv] sich ausdenken; sich etwas einfallen lassen <III U3, 68>
I don't think so. [aɪ dəʊnt 'θɪŋk səʊ] Ich glaube nicht. II
I think so. [aɪ 'θɪŋk səʊ] Ich glaube. II

third [θɜːd] dritte I

thirsty ['θɜːsti] durstig II

thirteen [θɜː'tiːn] dreizehn I

thirty ['θɜːti] dreißig I

this [ðɪs] das; dies I
like this [laɪk 'ðɪs] so; auf diese Weise III U3, 62
this way [ðɪs 'weɪ] in diese Richtung II

those [ðəʊz] jene II

though [ðəʊ] jedoch <III U1, 24>

thought [θɔːt] simple past, past participle von to think II

a/one **thousand** [ə/wʌn 'θaʊznd] eintausend; tausend II

three [θriː] drei I

throat [θrəʊt] Hals II
sore throat [ˌsɔː 'θrəʊt] Halsschmerzen II

through [θruː] durch II

Thursday ['θɜːzdeɪ] Donnerstag I

ticket ['tɪkɪt] Karte II; Fahrschein; Eintrittskarte III U1, 15
return ticket [rɪ'tɜːn ˌtɪkɪt] Hin- und Rückfahrkarte III U5, 101
single ticket ['sɪŋgl ˌtɪkɪt] einfache Fahrkarte III U5, 101

to **tidy** (up) [taɪdi 'ʌp] aufräumen; in Ordnung bringen II

tiger ['taɪgə] Tiger I

tight [taɪt] eng; fest II

time [taɪm] Zeit; Uhrzeit I; Mal III U1, 21
free time [fri: 'taɪm] Freizeit I
on time [ɒn 'taɪm] pünktlich III U5, 100
time travel ['taɪm ˌtrævl] Zeitreise III U4, 79
It's time to go. [ɪts ˌtaɪm tə 'gəʊ] Es ist Zeit zu gehen. I
the first time [ðə ˌfɜːst 'taɪm] das erste Mal I
What time is it? [wɒt 'taɪm_ɪz_ɪt] Wie spät ist es?; Wie viel Uhr ist es? I

timetable ['taɪmˌteɪbl] Stundenplan I; Fahrplan III U5, 100

tiny ['taɪni] klein; winzig III U1, 17

tip [tɪp] Tipp III U3, 58; Ratschlag <I>
language tip [ˌlæŋgwɪdʒ 'tɪp] Grammatikhinweis <I>

tired [taɪəd] müde I

tissue ['tɪʃuː] Taschentuch III U4, 81

title ['taɪtl] Titel; Überschrift <II>

to [tuː] in; nach; zu; vor (bei Uhrzeitangaben) I

to [tʊ] bis II

to [tuː] um zu <III U1, 24>

today [tə'deɪ] heute I

together [tə'geðə] zusammen; gemeinsam I

toiletries ['tɔɪlɪtriz] Toilettenartikel; Hygieneartikel <III U5, 206>

told [təʊld] simple past von to tell I

tomato (sg) [tə'mɑːtəʊ], **tomatoes** (pl) [tə'mɑːtəʊz] Tomate II

tomorrow [tə'mɒrəʊ] morgen II

tongue twister ['tʌŋ ˌtwɪstə] Zungenbrecher <III U1, 13>

tonne [tʌn] Tonne II

too [tuː] auch I; zu II
too much [tuː 'mʌtʃ] zu sehr II

took [tʊk] simple past von to take II

tool [tuːl] Werkzeug II

tooth (sg) [tuːθ], **teeth** (pl) [tiːθ] Zahn III U2, 39

toothbrush ['tuːθbrʌʃ] Zahnbürste III U5, 96

toothpaste ['tuːθpeɪst] Zahnpasta III U5, 97

toothpick ['tuːθpɪk] Zahnstocher II

top [tɒp] Top; Oberteil II

topic ['tɒpɪk] Thema <II>

torch [tɔːtʃ] Taschenlampe I

tornado [tɔː'neɪdəʊ] Tornado <III U3, 73>

caber **toss** ['keɪbə ˌtɒs] Baumstammwerfen <III U3, 130>

*to **keep in touch** [ˌkiːp ɪn 'tʌtʃ] in Verbindung bleiben II

tough [tʌf] hart III U2, 34

tour [tʊə] Tour; Fahrt; Reise; Rundgang <III U1, 30>

tourist ['tʊərɪst] Tourist; Touristin I
Tourist Information Centre [ˌtʊərɪst ˌɪnfə'meɪʃn ˌsentə] Touristeninformation I

to **tow away** ['təʊ ˌəweɪ] abschleppen <III U4, 86>

towel ['taʊəl] Handtuch III U5, 96

towel

tower ['taʊə] Turm II
    clock tower ['klɒk ˌtaʊə] Uhrenturm II
town [taʊn] Stadt I
toy [tɔɪ] Spielzeug III U2, 39
    cuddly toy ['kʌdli ˌtɔɪ] Kuscheltier III U2, 39
tractor ['træktə] Traktor I
tradition [trə'dɪʃn] Tradition III U3, 53
traffic light ['træfɪk ˌlaɪt] (Verkehrs-) Ampel <III U1, 178>
traffic ['træfɪk] Verkehr III U1, 16
train [treɪn] Zug I
    to go by (train) [ˌgəʊ baɪ ('treɪn)] mit (dem Zug) fahren I
trained [treɪnd] ausgebildet <III U1, 126>
trainer ['treɪnə] Turnschuh I
training ['treɪnɪŋ] Training III U2, 41
tram [træm] Straßenbahn III U5, 100
public **transport** [ˌpʌblɪk 'trænspɔːt] öffentliche Verkehrsmittel III U5, 100
time **travel** ['taɪm ˌtrævl] Zeitreise III U4, 79
to **travel** ['trævl] reisen II; fahren III U5, 103
traveller ['trævlə] Reisender; Reisende <III U1, 17>
tray [treɪ] Tablett II
treasure ['treʒə] Schatz II
treat [triːt] Leckerbissen <III U3, 66>
tree [triː] Baum I
    tree house ['triː ˌhaʊs] Baumhaus I
trick [trɪk] Trick; Streich I; Kunststück III U2, 41
    Trick or treat! [ˌtrɪk ə 'triːt] Süßes, sonst gibt's Saures! I
trip [trɪp] Ausflug I; Trip; Fahrt III U2, 34; Reise III U3, 58
    boat trip ['bəʊt ˌtrɪp] Bootsfahrt; Schiffsfahrt II
    to take a trip [ˌteɪk ə 'trɪp] eine Fahrt machen III U2, 34
trouble ['trʌbl] Schwierigkeiten; Problem; Ärger III U2, 33

to get into trouble [ˌget ˌɪntə 'trʌbl] in Schwierigkeiten geraten <III U2, 128>
trousers (pl) ['traʊzəz] Hose I
truck [trʌk] Wagen; Karre III U1, 21
true [truː] wahr II
truth [truːθ] Wahrheit <III U4, 77>
to **try** [traɪ] ausprobieren III U2, 33
    to try on [ˌtraɪ 'ɒn] anprobieren II
    to try out [traɪ 'aʊt] ausprobieren III U2, 43
T-shirt ['tiː ʃɜːt] T-Shirt I
TTYL (Talk to you later!) ['tɔːk tə ju ˌleɪtə] Wir reden später! II
tube [tjuːb] Schlauch; Rohr III U3, 55
Tuesday ['tjuːzdeɪ] Dienstag I
    on Tuesday [ˌɒn 'tjuːzdeɪ] am Dienstag I
tuna ['tjuːnə] Thunfisch II
tunnel ['tʌnl] Tunnel III U1, 20
(wind) **turbine** [(wɪnd) 'tɜːbaɪn] Windrad III U3, 53
Your **turn.** [jɔː 'tɜːn] Du bist dran. <I>
to **turn** [tɜːn] abbiegen III U1, 12
    to turn left (into …) [ˌtɜːn 'left] (nach) links abbiegen I
    to turn right (into …) [ˌtɜːn 'raɪt] rechts abbiegen I
*to take **turns** [teɪk 'tɜːnz] sich abwechseln <II>
tutor ['tjuːtə] Klassenlehrer; Klassenlehrerin I
    tutor group ['tjuːtə ˌgruːp] Klasse I
TV [ˌtiː'viː] Fernseher I
    TV show [ˌtiː'viː ˌʃəʊ] Fernsehsendung II
    TV studio [ˌtiː'viː ˌstjuːdiəʊ] Fernsehstudio II
    to watch TV [ˌwɒtʃ tiː'viː] fernsehen I
tweet [twiːt] Pieps III U1, 22
twelve [twelv] zwölf I
twenty ['twenti] zwanzig I
    twenty-one [ˌtwenti'wʌn] einundzwanzig I
to **twist** [twɪst] verdrehen; verzerren II
two [tuː] zwei I

type [taɪp] Sorte; Typ; Art III U1, 31
to **type** [taɪp] tippen <III U2, 47>
typically ['tɪpɪkli] typisch <III U3, 66>
tyre [taɪə] Reifen III U3, 55

U

umbrella [ʌm'brelə] Regenschirm II
umpire ['ʌmpaɪə] Schiedsrichter; Schiedsrichterin <III U5, 109>
uncle ['ʌŋkl] Onkel II
uncomfortable [ʌn'kʌmftəbl] unbequem; unangenehm II
under ['ʌndə] unter I
underground ['ʌndəgraʊnd] U-Bahn II
underlined [ʌndə'laɪnd] unterstrichen <III U3, 73>
*to **understand** [ʌndə'stænd] verstehen II
understood [ʌndə'stʊd] simple past, past participle von to understand II
unemployment (no pl) [ˌʌnɪm'plɔɪmənt] Arbeitslosigkeit <III U4, 133>
unfair [ʌn'feə] unfair III U1, 16
unfashionable [ʌn'fæʃnəbl] unmodisch II
unfriendly [ʌn'frendli] unfreundlich III U2, 35
unhappy [ʌn'hæpi] unglücklich II
uniform ['juːnɪfɔːm] Uniform I
unit ['juːnɪt] Lektion; Kapitel <I>
unreal [ʌn'rɪəl] irreal <III U5, 101>
untied [ʌn'taɪd] nicht zugebunden <III U1, 17>
until [ʌn'tɪl] bis I
up [ʌp] hinauf; oben II
to **upload** ['ʌpləʊd] ins Internet stellen; hochladen II
upper ['ʌpə] obere III U4, 92
us [ʌs] uns I
to **use** [juːz] benutzen; verwenden II
used to (live) ['juːst tə] (wohnte) früher III U1, 16
useful ['juːsfl] nützlich; hilfreich III U4, 76

usually ['juːʒli] normalerweise;
gewöhnlich II

V

no **vacancies** [ˌnəʊ 'veɪknsiz] kein
Zimmer frei <III U4, 86>
in **vain** [ɪn 'veɪn] umsonst; vergeblich
<III U5, 101>
valid ['vælɪd] gültig III U5, 100
van [væn] Lieferwagen; Transporter
III U4, 93
vegetable (veg) ['vedʒtəbl] Gemüse II
vegetarian [ˌvedʒɪ'teəriən] Vegetarier;
Vegetarierin I
veggie bean cake [ˌvedʒi 'biːn keɪk]
vegetarisches Bohnengericht II
vehicle ['vɪəkl] Fahrzeug <III U4, 86>
version ['vɜːʃn] Version <III U1, 27>
very ['veri] sehr I
vet [vet] Tierarzt; Tierärztin II
Victorian era [vɪkˌtɔːriən 'ɪərə] viktorianisches Zeitalter III U1, 25
video ['vɪdiəʊ] Video II
video chat ['vɪdiəʊ ˌtʃæt] Video-
Chat III U3, 67
viewing ['vjuːɪŋ] Hör-/Sehverstehen
<I>
viewing skills ['vjuːɪŋ ˌskɪlz] Fertigkeit Hör-/Sehverstehen <I>
the **Vikings** [ðə 'vaɪkɪŋz] die Wikinger
III U1, 11
Viking ['vaɪkɪŋ] Wikinger; Wikingerin
<III U5, 134>
village ['vɪlɪdʒ] Dorf III U1, 16
violence (no pl) ['vaɪələns] Gewalt
<III U4, 133>
violent ['vaɪələnt] gewaltsam; gewalt-
tätig; brutal <III U4, 132>
visa ['viːzə] Visum; Einreisebewilli-
gung <III U5, 206>
to **visit** ['vɪzɪt] besuchen II
visitor ['vɪzɪtə] Besucher; Besucherin
II
voice [vɔɪs] Stimme III U1, 22
volleyball ['vɒlibɔːl] Volleyball II

volunteer [ˌvɒlən'tɪə] Freiwilliger;
Freiwillige; ehrenamtlicher Helfer;
ehrenamtliche Helferin III U2, 33
voyage ['vɔɪɪdʒ] Reise; Fahrt III U4, 84

W

to **wait** [weɪt] warten II
to wait for [weɪt 'fɔː] warten auf II
I can't wait [aɪ ˌkɑːnt 'weɪt] ich
kann es kaum erwarten III U5, 100
waiter ['weɪtə] Kellner II
*to **wake up** [weɪk ˌʌp] aufwachen II
walk [wɔːk] Spaziergang III U3, 61
to go for a walk [gəʊ fər ə 'wɔːk]
spazieren gehen I
night walk ['naɪt wɔːk] Nachtwanderung I
a five minute walk [ə 'faɪv mɪnɪt
ˌwɔːk] fünf Minuten zu Fuß
III U1, 12
to take the dog for a walk [teɪk
ðə dɒg fɔːr ə 'wɔːk] den Hund
ausführen I
to **walk** [wɔːk] gehen; laufen I
walking ['wɔːkɪŋ] Wandern III U3, 61
wall [wɔːl] Mauer; Wand II
to **want** (to) ['wɒnt] wollen I
wardrobe ['wɔːdrəʊb] Kleiderschrank I
warm [wɔːm] warm I
was [wɒz] simple past von to be I
to **wash** [wɒʃ] (sich) waschen; spülen
III U5, 98
washable ['wɒʃəbl] waschbar
<III U3, 193>
*to do the **washing** up [ˌduː ðə
'wɒʃɪŋ ˌʌp] abspülen II
to **watch** [wɒtʃ] anschauen I; aufpassen auf; zuschauen; beobachten II
to watch TV [ˌwɒtʃ tiː'viː] fernsehen I
bird **watching** ['bɜːd ˌwɒtʃɪŋ] Vogelbeobachtung III U3, 61
mineral **water** ['mɪnrl ˌwɔːtə] Mineralwasser III U4, 81
water ['wɔːtə] Wasser III U2, 33

waterproofs ['wɔːtəpruːfs] Regenbe-
kleidung <III U2, 186>
wave [weɪv] Welle I; <III U3, 72>
to **wave** [weɪv] winken II
wax [wæks] Wachs <III U1, 30>
way [weɪ] Weg; Art und Weise
III U1, 12
No way! [ˌnəʊ 'weɪ] Auf keinen
Fall!; Was?!; Echt?! III U3, 58
way in [ˌweɪ 'ɪn] Einstieg <I>
asking the way [ɑːskɪŋ ðə 'weɪ]
nach dem Weg fragen I
Can you tell me the way to …?
[kæn ju: ˌtel mi ðə 'weɪ tə] Kannst
du mir sagen, wie ich … komme? I
this way [ðɪs 'weɪ] in diese Richtung II
way to go ['weɪ tə ˌgəʊ] super II
we [wiː; wi] wir I
weak [wiːk] schwach III U2, 35
wealth [welθ] Reichtum III U5, 105
*to **wear** [weə] tragen I
weather ['weðə] Wetter I
web [web] Spinnennetz; Netz
III U3, 63
website ['websaɪt] Website II
wedding ['wedɪŋ] Hochzeit II
Wednesday ['wenzdeɪ] Mittwoch I
week [wiːk] Woche I
on **weekdays** [ɒn 'wiːkdeɪz] unter der
Woche; an Werktagen III U5, 96
weekend ['wiːkend] Wochenende I
at the weekend [ət ðə ˌwiːk'end]
am Wochenende I
weekly ['wiːkli] wöchentlich III U5, 101
to **weigh** [weɪ] wiegen II
to **welcome** ['welkəm] willkommen
heißen <III U4, 132>
You're welcome. [jɔː 'welkəm] Gern
geschehen. I
welcome (to) ['welkəm tʊ] willkommen (bei/in) I
well [wel] gut II
Well done! [ˌwel 'dʌn] Gut
gemacht! I
well [wel] na ja I
Well, look … [wel 'lʊk] Na ja,
schau mal … nach. I

well

Welsh [welʃ] Walisisch; walisisch; Waliser; Waliserin III U2, 32

went [went] simple past von *to go* I

were [wɜ:] simple past von *to be* I

west [west] Westen III U1, 17

westbound ['wesbaʊnd] in Richtung Westen <III U5, 207>

wet [wet] nass I

what [wɒt] was I; welche II; wie III U1, 12

What about you? [wɒt‿əbaʊt 'ju:] Und du? II

What must you be like? [wɒt ˌmʌst ju 'bi: laɪk] Wie musst du sein? III U2, 37

what sth was like [wɒt … 'wəz laɪk] wie etwas war III U1, 12

What time is it? [wɒt 'taɪm‿ɪz‿ɪt] Wie spät ist es?; Wie viel Uhr ist es? I

What to … ['wɒt tə] Was man … II

What's your name? [wɒts jə 'neɪm] Wie heißt du? I

What's wrong? [wɒts 'rɒŋ] Was ist los?; Was stimmt nicht? II

wheel [wi:l] Rad III U3, 55

big wheel [bɪg 'wi:l] Riesenrad II

wheelchair ['wi:ltʃeə] Rollstuhl III U2, 43

when [wen] wenn; als II

when [wen] wann I

where [weə] wo, wohin, woher I

Where are you from? [ˌweər‿ə ju 'frɒm] Woher kommst du? I

wherever [weə'revə] wo(hin) auch immer; egal wo(hin); überall wo(hin) III U5, 107

which [wɪtʃ] welche II

which [wɪtʃ] die; der; dem; den; das III U3, 54

while [waɪl] während II

white [waɪt] weiß I

who [hu:] wer I

who [hu:] die; welche II; der; dem; den III U3, 54

whose [hu:z] dessen; deren III U3, 54

why [waɪ] warum II

will [wɪl] werden II

*to **win** [wɪn] gewinnen; siegen I

wind [wɪnd] Wind I

wind farm ['wɪnd fɑ:m] Windpark III U3, 53

window ['wɪndəʊ] Fenster I

windowsill ['wɪndəʊsɪl] Fenstersims <III U1, 17>

windsurfing ['wɪndsɜ:fɪŋ] Windsurfen <III U2, 186>

windy ['wɪndi] windig I

winner ['wɪnə] Gewinner; Gewinnerin I

winter ['wɪntə] Winter I

wish [wɪʃ] Wunsch <III U3, 61>

Best wishes, [ˌbest 'wɪʃɪz] Mit den besten Wünschen, I

to **wish** [wɪʃ] wünschen III U1, 25

witch [wɪtʃ] Hexe I

with [wɪð] mit I

with special needs [wɪθ ˌspeʃl 'ni:dz] mit Behinderung; mit besonderen Bedürfnissen III U5, 95

without [wɪ'ðaʊt] ohne III U4, 76

woke up [ˌwəʊk‿'ʌp] simple past von *to wake up* II

woman *(sg)* ['wʊmən], **women** *(pl)* ['wɪmɪn] Frau II

women's national team [ˌwɪmɪnz 'næʃnl ti:m] Frauen-Nationalmannschaft <III U1, 24>

won [wʌn] past participle von *to win* II

It **won't** be long. [ɪt ˌwəʊnt bi 'lɒŋ] Es wird nicht lange dauern. II

won't (= will not) [wəʊnt] nicht werden II

won't matter [ˌwəʊnt 'mætə] wird nicht von Bedeutung sein; wird nichts ausmachen <III U5, 101>

wonderful ['wʌndəfl] wunderbar III U5, 105

wood [wʊd] Holz III U3, 54; Wald II

wool [wʊl] Wolle I

word [wɜ:d] Wort <I>

wore [wɔ:] simple past von *to wear* I

work [wɜ:k] Arbeit I

to **work** [wɜ:k] arbeiten I

worker ['wɜ:kə] Arbeiter; Arbeiterin II

workshop ['wɜ:kʃɒp] Workshop II

acting workshop ['æktɪŋ ˌwɜ:kʃɒp] Schauspielworkshop II

world [wɜ:ld] Welt II

in the world [ɪn ðə 'wɜ:ld] auf der Welt II

worried ['wʌrid] beunruhigt; besorgt II

to **worry** ['wʌri] sich Sorgen machen I

Don't worry. [dəʊnt 'wʌri] Mach dir keine Sorgen. II

worst [wɜ:st] schlimmste; schlechteste III U1, 16

would [wʊd] würde(n) II

would like [wʊd 'laɪk] würde(n) gern; hätte(n) gern II

I wouldn't like (to) … [aɪ 'wʊdnt laɪk (tə)] ich möchte nicht …; ich würde nicht gerne … I

Would you like (to)…? [ˌwʊd jə 'laɪk (tə)] Möchtest du? I

wound [wu:nd] Wunde; Verletzung <III U2, 187>

wrap [ræp] Wrap II

*to **write** [raɪt] schreiben I

to write down [raɪt 'daʊn] aufschreiben <III U1, 24>

writer ['raɪtə] Schriftsteller; Schriftstellerin II; Verfasser; Verfasserin; Autor; Autorin III U2, 50

writing ['raɪtɪŋ] Schreiben <I>

wrong [rɒŋ] falsch I

to get a job wrong [ˌget‿ə dʒɒb 'rɒŋ] einen Auftrag vermasseln III U2, 50

is something wrong [ɪz 'sʌmθɪŋ rɒŋ] stimmt etwas nicht II

What's wrong? [wɒts 'rɒŋ] Was ist los?; Was stimmt nicht? II

wrote [rəʊt] simple past von *to write* II

Y

yeah *(infml)* [jeə] ja II

year [jɪə] Jahr; Jahrgangsstufe; Klasse I

yellow ['jeləʊ] gelb I

p pen • b bed • t ten • d dad • k cat • g grey • tʃ chair • dʒ joke • f fan • v very • θ three • ð the

yes [jes] ja I
yesterday [ˈjestədeɪ] gestern I
yet [jet] schon II
   not … yet [nɒt … ˈjet] noch nicht II
yogurt [ˈjɒgət] Joghurt II
you [juː] du; Sie; ihr; dich; euch; dir;
   Ihnen I
   Would you like (to)…? [ˌwʊd jə
   ˈlaɪk (tə)] Möchtest du? I
   You're right. [jɔː ˈraɪt] Du hast
   recht. I
   You're welcome. [jɔː ˈwelkəm] Gern
   geschehen. I
young [jʌŋ] jung II
Your turn. [jɔː ˈtɜːn] Du bist dran. II
your [jɔː] dein; euer I
   Your turn. [jɔː ˈtɜːn] Du bist dran.
   <I>
yours [jɔːz] deine; eure; Ihre II
yourself [jɔːˈself] dich selbst II
yourselves [jɔːˈselvz] selber; ihr/euch/
   Sie/sich (selbst) III U2, 152
   Help yourselves! [ˌhelp jɔːˈselvz]
   Bedient euch!; Bedienen Sie sich!
   II
youth (no pl) [juːθ] Jugend; Jugend-
   III U5, 94

Z

zebra [ˈzebrə] Zebra I
zero [ˈzɪərəʊ] null I
zip line [ˈzɪp ˌlaɪn] Seilrutsche
   III U2, 32
zoo [zuː] Zoo; Tierpark I
   at the zoo [ət ðə ˈzuː] im Zoo I
zookeeper [ˈzuːˌkiːpə] Tierpfleger;
   Tierpflegerin I
to zoom in [ˈzuːm ˌɪn] heranzoomen
   <I>

Boys' names

Alan [ˈælən] III U5, 103
Alex [ˈælɪks] II
Ashley [ˈæʃli] III U4, 76
Barry [ˈbæri] I
Bart [bɑːt] III U1, 21

Ben [ben] I
Bertie [ˈbɜːti] <III U5, 135>
Billy [ˈbɪli] III U1, 20
Brad [bræd] II
Conor [ˈkɒnə] III U5, 96
Dan [dæn] III U4, 80
Dave [deɪv] I
Desmond [ˈdezmənd] I
Dylan [ˈdɪlən] III ZI 9
Edward [ˈedwəd] <III U1, 126>
Frank [fræŋk] I
Fred [fred] I
George [dʒɔːdʒ] III U4, 75
Harold [ˈhærəld] <III U1, 126>
Harry [ˈhæri] III U3, 58
Howard [ˈhaʊəd] III U2, 129
Ian [ˈiːən] III U4, 80
Jahangir [ˈdʒəhæŋgɪr] I
Jake [dʒeɪk] III U3, 58
Jamie [ˈdʒeɪmi] I
Jay [dʒeɪ] I
Jim [dʒɪm] I
Jinsoo [ˈdʒɪnsuː] I
Joe [dʒəʊ] II
John [dʒɒn] <III U2, 129>
John [dʒɒn] III U4, 85
Jonas [ˈdʒəʊnəs] III U1, 20
Keith [kiːθ] III U5, 95
Leo [ˈliːəʊ] III U5, 96
Lewis [ˈlʊɪs] III ZI 9
Luke [luːk] I
Malcolm [ˈmælkəm] <III U3, 130>
Mark [mɑːk] III U2, 34
Marley [ˈmɑːli] I
Nathan [ˈneɪθn] I
Nick [nɪk] II
Patrick [ˈpætrɪk] III ZI 9
Richard [ˈrɪtʃəd] III U2, 42
Sam [sæm] I
Sean [ʃɔːn] III U4, 87
Seb [seb] III U4, 79
Shahid [ˈʃɑːhɪd] I
Sid [sɪd] I
Simon [ˈsaɪmən] I
Steve [stiːv] III U4, 79
Tim [tɪm] I
Tom [tɒm] I
William [ˈwɪljəm] <III U1, 126>

Girls' names

Abby [ˈæbi] III U3, 58
Alicia [əˈlɪʃə] I
Alva [ˈælvə] III U3, 67
Beth [beθ] III U2, 34
Billy [ˈbɪli] III U5, 104
Carol [ˈkærl] III U4, 79
Ciara [ˈkɪərə] III U5, 107
Claire [kleə] I
Daisy [ˈdeɪzi] III U1, 16
Dianne [daɪˈæn] <III U3, 59>
Ellie [ˈeli] III U2, 43
Emily [ˈemɪli] III ZI 9
Gwen [gwen] II
Hannah [ˈhænə] I
Hayley [ˈheɪli] III U5, 107
Helen [ˈhelɪn] III U5, 103
Holly [ˈhɒli] I
Irina [iˈriːnə] I
Jamila [dʒəˈmiːlə] II
Janet [ˈdʒænɪt] I
Julie [ˈdʒuːli] III U4, 74
Kate [keɪt] III U5, 103
Katie [ˈkeɪti] III U3, 58
Kim [kɪm] III U2, 41
Laura [ˈlɔːrə] I
Lucy [ˈluːsi] I
Maddy [ˈmædi] III U5, 96
Maggie [ˈmægi] III U4, 75
Maisie [ˈmeɪzi] II
Mary [ˈmeəri] I
Megan [ˈmegən] III U2, 40
Mina [ˈmiːnə] II
Molly [ˈmɒli] II
Niamh [niːv] III U5, 104
Nichola [ˈnɪklə] II
Nisha [ˈnɪʃə] III U5, 104
Olivia [ɒlˈɪviə] I
Pamela [ˈpæmələ] II
Parule [ˈpəruːl] I
Polly [ˈpɒli] II
Rachel [ˈreɪtʃl] I
Rosie [ˈrəʊzi] I
Sally [ˈsæli] I
Sarah [ˈseərə] III U4, 74
Sharon [ˈʃærən] III U1, 13
Sonya [ˈsɒnjə] III U5, 104

Sonya

Sophie [ˈsəʊfi] III ZI 9
Susan [ˈsuːzn] <III U2, 129>
Violet [ˈvaɪələt] III U1, 25

Surnames

Adams [ˈædəmz] III U2, 38
Ahern [əˈhɜːn] <III U5, 135>
Archer [ˈɑːtʃə] <III U1, 127>
Azad [ˈæzæd] I
Becket [ˈbekɪt] III U2, 45
Brown [braʊn] III U4, 74
Burgess [ˈbɜːdʒəs] II
Darcy [ˈdɑːsi] <III U1, 127>
Elliot [ˈeliət] I
Fox [fɒks] III U1, 20
Fraser [ˈfreɪzə] I
Green [griːn] II
Hanley [ˈhænli] III U5, 95
Hardy [ˈhɑːdi] II
Jenkins [ˈdʒeŋkɪnz] III U1, 12
Kapoor [ˈkæpɔː] I
Link [lɪŋk] III U2, 129
MacGowan [məˈgaʊən] III U3, 61
McCane [məˈkeɪn] II
Merchant [ˈmɜːtʃnt] <III U2, 129>
Miller [ˈmɪlə] I
Nair [neə] II
O'Brian [əˈbraɪən] III U5, 96
Preston [ˈprestən] I
Reedman [ˈriːdmən] II
Richardson [ˈrɪtʃədsn] I
Safi [ˈsæfi] I
Simpson [ˈsɪmsən] III U4, 85
Smith [smɪθ] III U2, 42
Swindon [ˈswɪndən] I
Taylor [ˈteɪlə] <III U2, 129>
Thomas [ˈtɒməs] III U2, 38
Thompson [ˈtɒmpsn] III U4, 80
Warren [ˈwɒrn] I
Welch [weltʃ] I
Yeates [jeɪts] III U2, 42

Place names

Africa [ˈæfrɪkə] Afrika I
America [əˈmerɪkə] Amerika II
Australia [ɒsˈtreɪliə] Australien I

Ballyronan [ˌbælɪˈrəʊnən] Ort in Nordirland III U4, 80
Bannockburn [ˈbænəkbɜːn] Ort in Schottland III U3, 64
Bavaria [bəˈveəriə] Bayern II
Belfast [belˈfɑːst] Hauptstadt von Nordirland III U4, 74
Berlin [bɜːˈlɪn] Berlin II
Birmingham [ˈbɜːmɪŋəm] Stadt in der Mitte Englands II
Boston [ˈbɒstən] Stadt in den USA III U3, 54
Bramford [ˈbræmfəd] Dorf in Nordengland III U1, 16
Brighton [ˈbraɪtn] Küstenort in Südengland II
Bristol [ˈbrɪstl] Stadt in Südwestengland II
The British Isles [ðə ˌbrɪtɪʃ ˈaɪlz] die Britischen Inseln III ZI 8
Cambridge [ˈkeɪmbrɪdʒ] Stadt in Ostengland <III U1, 24>
Canada [ˈkænədə] Kanada III U3, 54
Cardiff [ˈkɑːdɪf] Hauptstadt von Wales III U2, 33
Cork [ˈkɔːk] Stadt in Irland III U5, 95
Cornwall [ˈkɔːnwɔːl] Grafschaft in Südwestengland II
Culloden [kəˈlɒdn] Ort in Schottland III U3, 64
Denmark [ˈdenmɑːk] Dänemark III U1, 11
Devon [ˈdevn] Grafschaft in Südwestengland I
Donegal [ˌdɒnɪˈgɔːl] Ort in Irland III U5, 104
Dublin [ˈdʌblɪn] Hauptstadt von Irland III U4, 76
Edinburgh [ˈedɪnbrə] Hauptstadt von Schottland III U3, 52
England [ˈɪŋglənd] England I
Europe [ˈjʊərəp] Europa II
France [frɑːns] Frankreich III U1, 11
Germany [ˈdʒɜːməni] Deutschland I
Glasgow [ˈglɑːzgəʊ] Stadt in Schottland III U3, 61
Goldenbridge [ˌgəʊldnˈbrɪdʒ] Stadtteil von Dublin III U5, 100

Great Britain [ˌgreɪt ˈbrɪtn] Großbritannien III ZI 8
Greenwich [ˈgrenɪdʒ] Stadtteil im Südosten Londons I
Hastings [ˈheɪstɪŋz] Stadt in Südostengland III U1, 11
India [ˈɪndiə] Indien I
Inverness [ˌɪnvəˈnes] Ort in Nordschottland III U3, 58
Isle of Skye [ˌaɪl əv ˈskaɪ] Insel in Nordwestschottland III U3, 61
Isle of Wight [ˈaɪl əv ˌwaɪt] Insel südlich von England II
Italy [ˈɪtəli] Italien II
Jamaica [dʒəˈmeɪkə] Jamaika II
Lisburn [ˈlɪzbɜːn] Stadt in Nordirland III U4, 92
Llandudno [lænˈdɪdnəʊ] Küstenort in Wales III U2, 38
London [ˈlʌndən] Hauptstadt von England I
Manchester [ˈmæntʃɪstə] Stadt im Norden von England II
Margate [ˈmɑːgeɪt] Ausflugsort in England I
Milltown [ˈmɪltaʊn] Stadtteil von Dublin III U5, 101
New York [ˌnjuː ˈjɔːk] Großstadt in den USA III U4, 84
Newcastle [ˈnjuːˌkɑːsl] Stadt in Nordostengland III U1, 16
Northampton [nɔːˈθæmtən] Stadt in Mittelengland III U5, 104
Northern Ireland [ˌnɔːðn ˈaɪələnd] Nordirland III ZI 8
Norway [ˈnɔːweɪ] Norwegen III U1, 11
Paris [ˈpærɪs] Paris II
Poland [ˈpəʊlənd] Polen II
Powys [ˈpəʊɪs] Stadt in Wales III U2, 34
Randalstown [ˈrændlztaʊn] Ort in Nordirland III U4, 75
The Republic of Ireland [ðə rɪˌpʌblɪkˌ əvˈaɪələnd] Irland III ZI 8
Rugby [ˈrʌgbi] Stadt in Mittelengland <III U1, 24>
Scotland [ˈskɒtlənd] Schottland II
Senlac Hill [ˌsenlæk ˈhɪl] Ort in der Nähe von Hastings <III U1, 126>

p pen • b bed • t ten • d dad • k cat • g grey • tʃ chair • dʒ joke • f fan • v very • θ three • ð the

Snowdonia [snəʊˈdəʊniə] *National-park in Nordwales* III U2, 36

South Pole [ˈsaʊθ ˌpəʊl] *Südpol* II

Southampton [saʊˈθæmtən] *Hafen-stadt in Südengland* III U4, 84

Spain [speɪn] *Spanien* II

Stamford Bridge [ˈstæmfəd ˌbrɪdʒ] *Ort in Nordengland* <III U1, 126>

Stirling [ˈstɜːlɪŋ] *Ort in Schottland* III U3, 64

Turkey [ˈtɜːki] *Türkei* II

The **United Kingdom** [ðə juːˌnaɪtɪd ˈkɪŋdəm] *Vereinigtes Königreich von Großbritannien und Nordirland* III ZI 8

USA (United States of America) [juːesˈeɪ (juːˌnaɪtɪd ˌsteɪts əv əˈmerɪkə)] *USA (Vereinigte Staaten von Amerika)* III U3, 54

Wales [weɪlz] *Wales* III ZI 8

York [jɔːk] *Stadt in Nordengland* III U1, 11

Other names

Abbey Street [ˈæbi ˌstriːt] *Straße in Dublin* III U5, 100

Arsenal [ˈɑːsnl] *Name einer Fußball-mannschaft* <III U1, 24>

The **Baker** [ðə ˈbeɪkə] *Filmname* III U2, 50

Baker Street [ˈbeɪkə ˌstriːt] *Straßen-name* I

Bayeux Tapestry [baɪjɜː ˈtæpɪstri] *Bayeuxteppich* <III U1, 127>

Alexander Graham **Bell** [ˌælɪgzaːndə ˈgreɪəm bel] *Erfinder des Telefons* III U3, 54

Ben Nevis [ben ˈnevɪs] *höchster Berg Schottlands* <III U3, 72>

Big Ben [ˌbɪg ˈben] *Sehenswürdigkeit in London* II

Bollywood [ˈbɒliwʊd] *indische Filmin-dustrie: Bombay + Hollywood* II

Bond Street [ˈbɒnd ˌstriːt] *Londoner Straßenname* II

Brandenburg Gate [ˈbrændənbɜːg ˌgeɪt] *Brandenburger Tor* II

Buckingham Palace [ˌbʌkɪŋəm ˈpælɪs] *Buckingham-Palast* <III U1, 30>

The **Busy Bookworm** [ðə ˌbizi ˈbʊkwɜːm] *Name einer Buchhand-lung* III U1, 14

Caldicot Castle [ˈkɑːldɪkɒt ˌkaːsl] *Burgruine in Wales* III U2, 42

Camden Market [ˌkæmdən ˈmaːkɪt] *Markt im Londoner Stadtteil Camden* II

Captain Sparrow [ˌkæptɪn ˈspærəʊ] *Filmfigur* II

Cats [kæts] *Musicalname* <III U3, 73>

The **Channel Tunnel** [ðə ˌtʃænl ˈtʌnl] *Ärmelkanaltunnel* III ZI 8

Chelsea [ˈtʃelsi] *Name einer Fußball-mannschaft* <III U1, 24>

Lewis **Clarke** [ˌlʊɪs ˈklaːk] *Personen-name* II

Connolly [ˈkɒnli] *Bahnhof in Dublin* III U5, 101

Cutty Sark [ˌkʌti ˈsaːk] *Museumsschiff in Greenwich* I

Duke of Normandy [ˌdjuːk əv ˈnɔːməndi] *Herzog der Normandie* <III U1, 126>

Edward I [ˌedwəd ðə ˈfɜːst] *König von England (1272-1307)* III U3, 62

Elizabeth Tower [ɪˌlɪzəbəθ ˈtaʊə] *Sehenswürdigkeit in London* II

European Union [jʊərəpiːən ˈjuːnjən] *Europäische Union* III U5, 94

George's Dock [ˈdʒɔːdʒɪz ˌdɒk] *Hafen in Dublin* III U5, 101

Giant's Causeway [ˌdʒaɪənts ˈkɔːzweɪ] *Sehenswürdigkeit in Nordirland* III U4, 74

The **Globe Theatre** [ðə ˌgləʊb ˈθɪətə] *das Globe-Theater* II

Green Park [ˌgriːn ˈpaːk] *Park in Lon-don* <III U1, 30>

Greenwich Market [ˈgrenɪdʒ ˌmaːkɪt] *überdachter Markt in Greenwich* I

Greenwich Park [ˈgrenɪdʒ ˌpaːk] *Park in Greenwich* I

Greenwich Shopping Park [ˌgrenɪdʒ ˈʃɒpɪŋ paːk] *Einkaufszentrum in Greenwich* II

Hadrian's Wall [ˌheɪdriənz ˈwɔːl] *Sehenswürdigkeit in Nordengland* III U1, 10

Harley Street [ˈhaːli ˌstriːt] *Londoner Straßenname* II

Harrods [ˈhærədz] *Kaufhaus in London* II

Henry II [ˌhenri ðə ˈseknd] *König von England (1154-1189)* <III U5, 134>

Henry VIII [ˌhenri ði ˈeɪtθ] *König von England (1509-1547)* <III U5, 134>

High Road [ˈhaɪ ˌrəʊd] *Straßenname* II

the **Highlands** [ðə ˈhaɪləndz] *Bergre-gion in Schottland* III U3, 58

Hollywell School [ˈhɒliwel ˌskuːl] *Schulname* <III U4, 88>

Hollywood [ˈhɒliwʊd] *Zentrum der amerikanischen Filmindustrie (in Los Angeles)* II

Hyde Park [ˌhaɪd ˈpaːk] *Park in Lon-don* <III U1, 30>

Irish Sea [ˌaɪrɪʃ ˈsiː] *Irische See* III U5, 105

Jedward [ˈdʒedwəd] *irische Popgruppe* <III U5, 101>

John Dunlop [ˌdʒɒn ˈdʌnlɒp] *Erfinder der Gummireifen* III U3, 55

John Lewis [ˌdʒɒn ˈluːɪs] *Name einer Kaufhauskette* II

Kilkenny [kɪlˈkeni] *Tiername* III U1, 18

Lancelot [ˈlaːnsəlɒt] *Name eines Ritters* III U2, 42

Lionheart [ˈlaɪənhaːt] *Löwenherz* III U2, 42

Loch Ness [ˌlɒk ˈnes] *See in Schottland* III U3, 58

The **London Eye** [ðə ˌlʌndən ˈaɪ] *Rie-senrad in London* II

London Underground [ˈlʌndən ˌʌndəgraʊnd] *Londoner U-Bahn* II

Lough Neagh [ˌlɒx ˈneɪ] *See in Nordir-land* III U4, 75

Madame Tussauds [ˌmædəm tʊˈsɔːdz] *Wachsfigurenmuseum in London* <III U1, 30>

Manchester City [ˌmæntʃɪstə ˈsɪti] *Name einer Fußballmannschaft* III U1, 16

Mount

Mount Snowdon [ˌmaʊnt ˈsnəʊdn] *höchster Berg in Wales* III U2, 32

Nessie [ˈnesi] *Ungeheuer, das angeblich in Loch Ness wohnt* III U3, 58

Nessie's Nest [ˌnesiz ˈnest] *Name einer Frühstückspension* III U3, 61

No Tree Hostel [ˌnəʊ tri: ˈhɒstl] *Name einer Herberge* III U3, 61

Norman Conquest [ˌnɔ:mən ˈkɒŋkwest] *Normannische Eroberung Englands* <III U1, 126>

Notting Hill Carnival [ˌnɒtɪŋ hɪl ˈkɑ:nɪvl] *jährlicher Karneval im Londoner Stadtteil Notting Hill* I

The **O2** [ði ˈəʊˌtu:] *Konzertarena in London* II

O'Connell Street [əˈkɒnl ˌstri:t] *Straße in Dublin* III U5, 100

Paddy [ˈpædi] *Kosename für Patrick* III U5, 105

Portobello Road Market [ˌpɔ:təbeləʊ rəʊd ˈmɑ:kɪt] *Straßenmarkt in London* <III U1, 30>

Prince George Theatre [ˌprɪns dʒɔ:dʒ ˈθɪətə] *Theater in London* II

Red Line [ˈred ˌlaɪn] *Straßenbahnlinie in Dublin* III U5, 100

Red Nose Day [red nəʊz ˈdeɪ] *Spendenmarathon* I

River Humber [ˌrɪvə ˈhʌmbə] *Fluss im Nordosten Englands* II

River Severn [ˌrɪvə ˌsevn] *Fluss im Südwesten Englands* II

River Thames [ˌrɪvə ˈtemz] *Fluss in London* II

RNLI (Royal National Lifeboat Institution) [ˈɑ:r en el ˌaɪ] *briti-*

sche Seenotrettungsorganisation <III U2, 128>

Robert the Bruce [ˈrɒbət də ˌbru:s] *König von Schottland (1306–1329)* III U3, 52

Rushy Park Coal Mine [ˌrʌʃi pɑ:k ˈkəʊl maɪn] *Name eines Kohlebergwerks* III U1, 20

Sackville Place [ˈsækvɪl ˌpleɪs] *Straßenname in Dublin* III U5, 100

Saint Patrick [snt ˈpætrɪk] *Schutzheiliger von Irland* <III U5, 134>

Selfridges [ˈselfrɪdʒɪz] *Name einer Kaufhauskette* II

William **Shakespeare** [ˌwɪljəm ˈʃeɪkspɪə] *englischer Schriftsteller* II

The **Shambles** [ðə ˈʃæmblz] *Einkaufsstraße in York* III U1, 12

The **Shard** [ðə ˈʃɑ:d] *Name eines Gebäudes in London* II

Sherlock [ˈʃ3:lɒk] *Tiername* I

South Kensington [saʊθ ˈkenzɪŋtən] *Londoner U-Bahn-Haltestelle* <III U1, 30>

Spiderman [ˈspaɪdəmæn] *Spiderman* II

The **Spire** [ðə ˈspaɪə] *Monument und Wahrzeichen von Dublin* III U5, 100

St Patrick's Day [sn ˈpætrɪks ˌdeɪ] *Feiertag in Irland am 17. März* III U5, 95

St Paul's Cathedral [sənt ˈpɔ:lz ˌkəθi:drəl] *St. Pauls Kathedrale* II

Stonehenge [ˌstəʊnˈhendʒ] *Sehenswürdigkeit in Südwestengland* III U1, 10

Thomas Tallis School [ˌtɒməs ˈtælɪs ˌsku:l] *Schulname* I

Tigerboy III [ˈtaɪgəˌbɔɪ ˈθri:] *Filmname* III U4, 79

Titanic [taɪˈtænɪk] *Schiffsname* III U4, 75

The **Tower of London** [ðə ˌtaʊər əv ˈlʌndən] *Sehenswürdigkeit in London* II

Victoria Station [vɪkˌtɔ:riə ˈsteɪʃn] *Londoner Bahnhof* <III U1, 25>

Victoria Station [vɪkˌtɔ:riə ˈsteɪʃn] *Londoner Bahnhof* III U5, 107

Viking Centre [ˈvaɪkɪŋ ˌsentə] *Wikingermuseum in York* III U1, 12

The **Voice of Ireland** [ðə ˌvɔɪs əv ˈaɪələnd] *Name einer Fernsehsendung* III U5, 95

Emma **Watson** [ˌemə ˈwɒtsn] *Schauspielerin* II

Wembley [ˈwembli] *Name eines Fußballstadions in London* II

Westminster Abbey [ˈwestmɪnstərˌæbi] *Kirche im Londoner Stadtteil Westminster* II

Westminster Cathedral [ˈwestmɪnstə ˌkəθi:drəl] *Dom im Londoner Stadtteil Westminster* II

The **White Star Line** [ðə ˌwaɪt stɑ: ˈlaɪn] *Baufirma der Titanic* III U4, 84

Whitelee [ˌwaɪtˈli:] *Name eines Windparks in Schottland* III U3, 53

Zip World [ˈzɪp ˌw3:ld] *Erlebniswelt in Nordwales* <III U2, 44>

A

abbiegen to turn III U1, 12
Abend evening I
Abendessen dinner II
(frühes) Abendessen tea I
abends in the evenings III U4, 76
Abenteuer adventure III U2, 32
aber but I
abfahren leave II
Abfall rubbish II
den Tisch abräumen to clear the
    table II
abschicken *(einen Brief)* to post
    III U4, 80
Abschieds- leaving II
Abschiedsrede farewell speech II
absichtlich on purpose II
abspülen *to do the washing up II
Abteilung department II
acht eight I
Achterbahn roller coaster II
achtzehn eighteen I
achtzig eighty I
Adapter adaptor III U5, 96
Adresse address II
Affe monkey I
Aktenkoffer briefcase III U2, 45
Aktentasche briefcase III U2, 45
Aktivität activity I
albern silly II
alle all I
alle everyone II; every III U4, 75
Allergie allergy II
allergisch gegen allergic to II
alles klar all right II
alles everything II
Alphabet alphabet I
als than; as II
als when II
als Nächstes next II
also so I
alt old I
    Wie alt bist du? How old are you? I
Alter age I
Altglascontainer bottle bank II
Aluminium aluminium III U3, 55
am on; at I

am Wochenende at the weekend I
am 7. Juli on 7th July I
am Dienstag on Tuesday I
an on; at I
    an Bord on board III U4, 84
Ananas pineapple III U5, 107
Andenken souvenir III U1, 12
andere other I
    ein andere another II
anderen others II
anderer Meinung sein to disagree II
(sich) ändern to change III U3, 54
    seine Meinung ändern to change
    one's mind III U4, 81
Anfang start III U2, 51; beginning
    III U5, 105
anfangen to start II
Anführer leader III U3, 65
Anführerin leader III U3, 65
angenehm comfortable II
angezogen (wie) dressed III U5, 105
Angst haben *to be scared III U2, 34
Angst haben *to be afraid II
ängstlich afraid II
anhören to listen (to) I
ankommen to arrive II
Ankündigung announcement II
anlegen *to put on III U2, 39
anmalen to paint II
Anmeldeformular entry form II
anprobieren to try on II
Anruf call III U5, 104
anrufen to call II; to phone I
Anrufer caller III U2, 38
Anruferin caller III U2, 38
anschauen to watch; to look at I; *to
    have a look II
sich anschließen to join III U5, 96
Anspitzer pencil sharpener I
anstoßen *to hit III U2, 40
Antwort answer I
antworten to answer I
anziehen *to put on III U2, 39
    sich anziehen to get dressed II
Apfel apple I
April April I
Arbeit work I; job II
arbeiten to work I

Arbeiter worker II
Arbeiterin worker II
Archiv archive II
Ärger trouble III U2, 33
Armee army III U3, 62
armselig miserable III U5, 105
Art sort II; type III U1, 31
Art und Weise way III U1, 12
Arzt doctor II
Ärztin doctor II
atmen to breathe III U1, 22
auch too I
    auch nicht not … either III U3, 58
auf on; at I
    auf diese Weise like this III U3, 62
    auf einmal suddenly II
    Auf Wiedersehen. Goodbye. I
    auf der Welt in the world II
    Auf keinen Fall! No way! III U3, 58
auffallend striking III U5, 100
Aufgabe job II
aufgeben *to give up III U3, 63
aufgeben *(einen Brief)* to post
    III U4, 80
aufgeregt excited; nervous II
aufheben to pick up III U1, 22
jmdn. aufheitern to cheer sb up
    III U5, 105
aufhören to stop I; to finish II
    Hör(t) auf! Stop it! II
Aufkleber sticker II
aufmachen to open I
jmdn. aufmuntern to cheer sb up
    III U5, 105
aufpassen to look after II
    aufpassen auf to watch II
aufräumen to tidy (up) II
aufregend exciting I
aufstehen *to get up I
einen Auftrag vermasseln *to get a
    job wrong III U2, 50
aufwachen *to wake up II
aufwachsen *to grow up III U3, 54
Auge eye II
    Ich traute meinen Augen nicht. I
    couldn't believe my eyes. III U5, 105
Augenblick moment II

August

August August I

im August in August I
aus from I
aus Deutschland German III U5, 98
hergestellt sein aus to be made of
III U3, 54
auschecken to check out III U3, 59
Auseinandersetzung argument II
Ausflug trip I
den Hund **ausführen** to take the dog
for a walk I
ausgeben *(Geld)* *to spend II
ein **ausgefüllter** Tag a busy day I
ausgehen *(Ware)* *to run out of
III U4, 81
ausleihen to borrow II
ausprobieren to try III U2, 33; to try
out III U2, 43
ausruhen to rest II
Ausrüstung equipment III U2, 34
aussehen to look II
außer except III U5, 96
Außerirdische alien I
Außerirdischer alien I
Aussichtspunkt lookout point II
aussteigen *to get off II
einen Turnierzweikampf **austragen**
to joust III U2, 43
Ausverkauf sale II
auswählen *to choose II
Ausweis ID III U5, 97
Auto car I
Autofahrt drive III U1, 17
Automat machine II
Autor writer III U2, 50
Autorin writer III U2, 50

B

Bach stream II
Bäcker baker III U2, 50
Bäckerei baker's III U1, 13
Bäckerin baker III U2, 50
Bad(ezimmer) bathroom I
Bahnhof station I
bald soon II
Bis **bald**! See you!; See you soon! I
Ball ball II
Banane banana I

Band band II
Bank bench III U4, 87
Basketball basketball II
Bauarbeiter builder II
Bauarbeiterin builder II
Bauch stomach II
Bauchschmerzen stomach ache II
Bauchweh stomach ache II
bauen *to build II
Bauer farmer I
Bäuerin farmer I
Bauernhof farm I
Baum tree I
Baumhaus tree house I
Baumwolle cotton III U3, 55
beängstigend scary I
beantworten to answer I
bedauern *to feel sorry III U5, 105
bedeuten *to mean III U2, 33
Bedienen Sie sich! Help yourselves!
II
sich bedienen to help oneself
III U5, 96
Bedient euch! Help yourselves! II
mit besonderen **Bedürfnissen** with
special needs III U5, 95
sich **beeilen** to hurry III U2, 38; to
rush III U5, 105
beeindrucken to impress III U5, 107
beenden to finish II
befolgen to follow III U5, 102
befragen to interview I
Befragung interview II
begeistert excited II
Beginn beginning III U5, 105
beginnen to start II
mit **Behinderung** with special needs
III U5, 95
bei at I
bei Bewusstsein awake III U2, 38
Bein leg II
beinahe almost III U1, 25
bekommen *to get I
beliebt popular III U2, 33
bemerkenswert striking III U5, 100
benutzen to use II
beobachten to watch II
bequem comfortable II

bereit ready I
bereits already II
Berg mountain III U1, 17
Bergarbeiter miner III U1, 20
Bergarbeiterin miner III U1, 20
bergen to save III U4, 85
Bergwerk mine III U1, 16
Beruf job II
berühmt famous I
Besatzung crew III U4, 84
beschäftigt busy I
eine **Besichtigungstour** machen *to
go sightseeing II
besitzen *to have I; to own II
mit **besonderen** Bedürfnissen with
special needs III U5, 95
besonders special I
besorgt worried II
Besorgungen machen *to do the
shopping II
beste best II
besteigen to climb III U2, 34
bestellen to order II
die **besten** the best II
besuchen to visit II
Besucher visitor II
Besucherin visitor II
betreiben *to run III U4, 75
Bett bed I
ins Bett gehen to go to bed I
beunruhigt worried II
bevor before II
(sich) **bewegen** to move III U2, 39
Bewegung move III U5, 100
bewerten to rate III U2, 51
Bewohner inhabitant III U1, 16
Bewohnerin inhabitant III U1, 16
bei **Bewusstsein** awake III U2, 38
Bezahlautomat payment machine II
bezahlen *to pay II
Bibliothek library III U1, 15
Bild picture I
billig cheap II
Biologie Biology I
bis to II
bis zu before II
bis (spätestens) by III U5, 100
Bis bald! See you!; See you soon! I

bis until I
ein **bisschen** a little; a bit II
bitte please I
 Bitte schön. Here you are. I
blau blue I
der **blaue** the blue one II
bleiben to stay II
 etw. bleiben lassen to give sth a
 miss III U2, 50
 in Verbindung bleiben to keep in
 touch II
Bleistift pencil I
Blog blog II
bloß only III U1, 16
Blume flower III U5, 104
Bluse blouse I
bluten *to bleed III U2, 38
Boden ground III U3, 64
Bonbon sweet I
Boot boat II
Bootsfahrt boat trip II
an **Bord** on board III U4, 84
böse angry II; bad III U2, 38; naughty
 III U2, 43
Boss boss II
Box box I
Bratwurst sausage II
brauchen to need II
 nicht brauchen needn't I
braun brown I
brechen *to break II
brennen *to burn III U2, 39
Brief letter III U4, 80
Briefmarke stamp III U4, 80
bringen *to bring II
britisch British II
Broschüre brochure III U1, 31
belegtes **Brot** sandwich I
Brot bread II
Brotlaib loaf III U4, 80
Brücke bridge II
Bruder brother I
Buch book I
Bücherei library III U1, 15
Buchstabe letter III U4, 80
buchstabieren *to spell I
Büfett buffet III U3, 58
Bühne stage II

bunt colourful II
Burg castle II
Büro office II
Bus bus I
 im Bus on the bus II
Bushaltestelle bus stop II
Butter butter I

C

Cache *(Geheimschatz)* cache I
Café café I
Cafeteria cafeteria I
Camp camp II
campen gehen *to go camping II
Camping camping III U2, 36
Campingplatz campsite III U3, 58
Center centre III U1, 16
Chance chance II
chatten to chat II
Chef boss II
Chefkoch head chef II
Chili chilli II
circa about II
Cola coke I
Comic(heft) comic II
Computer computer I
Computerspiel computer game I
cool cool I
Cousin cousin II
Cousine cousin II
Crew crew III U4, 84
Curry curry II

D

da there I
 da drüben over there II
da because I
Dach roof II
Dachboden attic I
damals then III U1, 10
Dampfmaschine steam engine
 III U3, 57
danach then; after that I; after
 III U4, 84
Danke. Thanks.; Thank you. I
dann then I

das the I
das this; that I; which III U3, 54
dass that III U1, 22
Datei file II
Datum date I
dauern *to take III U1, 10
decken *to lay II
dein your I
deine yours II
dem who; which III U3, 54
den who; which III U3, 54
denken *to think I
Denkmal monument II
dennoch still III U2, 43
der the I
der who; which III U3, 54
deren whose III U3, 54
derselbe the same II
Desaster disaster III U4, 84
deshalb so I
dessen whose III U3, 54
Deutsch German I
deutsch German III U5, 98
Deutschland Germany I
Dezember December I
dich you I
 dich selbst yourself II
die the I
die who II; which III U3, 54
Dienst service III U2, 38
Dienstag Tuesday I
 am Dienstag on Tuesday I
dies this I
diese these II
Ding thing II
dir you I
Donnerstag Thursday I
doof silly III U4, 76
Dorf village III U1, 16
dort there I
 dort drüben over there II
eine **Dose** … a can of I
Dr. *(Anrede)* Dr III U4, 85
Drama drama III U2, 51
drängeln to push III U5, 102
draußen halten *to keep out III U3, 62
draußen outside III U3, 58
dreckig dirty I

dreckig

Drehort location III U2, 50
drei three I
dreißig thirty I
dreizehn thirteen I
dritte third I
du you I
Dudelsack bagpipes *(pl)* III U3, 53
dumm silly III U4, 76
dunkel dark I
Dunkelheit dark III U1, 20
durch through II
Durcheinander mess I
Durchsage announcement II
dürfen may II
    nicht/nie dürfen must not/never
    III U3, 63
    nicht dürfen mustn't III U5, 100
durstig thirsty II
Dusche shower III U5, 97
Duschgel shower gel III U5, 97
DVD DVD II

E

echt real II
Echt?! No way! III U3, 58
echt really II
Ecke corner III U4, 92
Es ist **egal.** It doesn't matter. II
egal wo(hin) wherever III U5, 107
ehrenamtliche Helferin volunteer
    III U2, 33
ehrenamtlicher Helfer volunteer
    III U2, 33
Ei egg II
eifersüchtig jealous II
eigene own II
eigentlich actually III U5, 105
Eigentümer landlord II
eilen to rush III U5, 105
ein a; an I
    ein bisschen a bit II
    ein paar a few III U3, 58
    ein wenig a bit II
einander each other III U2, 34
einchecken to check in III U3, 59
eindringen (in) to invade III U1, 11
eine a; an I

einfach easy I; plain II; simple
    III U3, 58
einfache Fahrkarte single ticket
    III U5, 101
einflussreich important III U2, 33
einfügen to paste II
einhundert a/one hundred I
einige some I
einige a few III U3, 58
Einkäufe machen *to do the shop-
    ping II
Einkaufen shopping I
einkaufen gehen *to go shopping II
Einkaufszentrum shopping centre I
Einkaufszettel shopping list I
einladen to invite I
Einladung invitation I
einmal once III U5, 105
    auf einmal suddenly II
    noch einmal again; once more II
einmarschieren (in) to invade
    III U1, 11
einpacken to pack; to pack up II
eins one I
einsam lonely III U4, 76
einschlafen *to fall asleep III U1, 25
einsetzen *to put in I
einst once III U5, 105
einstufen to rate III U2, 51
Eintrittskarte ticket III U1, 15
nicht **einverstanden** sein to disagree
    II
Einwohner inhabitant III U1, 16
Einwohnerin inhabitant III U1, 16
einzige only II
Eis ice cream II
Eisberg iceberg III U4, 84
Eiscreme ice cream II
Elefant elephant I
elegant chic I
Elektrizität electricity III U3, 53
elend miserable III U5, 105
elf eleven I
Eltern parents *(pl)* II
E-Mail e-mail II
Empfang signal III U3, 67
Ende end II; ending III U2, 45
enden to finish II

endlich at last II
eng tight II
aus **England** English I
die **Engländer** the English III U1, 11
Englisch English I
entfernt away II
entlang down III U1, 12
entlang along I
(sich) **entscheiden** to decide III U3, 58
sich **entschuldigen** *to say sorry II
Entschuldigung. Sorry.; Excuse me. I
entspannt relaxed II
er he I
    er selbst himself III U2, 34
Erdbeere strawberry II
Erdboden ground III U3, 64
Erdkunde Geography I
Erdnussbutter peanut butter III U4, 81
etwas **erfahren** über to learn about
    sth III U1, 12
erfinden to invent III U3, 54
Erfinder inventor III U3, 52
Erfinderin inventor III U3, 52
Erfindung invention III U3, 54
Erfolg success III U3, 54
erfolgreich successful III U2, 35
erforschen to explore II
Ergebnis result II
ergreifen to grab III U5, 105
sich **erinnern** (an) to remember II
erklären to explain III U5, 104
erkunden to explore II
ernst serious III U3, 58
    Im Ernst? Are you serious? III U3, 58
erraten to guess II
erschöpft exhausted III U2, 35
erschrecken to scare II; to jump
    III U2, 42
erschrocken sein *to be scared
    III U2, 34
erst only III U1, 16
erstaunlich amazing III U3, 63
erste first I
    das erste Mal the first time I
als **Erstes** first I
Erwachsene adult III U4, 75
Erwachsener adult III U4, 75
erwarten to expect III U2, 45

ich kann es kaum erwarten I can't wait III U5, 100
erzählen *to tell I
Erzähler narrator I
Erzählerin narrator I
es it I
 Mir geht es gut. I'm fine. II
es gibt there is (= there's); there are I
Essen food I; meal II
 Essen zum Mitnehmen takeaway II
essen *to eat I
Essensstand food stall II
Esslöffel tablespoon II
Esszimmer dining room I
etwa about II
etwas something; some I
euch you I
euer your I
eure yours II
Euro (Währung) euro III U5, 94
ewig forever II
exakt exact III U4, 81
explodieren to explode III U1, 20
Explosion explosion III U1, 20

F

Fabel fable III U5, 105
Fabrik factory III U1, 16
Fahne flag II
fahren *to go I; *to ride II; to travel III U5, 103
 gegen etw. fahren to hit III U4, 84
 mit (dem Zug) fahren to go by (train) I
Fahrer driver III U5, 102
Fahrerin driver III U5, 102
einfache Fahrkarte single ticket III U5, 101
Fahrplan timetable III U5, 100
Fahrpreis fare III U5, 100
Fahrrad bike I
Fahrschein ticket III U1, 15
Fahrt ride II; drive III U1, 17; trip III U2, 34; journey III U5, 100; voyage III U4, 84

eine Fahrt machen to take a trip III U2, 34
Fakt fact II
fallen *to fall I; *to fall (over) III U2, 38
falsch wrong I
Faltblatt flyer II
Familie family I
Fan fan I
Fantasie fantasy II
Fantasieausflug fantasy trip I
fantastisch fantastic II
 Du bist fantastisch. You're a star. II
Fantasy fantasy II
Farbe colour I
Fasching carnival I
fast almost III U1, 25
Fastfood-Restaurant fast food restaurant I
Februar February I
Federmäppchen pencil case I
fegen *to sweep II
Feier party I
feiern to celebrate I
Feind enemy III U2, 50
Feindin enemy III U2, 50
Fels rock III U2, 38
Fenster window I
Ferien holiday II
fernsehen to watch TV I
Fernseher TV I
Fernsehsendung TV show II
Fernsehstudio TV studio II
fertig ready I
fertigstellen to finish II
fest tight II; solid III U3, 55
festhalten *to hold III U2, 43
feststecken *to be stuck I
Feuer fire II
Feuerwehrauto fire engine II
Film film; movie I
Filzstift felt-tip I
finden *to find I
 ich kann … nicht finden I can't find … I
Finger finger III U2, 39
Fingerabdruck fingerprint II
Firma company II
Fisch fish I

Pommes mit Fisch fish and chips I
fit fit III U2, 34
Fitnessraum gymnasium III U4, 84
Flagge flag II
Flamingo flamingo I
eine Flasche … a bottle of I
Fledermaus bat I
Fleisch meat I
fliegen *to fly II
fließend fluent III U2, 33
Flohmarkt jumble sale II
Flughafen airport II
Flugzeug plane II
Flur corridor III U2, 42
Fluss river I
flüssig fluent III U2, 33
Flyer flyer II
folgen to follow III U5, 102
Fön hairdryer III U5, 97
in Form fit III U2, 34
Foto photo I
 ein Foto machen to take a photo I
Frage question I
fragen to ask I
Frankreich France III U1, 11
Französisch French I
Frau woman II
Frau (Anrede) Mrs; Ms I
frech cheeky III U2, 34; naughty III U2, 43
im Freien outside III U3, 58
Freiland- free range II
Freiluft- outdoor III U2, 34
Freitag Friday I
Freiwillige volunteer III U2, 33
Freiwilliger volunteer III U2, 33
Freizeit free time I
Freizeitpark theme park I
Freude fun I
Freund friend I
Freundin friend I
freundlich friendly III U2, 35
Freundschaften schließen *to make friends I
Frieden peace III U3, 65
frieren *to freeze III U3, 58, *to get cold III U3, 60
Frisbeescheibe frisbee I

frisch fresh II

Friseur hairdresser II

Friseurin hairdresser II

froh happy I; glad II

Frucht fruit I

früh early III U3, 60

(wohnte) **früher** used to (live) III U1, 16

Frühlingsrolle spring roll II

Frühstück breakfast I

frühstücken *to have breakfast I

Frühstückspension bed and breakfast (B & B) III U3, 58

(sich) **fühlen** *to feel II

führen *to run III U4, 75

Führer leader III U3, 65

Führerin leader III U3, 65

Füller pen I

fünf five I

fünfzehn fifteen I

fünfzig fifty I

für for I

für immer forever II

furchtbar awful I; horrible; dreadful III U4, 77

sich **fürchten** *to be afraid II

Fuß foot I

zu Fuß gehen to go on foot I

Fußball football I

Fußgelenk ankle II

Fußknöchel ankle II

füttern *to feed I

G

Gabel fork II

Gang corridor III U2, 42

ganz quite III U2, 34

den **ganzen** Tag all day III U3, 58

Garten garden I

Gas gas III U1, 20

Gast guest III U2, 33

Gasthaus pub III U5, 94

Gebärdensprache sign language III U5, 95

Gebäude building II

es **gibt** there is (= there's); there are I

geben *to give I

jmdm. das Gefühl geben, etw. zu sein to make sb feel like sth III U2, 43

geboren werden *to be born III U3, 52

(in der Pfanne) **gebraten** fried II

Geburtstag birthday I

Alles Gute zum Geburtstag! Happy birthday! I

Gedicht poem III U5, 105

geduldig patient III U2, 35

gefährlich dangerous III U2, 34

gefällt mir I like I

gefällt mir nicht I don't like I

Gefängnis prison II

gefrieren *to freeze III U3, 58

jmdm. das **Gefühl** geben, etw. zu sein *to make sb feel like sth III U2, 43

gegen against III U1, 11; around III U5, 96

gegen etw. fahren to hit III U4, 84

sich **gegenseitig** each other III U2, 34

gegenüber opposite I

geheim secret II

Geheimnis mystery I; secret II

gehen *to go; to walk I

campen gehen to go camping II

gehen um to be about III U1, 31

ins Bett gehen to go to bed I

spazieren gehen to go for a walk I

zu Fuß gehen to go on foot I

Wie geht es dir? How are you? I

gehörlos deaf III U3, 54

Mir **geht** es gut. I'm fine. II

Geist ghost II

Gel gel III U5, 97

gelassen relaxed II

gelb yellow I

Geld money I

Geldschein note II

Gelegenheit chance II

gemeinsam together I

Gemüse vegetable (veg) II

Obst- und **Gemüseladen** greengrocer's III U1, 13

gemustert patterned II

gemütlich cosy III U3, 58

genau exact III U4, 81

genießen to enjoy III U3, 53

genug enough III U2, 34

genügend enough III U2, 34

Geografie Geography I

gerade right now III U5, 98

geradeaus straight on I

Geräusch noise I; sound III U3, 54

Gericht dish II

gern haben to like I

Gern geschehen. You're welcome. I

ich würde gerne … I'd like (to) … (= I would like to) I

Geschäft shop I

geschehen to happen II

Geschenk present I

Geschichte History; story I; history III U1, 12

Gesellschaft company II

Gesicht face I

gestern yesterday I

Getränk drink II

gewinnen *to win I

Gewinner winner I

Gewinnerin winner I

gewöhnlich usually II

Gewürz spice II

Gips cast III U2, 39

Giraffe giraffe I

Gitarre guitar III U5, 95

Glas glass II; jar III U4, 80

glauben to believe II

Ich glaube nicht. I don't think so. II

Ich glaube. I think so. II

gleich the same II

jetzt **gleich** right now III U5, 98

Glocke bell II

viel **Glück** good luck II

glücklich happy I

Glückstag lucky day II

Glückwunsch! Congratulations! II

Glühbirne light bulb III U3, 57

Gold gold III U5, 104

Gold- gold III U5, 104

golden gold III U5, 104

Grab grave III U1, 11

grau grey I

greifen to grab III U5, 105

Grill barbecue I

groß high; big I; tall; large II
großartig great I; fantastic II
Größe size II
Großeltern grandparents *(pl)* II
Großmutter grandmother II
Großstadt city II
Großvater grandfather II
grün green I
Grund reason III U2, 51
    Gründe angeben to give reasons
    III U2, 51
    Gründe nennen to give reasons
    III U2, 51
gründen to start III U3, 55
Gruppe group; team I
gruselig scary I
Grüße … von mir. Say hi to … I
gültig valid III U5, 100
Gummi rubber III U3, 55
gut good I; fine II; nice III U3, 58
    Gut gemacht! Well done! I
    gut sein in to be good at I
    Guten Morgen. Good morning. II
    gut sein bei to be good at I
gut well II
Mir geht es gut. I'm fine. II

H

Haar hair III U5, 98
Haarbürste hairbrush III U5, 97
Haare hair III U5, 98
    sich die Haare schneiden lassen to
    have a haircut II
Haargel hair gel III U5, 97
Haarglätter hair straightener I
Haarschnitt haircut II
haben *to have I
    Angst haben to be scared III U2, 34
    hast du have you got II
    hätte(n) gern would like II
    Du hast recht. You're right. I
    Mitleid **haben** mit *to feel sorry
    III U5, 105
Hafen harbour II
Hafer oat III U3, 53
Haferbrei porridge III U3, 53
Hai shark I

halb half III U1, 16
    eine halbe Million half a million
    III U1, 16
halb (drei) half past (two) I
(die) Hälfte half III U4, 84
Hallen- indoor III U2, 34
Hallo. Hello.; Hi. I
Hals throat II
Halsband collar I
Halsschmerzen sore throat II
Halt stop III U5, 100
halten *to keep II; *to hold III U2, 43
Haltestelle stop II
Hamburger burger II
Hand hand III U2, 40
handeln von *to be about III U1, 31
Handtuch towel III U5, 96
Handy mobile (phone) I
hängen *to hang II
hart hard II; tough III U2, 34
hassen to hate I
hassen to hate III U4, 76
häufig often I
Hauptgericht main course II
Hauptstadt capital (city) III U2, 33
Haus house I
    zu Hause at home; around the
    house I
Hausaufgabe(n) machen *to do
    homework I
Häuschen cottage III U3, 53
Hausmeister caretaker I
Hausmeisterin caretaker I
Haustier pet I
Heer army III U3, 62
Heft book I
Heim home I
Heimweh haben *to be homesick
    III U5, 104
heiraten *to get married II
heiß hot I
heißen *to be called II
    Ich heiße … My name is … I
    Wie heißt du? What's your name? I
Held hero III U3, 64
helfen to help I
ehrenamtliche Helferin volunteer
    III U2, 33

ehrenamtlicher Helfer volunteer
    III U2, 33
Helikopter helicopter I
Helm helmet I
Hemd shirt II
heraus out II
herausfinden *to find; *to find out I
herauskommen *to get out III U1, 22
herausnehmen *to take out I
Herberge hostel III U3, 59
hereinkommen *to get in I
hergestellt sein aus *to be made of
    III U3, 54
Herr *(Anrede)* Mr I
herrlich lovely II
herum around III U1, 19
herumkommen *to get around
    III U5, 100
herunter down III U1, 12
herunterladen to download II
hervorkommen *to come out II
heute today I
heutzutage now II
Hexe witch I
hier here I
hiesig local III U3, 58
Hilfe help II
hilfreich useful III U4, 76
Himbeere raspberry III U4, 80
hinauf up II
hinbringen *to take II
in … hinein inside II
Hin- und Rückfahrkarte return ticket
    III U5, 101
hinfallen *to fall I; *to fall (over)
    III U2, 38
zu … hinfügen to bookmark II
hinter behind II
Hintergrund background III U4, 92
im Hintergrund in the background
    III U4, 92
hinunter down III U1, 12
Hinweis clue I
hinzufügen to add II
Hip-Hop *(Musik)* hip hop III U5, 95
Hobby hobby III ZI 9
hoch high I; tall II
hochladen to upload II

Hochzeit wedding II
hoffen to hope II
hoffnungsvoll hopeful III U4, 77
höflich polite II
Höhe height II
Höhle cave II
Holz wood III U3, 54
hören to listen (to); *to hear I
Hose trousers *(pl)* I
  kurze Hose shorts *(pl)* I
Hotel hotel II
Hotelfachschule catering college II
hübsch beautiful I; pretty; lovely II
Hubschrauber helicopter I
Huhn chicken I
Hühnchen chicken II
Hund dog I
Hundekeks dog biscuit II
hundert a/one hundred I
hungrig hungry I
husten to cough III U1, 21
Hut hat II
hüten to look after II

I

ich I; me I
  ich mag I like I
  ich möchte … I'd like (to) … (= I would like to) I
  ich würde gerne … I'd like (to) … (= I would like to) I
  ich würde lieber I'd rather III U1, 25
  ich würde nicht gerne … I wouldn't like (to) … I
Idee idea I
  Irgendeine Idee? Any idea? I
ihm him I
ihn him I
Ihnen you I
ihr you; her; their I; its III U3, 52
ihre hers II; theirs III U5, 99
Ihre yours II
im in I
  im August in August I
  im Freien outside III U3, 58
  im Bus on the bus II

im Süden von in the south of III U1, 10
Im Ernst? Are you serious? III U3, 58
Imbiss snack I
immer always I
  für immer forever II
in in; to; at I; inside III U1, 31
  in … hinein inside II
  in der Schule at school I
  in Form fit III U2, 34
  in Ordnung fine; all right II
  in der Mitte von in the centre of III U1, 16
Indien India I
indisch Indian II
Industrie industry III U1, 11
industrielle Revolution Industrial Revolution III U1, 11
Informatik IT (Information Technology) I
Information information desk II
Ingenieur engineer II
Ingenieurin engineer II
Inhalt content III U2, 50
innen in inside III U1, 31
Innen- indoor III U2, 34
im **Innern** inside III U1, 31
Insekt insect III U3, 58
Insel island II
intelligent clever II; smart; intelligent III U4, 77
interessant interesting I
sich **interessieren** für *to be interested in III U1, 12
interessiert sein an *to be interested in III U1, 12
Internet internet II
  im Internet surfen to surf the internet II
  ins Internet stellen to upload II
Internettagebuch blog II
Interview interview II
interviewen to interview I
irgendein any II
  Irgendeine Idee? Any idea? I
irgendetwas anything II
irgendwelche any II
Irisch Irish III U5, 94

irisch Irish III U5, 94

J

ja yes I; yeah *(infml)* II
Jacke coat I; jacket II
Jahr year I
Jahrgangsstufe year I
Jahrhundert century III U1, 25
jamaikanisch Jamaican II
jämmerlich miserable III U5, 105
Januar January I
Jeans jeans *(pl)* I
jede every I
jeder everyone I
jedoch however III U4, 85
jemals ever II
jene those II
jetzt now I
  jetzt gleich right now III U5, 98
Job job II
Joghurt yogurt II
Jugend youth *(no pl)* III U5, 94
Jugend- youth *(no pl)* III U5, 94
Jugend- teen II
Jugendliche teen II; teenager III U2, 33
Jugendlicher teen II; teenager III U2, 33
Jugendzentrum activity centre III U2, 34
Juli July I
  am 7. Juli on 7th July I
jung young II
Junge boy I
Juni June I
Juror judge II
Jurorin judge II
Juwelierladen jeweller's III U1, 13

K

Käfig cage I
kalt cold I
Kamel camel III U4, 82
Kamm comb III U5, 97
Kampf battle III U1, 11; fight III U2, 50
kämpfen *to fight III U3, 52

Kanarienvogel canary III U1, 20
Kanone cannon II
Kanonenkugel cannon ball II
Kanufahren canoeing I
Kapitän captain I
Kapitänin captain I
Kappe cap I
kaputt machen *to break II
Karneval carnival I
Karotte carrot II
Karre truck III U1, 21
Karte ticket; card II
Kartoffel potato II
Kartoffelbrei mashed potatoes II
Kartoffelchip crisp I
Karton cardboard III U3, 55
Käse cheese I
Käsekuchen cheesecake II
Katastrophe disaster III U4, 84
Katholik Catholic III U4, 74
Katholikin Catholic III U4, 74
katholisch Catholic III U4, 74
Katze cat I
kaufen *to buy I
Kaufhaus department store II
Kaugummi chewing gum I
kein no I
keine no I
kein not … any II
Keks biscuit II
Kellner waiter II
kennen lernen *to meet I; *to get to
know II
Kerze candle I
Ketchup ketchup II
sieben **Kilogramm** täglich 7 kilo-
grams a day I
40 **Kilometer** pro Stunde 40 kilomet-
res an hour I
Kilt kilt III U3, 53
Kind kid II
Kinder children *(pl)* II
Kinderzimmer bedroom I
Kino cinema I
Kirche church II
Kiste box I
alles **klar** all right II

Klasse year; tutor group I; class
III U2, 36
Klassenlehrer tutor I
Klassenlehrerin tutor I
Klassenzimmer classroom I
Klebstoff glue I
Kleeblatt shamrock III U5, 104
Kleid dress II
Kleider *(Pl.)* clothes *(pl)* I
Kleiderschrank wardrobe I
Kleidung clothes *(pl)* I; outfit
III U5, 105
klein little II; tiny III U1, 17; small
III U2, 35
Klettern rock climbing I
klettern to climb III U2, 34
klicken to click I
klingeln *to ring II
klingen to sound II
Kloß dumpling II
Klub club II
klug clever II; smart; intelligent
III U4, 77
Kneipe pub III U5, 94
Knie knee III U2, 39
Knoblauch garlic II
knuddelig cuddly III U2, 39
Koch chef II
Kochbanane plantain II
kochen to cook II
Köchin chef II
Koffer suitcase II
Kohl cabbage II
Kohle coal III U1, 16
Kombination combination II
komisch funny I
kommen *to come I
ich komme aus … I'm from … I
Kannst du mir sagen, wie ich …
komme? Can you tell me the way
to …? I
Woher kommst du? Where are you
from? I
Kommentar comment II
Komödie comedy III U2, 50
Kontiture jam III U4, 80
König king III U1, 11
Königin queen III U1, 31

königlich royal II
können can I; may II
nicht weg **können** *to be stuck I
nicht können can't I; cannot
III U2, 45
ich kann … nicht finden I can't
find … I
Ich konnte nicht anders als … I
couldn't help but … III U5, 105
Kannst du mir sagen, wie ich …
komme? Can you tell me the way
to …? I
Könntest du das bitte wiederholen? Can you say that again,
please? I
konnte could III U1, 21
könnten could III U3, 58
kontrollieren to check III U4, 81
Konzert concert II
Kopf head II
Kopfsalat lettuce II
Kopfschmerzen headache II
kopfüber head first III U1, 18
Kopfweh headache II
Kopie copy II
kopieren to copy II
Korbball netball I
Körper body III U5, 97
Körperlotion body lotion III U5, 97
korrekt right I
Korridor corridor III U2, 42
kosten *to cost III U4, 75
… kostet 99 Pence … is 99p I
Wie viel (kostet/kosten) …? How
much (is/are) …? I
kostenlos free III U4, 75
köstlich delicious II
Kostüm costume; fancy dress I
krank ill II; sick III U1, 11
Krankenhaus hospital I
Krankenpfleger nurse II
Krankenschwester nurse II
Krankenwagen ambulance III U2, 38
Kraut cabbage II
Kreis circle III U1, 10
Kricket cricket II
Kritik review III U2, 50
Krokodil crocodile I

Küche kitchen I
Kuchen cake I; pie II
Kuh cow III U1, 16
kühl cool I
kühlen to cool III U2, 39
Kühlschrank fridge III U5, 96
sich **kümmern** (um) to care (for)
III U5, 95
Kunde customer III U4, 80
Kundin customer III U4, 80
Kunst Art I
Künstler artist III U5, 98
Künstlerin artist III U5, 98
Kunststoff plastic III U3, 54
Kunststück trick III U2, 41
Kuppel dome II
Kurs course III U5, 95
kurz short II
kurze Hose shorts (pl) I
kurz shortly III U4, 84
Kuscheltier cuddly toy III U2, 39
Kuss kiss II
Küste coast III U2, 33
an der Küste on the coast III U1, 17

L

lachen to laugh II
Ladegerät charger III U5, 97
Laden shop I
Tante-Emma-Laden corner shop I
Lage location III U2, 50
Lager camp II
Lamm lamb II
Lampe lamp I
Land country I; land II; countryside
III U3, 53
Landkarte map I
ländliche Gegend country I
Landschaft countryside III U3, 53
Landwirt farmer I
Landwirtin farmer I
lang long I
langsam slow III U2, 34
langweilig boring I
Lasagne lasagne II
lassen leave II

etw. bleiben lassen to give sth a
miss III U2, 50
lass(t) uns let's (= let us) I
laufen *to run; to walk I
Laut sound III U3, 54
laut noisy III U1, 16; loud III U2, 35
läuten *to ring II
Leben life I
leben to live I
Lebensmittel food I
lecker nice III U3, 58; tasty III U4, 80
Leder leather III U3, 55
legen *to put II
Lehrer teacher I; instructor III U2, 35
Lehrerin teacher I; instructor
III U2, 35
leicht easy I
leid tun *to be sorry III U4, 87
Tut mir leid. Sorry. I
leihen *to lend II
leise quiet III U1, 16
leiten *to run III U4, 75
Leiter ladder I
lernen to learn II
kennen lernen to meet I; to get to
know II
lesen *to read I
letzte last I
Leute people I; guys II
Liebe(r) …, (Anrede in Briefen) Dear
…, I
lieben to love I
ich würde **lieber** I'd rather III U1, 25
Liebesgeschichte romance III U2, 51
Lieferwagen van III U4, 93
Lieblings- favourite I
liegen to rest II
lila purple I
Limonade lemonade II
Lineal ruler I
Linie line III U5, 100
links left III U1, 12
links on the left I
auf der linken Seite on the left I
Liste list II
LKW-Fahrer lorry driver II
LKW-Fahrerin lorry driver II
Loch hole I

locker relaxed; loose II
Löffel spoon II
lokal local III U3, 58
lose loose II
lösen to solve I
Löwe lion I
Luft air III U3, 55
Luftballon balloon I
Lunchpaket packed lunch II
lustig funny I

M

machen *to do; *to make I
ein Foto machen to take a photo I
Hausaufgabe(n) machen to do
homework I
kaputt machen to break II
sich Notizen machen to take
notes I
Mach dir keine Sorgen. Don't
worry. II
Mach dir nichts draus. Never
mind. II
Macht nichts. Never mind. II
Mädchen girl I
Magen stomach II
Magie magic II
Mahlzeit meal II
Mai May I
Mal time III U1, 21
das erste Mal the first time I
malen to paint II
Mama mum I; mama II
manchmal sometimes II
Mann man I
Mannschaft crew III U4, 84
Märchen fable III U5, 105
Marke brand III U4, 81
Markt market II
Marmelade jam III U4, 80
März March I
Maschine machine II
Mathe Maths I
Matsch mud II
Mauer wall II
Maus mouse I
Mayonnaise mayonnaise II

meckern to nag III U4, 76
Medikamente medicine III U2, 39
Medizin medicine III U2, 39
Meer sea I
   am Meer at the seaside I
Meerschweinchen guinea pig II
Mehl flour I
mehr more II
Meile mile II
mein my I
meine mine II
meinen *to mean III U2, 33
meins mine II
Meinung opinion III U2, 50
   seine Meinung ändern to change
   one's mind III U4, 81
   anderer Meinung sein to disagree
   II
eine **Menge** a lot of I
   jede Menge lots of I; lots III U2, 43
Mensa cafeteria I
Mensch person II
Menschenmenge crowd II
sich **merken** to remember II
merkwürdig funny I; strange II
Messer knife II
Metall metal III U3, 54
Meter metre I
Metzgerei butcher's III U1, 13
mich me I
Miete rent II
Mikrowelle microwave II
Milch milk II
Milchmischgetränk milkshake
   III U4, 76
Milchshake milkshake III U4, 76
mild mild I
Milliarde billion II
Million million III U1, 11
   eine halbe Million half a million
   III U1, 16
Mineralwasser mineral water
   III U4, 81
Minute minute II
mir me I
Mir geht es gut. I'm fine. II
mit with I

mit besonderen Bedürfnissen with
   special needs III U5, 95
   Mit den besten Wünschen, Best
   wishes, I
mitbringen *to bring II
Mitleid haben mit *to feel sorry
   III U5, 105
Mittagessen lunch I; dinner II
Mittagspause lunchtime I
Mittagszeit lunchtime I
Mitte centre III U1, 16; middle
   III U4, 92
   in der Mitte in the middle III U4, 92
   in der Mitte von in the centre of
   III U1, 16
Mitternacht midnight III U4, 84
Mittwoch Wednesday I
modern modern I
modisch fashionable II
mögen to like I; to enjoy III U2, 50
   gern mögen to love I
   nicht mögen to hate III U4, 76
   ich mag I like I
   ich mag nicht I don't like I
   ich möchte nicht … I wouldn't like
   (to) … I
   ich möchte … I'd like (to) … (= I
   would like to) I
   Möchtest du? Would you like
   (to)…? I
Möglichkeit chance II
Moment moment II
Monat month I
monatlich monthly III U5, 101
Monster monster III U3, 58
Montag Monday I
Mörder murderer III U2, 50
Mörderin murderer III U2, 50
Morgen morning I
   Guten Morgen. Good morning. II
morgen tomorrow II
Moschee mosque II
Motorrad motorbike I
Moussaka moussaka II
müde tired I
Müll rubbish II
Mund mouth II
Münze coin III U4, 79

Münzgeld change II
Münztelefon pay phone III U3, 67
Museum museum II
Musik music I
Musik- musical III U5, 95
musikalisch musical III U5, 95
Musikgruppe band II
Müsli cereal III U5, 96
Muslim Muslim I
Muslimin Muslim I
müssen must I; *to have to II
   nicht müssen needn't I
mutig brave III U3, 63
Mutter mother I
Mutti mum I
Mütze cap I

N

na ja well I
   Na ja, schau mal … nach. Well,
   look … I
nach to; after I
nach *(bei Uhrzeitangaben)* past I
Nachbar neighbour III U3, 67
Nachbarin neighbour III U3, 67
Nachmittag afternoon I
   am Nachmittag in the afternoon I
nachmittags p.m. II
Nachricht message II
Nachricht(en) news II
Nachspeise dessert; pudding II
nachsprechen *to say I
nächste next I
als **Nächstes** next II
Nacht night I
Nachtwanderung night walk I
Nagel nail III U5, 97
Nagelschere nail scissors III U5, 97
nah near III U1, 15
in der **Nähe** close III U1, 17
   in der Nähe von near I
nahe close III U1, 17
Name name I
Nase nose I
   die Nase voll haben (von) to be
   fed up (with) III U4, 76
nass wet I

National- national III U5, 104
national national III U5, 104
Natur nature III U3, 53
natürlich of course II
Naturwissenschaft Science I
neben next to I
neblig foggy I
nehmen *to take II
neidisch jealous II
nein no I
nennen *to say I
   genannt werden to be called II
nervös nervous II
nett nice; friendly III U2, 35
   Nett, dich kennen zu lernen. Nice
   to meet you. I
Netz web III U3, 63
neu new I
Neuigkeit(en) news II
neun nine I
neunzehn nineteen I
neunzig ninety I
nicht not I
   auch nicht not … either III U3, 58
   nicht dürfen mustn't III U5, 100
   nicht können can't I; cannot
   III U2, 45
   nicht mögen to hate III U4, 76
   nicht werden won't (= will not) II
   ich kann … nicht finden I can't
   find … I
   nicht einverstanden sein to
   disagree II
   nicht mehr not … any more
   III U4, 76
   nicht wahr? isn't it? II
Nichte niece III U4, 80
nichts nothing III U1, 21
nie never I
niedlich cute II
niedrig low II
niemals never I
niemand nobody III U3, 58
niemand no one I
noch even II
   noch ein another II
   noch einmal again II
   noch nicht not … yet II

noch einmal once more II
Norden north III U1, 10
Nordwesten northwest III U1, 16
nordwestlich northwest of III U4, 75
nörgeln to nag III U4, 76
normalerweise usually II
Normanne Norman III U1, 11
die **Normannen** the Normans
   III U1, 11
Normannin Norman III U1, 11
Notdienst emergency service
   III U2, 38
Notfall emergency III U2, 38
sich **Notizen** machen *to take notes I
Notruf emergency call III U2, 38
November November I
Nudelauflauf pasta bake II
Nudeln pasta II
null zero I
null *(bei Uhrzeiten und Telefonnum-*
   mern) oh I
Nummer number I
nun now I
nur just II; only III U1, 16
Nuss nut I
nützlich useful III U4, 76

O

oben up II
obere upper III U4, 92
Oberteil top II
Obst fruit I
   Obst- und Gemüseladen
   greengrocer's III U1, 13
oder or I
Ofenkartoffel jacket potato II
öffentliche Verkehrsmittel public
   transport III U5, 100
öffnen to open I
oft often I
ohne without III U4, 76
Ohr ear II
oje oh dear III U4, 80
okay OK I
Oktober October I
Oma grandma II
Onkel uncle II

online online II
Opa grandad III U4, 75
Operation operation III U2, 39
optimistisch optimistic III U4, 77
Orange orange I
orange orange I
Orchester orchestra III U5, 94
Ordinalzahl ordinal number I
in **Ordnung** bringen to tidy (up) II
   in Ordnung fine; all right II
organisieren to organize II
Ort place I
örtlich local III U3, 58
Osten east III U1, 17
Outdoor- outdoor III U2, 34
Outfit outfit III U5, 105

P

ein **Paar** a pair of II
ein **paar** a few III U3, 58
packen to pack; to pack up II
eine **Packung** … a packet of I
panisch werden to panic II
Papa dad I
Papier paper III U3, 55
Pappe cardboard III U3, 55
Parade parade III U5, 104
Parfüm perfume III U5, 97
Park park I
Partner partner III U5, 99
PartnerIn partner III U5, 99
Party party I
Passagier passenger II
Passagierin passenger II
passen to suit; to fit II
passieren to happen II
Pasta pasta II
Pastete pasty; pie II
Patient patient II
Patientin patient II
in der **Pause** at break I
   Pause machen to take a break II
Pausenhof playground I
Pence *(brit. Währungseinheit)* pence I
   … kostet 99 Pence … is 99p I
Person person II
Personalausweis ID III U5, 97

persönlich personal III U5, 97
Pfannkuchen pancake II
Pfeffer pepper II
Pferd horse I
Pfirsich peach I
Pflanze plant III U2, 33
Pflaster plaster III U2, 39
Pfund *(brit. Währungseinheit)*
  pound I
  das macht 2 Pfund und 24 Pence
  that's £2.24 I
Picknick picnic I
Pieps tweet III U1, 22
Pinguin penguin I
pink pink I
Pirat pirate I
Piratin pirate I
Pirogge pierogi II
Pizza pizza I
Plan plan II
planen to plan II
Plastik plastic III U3, 54
Platz place I; square II
plaudern to chat II
plötzlich suddenly II
Polizei police III U2, 38
Polizeibeamter police officer I
Polizeibeamtin police officer I
Pommes chips *(pl)* I
  Pommes mit Fisch fish and chips I
Popcorn popcorn I
positiv positive III U4, 76
Postamt post office I
Poster poster I
Postkarte postcard I
Pranger stocks III U2, 43
präsentieren to present I
Preis prize; price II
Prise pinch II
pro Stück each II
Problem problem I; trouble III U2, 33
Projekt project III U5, 98
Prospekt brochure III U1, 31
Protestant Protestant III U4, 74
Protestantin Protestant III U4, 74
protestantisch Protestant III U4, 74
prüfen to test II
Pudding pudding II

pünktlich on time III U5, 100
putzen to clean I

Q

Quittung receipt II

R

Rad wheel III U3, 55
Radfahren cycling III U3, 61
Radiergummi eraser I
Radio radio III U3, 67
Rafting rafting III U2, 33
rappen to rap II
Rapper rapper III U5, 98
Rapperin rapper III U5, 98
rasten to rest II
Rat advice III U2, 51
raten to guess II
Ratschlag advice III U2, 51
Rätsel mystery I
Rauch smoke III U2, 42
Raum room I
(Taschen-) Rechner calculator I
Rechnung bill III U3, 59
Du hast **recht**. You're right. I
  recht haben to be right II
rechts on the right I; right III U1, 12
  auf der rechten Seite on the right I
Rechtschreibung spelling I
Rede speech III U3, 54
reden (mit) to talk (to) I
Regal shelf I
Regalbrett shelf I
Regel rule III U2, 34
Regenbogen rainbow III U5, 104
Regenmantel raincoat III U5, 97
Regenschirm umbrella II
Regisseur director II
Regisseurin director II
regnen to rain I
reich rich III U3, 54
reichen to pass II
Reichtum wealth III U5, 105
Reifen tyre III U3, 55
in die richtige **Reihenfolge** bringen
  *to put in the right order I

Reis rice II
Reise trip III U3, 58; voyage III U4, 84;
  journey III U5, 100
reisen to travel II
Reiten horse riding I
reiten *to ride II
Religionsunterricht RE (Religious
  Education) I
Rennen race I
rennen *to run I
reparieren to repair III U3, 67
Reporter reporter III U2, 42
Reporterin reporter III U2, 42
Republik republic III U5, 94
Requisit prop III U2, 45
reservieren *to make a reservation
  III U3, 59
Reservierung reservation III U3, 59
Restaurant restaurant II
  Fastfood-Restaurant fast food
  restaurant I
retten to save III U4, 85
Rettungsboot lifeboat III U2, 33
Rettungsdienst emergency service
  III U2, 38
Rezept recipe II
richtig right I; real II
das **Richtige** tun *to do the right
  thing III U2, 38
in diese **Richtung** this way II
riechen *to smell III U1, 20
Riese giant III U4, 75
riesengroß huge III U1, 17
Riesenrad big wheel II
riesig huge III U1, 17
Rindfleisch beef II
Ring circle III U1, 10
Ritt ride II
Ritter knight III U2, 42
Rock skirt I
Rohr tube III U3, 55
Rolle part II
Rollstuhl wheelchair III U2, 43
Rolltreppe escalator II
die **Römer** the Romans III U1, 10
rosa pink I
rot red I

rot

Hin- und **Rückfahrkarte** return ticket III U5, 101

Ruf call III U5, 104

rufen to call; to shout II

Rugby rugby III U2, 34

Ruhe silence III U1, 20

ruhig quiet III U1, 16

Rührei scrambled egg II

rühren to stir II

ruinieren to ruin II

Rüstung armour III U2, 43

S

Sache thing II

Sack bag I

Saft juice II

sagen *to say; *to tell I

Salat salad II

Salz salt II

sammeln to collect I

Samstag Saturday I

samstags on Saturdays I

Sand sand II

Sandwich sandwich I

Sänger singer I

Sängerin singer I

sauber clean III U3, 53
    sauber machen to clean I

sauer sein *to be fed up (with) III U4, 76

Saxofon saxophone I

eine **Schachtel** … a box of I

Schaf sheep I

Schal scarf II

Schälchen bowl II

Schale bowl II

Schatz treasure II

(nach)**schauen** to look I

Schauspielen acting III U5, 95

Schauspieler actor II

Schauspielerei acting III U5, 95

Schauspielerin actor II

Schauspielworkshop acting workshop II

Schere scissors (pl) III U5, 97

schick chic I

schicken *to send I

schieben to push I

Schiff ship I

Schiffsbauer ship builder III U4, 84

Schiffsbauerin ship builder III U4, 84

Schiffsfahrt boat trip II

Schild sign III U2, 32

Schinken ham II

Schlacht battle III U1, 11

Schlaf sleep III U2, 39

schlafen *to sleep I; *to be asleep III U1, 25

Schlafzimmer bedroom I

schlagen *to hit II; *to beat III U3, 62

Schlamm mud I

Schlange snake I

schlau clever II; smart III U4, 77

Schlauch tube III U3, 55

schlecht ill II; bad III U2, 38

schlechteste worst III U1, 16

schlicht plain II

schließen to close I

schließlich in the end; finally II

schlimm bad III U2, 38

schlimmste worst III U1, 16

Schloss castle II

Schlumpf smurf I

Schluss end II; ending III U2, 45
    zum Schluss in the end; finally II

Schlussfolgerung conclusion III U2, 50

Schlussverkauf sale II

schmackhaft tasty III U4, 80

schmerzhaft sore II

Schmuck jewellery II

Schmuggler smuggler II

Schmugglerin smuggler II

schmutzig dirty I

Schnäppchen bargain II

schnappen to grab III U5, 105

schneiden *to cut III U2, 39
    sich die Haare schneiden lassen to have a haircut II

der/die/das **schnellste** the fastest I

schnell fast II; quick III U2, 34

schnell quickly II

Schokolade chocolate I
    eine Tafel Schokolade a bar of chocolate I

schön nice; beautiful I; fine; lovely II

schon already; yet II

Schon gut. Never mind. II

Schotte Scot III U3, 53

Schottenrock kilt III U3, 53

Schottin Scot III U3, 53

schottisch Scottish III U3, 53

Schrank cupboard III U5, 98

schrecklich awful I; horrible III U4, 77

Schrei shout I

schreiben *to write I
    eine SMS schreiben to text II

schreien to shout II

Schriftsteller writer II

Schriftstellerin writer II

Schritt step III U5, 102

schubsen to push III U5, 102

Schuh shoe II

Schule school I
    in der Schule at school I

Schüler student I

Schülerin student I

Schulfach subject I

Schulhof playground I

Schulstunde lesson I

Schüssel bowl II

schützen to protect III U3, 53

schwach weak III U2, 35

schwarz black I

Schweigen silence III U1, 20

schweigsam silent III U1, 21

Schweinefleisch pork II

schwer heavy; hard II

schwerhörig deaf III U3, 54

Schwert sword III U2, 43

Schwester sister I

schwierig difficult; hard II

Schwierigkeiten trouble III U2, 33

Schwimmbad swimming pool I

schwimmen *to swim II
    schwimmen gehen to go swimming I

Science-Fiction science fiction I

Scone (eine Art süßes Brötchen) scone II

sechs six I

sechzehn sixteen I

sechzig sixty I

See lake III U3, 53
sehen *to see I; to look II
Sehenswürdigkeit sight II
zu **sehr** too much II
sehr very I
   so sehr so much III U4, 76
Seide silk III U3, 55
Seife soap III U5, 97
Seil rope I
Seilrutsche zip line III U2, 32
sein *to be I
   hergestellt sein aus to be made of
   III U3, 54
   sauer sein to be fed up (with)
   III U4, 76
   sei still don't talk I
sein his I; its III U3, 52
seiner his II
seins his II
Seite side II
Sekunde second II
selber myself III U2, 34; ourselves;
   yourselves; themselves III U2, 152
ihr/euch/Sie/sich (**selbst**) yourselves
   III U2, 152
   dich selbst yourself II
   sie selbst herself; themselves
   III U2, 152
selbst myself; self III U2, 34
selbstbewusst confident III U4, 77
selbstsicher confident; sure of
   oneself III U4, 77
selbstverständlich of course II
seltsam strange II
senden *to send I
Senf mustard II
September September I
Serviette napkin II
setzen *to put II
   sich (hin)setzen to sit (down) I
Shampoo shampoo III U5, 96
Shirt shirt II
Shorts shorts (pl) I
sich each other; self III U2, 34
   sich (selbst) himself III U2, 34
   sich gegenseitig each other
   III U2, 34
   sich selbst herself III U2, 152

sicher sure II; safe III U2, 35
Sie you I
sie she I; them II
sie (Pl.) they I
   sie selbst herself III U2, 152
sieben seven I
siebzehn seventeen I
siebzig seventy I
siegen *to win I
Signal signal III U3, 67
singen *to sing I
sinken *to sink III U4, 84
Situation situation II
Sitzbank bench III U4, 87
Skateboard skateboard III U2, 41
Ski fahren to ski II
Skifahren skiing III U2, 32
SMS message II
   eine SMS schreiben to text II
Textnachricht (**SMS**) text message I
SMS-Schreiber texter II
SMS-Schreiberin texter II
Snack snack I
so like that I; so II
   so sehr so much III U4, 76
so … wie as … as II
so like this III U3, 62
Socke sock I
soeben just II
Sofa sofa II
sofort right now III U5, 98
Software software II
sogar even II
Sohn son III U3, 64
Soldat soldier III U3, 62
Soldatin soldier III U3, 62
sollte should III U2, 38
Sommer summer II
Sonderangebot special offer III U4, 80
Sonne sun III U1, 11
sonnenbaden to sunbathe II
Sonnenbrille sunglasses (pl) II
sonnig sunny I
Sonntag Sunday I
sich **Sorgen** machen to worry I
Mach dir keine **Sorgen.** Don't worry.
   II
Sorte sort II; type III U1, 31

Soße sauce II
Souvenir souvenir III U1, 12
Souvenirladen souvenir shop
   III U1, 12
Spaghetti spaghetti II
spannend exciting I
Spaß fun I
   zum Spaß for fun III U2, 43
Wie **spät** ist es? What time is it? I
   (zu) spät late II
später later I; after III U4, 84
spazieren gehen *to go for a walk I
Spaziergang walk III U3, 61
speichern to save II
Speise dish II
Speisekarte menu II
speziell special I
Spiegel mirror III U5, 97
Spiel game I
spielen to play I; to act II
Spieler player II
Spieler (Computer) gamer II
Spielerin player II
Spielerin (Computer) gamer II
Spielfeld court III U4, 87
Spielkarte card II
Spielplatz playground I
Spielzeug toy III U2, 39
Spinne spider III U3, 63
Spinnennetz web III U3, 63
Sport sport I
Sportart sport III U2, 33
Sportgeschäft sports shop I
Sportunterricht PE (Physical Educa-
   tion) I
Sprache language II; speech III U3, 54
sprechen *to say I; *to speak III U1, 21
sprechen (mit) to talk (to) I
   sprechen über to talk about II
Spritze injection III U2, 39
spülen to wash III U5, 98
Spur clue I
Stadion stadium II
Stadt town I; city II
Stadtmitte city centre III U2, 33
Stadtplan map I
Stadtzentrum city centre III U2, 33
Stahl steel III U3, 55

Stahl

261

Standinhaber stallholder II
Standinhaberin stallholder II
Star star I
stark heavy II
Start start III U2, 51
starten to start II
staubsaugen to hoover II
stehen to suit; *to stand II
steigen to climb III U2, 34
Stein rock III U2, 38; stone III U1, 10
Stelle place I
stellen *to put II
sterben to die III U1, 21
Stern star III U2, 50
Stiefel boot II
Stift pen I
Stil style III U5, 95
still quiet III U1, 16
Stille silence III U1, 20
Stimme voice III U1, 22
stimmt's? isn't it? II
Stockwerk floor II
stolz (auf) proud (of) III U3, 65
(sich) **stoßen** to hit III U2, 40
Strand beach I
  den Strand nach Strandgut absuchen to go beach combing II
Straße road I; street III U1, 15
Straßenbahn tram III U5, 100
Streich trick I
streichen to paint II
Streit argument II; fight III U2, 50
(sich) **streiten** *to fight III U3, 52
Strom electricity III U3, 53
Stück piece II
  pro Stück each II
Stufe step II
Stuhl chair I
stumm silent III U1, 21
40 Kilometer pro **Stunde** 40 kilometres an hour I
Stundenplan timetable I
Sturm storm I
stürzen to rush III U5, 105
suchen to look for I
Süden south III U1, 10
  im Süden von in the south of III U1, 10

super cool I; way to go II
Superman superman I
Supermarkt supermarket II
Suppe soup II
surfen to surf II
  im Internet surfen to surf the internet II
süß cute II; sweet III U5, 96
Süßes, sonst gibt's Saures! Trick or treat! I
Süßigkeit sweet I
Sweatshirt sweatshirt I
Szene scene II

T

Tablett tray II
Tablette tablet II
Tafel board I
  eine Tafel Schokolade a bar of chocolate I
Tag day I
  ein ausgefüllter Tag a busy day I
  eines Tages one day III U1, 21
  den ganzen Tag all day III U3, 58
Tagebuch diary I
täglich daily III U5, 101
  vier Stunden täglich four hours a day I
Taktik tactic III U3, 64
talentiert talented III U2, 35
Talentwettbewerb talent show I
Tante aunt II
tanzen to dance I
Tänzer dancer I
Tänzerin dancer I
tapfer brave III U3, 63
Tasche bag I
Taschenlampe torch I
Taschentuch tissue III U4, 81
Tasse cup II
Tätigkeit job II
Tatsache fact II
tatsächlich actually III U5, 105
taub deaf III U3, 54
tausend a/one thousand II
Taxi taxi II
Team team I

Teamwork teamwork II
Technik Design Technology (DT) I
Techniker engineer II
Technikerin engineer II
Tee tea I
Teelöffel teaspoon II
Teenager teen II; teenager III U2, 33
Teenagerin teenager III U2, 33
Teil part II
teilen to share III U5, 96
teilnehmen (an) *to take part (in) III U5, 100
Telefon phone II; telephone III U3, 54
  ans Telefon gehen to answer the phone III U2, 45
Telefonanruf phone call I
telefonieren to phone I
Telefonnummer phone number III U2, 38
Telefonzelle telephone box II
Teller plate II
Tennis tennis I
Teppich carpet I
testen to test II
teuer expensive II
Text lines; text II
texten to text II
Textnachricht (SMS) text message I
Theater theatre; drama II
Theaterstück play II
Thunfisch tuna II
Tier animal I
Tierarzt vet II
Tierärztin vet II
Tierhandlung pet shop III U1, 13
Tierheim animal rescue shelter I
Tierpark zoo I
Tierpfleger zookeeper I
Tierpflegerin zookeeper I
Tiger tiger I
Tipp tip III U3, 58
Tisch table I
  den Tisch decken to lay the table II
Tischler carpenter II
Tischlerin carpenter II
Tischtennis table tennis II
Tochter daughter I

tödlich deadly III U1, 20
toll great; brilliant I; amazing III U3, 63
Tomate tomato II
Ton sound III U3, 54
Tonne tonne II
Top top II
Topf pot III U5, 104
tot dead III U1, 22
töten to kill III U1, 20
Tourist tourist I
Touristin tourist I
Touristeninformation Tourist Information Centre I
Tradition tradition III U3, 53
tragen *to wear I; to carry III U5, 103
trainieren to practise III U5, 96
Training practice I; training III U2, 41
Traktor tractor I
Transporter van III U4, 93
Ich **traute** meinen Augen nicht. I couldn't believe my eyes. III U5, 105
Traum dream II
träumen *to dream III U1, 25
traurig sad III U3, 65; down III U4, 77
treffen *to hit II
(sich) **treffen** to meet II
Trick trick I
trinken *to drink II
Trinkhalm straw II
Trip trip III U2, 34
trocken dry III U2, 35
Trommel- drumming III U5, 100
Tschüss! Bye!; See you! I
T-Shirt T-shirt I
Tuch scarf II
tun *to do; *to make I
leid tun to be sorry III U4, 87
Tut mir leid. Sorry. I
Was kann ich für dich tun? How can I help you? I
Tunnel tunnel III U1, 20
Tür door II
Türkei Turkey II
Türklingel doorbell I
Turm tower II
Turnier competition III U5, 95
turnieren to joust III U2, 43

Turnierzweikampf jousting III U2, 43
einen Turnierzweikampf austragen to joust III U2, 43
Turnschuh trainer I
eine **Tüte …** a packet of I
Tüte bag I
Typ type III U1, 31

U

U-Bahn underground II
üben to practise III U5, 96
über about; across II
überall wo(hin) wherever III U5, 107
sich **übergeben** *to be sick I
überleben to survive III U4, 84
überlegen to guess II
übernachten to stay II
Übernachtung sleepover I
überprüfen to check III U4, 81
überqueren to cross III U1, 12
überrascht surprised II
Überraschung surprise I
U-Boot submarine I
Übung practice I
Übungsheft exercise book I
Uhr clock II
Wie viel Uhr ist es? What time is it? I
Uhr (Zeitangabe bei vollen Stunden) o'clock I
Uhrenturm clock tower II
Uhrzeit time I
um at I
umfallen *to fall (over) III U2, 38
Umfrage survey II
umher around III U1, 19
umrühren to stir II
umsteigen to change III U5, 100
umziehen to move (house) II
Umzug parade III U5, 104
unangenehm uncomfortable II
unbequem uncomfortable II
und and I
Und du? What about you? II
unfair unfair III U1, 16
Unfall accident III U2, 38
unfreundlich unfriendly III U2, 35

ungefähr about II
ungefähr um around III U5, 96
ungefährlich safe III U2, 35
Ungeheuer monster III U3, 58
unglaublich amazing III U3, 63
Unglück disaster III U4, 84
unglücklich unhappy II
Uniform uniform I
unmodisch unfashionable II
unmöglich impossible III U3, 62
Unordnung mess I
uns us I
unser our I
unsere ours III U5, 96
unter under I
untere lower III U4, 92
untergehen *to sink III U4, 84
Unterricht lesson I; class III U5, 102
unterwegs out and about I
Urlaub holiday II
Ururopa great-great-grandad I

V

Vanillesauce custard II
Vater father I
Vati dad I
Vegetarier vegetarian I
Vegetarierin vegetarian I
verändern to change III U3, 54
verängstigt scared I
verärgert angry II; annoyed III U4, 77
Verband bandage III U2, 39
verbessern to correct I
verbinden to connect III U3, 67
in **Verbindung** bleiben *to keep in touch II
verbrennen *to burn III U2, 39
verbringen (Zeit) *to spend II
verdrehen to twist II
Verein club II
Verfasser writer III U2, 50
Verfasserin writer III U2, 50
Vergangenheit past III U1, 16
vergessen *to forget I
vergleichen to compare I
verkaufen *to sell III U1, 13

Verkäufer shop assistant II; assistant III U4, 83

Verkäuferin shop assistant II; assistant III U4, 83

Verkehr traffic III U1, 16

öffentliche **Verkehrsmittel** public transport III U5, 100

verkleidet (als) dressed III U5, 105

Verkleidung fancy dress I

verlassen leave II

verlegen embarrassed II

verletzen *to hurt II

sich **verlieben** (in) *to fall in love (with) III U2, 50

verlieren *to lose II

einen Auftrag **vermasseln** *to get a job wrong III U2, 50

vermissen to miss II

Vermittlung operator III U2, 38

vernünftig intelligent III U4, 77

verrenken to sprain III U2, 39

verrückt crazy I

jmdn. verrückt machen to drive sb crazy III U4, 76

verstauchen to sprain III U2, 39

(sich) **verstecken** *to hide III U2, 50

verstehen *to understand II; *to get III U4, 80

Versuch experiment II

vervollständigen to complete I; to finish II

verwenden to use II

verwirrt confused III U1, 25

verzerren to twist II

auf etw. **verzichten** *to give sth a miss III U2, 50

Vesper packed lunch II

Video video II

Video-Chat video chat III U3, 67

viel much; lots of; a lot of I; lots III U2, 43

viel a lot of III U1, 16

viele many II

wie viele how many II

vielleicht may II

vielleicht maybe II

vier four I

vierte fourth I

Viertel nach quarter past I

Viertel vor quarter to I

vierzehn fourteen I

vierzig forty I

viktorianisches Zeitalter Victorian era III U1, 25

violett purple I

Vogel bird III U3, 61

Vogelbeobachtung bird watching III U3, 61

Volleyball volleyball II

völlig quite III U2, 34

von from I; by II

ein Foto von a photo of I

vor ago II

vor (bei Uhrzeitangaben) to I

vorbei (an) past III U1, 12

vorbereiten to prepare III U5, 96

Vordergrund foreground III U4, 92

im Vordergrund in the foreground III U4, 92

Vorgehensweise tactic III U3, 64

vorhaben *to be up to III U3, 67

vorher before II

vorhersagen to foretell III U5, 105

Vormittag morning I

vormittags a.m. II

vorsichtig sein *to be careful II

Vorsingen audition II

Vorspielen audition II

Vorsprechen audition II

Vortanzen audition II

vorziehen to prefer II

W

wach awake III U2, 38

Wagen truck III U1, 21

wählen *to choose II

wahr true II

während during III U1, 11

während while II

wahrscheinlich probably III U4, 75

Wald wood II

Waliser Welsh III U2, 32

Waliserin Welsh III U2, 32

walisisch Welsh III U2, 32

Walisisch Welsh III U2, 32

Wand wall II

Wandern hiking III U3, 58; walking III U3, 61

wandern to hike II

Wandgemälde mural III U4, 74

wann when I

warm warm I

warten to wait II

warten auf to wait for II

Warteschlange queue II

warum why II

was what I

Was kann ich für dich tun? How can I help you? I

Was man … What to … II

Was ist los? What's wrong? II

Was stimmt nicht? What's wrong? II

Was?! No way! III U3, 58

Waschbär raccoon I

(sich) **waschen** to wash III U5, 98

Wasser water III U2, 33

Website website II

Wechselgeld change II

Hier ist dein Wechselgeld. Here's your change. I

wechseln to change II

Wecker alarm clock I

Weg way III U1, 12

nach dem Weg fragen asking the way I

nicht **weg** können *to be stuck I

weg away II

wegen because of III U2, 37

weglaufen *to run away III U2, 50

weh tun *to hurt II

Weihnachten Christmas I

Weihnachtstheaterstück pantomime II

weil because I

auf diese **Weise** like this III U3, 62

weiß white I

weit far III U1, 12

welche which; what; who II

Welle wave I

wellenreiten to surf II

Welt world II

auf der Welt in the world II

ein **wenig** a bit II
wenige a few III U3, 58
weniger less III U4, 80
wenn when; if II
wer who I
werden will; *to become II
   nicht werden won't (= will not) II
Werft shipyard III U4, 84
Werk factory III U1, 16
an **Werktagen** on weekdays III U5, 96
Werkzeug tool II
Westen west III U1, 17
Wettbewerb competition III U5, 95
Wetter weather I
Wettrennen race I
wichtig important III U2, 33
wie like II
wie as II
   so … wie as … as II
wie how I; what III U1, 12
   wie viele how many II
   Wie alt bist du? How old are you? I
   Wie bitte? Pardon? I
   wie etwas war what sth was like III U1, 12
   Wie geht es dir? How are you? I
   Wie heißt du? What's your name? I
   Wie man … How to … II
   Wie musst du sein? What must you be like? III U2, 37
   Wie spät ist es? What time is it? I
   Wie viel (kostet/kosten) …? How much (is/are) …? I
   Wie viel Uhr ist es? What time is it? I
wieder again II
wiederholen to repeat III U4, 80
   Könntest du das bitte wiederholen? Can you say that again, please? I
Auf **Wiedersehen**. Goodbye. I
wiegen to weigh II
die **Wikinger** the Vikings III U1, 11
willkommen (bei/in) welcome (to) I
Wind wind I
windig windy I
Windpark wind farm III U3, 53
Windrad (wind) turbine III U3, 53

winken to wave II
Winter winter I
winzig tiny III U1, 17
wir we I
wirklich real II
wirklich actually III U5, 105
Wirklich? Really? I
wirr confused III U1, 25
Ich **weiß** (es) nicht! I don't know! I
   Weißt du was? Guess what? I
Wissenschaft Science I
Witz joke I
witzig funny I
wo where I
   wo(hin) auch immer wherever III U5, 107
Woche week I
   unter der Woche on weekdays III U5, 96
Wochenende weekend I
   am Wochenende at the weekend I
wöchentlich weekly III U5, 101
woher where I
   Woher kommst du? Where are you from? I
wohin where I
wohnen to live I
Wohnung flat I
Wohnwagen caravan III U3, 59
Wohnzimmer living room I
Wolke cloud III U2, 42
wolkig cloudy I
Wolle wool I
wollen to want (to) I
Workshop workshop II
Wrap wrap II
wund sore II
Mit den besten **Wünschen**, Best wishes, I
wünschen to wish III U1, 25
würde(n) would II
   würde(n) gern would like II
   ich würde gerne … I'd like (to) … (= I would like to) I
   ich würde nicht gerne … I wouldn't like (to) … I
Wurst sausage II
wütend angry II; furious III U4, 77

Z

Zahl number I
Zahn tooth III U2, 39
Zahnbürste toothbrush III U5, 96
Zahnpasta toothpaste III U5, 97
Zahnstocher toothpick II
Zauberei magic II
Zebra zebra I
zehn ten I
Zeichen sign III U2, 32; signal III U3, 67
Zeichensprache sign language III U5, 95
zeichnen *to draw II
zeigen *to show II
Zeit time I
viktorianisches **Zeitalter** Victorian era III U1, 25
Zeitpunkt date I
Zeitreise time travel III U4, 79
Zeitschrift magazine I
Zeitschriftenladen newsagent's III U1, 13
Zelt tent II
Zelten camping III U2, 36
Zeltplatz campsite III U3, 58
Zentimeter (cm) centimetre (cm) I
Zentrum centre III U1, 16
zerstören to ruin II
Ziege goat III U1, 16
ziehen to pull I
ziemlich quite III U2, 34
Zimmer room I
Zimmerdecke ceiling I
Zimmerin carpenter II
Zimmermann carpenter II
Zitrone lemon II
Zoo zoo I
   im Zoo at the zoo I
zornig angry II
zu too II
   zu sehr too much II
zu to I
   zu Hause back home II
zubereiten to prepare III U5, 96
zuerst first I
Zug train I

mit (dem Zug) fahren to go by (train) I
Zuhause home I
zuhören to listen (to) I
zum Schluss finally II
    zum Spaß for fun III U2, 43
zumachen to close I
zuordnen to match I
zurück back III U2, 41

zurückzahlen *to pay back II
zusammen together I
zusammen everyone II
zusammenzucken to jump III U2, 42
Zusatz- extra II
zusätzlich extra II
zuschauen to watch II
zustimmen to agree II
Zutat ingredient II

zuvor before II
zwanzig twenty I
zwei two I
zweite second I
Zwiebel onion II
zwischen between II
zwölf twelve I

Lösungen Extra practice

Seite 28

1 Write the name of the places.
1. Hadrian's Wall, 2. York, 3. Manchester,
4. Stonhenge, 5. Hastings

2 Where do you go to ...
1. baker's
2. sports shop
3. clothes shop
4. card shop
Which shop don't you need? shoe shop

3 Write Ben's sentences.
1. I never get up before 8 p.m.
2. I usually fly to different places.
3. But sometimes I also walk.
4. I always eat little animals for breakfast.
5. Cheese? No, I never have that.
6. I usually go to bed in the morning.

4 Write Ben's sentences.
1. Does your friend sometimes buy T-shirts at the new clothes shop?
2. Do you sometimes go shopping in the York Sweet Shop?
3. Do they often play football after school?
4. Does she usually buy bread at the baker's on the weekend?
5. Does the new shoe shop always open at 10 p.m.?
6. Does your family usually walk to the card shop?

Seite 29

5 Find the way.
a) 1. swimming pool
   2. park
   3. café
b) 1. opposite
   2. next to
   3. corner
   4. cross, right

6 Write sentences about Hannah.
1. Hannah didn't get up at 9 a.m. So she was late.
2. Hannah met her friend on the bus.
3. They went shopping and had lots of ice cream.
4. Hannah didn't call her mum at 4 p.m.
5. They went back home at 5 p.m. Hannah's mum was angry.
6. So they didn't go to the cinema in the evening.

7 Write the questions.
1. Did you forget your mobile?
2. Did you buy a new T-shirt?
3. Did you go to the library?
4. Did you have a good time together?
5. Did you buy cheese and tomatoes?

Seite 48

1 What's the word?
1. capital
2. canoeing, rafting
3. road signs
4. lifeboats
5. rugby
6. rules
7. volunteers
8. outdoor
9. rock climbing

2 What did the rock climbing instructor say?
1. carefully
2. loudly
3. good
4. hard
5. easy
6. slowly
7. careful
8. wet
9. tired

3 Match the parts of the dialogue.
1. F; 2. E; 3. D; 4. B; 5. A; 6. G; 7. C

Seite 49

4 Write about accidents.
a) 1. have an accident
   2. break my arm
   3. cut my finger
   4. twist my knee
   5. burnt my finger
   6. sprain my ankle

b) 1. I've had an accident.
   2. I've burnt my arm.
   3. I'v cut my finger.
   4. I've twisted my knee.
   5. I've burnt my finger.
   6. I've sprain my ankle.

5 What have the people done? What haven't they done yet?

1. Claire has bought some tablets. She hasn't taken them yet.
2. Nick has burnt his hand. He hasn't cooled it yet.
3. Molly has twisted her knee. She hasn't put a bandage on it yet.
4. Joe has gone to the doctor. He hasn't seen the doctor yet.

6 Complete the text.

Megan loves outdoor activities and sports. She has already tried many things (1). She has started (2) to play tennis when she was (3) ten years old. Two years ago she rode (4) her bike up Mount Snowdon. But canoeing is her favourite and she has already won (5) lots of prizes. Last year she had (6) an accident and broke (7) her arm. But it has got (8) better quickly and she has already been (9) on the river again this year. Have you ever gone (10) canoeing?

Seite 70

1 Match the sentence parts.

1. C; 2. F; 3. G; 4. B; 5. H; 6. E; 7. D; 8. A

2 What's the material?

1. This chair is made of wood.
2. This magazine is made of paper.
3. This fork is made of metal.
4. This bag is made of plastic.
5. This bag is made of leather.
6. This spoon is made of wood.
7. This eraser is made of rubber.
8. This T-shirt is made of cotton.

3 Complete the sentences.

1. A kilt is a skirt which is for men.
2. Robert the Bruce was a king who fought against the English.
3. Edinburgh is a Scottish city which is very old.
4. Porridge is a dish which has oats in it.
5. Scotland is a country which doesn't have much sun.
6. A cottage is a house which is small and often in the country.
7. An inventor is a person who invents machines and other things.

Seite 71

4 Use whose to make one sentence out of two.

1. Inventors are important persons whose ideas make life easies.
2. Bell was a famous inventor whose wife and his mother were both deaf.
3. Bell was a teacher whose wish was to help people who couldn't hear well.
4. Bell became a famous man whose invention changed the world forever.

5 Complete the sentences.

1. If we don't want to pay much, we will stay at a campsite.
2. We will freeze if we stay at a campsite.
3. There won't be any insects if we go to a cosy B & B.
4. If we are in a hotel, we will have our own bathroom.
5. We won't get nice food if we stay at a campsite.
6. If we choose a hotel, we won't have money for anything else.
7. We will take a cottage if a hotel room is too expensive.
8. If we see the Loch Ness monster, everyone will be happy.

6 Make sentences.
1. If I go to Scotland, I will visit Edinburgh.
2. If I see Nessie, I'll take a photo.
3. If I have money, Ill go shopping.
4. If I stay in a B & B, I'll eat porridge.
5. If it's wet tomorrow, I won't go into the mountains.
6. If I go to the museum, I'll learn about history.

Seite 90

1 Find the places.
1. Northern Ireland
2. bed and breakfast
3. Lough Neagh
4. Giant's Causeway
5. Maggie's shop
6. Belfast

2 Find the adjectives and make a new word.
1. smart
2. confident
3. fed up
4. furious
5. horrible
6. sad
7. optimistic
8. tourist

3 What would they do?
1. If Julie lived in a B & B, she would talk to the tourists.
2. If Sarah's parents had more time, it would be more fun.
3. If Sarah's mum didn't nag her, Sarah would feel better.
4. If Ashley didn't help Sarah, it would be horrible.
5. If Julie lived nearer, Sarah wouldn't miss her.
6. If Julie visited Sarah, she would ask silly questions.
7. If Sarah and her family lived in Belfast, Sarah would see her friend more often.

4 Complete the shopping dialogue.
1. like
2. jar
3. else
4. are
5. change
6. you

Seite 91

5 Write a shopping list.
two bottles of orange juice, two loaves of bread, a jar of strawberry jam, a bottle of mineral water, a jar of peanut butter, a packet if tissues

6 Compare the things.
1. Northern Ireland isn't as big as Scotland.
2. The train is faster than the car.
3. Rice is as good as pasta.
4. Rugby isn't as popular as football in Northern Ireland.
5. Belfast isn't as warm as Berlin today.
6. Orange juice is more expensive than mineral water.

7 Complete the dialogue in the supermarket.
1. any
2. some
3. some
4. any
5. some
6. any
7. any
8. some

Seite 110

1 Find the words.
1. competition
2. St Patrick's day; green
3. pubs
4. dance; courses
5. EU (European Union)
6. orchestra

2 What is it?
1. toothpaste
2. kitchen
3. bed
4. fridge
5. shampoo
6. tea
7. hairdryer

3 Put in the right forms.
1. 'm (am) doing
2. cooks
3. have
4. 's (is) practising
5. 's (is) wearing
6. uses
7. 's (is) shouting
8. rains

Seite 111

4 Match and make sentences.

a) 1. get off (around)
   2. public transport
   3. get around (off)
   4. bus timetable
   5. plan the journey
   6. pay the fare

b) 1. plan the journey
   2. get off
   3. pay the fare
   4. bus timetable
   5. public transport
   6. get around

5 Concert rules. Must or mustn't?

1. mustn't
2. must
3. mustn't
4. mustn't
5. must
6. mustn't
7. mustn't
8. mustn't

6 Put in the right word.

1. must
2. needn't
3. mustn't
4. must
5. needn't
6. mustn't
7. needn't
8. must

Lösungen Zoom in (Seite 8)

1. England, Wales, Scotland, Northern Ireland and the Republic of Ireland
2. England
3. The Republic of Ireland
4. Scotland
5. Northern Ireland
6. Scotland
7. London
8. The Republic of Ireland
9. England

Bildquellennachweis

Cover.1 plainpicture GmbH (Ableimages/Jutta Klee), Hamburg; **Cover.2** plainpicture GmbH (Bias), Hamburg; **2.1** plainpicture GmbH (Robert Harding), Hamburg; **3.1** Mauritius Images (Alamy), Mittenwald; **3.2** Getty Images (The Image Bank/Victoria Snowber), München; **4.1** plainpicture GmbH (Cultura), Hamburg; **4.2** Getty Images (Joe Daniel Price), München; **5.1** Alamy Images (GL Archive), Abingdon, Oxon; **9.1** plainpicture GmbH (Bias), Hamburg; **9.2** plainpicture GmbH (Design Pics/Wayne Hutchinson), Hamburg; **9.3** plainpicture GmbH (Westend61/lyzs), Hamburg; **9.4** plainpicture GmbH (Design Pics/The Irish Image Collection), Hamburg; **9.5** Corbis (Lola Akinmade Akerstrom/National Geographic Creative), Berlin; **9.6** Thinkstock (Jessica Hunnicutt), München; **9.7** iStockphoto (Guillermo Perales Gonzalez), Calgary, Alberta; **9.8** iStockphoto (kati1313), Calgary, Alberta; **9.9** Thinkstock (Brian Doty), München; **9.10** iStockphoto (jcarter), Calgary, Alberta; **10.1** plainpicture GmbH (Arcaid), Hamburg; **10.2** plainpicture GmbH (Robert Harding), Hamburg; **11.1** Getty Images (Iconica/Arctic-Images), München; **11.2** Alamy Images (Carolyn Clarke), Abingdon, Oxon; **11.3** Getty Images, München; **12.1** Alamy Images (Simon Dack), Abingdon, Oxon; **12.2** plainpicture GmbH (Robert Harding), Hamburg; **12.3** Alamy Images (Steve Morgan), Abingdon, Oxon; **12.4** shutterstock.com (Alastair Wallace), New York, NY; **16.1** plainpicture GmbH (alt6/Suzanne Rochette), Hamburg; **16.2** shutterstock.com (Julija Sapic), New York, NY; **19.1** Getty Images (Photodisc), München; **19.2** Klett-Archiv (Thomas Weccard), Stuttgart; **24.1** Corbis (Imaginechina), Berlin; **24.2** Getty Images (E+), München; **25.1** February Films, London; **25.2** February Films, London; **25.3** February Films, London; **27.1** Weccard, Thomas, Ludwigsburg; **28.1** plainpicture GmbH (Robert Harding), Hamburg; **28.2** Getty Images (Iconica/Arctic-Images), München; **28.3** Getty Images, München; **28.4** plainpicture GmbH (Arcaid), Hamburg; **28.5** plainpicture GmbH (Arcaid), Hamburg; **30.1** Corbis (Steven Vidler), Berlin; **30.2** Mauritius Images (Alamy), Mittenwald; **30.3** Getty Images (Brendan Hoffman), München; **30.4** Mauritius Images (Alamy), Mittenwald; **32.1** Getty Images (Cultura), München; **32.2** Mauritius Images (Alamy), Mittenwald; **33.1** Getty Images (Robert Harding), München; **33.2** Mauritius Images (Alamy), Mittenwald; **33.3** Corbis (Andrew Fox), Berlin; **34.1** Fotolia.com (goodluz), New York; **34.1** Getty Images (Cultura), München; **36.1** Alamy Images (John Robertson), Abingdon, Oxon; **36.2** Mauritius Images (Alamy), Mittenwald; **37.1** plainpicture GmbH (Johner), Hamburg; **37.1** shutterstock.com (Elena Elisseeva), New York, NY; **37.2** Thinkstock/iStock/Wojciech Gajda, Getty Images RF/PhotoDisc, shutterstock/Worytko Pawel; **39.1** shutterstock.com (PathDoc), New York, NY; **42.1** Fotolia.com (BasPhoto), New York; **42.2** Getty Images (Cultura), München; **43.1** Alamy Images (James Davies), Abingdon, Oxon; **43.2** Alamy Images (Cultura Creative), Abingdon, Oxon; **44.1** Corbis, Berlin; **45.1** February Films, London; **46.1** Corbis (Ed Bock), Berlin; **46.2** Corbis (Ed Bock), Berlin; **46.3** Corbis (Ed Bock), Berlin; **46.4** Corbis (Ed Bock), Berlin; **46.5** Corbis (Ed Bock), Berlin; **46.6** Corbis (Ed Bock), Berlin; **46.7** Corbis (Ed Bock), Berlin; **47.1** Corbis (Ed Bock), Berlin; **47.2** Corbis (Ed Bock), Berlin; **47.3** Corbis (Ed Bock), Berlin; **47.4** Corbis (Ed Bock), Berlin; **47.5** Corbis (Ed Bock), Berlin; **47.6** Corbis (Ed Bock), Berlin; **47.7** Corbis (Ed Bock), Berlin; **48.1** iStockphoto (MivPiv), Calgary, Alberta; **49.1** iStockphoto (saxifrag), Calgary, Alberta; **49.2** dreamstime.com (Maxximmm), Brentwood, TN; **49.3** iStockphoto (Steve Debenport), Calgary, Alberta; **49.4** Thinkstock (Ryan McVay), München; **49.5** Thinkstock (Wavebreakmedia Ltd), München; **52.1** Getty Images (John Lawson/Moment), München; **52.2** Getty Images (AWL Images), München; **53.1** CC-BY-SA-4.0 (Rosser1954/keine Änderungen), Mountain View; **53.2** Getty Images (2010 Billy Currie), München; **53.3** Getty Images (The Image Bank/Victoria Snowber), München; **54.1** Thinkstock (Photos.com), München; **54.2** Picture-Alliance (Everett Collection), Frankfurt; **54.3** Thinkstock (istock/passigatti), München; **54.4** iStockphoto (davincidig), Calgary, Alberta; **54.5** Thinkstock (istock/NatalyaAksenova), München; **54.6** Thinkstock (istock/TimZillion), München; **54.7** Thinkstock (istock/thumb), München; **54.8** Thinkstock (istock/rvlsoft), München; **57.1** Fotosearch Stock Photography (Eclecti Collection RF), Waukesha, WI; **57.2** Thinkstock (iStock/Digital Paws Inc.), München; **57.3** Fotolia.com (Diogo Barbosa), New York; **58.1** Avenue Images GmbH (Banana Stock), Hamburg; **60.1** iStockphoto (clubfoto), Calgary, Alberta; **60.2** Thinkstock (Eli Franssens), München; **61.1** Thinkstock (iStock/Nastco), München; **61.2** Klett-Archiv, Stuttgart; **61.3** Thinkstock (istock/ffolas), München; **61.4** Thinkstock (istock/Juliane Jacobs), München; **61.5** Thinkstock (istock/andreusK), München; **61.6** Thinkstock (iStock/JaySi), München; **66.1** Mauritius Images (Alamy), Mittenwald; **66.2** Mauritius Images (Alamy), Mittenwald; **66.2** Mauritius Images (Hüttner + Consorten), Mittenwald; **66.3** shutterstock.com (Gencay M. Emin), New York, NY; **66.4** Thinkstock (iStockphoto), München; **66.5** shutterstock.com (Gencay M. Emin), New York, NY; **66.6** Thinkstock (iStockphoto), München; **67.1** iStockphoto (davincidig), Calgary, Alberta; **68.1** Thinkstock (Smitt), München; **68.2** Fotolia.com (laralova), New York; **70.1** Thinkstock (iStock/saknakorn), München; **70.2** Thinkstock (iStock/prapann), München; **70.3** shutterstock.com (shnjr52), New York, NY; **70.4** shutterstock.com (MNI), New York, NY; **70.5** shutterstock.com (MaleWitch), New York, NY; **70.6** shutterstock.com (Diana Taliun), New York, NY; **70.7** shutterstock.com (spaxiax), New York, NY; **70.8** shutterstock.com (Komkrit Noenpoempisut), New York, NY; **71.1** shutterstock.com (Gencay M. Emin), New York, NY; **71.2** iStockphoto (gremlin), Calgary, Alberta; **71.3** Fotolia.com (bzyxx), New York; **71.4** shutterstock.com (Egorov Igor), New York, NY; **71.5** Thinkstock (iStock/MartinM303), München; **71.6** Fotolia.com (lupico), New York; **72.1** shutterstock.com (John A Cameron), New York, NY; **72.2** Alamy Images (Alex Ekins Adventure Photography), Abingdon, Oxon; **72.3** dreamstime.com (Micka), Brentwood, TN; **73.1** PONS GmbH, Stuttgart, Stuttgart; **74.1** Getty Images (John Molloy), München; **74.2** plainpicture GmbH (Design Pics), Hamburg; **74.3** plainpicture GmbH (Cultura), Hamburg; **75.1** Corbis (Jon Boyes/incamerastock), Berlin; **75.2** plainpicture GmbH (Stockwerk/Dirk Kugelmeier), Hamburg; **75.3** Corbis (Hugh Rooney/http://www. eyeubiquitous. com/Eye Ubiquitous), Berlin; **76.1** Getty Images (John Molloy), München; **76.2** Getty Images (Stockbyte), München; **79.1** Alamy Images (Nikreates), Abingdon, Oxon; **87.1** February Films, London; **87.2** February Films, London; **87.3** February Films, London; **88.1** Fotolia.com (sharynos), New York; **89.1** Klett-Archiv (Peter Nierhoff), Stuttgart; **94.1** Getty Images (Joe Daniel Price), München; **94.2** Alamy Images (imageBROKER), Abingdon, Oxon; **95.1** shutterstock.com (TDC Photography), New York, NY; **95.2** plainpicture GmbH (Hero Images), Hamburg; **95.3** iStockphoto (Carmine Salvatore), Calgary, Alberta; **96.1** shutterstock.com (Tracy Whiteside), New York, NY; **96.2** shutterstock.com (RyFlip), New York, NY; **100.1** plainpicture GmbH (Westend61), Hamburg; **101.1** TRANSDEV Ireland, Dublin; **102.1** Thinkstock (Steeve ROCHE), München; **103.1** Thinkstock (istock/worac), München; **106.1** Picture-Alliance (Jens Kalaene/dpa), Frankfurt; **108.1** shutterstock.com (Aleksandar Mijatovic), New York, NY; **108.2** Thinkstock (iStockphoto), München; **108.3** shutterstock.com (ruskpp), New York, NY; **108.4** shutterstock.com (

Gencay M. Emin), New York, NY; **108.5** shutterstock.com (Jim Barber), New York, NY; **108.6** Thinkstock (iStockphoto), München; **110.1** iStockphoto (edfuentesg), Calgary, Alberta; **110.2** Thinkstock (CEZARY ZAREBSKI), München; **110.3** Alamy Images (Alex Segre), Abingdon, Oxon; **110.4** Thinkstock (Benis Arapovic), München; **110.5** Getty Images (Cultura), München; **110.6** shutterstock.com (Pavel L Photo and Video), New York, NY; **116.1** Thinkstock (Photos.com), München; **119.1** Thinkstock (iStock Editorial/IR_Stone), München; **119.2** Fotolia.com (Calin Bocian), New York; **119.3** shutterstock.com (Anneka), New York, NY; **119.4** Corbis (Steve Raymer/National Geographic Creative), Berlin; **119.5** shutterstock.com (Ilaszlo), New York, NY; **120.1** Thinkstock (iStock/Nastco), München; **120.2** Klett-Archiv, Stuttgart; **120.3** Thinkstock (istock/ffolas), München; **120.4** Thinkstock (istock/Juliane Jacobs), München; **120.5** Thinkstock (istock/andreusK), München; **120.6** Thinkstock (iStock/JaySi), München; **124.1** TRANSDEV Ireland, Dublin; **125.1** Thinkstock (istock/worac), München; **127.1** Alamy Images (GL Archive), Abingdon, Oxon; **128.1** shutterstock.com (antb), New York, NY; **128.1** Mauritius Images (Matthew Horwood/Alamy), Mittenwald; **128.2** shutterstock.com (Peter Raymond Llewellyn), New York, NY; **128.2** Mauritius Images (Jack Sullivan/Alamy), Mittenwald; **129.1** Getty Images (Moment), München; **129.2** plainpicture GmbH (Thorsten Rother), Hamburg; **129.3** Fotolia.com (PT Images), New York; **129.4** Thinkstock (umdash9), München; **130.1** Getty Images (Stockbyte), München; **130.2** Getty Images (Stockbyte), München; **131.1** Getty Images (The Image Bank), München; **131.2** iStockphoto (Liz Leyden), Calgary, Alberta; **131.3** Getty Images (Moment Open), München; **132.1** shutterstock.com (VanderWolf Images), New York, NY; **132.2** Getty Images (Stockbyte), München; **132.3** Getty Images (Christopher Pillitz), München; **133.1** Corbis (Artur Widak/NurPhoto), Berlin; **133.2** Corbis (Ralph White), Berlin; **133.2** Mauritius Images (Marco Secchi/Alamy), Mittenwald; **134.1** Getty Images (Matt Cardy), München; **134.2** Mauritius Images (Brickley Pix/Alamy), Mittenwald; **134.3** Getty Images (Universal Images Group), München; **134.4** Getty Images (Hulton Fine Art Collection), München; **134.5** Corbis, Berlin; **134.5** Alamy Images (imageBROKER/Dr. Wilfried Bahnmüller), Abingdon, Oxon; **135.1** Corbis, Berlin; **135.1** Mauritius Images (Ian Shipley IRE/Alamy), Mittenwald; **135.2** Alamy Images (jeremy sutton-hibbert), Abingdon, Oxon; **135.3** plainpicture GmbH (STOCK4B), Hamburg; **135.4** Getty Images (Cultura), München; **136.1** Klett-Archiv (Axel Reis), Stuttgart; **136.2** Klett-Archiv, Stuttgart; **136.3** Klett-Archiv (Axel Reis), Stuttgart; **136.4** Klett-Archiv (Axel Reis), Stuttgart; **136.5** Klett-Archiv (Axel Reis), Stuttgart; **137.1** Klett-Archiv (Axel Reis), Stuttgart; **137.2** Klett-Archiv (Axel Reis), Stuttgart; **137.3** Klett-Archiv (Axel Reis), Stuttgart; **137.4** Klett-Archiv (Axel Reis), Stuttgart; **137.5** Klett-Archiv, Stuttgart; **137.6** Klett-Archiv (Axel Reis), Stuttgart; **137.7** Klett-Archiv (Axel Reis), Stuttgart; **137.8** Klett-Archiv (Axel Reis), Stuttgart; **138.1** Thinkstock (Brand X Pictures/Jupiterimages), München; **138.2** Thinkstock (istock/Krzysztof Slusarczyk), München; **138.3** shutterstock.com (Leemonton), New York, NY; **138.4** Thinkstock (iStockphoto), München; **139.1** Thinkstock (iStock/blueringmedia), München; **139.2** Thinkstock (iStock/graphicsdunia4you), München; **144.1** Alamy Images (Ivy Close Images), Abingdon, Oxon; **172.1** dreamstime.com (Indos82), Brentwood, TN; **179.1** picturemaxx.net (RF), München; **179.2** Thinkstock (Medioimages/Photodisc), München; **179.3** Getty Images RF (Photodisc), München; **179.4** Thinkstock (iStockphoto), München; **186.1** Thinkstock (iStock/Michael Braun), München; **186.2** Thinkstock (Comstock), München; **186.3** Fotolia.com (Steve Lovegrove), New York; **186.4** Thinkstock (Lifesize), München; **186.5** Thinkstock (istockphoto), München; **186.6** Fotolia.com (Ints), New York; **186.7** Thinkstock (iStockphoto), München; **186.8** shutterstock.com (RF/McNally), New York, NY; **186.9** February Films (Elke Bock), London; **186.10** shutterstock.com, New York, NY; **186.11** Corbis RF (RF), Berlin; **186.12** Thinkstock (Comstock), München; **186.13** Fotolia.com (philippe Devanne), New York; **186.14** Thinkstock (mavrek), München; **186.15** iStockphoto (Liz Leyden), Calgary, Alberta; **186.16** Avenue Images GmbH (Image Source), Hamburg; **186.17** Avenue Images GmbH (Fancy RF), Hamburg; **186.18** shutterstock.com (Stefan Schurr), New York, NY; **186.19** dreamstime.com (Denyskuvaiev), Brentwood, TN; **186.20** Corbis (Gary Kufner), Berlin; **186.21** Getty Images RF (PhotoDisc), München; **186.22** Avenue Images GmbH (Ingram Publishing), Hamburg; **186.23** iStockphoto (Webphotographeer), Calgary, Alberta; **186.24** Thinkstock (iStockphoto), München; **186.25** creativ collection Verlag GmbH, Freiburg; **186.26** Avenue Images GmbH (image source), Hamburg; **186.27** Ingram Publishing, Tattenhall Chester; **186.28** Thinkstock (iStock/Ljupco), München; **186.29** Fotolia.com (mustgo), New York; **186.30** shutterstock.com (Cathleen A Clapper), New York, NY; **186.31** Thinkstock (Jupiterimages), München; **193.1** Klett-Archiv (Wolfgang Schaar, Grafing), Stuttgart; **194.1** shutterstock.com (Anneka), New York, NY; **194.2** iStockphoto (onfilm), Calgary, Alberta; **194.3** picturemaxx.net (RF), München; **194.4** Thinkstock (Medioimages/Photodisc), München; **194.5** Getty Images RF (Photodisc), München; **194.6** Thinkstock (iStockphoto), München; **206.1** shutterstock.com (Pack), New York, NY; **207.1** Thinkstock (iStockphoto), München; **207.2** iStockphoto (Lorraine Boogich), Calgary, Alberta; **207.3** iStockphoto (ollo), Calgary, Alberta; **207.4** shutterstock.com (Jordan Tan), New York, NY; **207.5** Fotolia.com (ang17a), New York; **207.6** Fotolia.com (david hughes), New York; **207.7** Avenue Images GmbH (Banana Stock), Hamburg; **207.8** Corbis RF, Berlin; **207.9** dreamstime.com, Brentwood, TN; **207.10** iStockphoto (Nick free), Calgary, Alberta; **207.11** panthermedia.net (dieschu), München; **207.12** Fotolia.com (godfer), New York; **207.13** shutterstock.com (William Attard McCarthy), New York, NY; **U00/Vorsatz hinten.1** Visit York, York

Sollte es in einem Einzelfall nicht gelungen sein, den korrekten Rechteinhaber ausfindig zu machen, so werden berechtigte Ansprüche selbstverständlich im Rahmen der üblichen Regelungen abgegolten.

Textquellennachweis
S. 17: The City, GOSLING, JAKE NATHAN/Sheeran, Edward Christopher © BDI Music Limited/Sony ATV Music Publishing (UK) Limited, Platz Musikverlage GmbH, Hamburg/Sony/ATV Music Publishing, (Germany) GmbH, Berlin
S. 77: Let your tears fall, FURLER, SIA KATE/Kurstin, Gregory Allen © EMI April Music Inc/EMI Music Publishing Ltd/Kurstin Music, EMI Music Publishing Germany GmbH, Berlin
S. 101: Luminous, Gustafsson, Johan/Haeggstam, Fredrik Folke Alexander/Lundberg, Sebastian Per Emil © Universal Music Publishing AB, Universal Music Publishing GmbH, Berlin
S. 140–143: Siobhan Dowd, The London Eye Mystery, Corgi Yearling (Verlag) © Siobhan Dowd, 2007

Visit York
visityork.org